W9-BZK-859

Design Elements
A Graphic Style Manual

ROCKPORT

First published in the United States of America by
Rockport Publishers, a member of Quayside Publishing Group

100 Cummings Center, Suite 406-L

Beverly, MA 01915-6101

978.282.9590 *Telephone*

978.283.2742 *Facsimile*

www.rockpub.com

Library of Congress Cataloging-in-Publication Data

Samara, Timothy.
Design elements : a graphic style manual : understanding the rules and knowing when to break them / Timothy Samara.
p. cm.
ISBN-13: 978-1-59253-261-2 (flexibind)
ISBN-10: 1-59253-261-6 (flexibind)
1. Graphic design (Typography) 2. Layout (Printing) I. Title.

Z246 .S225
686.2'2—dc22 2006019038
CIP

ISBN-13: 978-1-59253-261-2
ISBN-10: 1-59253-261-6

10 9

Cover and text design
STIM Visual Communication New York

Printed in China

Design Elements

A Graphic Style Manual

TIMOTHY SAMARA

ROCKPORT PUBLISHERS

BEVERLY MASSACHUSETTS

contents

Credits for projects shown on the following page spread

A AdamsMorioka *United States*
B Mutabor *Germany*
C LSD *Spain*
D BBK Studio *United States*
E Muller *United Kingdom*
F Form *United Kingdom*

What It Is

A graphic designer is a communicator: someone who takes ideas and gives them visual form so that others can understand them. The designer uses imagery, symbols, type, color, and material—whether it's concrete, like printing on a page, or somewhat intangible, like pixels on a computer screen or light in a video—to represent the ideas that must be conveyed and to organize them into a unified message. Graphic designers perform this service on behalf of a company or other organization to help that entity get its message out to its audience and, in so doing, evoke a particular response. ■ Graphic design, as an industry, is a cousin to advertising, both of which were born from the tumultuous period of the Industrial Revolution of the late 1700s and early 1800s, when the working class—finding itself with time on its hands and money to spend in the pursuit of comfort—began to look for stuff to buy and things to do. Graphic design and advertising share one particular goal—to inform the public about goods, services, events, or ideas that someone believes will be important to them; but graphic design parts company with advertising when it comes to ultimate purpose. Once advertising informs its audience about some product or event, it cajoles the audience into spending money. Graphic design, however, simply seeks to clarify the message and craft it into an emotional experience. Granted, graphic design often is used by advertising as a tool to help sell goods and services; but the designing of messages is, at its core, its own endeavor altogether. ■ This purpose is what differentiates graphic design from other disciplines in the visual arts—a purpose defined by a client and manifested by a designer, rather than a purpose generated from within the designer. True, the fine arts patron historically was often a client to the great painters, but, up until the nineteenth century, artistic creation was understood to be

To understand the meaning of design is… to understand the part form and content play… and to realize that design is also commentary, opinion, a point of view, and social responsibility. To design is much more than simply to assemble, to order, or even to edit; it is to add value and meaning, to illuminate, to simplify, to clarify, to modify, to dignify, to dramatize, to persuade, and perhaps even to amuse.

Design is both a verb and a noun. It is the beginning as well as the end, the process and product of imagination.

Paul Rand Graphic designer.
From his book *Design, Form, and Chaos*,
Yale University Press, New Haven, 1993.

Gra

A

intrinsically a service industry. It wasn't until the 1830s that the mystique of the bohemian painter as "expresser of self" arose and, even more recently—since the mid 1970s—the idea of the graphic designer as "author." ■ In the fifty-odd years since the design industry began to ask business to take it seriously as a profession, the graphic designer has been touted as everything from visual strategist to cultural arbiter—shaping not only the corporate bottom line through clever visual manipulation of the brand-hungry public, but also the larger visual language of the postmodern environment. All these functions are important to graphic design... but, lest we forget the simplicity of the designer's true nature, let us return to what a graphic designer does. ■ A graphic designer assimilates verbal concepts and gives them form. A designer organizes the resulting form into a tangible, navigable experience. The quality of the experience is dependent on the designer's skill and sensibility in creating or selecting forms with which to manifest concepts, or messages. A designer is responsible for the intellectual and emotional vitality of the experience he or she visits upon the audience for such messages. The designer's task is to elevate the experience of the message above the banality of literal transmission and the confusing self-indulgent egoism of mere eye-candy or self-fulfillment—although these might be important to the designer. Beauty is a function, after all, of any relevant visual message. Just as prose can be dull and straightforward or well edited and lyrical, so too can a utilitarian object be designed to be more than just simply what it is. ■ Some time around 1932, Adolf Loos, the noted Viennese architect, said, "There is a great difference between an urn and a chamber pot, and in this difference there is leeway for culture." That's a lot of leeway. Designing is a discipline that integrates an enormous amount of knowledge and skill with intuition, but it's more than just the various aspects that go into it: understanding the fundamentals of form and composition; applying those fundamentals to evoke emotion and signify higher-order concepts; manipulating color messages; understanding semiotics and the relationship between different kinds of visual signs; controlling the pacing of material and informational hierarchy; integrating type and image for unified, coherent messaging; and planning the fabrication of the work and ensuring its physical quality as an object, whether it's printed, animated on screen, or built.

phic Design

Twenty Rules for Making Good Design

Rules can be broken—but never ignored.

David Jury Typographer and author

From the title page of his book ***About Face***
RotoVision SA: Switzerland, 2004

When people talk about "good" or "bad" design, they're referring to notions of quality that they've picked up from education and experience, and often from the experience of thousands of designers and critics before them. Sometimes these notions are aesthetic—"asymmetry is more beautiful than symmetry," for example, or "a neutral typeface is all you need"—and sometimes strictly functional—for example, "don't reverse a serif typeface from a solid background if it's less than 10 points in size, because it'll fill in." Both kinds of observation are helpful in avoiding pitfalls and striving to achieve design solutions that aren't hampered by irritating difficulties—to make every design be all that it can be. ■ Every time an attempt is made to cite rules governing what constitutes quality, however, people are bound to get their underwear in a knot: "That's so limiting!" To those people, I'll say this: get over it. ■ Rules exist—especially the ones set forth here—as guidelines, based on accumulated experience from many sources. As such, rules always come with exceptions and can be broken at any time, but not without a consequence. The consequence of breaking one rule might mean reinforcing another, and it might mean true innovation, in the right context—a context in which a revelation occurs that, oddly enough, will establish yet another rule. This is how human creativity works. ■ The importance of knowing which rules are considered important (at least historically), and why, is understanding the possible consequence of breaking them so that something unfortunate doesn't happen out of ignorance. In addition, rules act as guides in helping to build a communal discussion about interpreting and evaluating creative work. If everything is "good," then nothing really can be. Relativism is great, to a point, and then it just gets in the way of honest judgment; the result is a celebration of ubiquitous mediocrity. ■ By no means should any rule, including those that follow, be taken as Cosmic Law. If you're unconvinced, simply turn to page 248, where breaking every rule in this book is advocated wholeheartedly. But these rules are a starting point, an excellent list of issues to consider while you work. In the end, you will decide how and when to apply the rules, or not, as well as understand the results of either course of action.

Have a concept.

If there's no message, no story, no idea, no narrative, or no useful experience to be had, it's not graphic design. It doesn't matter how amazing the thing is to look at; without a clear message, it's an empty, although beautiful, shell. That's about as complicated as this rule can get. Let's move on.

One su kašike za zaljubljene - unikatne, vredne i u paru.

A restrained layout presents high-end flatware products in lushly styled and photographed environments to help convey their quality. Materials in the photographs—in this case, a spiral of espresso beans—are subtly repeated in the typography of the copy.

Jelena Drobac *Serbia*

Zippered plastic bags with evidence stickers package the books in a series of detective novels. The books themselves become artifacts of the crime novels.

Thomas Csano *Canada*

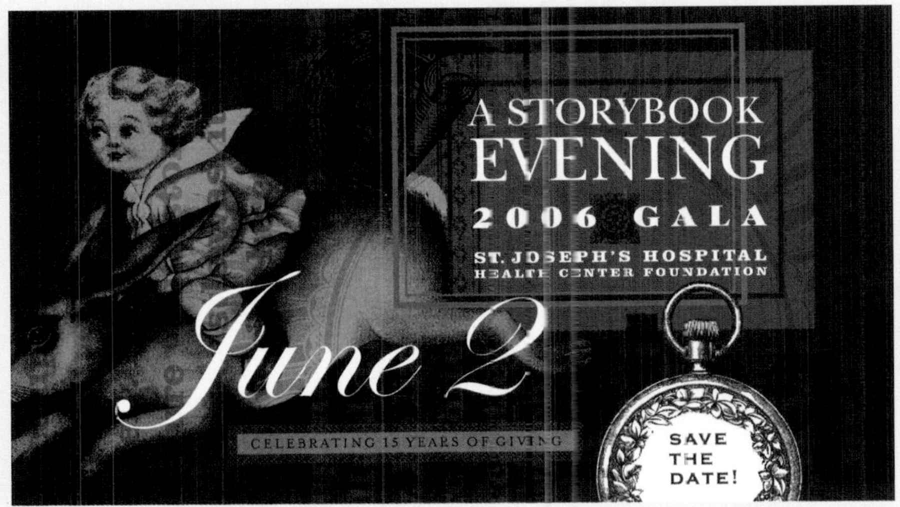

As rich and decorative as this postcard is, every detail included communicates the upcoming experience at a fund-raiser whose theme is fantasy literature: the watch suggests urgency; the child on the rabbit is a nod to children's stories; and the engravings and type texture create a mysterious space where participants' memories come alive.

Lexicon Graphix and STIM Visual Communication *United States*

Communicate— don't decorate.

Oooh... Neat! But what exactly is it? Somewhat related to Rule No. 1, this rule is about how you support the all-important concept. Form carries meaning, no matter how simple or abstract, and form that's not right for a given message will communicate messages that you don't intend—including the message that you don't know how to choose forms that are meaningful for your audience or that you don't care what's meaningful for them. It's all well and good to experiment with shapes and details and cool effects, but if you simply spackle them all over without considering what they mean and how they support or take away from the message, you end up with a jumbled mass of junk that no longer qualifies as design.

In this brochure, color and geometry provide the only visual forms to support a message about efficient business practice. The circular elements, though abstract, convey the meaning in the large quotation through their arrangement, size relationships, and color alone; no extras are needed.

And Partners *United States*

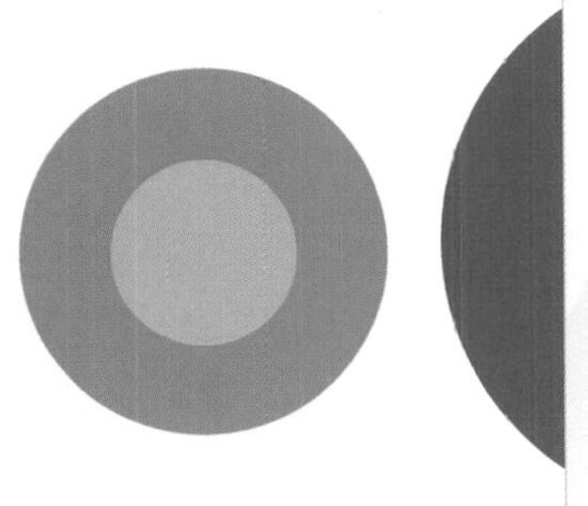

Seeing. Learn and build rapport by listening first, and talking second. Use the classic tools of probing — who, how, what, why, when and where — as well as statements like, "Tell me more," to keep them talking until you truly understand their challenges. Being. Avoid the temptation to show them how smart you are by telling them everything that Guy Carpenter can do for them, or risk appearing out of touch and overly complex. A solution defined by the problem will be better received than a solution in search of a problem.
Follow effective action with quiet reflection. From the quiet reflection will come even more effective action.
– Peter F. Drucker

3

Speak with one visual voice.

Make all the parts talk to each other… in the same language. Take a look at everything, from the big picture down to the tiniest detail, and ask yourself: "Does everything relate harmoniously to everything else?" Good design assumes that the visual language of the piece—its internal logic—is resolved to address all its parts so that they reinforce, restate, and reference each other, not only in shape or weight or placement, but conceptually as well. As soon as one element seems out of place, or just a leftover that hasn't been given any thought, it disconnects from the others, and the message is weakened.

Consistent use of color, typography, and application of the client's logo across branded print communications create a unified presence for a business entity that will be identified easily among its competitors.

Templin Brink Design
United States

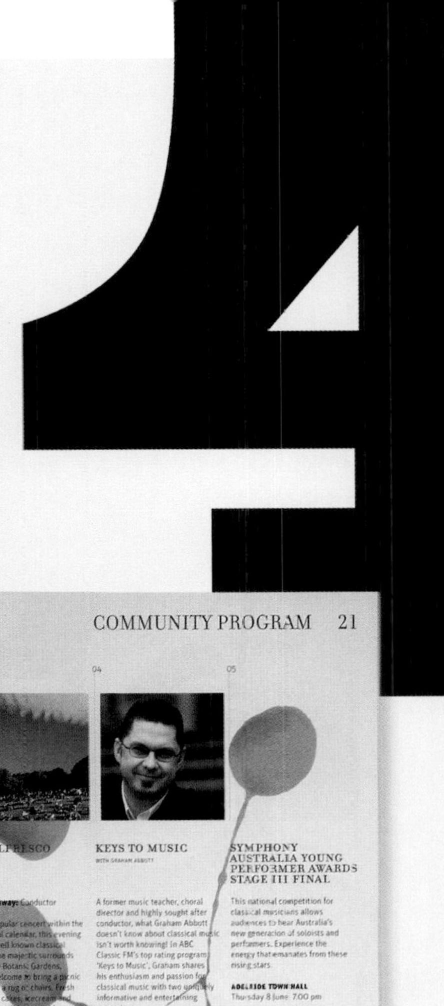

Use two typeface families maximum. OK, maybe three.

Choose typefaces for specific purposes. In doing that, you'll need to define what the purposes are, and you're likely to find that there are only two or three purposes for text in a project. Because a change in type family usually signals a change in meaning or function–restrain yourself! A single type family with a variety of weights and italics should be enough all by itself; adding a second is nice for texture, but don't overdo it. Too many typefaces are distracting and self-conscious and might confuse or tire the viewer.

This brochure for an orchestra balances exuberant abstract marks with quiet typography. Sans-serif text and notation provide ease of use while a stately serif adds warmth and contrast that visually complements the imagery.

Voice *Australia*

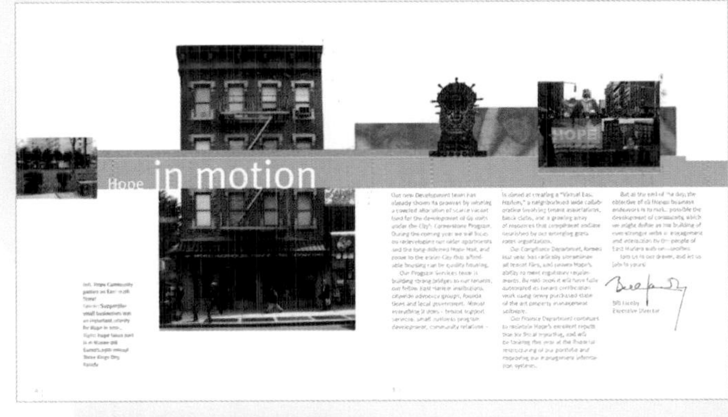

One type family alone can be used to great effect, as seen in this annual report. Employing only changes in size and color, the designer is able to present a clearly distinguished range of information with accessible, elegant restraint.

C. Harvey Graphic Design
United States

Viewers are likely to see this theater poster's title treatment from thirty strides away, followed by the theater's name and, in a sequence of decreasing contrast, weight, and size, the rest of the information. These type treatments, along with the movement created by the title and the supporting shapes, help move the viewer's eyes from most important item to least important.

Design Rudi Meyer *France*

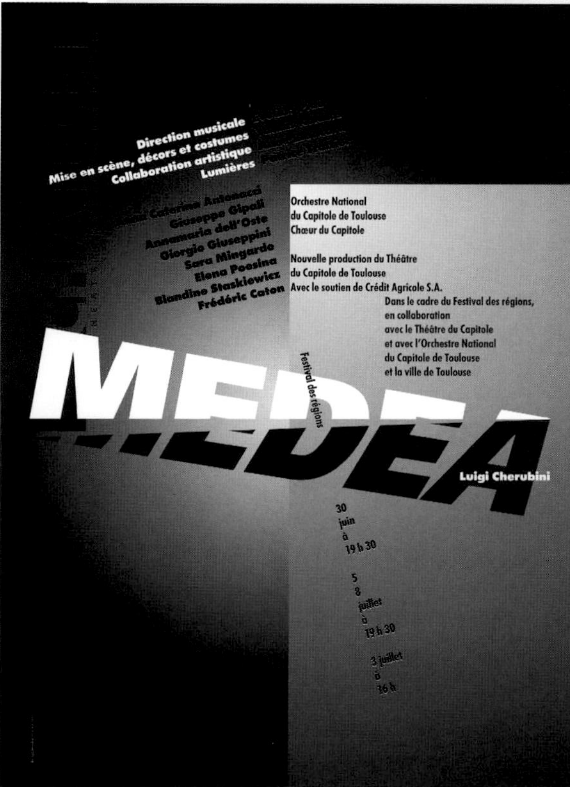

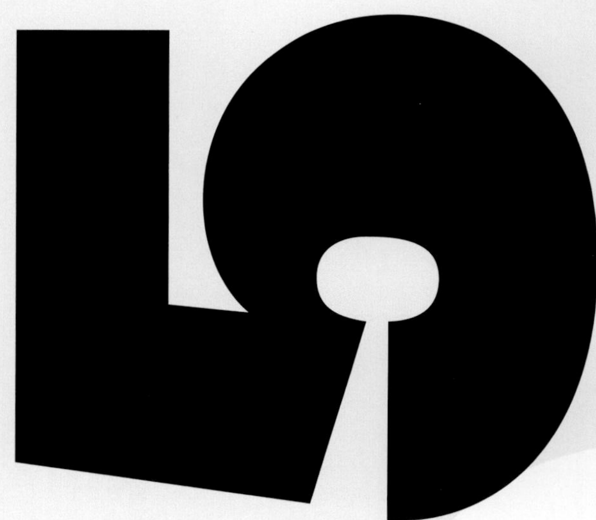

Use the one-two punch!

Focus viewers' attention on one important thing first, and then lead them through the rest. Once you capture the audience with a big shape, a startling image, a dramatic type treatment, or a daring color, steadily decrease the activity of each less important item in a logical way to help them get through it. This is establishing a "hierarchy"—the order in which you want them to look at the material—and it is essential for accessibility and ease of use. You're designing the thing to grab the audience's attention, to get them the information they need, and to help them remember it afterward. If there's no clear focus to start with, you've already lost the battle.

Pick colors on purpose.

Don't just grab some colors from out of the air. Know what the colors will do when you combine them and, more important, what they might mean to the audience. Color carries an abundance of psychological and emotional meaning, and this meaning can vary tremendously between cultural groups and even individuals. Color affects visual hierarchy, the legibility of type, and how people make connections between disparate items—sometimes called color coding—so choose wisely. Never assume that a certain color, or a combination of colors, is right for a particular job because of convention either. Blue for financial services, for example, is the standout color cliché of the past fifty years. Choose colors that are right, not those that are expected.

The muted rose tones in this fragrance packaging are feminine without being girlish; a slight shift toward brown in the typography creates a subtle, yet rich interaction. The complementary green-gold—almost a direct complement, but again, slightly off—presents rich contrast and hints at complexity and allure.

A10 Design *Brazil*

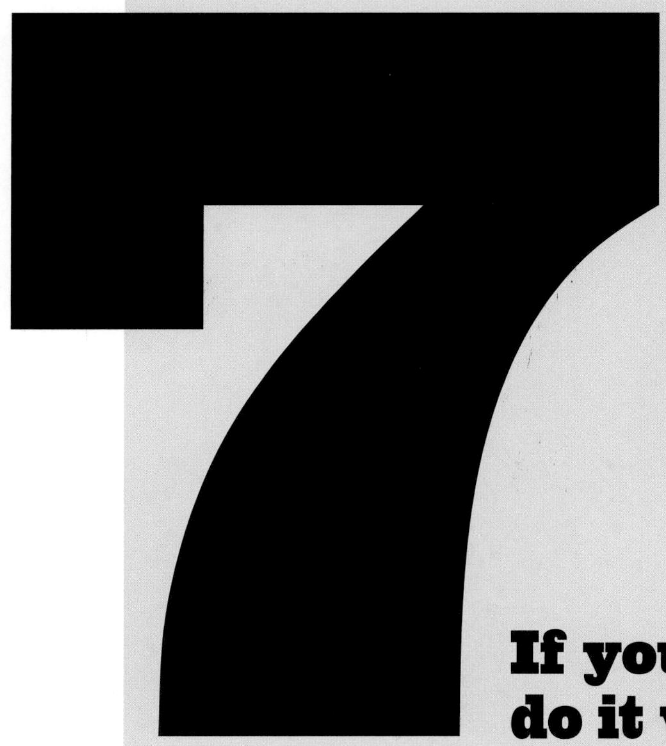

If you can do it with less, then do it.

This is a riff on an adage left over from Modernism, sometimes known as the "less is more" theory. It's not so much an aesthetic dogma now as it is a bit of common sense: the more stuff jammed into a given space, the harder it is for the average bear to see what they're supposed to be seeing. Plus, it's trashy; anybody can load a bunch of stuff onto a dull message and pretend it's a complex work of art, but there's a big difference between "complicated" and "complex," a state that often comes about in a simple context.

True art lies in the harmonic convergence of thoughtfulness and creativity applied to very little. If the concept and the form are truly beautiful, there can be very, very little of it to look at—without sacrificing a rich experience. Think about how much visual garbage gets thrown at someone walking down the street every day, and ask yourself: "Wouldn't it make more sense to delete some of that mush in favor of something sleek, clear, and noticeable?" Make more meaning out of what's there; don't gunk it up. If the idea is clear without adding, putting more stuff in is just "gilding the lily;" if the idea isn't there and it's not visually interesting, adding to it is simply trying to make "a silk purse from a sow's ear."

Exquisite, decisive control of the minimal elements, alignments, and the spaces around and between them creates a dynamic, almost architectural space that is active and three-dimensional... which is all you really need for a brochure for a contemporary architecture firm.

LSD *Spain*

Enpresa
gipuzkoarrarekiko
atxikimendua

El Compromiso
de Adegi
con la empresa
guipuzcoana

8

Negative space is magical—create it, don't just fill it up!

From within a confined space enclosed by the visual angles created by headline and body text, hands stretch outward to release a symbolic butterfly; the image's message is restated subtly by the compositional space with which it interacts.

Loewy *United Kingdom*

It's often said that negative space—sometimes called white space (even though there might not be any white around)—is more important than the stuff that's in it. For the most part, this is true. Space calls attention to content, separates it from unrelated content around it, and gives the eyes a resting place. Negative space is just as much a shape that you have to deal with in a composition as positive shapes, whether pictures or type. When you don't deal with it at all, negative space feels dead and disconnected from the visual material it surrounds. If the space gets filled up, the result is an oppressive presentation that no one will want to deal with. A lack of negative space overwhelms and confuses the audience, which is likely to get turned off.

Both the style—bold, all uppercase, sans serif—and placement of the type help complete the composition of this poster. The title does double duty as landing strip and identifier; the logo itself appears as an airplane (with the bowl of the numeral **5** creating its propeller); the angular quality of the numerals is placed in direct contrast with the curves of the cloud forms; and the small text at the top draws the diagonal motion of the other elements upward and activates the space at the top of the poster.

C+G Partners *United States*

Treat the type as image, as though it's just as important.

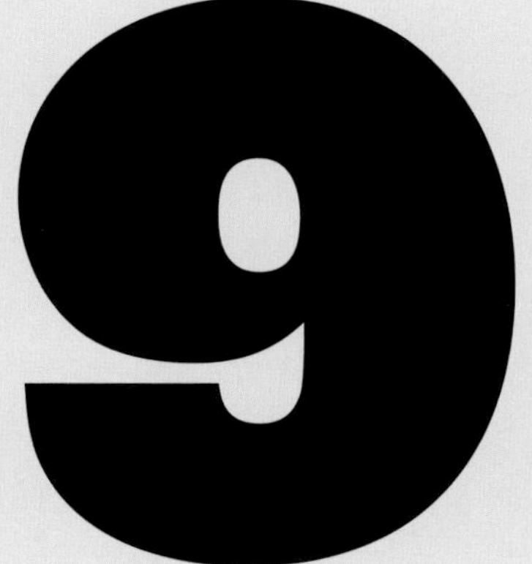

A sad commentary on typography today is that most of it fails in this regard: it's either unimaginatively separated from photography in the notorious "headline/picture/body-copy" strategy seen in countless ad campaigns during the past sixty years or insensitively slapped across images, in quirky typefaces, under the assumption that if it's big and on top of the photo, it's integrated. Time for a reality check! Type is visual material—made up of lines and dots and shapes and textures—that needs to relate compositionally to everything else included in the design, no matter how different they seem to be.

Make it legible, readable, or whatever you want to call it. It should go without saying that type that can't be read has no purpose, but, unfortunately, it bears repeating. Yes, typography can be expressive; yes, typography can be manipulated for inventive interconnection of structural elements within language; and yes, typography can resonate with its subcultural audience and reference this or that pop-cultural zeitgeist. Whatever! It must still transmit information. Back when typography was treated very rigidly and always in good taste, Beatrice Ward, an English type critic, likened it to a crystal wine goblet—a transparent vessel designed for utmost clarity, not for looks. Beatrice might be dead and her crystal goblet might have been replaced by the far less stuffy jelly jar, but the jelly jar still lets you see what kind of wine you're drinking.

Dramatic changes in type size, color blocking, and attention to details such as syllabic breaks and open leading make the type in these brochure spreads not only interesting but also easily read and easy to follow. Bars of color and bold weights help call out important information.

Cobra *Norway*

Type is only type when it's friendly.

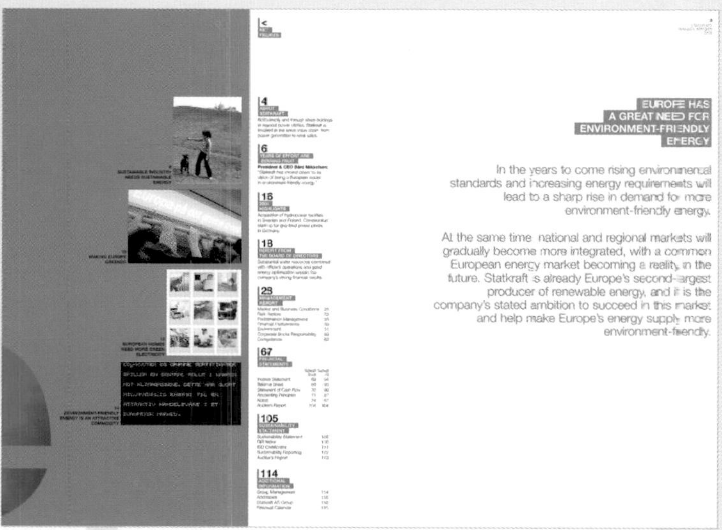

11

Be universal; remember that it's not about you.

UCLA Summer Sessions 1998
www.summer.ucla.edu

One of the reasons you like this poster so much is that it speaks to our common knowledge so clearly; it feels almost as if it hasn't been designed. A hot-colored circle floating over a cool blue horizon and punctuated by a refreshing yellow field pretty much explains itself.

AdamsMorioka *United States*

Talking to oneself is the domain of the fine artist. Being universal is the domain of the designer. A very large audience, not a few people who are "in the know," has to know what you mean with those shapes, that color, and that image you chose. Graphic design comes with an agenda–sometimes a small agenda, such as getting people to come to a film festival, and sometimes a big agenda, such as helping people find their way out of a burning building. The instant you forget–or shamelessly ignore–this little fact, you jeopardize the clarity of the message. It's not likely someone will die as a result, so let's put this in perspective. The worst that could happen is that millions of people will think your poster was really cool–although they can't remember what it was about, and your film festival clients won't hire you to achieve self-fulfillment on their dime again. But consider if you had been working on a way-finding system, and the neat inks you insisted on didn't have enough contrast in a smoky environment. As a result, twelve people asphyxiated trying to get out of the building.

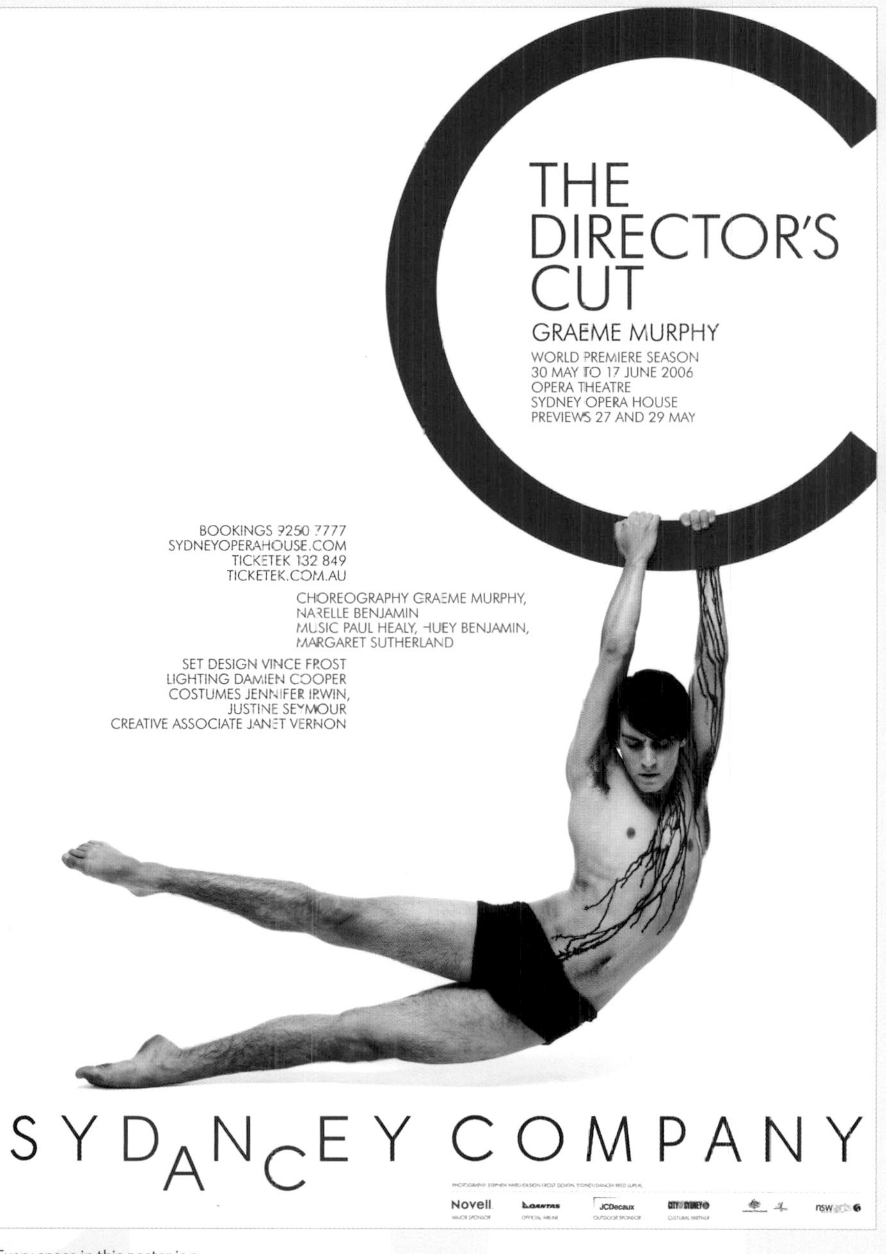

Every space in this poster is a different size; every element has a unique relationship with every other. Some material is dense and linear while other areas are open and round. Angles are juxtaposed tensely with curves, large masses with small. The result is a sequence of visual contrasts that engage the eyes by pushing and pulling at each other.

Frost Design *Australia*

12

Squish and separate.

Create contrasts in density and rhythm by pulling some material closer together and pushing other material further apart. Be rhythmic about it. Give the spaces between things a pulse by making some tighter and some looser unless, of course, you're trying to make something dull, lifeless, and uninteresting. In that case, everything should be about the same size, weight, color, and distance from everything else. Nothing kills a great idea like a dull layout that has no tension. "Without contrast," Paul Rand once said, "you're dead."

Soft, rippling transitions from deep black to luminous blue provide a sensuous backdrop for the bright, sparkling typography in this poster. By changing the sizes of type clusters, as well as the spaces between them, the designer also is able to introduce transitions in value that correspond to similar transitions in the image.

Paone Design Associates
United States

Take a suggestion from the world of photography: make sure there's a wide range of tonal value. Renowned landscape photographer Ansel Adams advocated a nine-zone system of tonal value, suggesting that any photograph without all nine zones didn't have enough, and therefore didn't live up to its potential. Furthermore, don't spread out the tonal range all over the place. Concentrate areas of extreme dark and light in separate places; create explosions of luminosity and deep undercurrents of darkness. Counter these with subtler transitions between related values. Above all, make distinctions between light and dark noticeable and clear.

13 Distribute light and dark like firecrackers and the rising sun.

Be decisive. Do it on purpose—or don't do it at all.

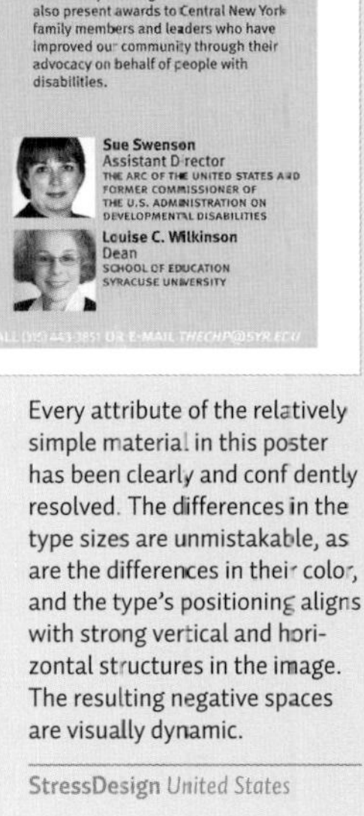

Every attribute of the relatively simple material in this poster has been clearly and confidently resolved. The differences in the type sizes are unmistakable, as are the differences in their color, and the type's positioning aligns with strong vertical and horizontal structures in the image. The resulting negative spaces are visually dynamic.

StressDesign *United States*

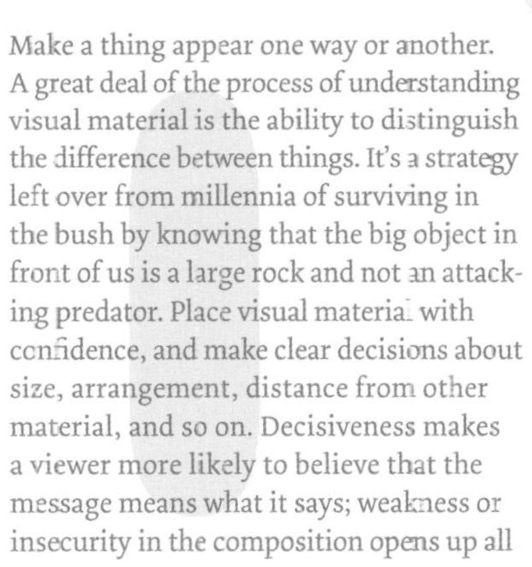

Make a thing appear one way or another. A great deal of the process of understanding visual material is the ability to distinguish the difference between things. It's a strategy left over from millennia of surviving in the bush by knowing that the big object in front of us is a large rock and not an attacking predator. Place visual material with confidence, and make clear decisions about size, arrangement, distance from other material, and so on. Decisiveness makes a viewer more likely to believe that the message means what it says; weakness or insecurity in the composition opens up all kinds of nasty thoughts in the viewer, even if he or she is intellectually unaware of the source–something feels off, unresolved, or not quite right. Suddenly, the viewer is trying to figure out what the issue is and not paying attention to the message itself. And that we just can't have.

The rough, visceral quality of this page spread belies the purposeful placement of forms. The designer has very objectively perceived the visual presence—weight, texture, movement, angularity, transparency, contour—of each element and has brought them into alignment and relationships that are harmonious and resolved.

Andreas Ortag *Austria*

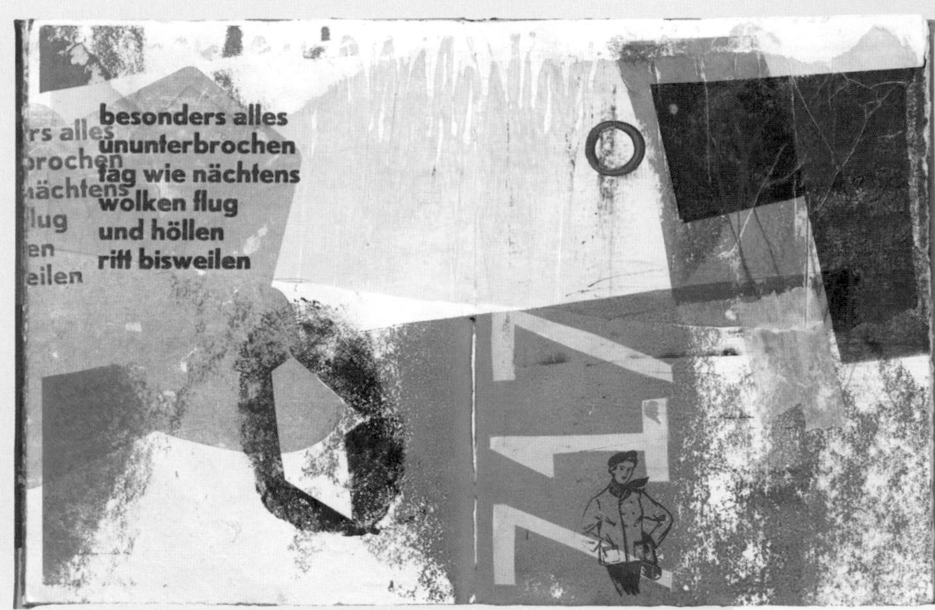

besonders alles
ununterbrochen
tag wie nächtens
wolken flug
und höllen
ritt bisweilen

15 Measure with your eyes: design is visual.

A thing is what it looks like—make it look the way it's supposed to look. The eyes are funny things; they're often fooled by visual stimuli, the notorious optical illusion. Oddly, optical illusions account for ninety percent of the visual logic of composition. Horizontal lines, for example, appear to drop in space and have to be adjusted upward to appear centered from top to bottom. Circular forms always look smaller than square forms that are mathematically the same height, so they must be faked a little larger than the square forms to appear the same size. Make decisions on behalf of your audience: Are the two elements the same size or not? Is the form touching the edge of the format or not? Are two elements aligning or not? If you intend one element to align with another, do it by eye—don't measure. If the viewer perceives the two items as aligning, it will assume they actually do. If you align two items by measuring and they don't look like they do, it doesn't matter that they're really lined up. The viewer will see two items that look like they should have aligned and will remember that some sloppy designer forgot to make sure that they did.

Commissioning illustration allows a designer to completely customize the imagery for a project. Plus, illustration—whether conventional drawing and painting or digital—need not be bound by the laws of nature.

Cyr Studio *United States*

Create images—don't scavenge.

16

Make what you need, and make it the best you can—or pay someone else to do it for you. Nothing is more banal or meaningless than a commonly used instance of stock photography that shows up everywhere. Try not to rely on what already exists, even though it might be cheaper or easier. Sometimes a simpler and more meaningful solution is no further away than a couple of dots and lines, or a personalized scribble that—while not slick, glossy, and full color (and lesser in meaning for your project because it was seen last week in a shopping-mall's newspaper ad, a billboard for used cars, or male enhancement product packaging)—might connect powerfully with the audience. Plus, you can say, quite proudly, that you did it all yourself.

17.09.
27.11.
SCHATTENSPIEL
KUNSTHALLEZUKIEL

All it takes to make an image new and original—even a bad one provided by a client—is a little manipulation. Whatever the source of this portrait, it's been given a new, specific life with a color change and a little texture.

Mutabor *Germany*

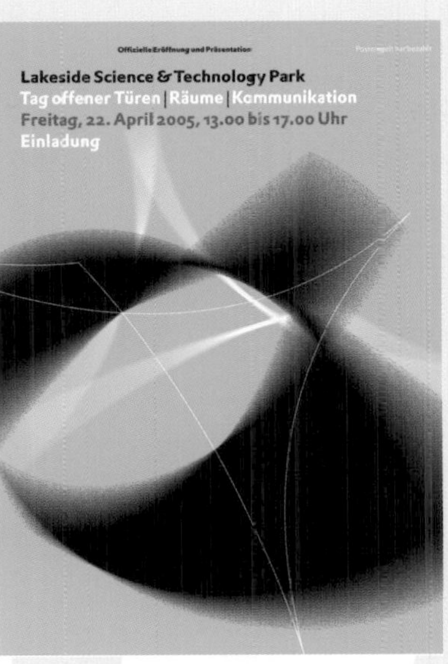

No photography or illustration available? Can't draw? No sweat. A designer with a strong understanding of how abstract form communicates—and what simple means (here, drawing software and a blur filter)—can transform uncomplicated visual elements into strikingly original and conceptually appropriate images.

Clemens Théobert Schedler *Austria*

Conservatoire
National
Supérieur d'Art
Dramatique
Atelier Danse
de 3e année dirigé
par
Caroline Marcadé
Un Bal Blanc Nacré
Mercredi 12
et jeudi 13 avril 2006
à 19h30

This poster defies nearly all trends currently in vogue: it's neither photographic nor illustrative; it's not flashy or glamorous; it's not technically complex; it doesn't look digital; and it's very nearly symmetrical. But it conveys energy and movement, and optically it's very powerful.

Apeloig Design *France*

17

Ignore fashion. Seriously.

Granted, this can be a tricky rule to follow because your job is to communicate to your audience who, unless time travel is now available to the public, exists today and only today, in the present. These people in the present have particular tastes and expectations about how they like their communications to look. Other designers around you are getting significant attention because their work is so now and cool and with it. Forget that. Look at it this way: if you design the project and style it around the meaning, not the audience's expectations of current stylistic conceits, several good things will come out of it. First, it's likely to mean more to the audience and be useful a lot longer, so it won't end up in a landfill as quickly, polluting the ecosystem. Second, it might even have the staying power to qualify for the history books. Nobody looks at the Pantheon, designed almost two thousand years ago, for example, and says, "Ewww, that's like, so First Century."

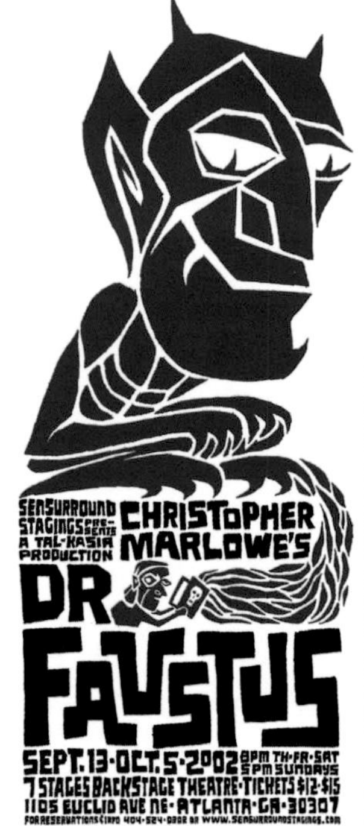

Although illustration is enjoying a rise in popularity, this particular illustration is not what's popular: flat, posterized, clearly digital images with complex texture and detail. This image, in honor of its subject, is nearly handmade in appearance and harks back to an earlier time.

Ames Brothers *United States*

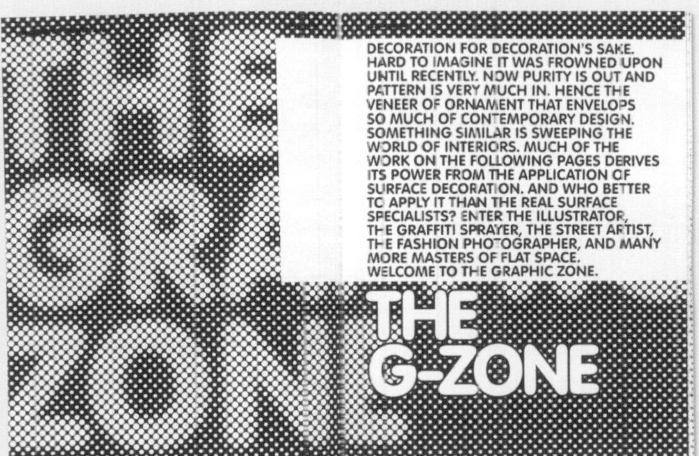

DECORATION FOR DECORATION'S SAKE. HARD TO IMAGINE IT WAS FROWNED UPON UNTIL RECENTLY. NOW PURITY IS OUT AND PATTERN IS VERY MUCH IN. HENCE THE VENEER OF ORNAMENT THAT ENVELOPS SO MUCH OF CONTEMPORARY DESIGN. SOMETHING SIMILAR IS SWEEPING THE WORLD OF INTERIORS. MUCH OF THE WORK ON THE FOLLOWING PAGES DERIVES ITS POWER FROM THE APPLICATION OF SURFACE DECORATION. AND WHO BETTER TO APPLY IT THAN THE REAL SURFACE SPECIALISTS? ENTER THE ILLUSTRATOR, THE GRAFFITI SPRAYER, THE STREET ARTIST, THE FASHION PHOTOGRAPHER, AND MANY MORE MASTERS OF FLAT SPACE. WELCOME TO THE GRAPHIC ZONE.
THE
G-ZONE

The extremely large type and texture in the background appear to pull to the left against the edge of the page while the white block appears to move to the right. The left alignment of the text block creates a vertical movement . . . never mind the ambiguous foreground and background state.

Coma *Netherlands*

By positioning the letters at staggered intervals around the format and then rotating the formation in the background, the designer creates not only a dynamic set of positive and negative intervals but also optical motion and a perception of shifting between background and foreground.

Stereotype Design *United States*

18

Move it! Static equals dull.

People make a weird assumption about two-dimensional visual stuff, and that is—it's flat and lifeless! Go figure. This is why painters and designers have been working like dogs for 1,000 years to create the illusion of three-dimensional movement on a flat surface: to fool the viewer into having a *moving* experience! If a layout is clearly flat and fails to offer a sense of movement or spatial interaction, a state that is relatively easy to achieve, the viewer's brain is likely to be uninterested enough to hang out and see what the message is. Static compositions say, "You've figured me out . . . so walk away, nothing to see here."

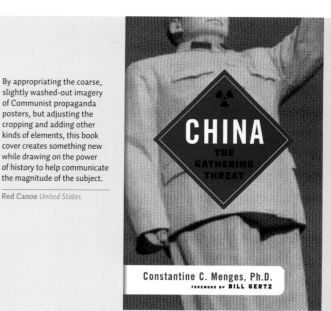

By appropriating the coarse, slightly washed-out imagery of Communist propaganda posters, but adjusting the cropping and adding other kinds of elements, this book cover creates something new while drawing on the power of history to help communicate the magnitude of the subject.

Red Canoe *United States*

19 Look to history, but don't repeat it.

The design of the past has its place. It's inspiring and important for a designer to consider how communication strategies and aesthetics have changed over time, and to understand how his or her own work fits into the continuum of thought and practice. Even more useful is the realization that somewhere along the way, another designer faced a similar problem... and solved it. To slavishly reproduce a particular period style because it's really cool—or worse, because the clients think that their "Circus Party" invitation should look like an 1846 wood-type poster—is just unacceptable. Learn from the work of others, but do your own work.

This cover for a reissued version of a significant art-movement text represents the energy and irreverence of the period and its style without mimicking it; instead of repetition and overlap, hallmarks of the style, this type is distorted and deformed.

Marek Okon *Canada*

Every letter has its own shape, and, at such a tremendous size in this poster, those shapes are all exaggerated; as a result, the repeated three-letter structure becomes intricate and asymmetrical as the viewer is able to appreciate the varied contours of black space around the forms. A dynamically irregular spatter of red dots introduces random movement and a sense of unexpected violence.

Studio International *Croatia*

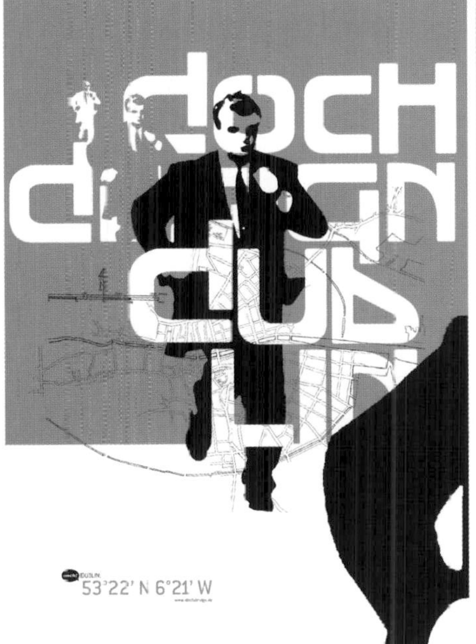

Although the black figure essentially is centered in the format, it participates in an asymmetrical arrangement of forms—both positive and negative—that moves compositional elements in a diagonal breaking of space from upper left to lower right. The line of type at the lower left enhances the asymmetrical quality of the arrangement.

Dochdesign *Germany*

It's true that symmetry occurs in nature—just look at our bodies—but that doesn't mean it's a good strategy for designing. Symmetrical visual arrangements are generally static and offer little movement (see Rule No. 18). Worse, symmetrical arrangements make integrating asymmetrical image material awkward, and limit a designer's flexibility in pacing and dealing with content that doesn't quite want to fit into the symmetrical mold. Last, but certainly not least: symmetry shouts very loudly that the designer is lazy and likes to let the format do the designing. The format has a center axis, and clearly everyone can see that. Why let the format tell you what to do? You tell the format who's boss.

Symmetry is the ultimate evil.

FORM SPACE

Chapter 1

> I am convinced that abstract form, imagery, color, texture, and material convey meaning equal to or greater than words.

Katherine McCoy

Graphic designer and former director, Cranbrook School of Design

AND

There is no longer agreement anywhere about art itself, and under these circumstances we must go back to the beginning, to concern ourselves with dots and lines and circles and all the rest of it.

Armin Hoffmann

Graphic designer and former director, Basel School of Design: 1946–1985

ACE

First Things First All graphic design—all image making, regardless of medium or intent—centers on manipulating form. It's a question of making stuff to look at and organizing it so that it looks good and helps people understand not just what they're seeing, but what seeing it means for them. "Form" is that stuff: shapes, lines, textures, words, and pictures. The form that is chosen or made, for whatever purpose, should be considered as carefully as possible, because every form, no matter how abstract or seemingly simple, carries meaning. Our brains use the forms of things to identify them; the form is a message. When we see a circle, for example, our minds try to identify it: Sun? Moon? Earth? Coin? Pearl? No one form is any better at communicating than any other, but the choice of form is critical if it's to communicate the right message. ■ In addition, making that form as beautiful as possible is what elevates designing above just plopping stuff in front of an audience and letting them pick through it, like hyenas mulling over a dismembered carcass. The term "beautiful" has a host of meanings, depending on context; here, we're not talking about beauty to mean "pretty"

Every form, no matter how abstract it appears, is meaningful. A circle, for example, is a continuous line, and its roundness is a very specific trait. A circle is therefore endless, organic, rotational, cellular, and a totality. A square, conversely, has angles and sides that are equal in measure, and is static. A square is therefore analytical, mathematical, unnatural, and finite.

Form is stuff—including all kinds of imagery and type.

The idea of formal beauty is highly subjective. Both these images can be considered beautiful, despite the fact that one is sensuous and "clean" and that the other is aggressive and "dirty."

or "serene and delicate" or even "sensuous" in an academic, Beaux-Arts, home-furnishings-catalog way. Aggressive, ripped, collaged illustrations are beautiful; chunky woodcut type is beautiful; all kinds of rough images can be called beautiful. Here, "beautiful" as a descriptor might be better replaced by the term "resolved,"–meaning that the form's parts are all related to each other and no part of it seems unconsidered or alien to any other part–and the term "decisive"–meaning that the form feels confident, credible, and on purpose. That's a lot to consider up front, so more attention will be given to these latter ideas shortly ■ Form does what it does somewhere, and that somewhere is called, simply, "space." This term, which describes something three-dimensional, applies to something that is, most often, a two-dimensional surface. That surface can be a business card, a poster, a Web page, a television screen, the side of a box, or a plate-glass window in front of a store. Regardless of what the surface is, it is a two-dimensional space that will be acted upon, with form, to become an apparent three-dimensional space. In painting, this space is called the "picture plane," which painters have historically imagined as a strange, membrane-like "window" between the physical world and the illusory depth of the painted environment. Coincidentally, this sense of illusory depth behind or below the picture plane applies consistently to both figurative and abstract imagery.

PEOPLE OFTEN OVERLOOK the potential of abstract form—or, for that matter, the abstract visual qualities of images such as photographs. This form study uses paper to investigate that very idea in a highly abstract way. What could this be? Who cares? It's about curl in relation to angle, negative space to positive strip. To understand how form works, the form must first be seen.

JRoss Design *United States*

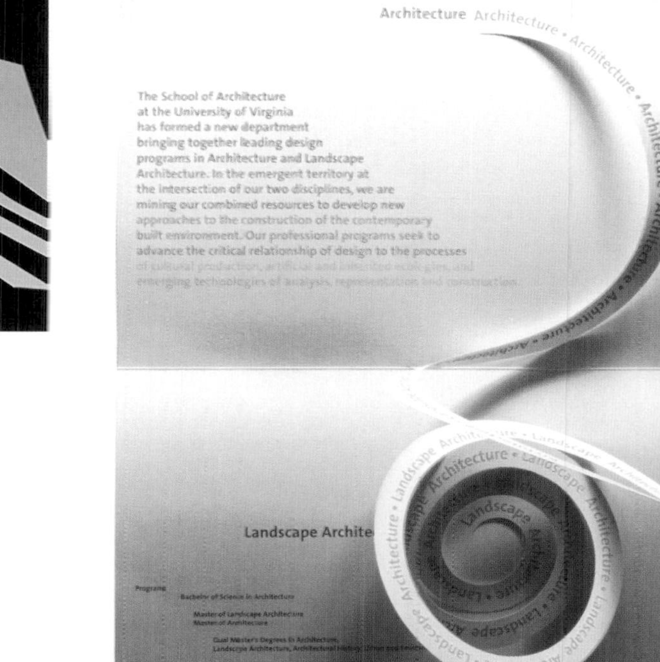

INVENTIVE USE OF a die-cut in this poster creates a surprising, inventive message about structure and organic design. The spiraling strip that carries green type becomes a plant tendril and a structural object in support of the poster's message. The dimensional spiral, along with its shadows, shares a linear quality with the printed type, but contrasts its horizontal and diagonal flatness.

Studio Works *United States*

LINE, MASS, AND TEXTURE communicate before words or a recognizable image. On this invitation for a calligraphy exhibit, the sense of pen gesture, flowing of marks, and the desert-like environment of high-contrast shadow and texture are all evident in a highly abstract composition.

VCU Qatar *Qatar*

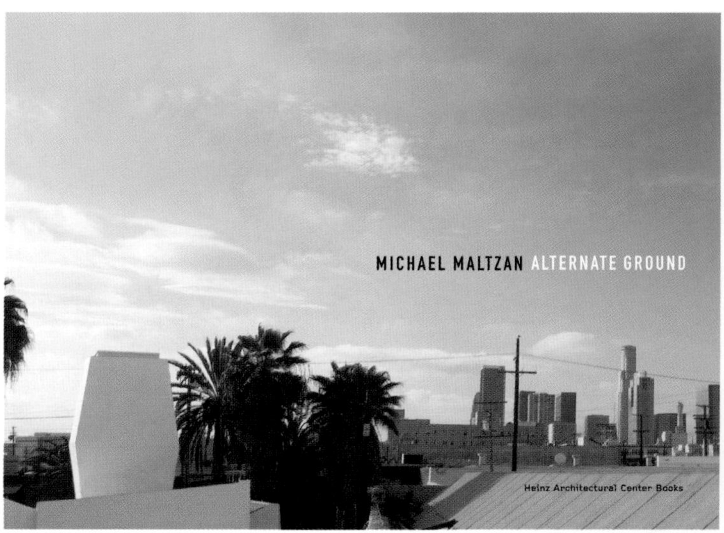

MICHAEL MALTZAN ALTERNATE GROUND
Heinz Architectural Center Books

ÅRSRAPPORT 2005
Vi skaper morgendagens medier. I dag.
SCHIBSTED

THE VERTICAL FORMAT of this annual report intensifies the human element as well as the vertical movement of flowers upward; the sense of growth is shown literally by the image, but expressed viscerally by the upward thrust of the format.

Cobra *Norway*

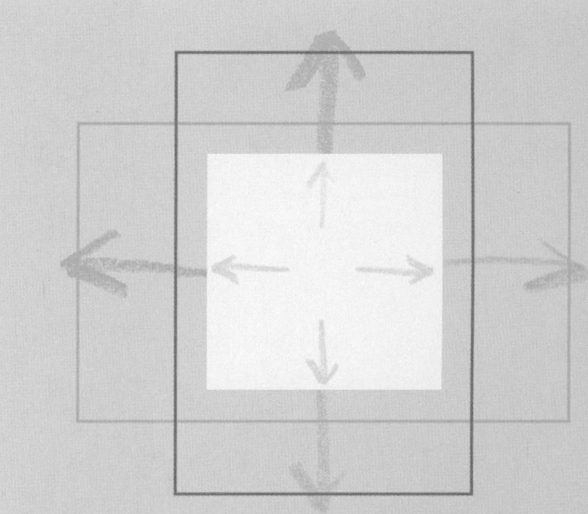

The shape of a space produces overall visual effects that will have a profound impact on the perception of form interaction within it. A square format is neutral in emphasis—no side exerts any more influence than any other. A vertical format is confrontational, creating an upward and a downward thrust. A horizontal format produces a calmer, lateral movement that is relatively inert compared to that of a vertical format.

The Shape of Space Also called the "format," the proportional dimensions of the space where form is going to do its thing is something to think about. The size of the format space, compared to the form within it, will change the perceived presence of the form. A smaller form within a larger spatial format—which will have a relatively restrained presence—will be perceived differently from a large form in the same format—which will be perceived as confrontational. The perception of this difference in presence is, intrinsically, a message to be controlled. The shape of the format is also an important consideration. A square format is neutral; because all its sides are of equal length, there's no thrust or emphasis in any one direction, and a viewer will be able to concentrate on the interaction of forms without having to pay attention to the format at all. A vertical format, however, is highly confrontational. Its shape produces a simultaneously upward and downward thrust that a viewer will optically traverse over and over again, as though sizing it up; somewhere in the dim, ancient hardwiring of the brain, a vertical object is catalogued as potentially being another person—its verticality mirrors that of the upright body. Horizontal formats are generally passive; they produce a calming sensation and imply lateral motion, deriving from an equally ancient perception that they are related to the horizon. If you need convincing, note the root of the word itself.

THE HORIZONTAL SHAPE of this book's format echoes the horizon that is prevalent in the photographs of the urban landscape that it documents. The horizontal frame becomes the camera eye, and it is relatively restful and contemplative.

Brett Yasko *United States*

THE SQUARE CD-ROM CASE is an appropriately neutral—and modular—format, considering the subject matter, pioneering Modernist architect Ludwig Mies van der Rohe. The circular CD-ROM obscures portions of the image in the tray but also adds its own layer.

Thomas Csano *Canada*

A small format enhances the presence, or apparent mass, of an element; a larger format decreases the presence of an element with the same physical size.

DYNAMIC, ANGULAR negative spaces contrast with the solidity of the letterforms' strokes and enhance the sharpness of the narrow channels of space that join them together.

Research Studios *United Kingdom*

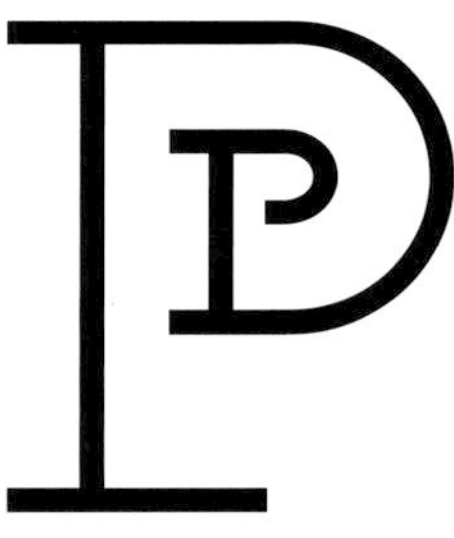

THE BLACK, LIGHTWEIGHT letter **P** in this logo, a positive form, encloses a negative space around a smaller version of itself; but that smaller version becomes the counterspace of a white, outlined **P.** Note the solid white "stem" in between the two.

Apeloig Design *France*

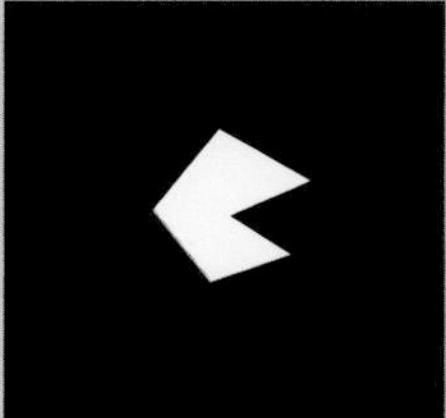

A positive (black) form on a negative (white) ground, and the reverse, retains its identity as positive if there is no other form or spatial break to define it as anything else. Note also how the white form on the black background appears larger than its same-sized black counterpart on the white field.

As a black (positive) form becomes larger within a negative (white) field, the leftover negative spaces become smaller and, eventually, might appear to be positive (white forms) in the context of a black field.

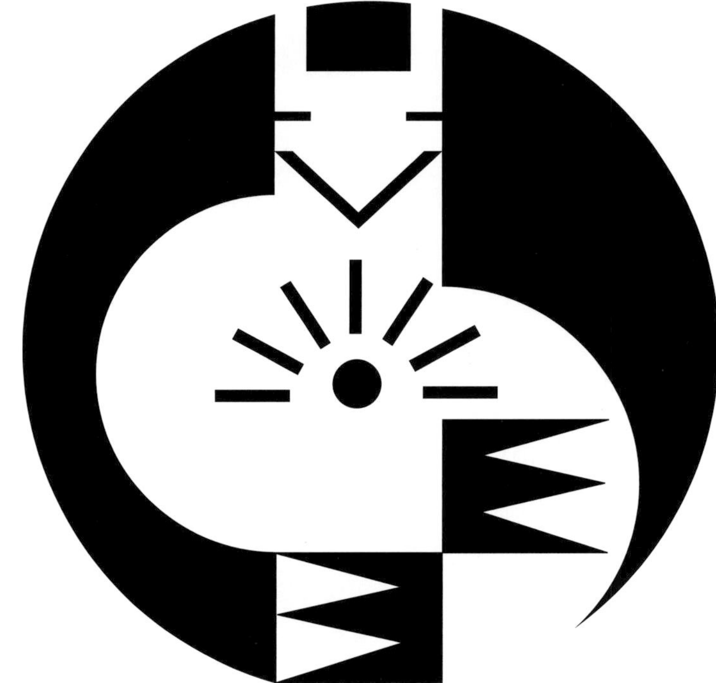

VARIED CONTRASTS IN positive and negative areas—such as those between the angular, linear beak; the round dot; the curved shoulders; and the sharp claws in this griffon image—spark interest and engage the viewer's mind.

Vicki Li *Iowa State University, United States*

Positive and Negative Form is considered a positive element, a solid thing or object. Space is considered negative—not in a bad way, but as the absence, or opposite, of form. Space is the "ground" in which form becomes a "figure." The relationship between form and space, or figure and ground, is complementary and mutually dependent; it's impossible to alter one and not the other. The confrontation between figure and ground defines the kind of visual activity, movement, and sense of three-dimensionality perceived by the viewer. All these qualities are inherently communicative—resolving the relationships between figure and ground is the first step in creating a simple, overarching message about the content of the designed work, before the viewer registers the identity of an image or the content of any text that is present. Organizing figure—the positive—in relation to the ground—or negative—is therefore one of the most important visual aspects of design because it affects so many other aspects, from general emotional response to informational hierarchy. ■ The figure/ground relationship must be understandable and present some kind of logic to the viewer; it must also be composed in such a way that the feeling this compositional, or visual, logic generates is perceived as appropriate to the message the designer is trying to convey. The logic of composition—the visual order and relationships of the figure and ground—is entirely abstract, but depends greatly on how the brain interprets the information that the viewer sees. Visual logic, all by itself, can also carry meaning. An extremely active relationship between figure and ground might be appropriate for one kind of communication, conveying energy, growth, and aggression; a static relationship, communicating messages such as quietness,

DARKER AND LIGHTER FIELDS of color are used interchangeably for light and shadow to define a three-dimensional space.

LSD *Spain*

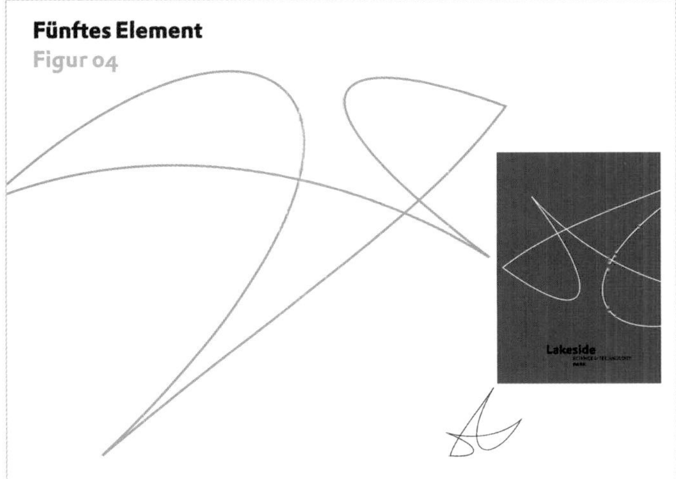

AS THE LINES OF this graphic form cross each other, the distinction between what is positive and what is negative becomes ambiguous. Some areas that appear to be negative at one glance become positive in the next.

Clemens Théobert Schedler *Austria*

restraint, or contemplation, might be equally appropriate in another context. ■ The degree of activity might depend on how many forms are interacting in a given space, the size of the forms relative to the space, or how intricate the alternation between positive and negative appears to be. However, a composition might have relatively simple structural qualities—meaning only one or two forms in a relatively restrained interaction—but unusual relationships that appear more active or more complex, despite the composition's apparent simplicity. ■ In some compositions, the figure/ground relationship can become quite complex, to the extent that each might appear optically to be the other at the same time. This effect, in which what appears positive one minute appears negative the next, is called "figure/ground reversal." This rich visual experience is extremely engaging; the brain gets to play a little game, and, as a result, the viewer is enticed to stay within the composition a little longer and investigate other aspects to see what other fun he or she can find. If you can recall one of artist M.C. Escher's drawings—in which white birds, flying in a pattern, reveal black birds made up of the spaces between them as they get closer together—you're looking at a classic example of figure/ground reversal in action. The apparent reversal of foreground and background is also a complex visual effect that might be delivered through very simple figure/ground relationships, by overlapping two forms of different sizes, for example, or allowing a negative element to cross in front of a positive element unexpectedly.

THE TWO MUSHROOM SHAPES appear to be positive elements, but they are actually the negative counterspaces of a lumpy letter M, which, incidentally, bears a resemblance to a mound of dirt.

Frost Design *Australia*

DESPITE THE FACT THAT most of the elements in this symbol are linear—and appear to occupy the same, flat spatial plane—the small figures toward the bottom appear to be in the foreground because one of them connects to the negative space outside the mark, and the line contours around these figures are heavier than those of the larger, crowned figure.

Sunyoung Park *Iowa State University, United States*

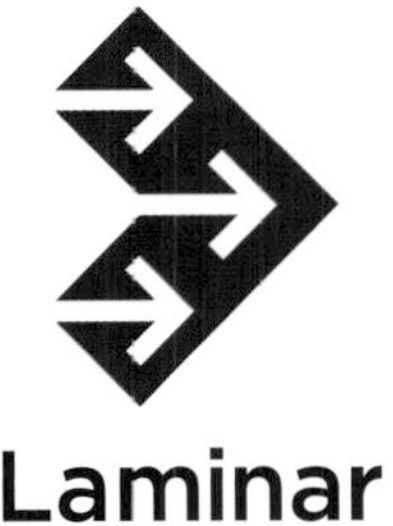

THE NEGATIVE ARROWS become positive against the large angled form.

John Jensen *Iowa State University; United States*

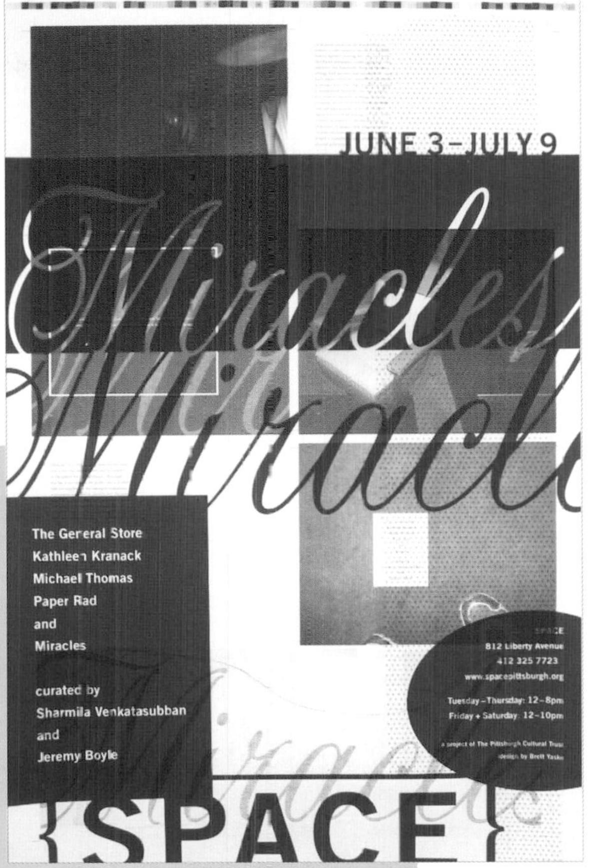

JUNE 3–JULY 9
Miracles
Miracle
The General Store
Kathleen Kranack
Michael Thomas
Paper Rad
and
Miracles
curated by
Sharmila Venkatasubban
and
Jeremy Boyle
812 Liberty Avenue
412 325 7723
www.spacepittsburgh.org
Tuesday–Thursday: 12–8pm
Friday + Saturday: 12–10pm
{SPACE{

POSITIVE AND NEGATIVE space, as they relate to type and ink, are used in an interesting repetition to create more ambiguous space in this poster. The red bar becomes flat against the photographs, but the reversed-out type seems to come forward, as does its positive repetition below. Although the photographs seem flat toward the top, they seem to drop into a deeper space down below, as they contrast the flat, linear quality of the script type.

Brett Yasko *United States*

Comparison of an active figure/ground relationship (left) with an inactive figure/ground relationship (right) hints at the potential for meaning to be perceived even in such a fundamentally simple, abstract environment. Compare these pairs of simple, opposing ideas between the two examples: loud/quiet; aggressive/passive; nervous/sedate; complex/simple; energetic/weak; and living/dead.

As shown earlier, cropping large forms within a smaller space may generate the perception of new forms that become positive, a simple example of figure/ground reversal.

The intrusion of a small shape of exterior negative space, relative to the positive form, causes the negative space to take on the quality of a positive white form while still allowing the eye to perceive the black form as positive overall. This complex figure/ground reversal presents rich optical possibilities in composition, even among relatively simple, or relatively few, form elements.

It is what it appears to be. Make decisions about forms based on their appearance rather than on intended effect or, worse, measurements. Form is optically deceptive and so must be judged according to what it looks like; this is all the viewer will have to go on as well. In this example, the three shapes—circle, square, and triangle—are first shown being mathematically the same height (top). You'll notice that the square appears larger than both the circle and the triangle. So, for all intents and purposes, it is. This optical illusion is a function of how our brains interpret rounded, angular, and square images relative to each other (see *Geometric Form*, page 54). If the goal here is to make all three shapes appear to be the same size, the circle and the triangle must be adjusted in size until they do (bottom). Only when all three shapes appear to be the same size are they really the same size—as far as the viewer is concerned.

CONSIDER EACH ELEMENT in this abstract page spread. Which form is descending? Which form is most in the background? Which form descends from right to left? Which form counteracts that movement? Which form moves from top to bottom? Which angles align and which do not? What effect does texture appear to have on the relative flatness or depth of the overall background color? Being able to describe what forms appear to be doing is crucial to understanding how they do it—and how to make them do it when you want to.

Andreas Ortag *Austria*

Clarity and Decisiveness Resolved and refined compositions create clear, accessible visual messages. Resolving and refining a composition means understanding what kind of message is being carried by a given form, what it does in space, and what effect the combination of these aspects has on the viewer. ■ First, some more definitions. To say that a composition is "resolved" means that the reasons for where everything is, how big the things are, and what they're doing with each other in and around space—the visual logic—is clear, and that all the parts seem considered relative to each other. "Refined" is a quirky term when used to describe form or composition; in this context, it means that the form or composition has been made to be more like itself—more clearly, more simply, more indisputably communicating one specific kind of quality. Like the term "beautiful," the quality of "refinement" can apply to rough, organic, and aggressive forms, as well as sensuous, elegant, and clean ones. It's not a term of value so much as an indicator of whether the form is as clear as possible. ■ This, of course, brings up the issue of "clarity," which has to do with whether a composition and the forms within it are readily understandable. Some of this understandability depends on the refinement of the forms, and some of it depends on the resolution of the relationships between form and space and whether these are "decisive," appearing to be on purpose and indisputable. A form or a spatial relationship can be called decisive if it is clearly one thing and not the other: for example, is one form larger or smaller than the one next to it, or are they both the same size? If the answer to this question is quick and nobody can argue with it—"The thing on the left is larger" or "Both things are the same size"—then the formal or spatial relationship is decisive. Being decisive with the visual qualities of a layout is important in design because the credibility of the message being conveyed depends on the confidence with which the forms and composition have been resolved. A weak composition, one that is indecisive, evokes uneasiness in a viewer, not just boredom. Uneasiness is not a good platform on which to build a complicated message that might involve persuasion.

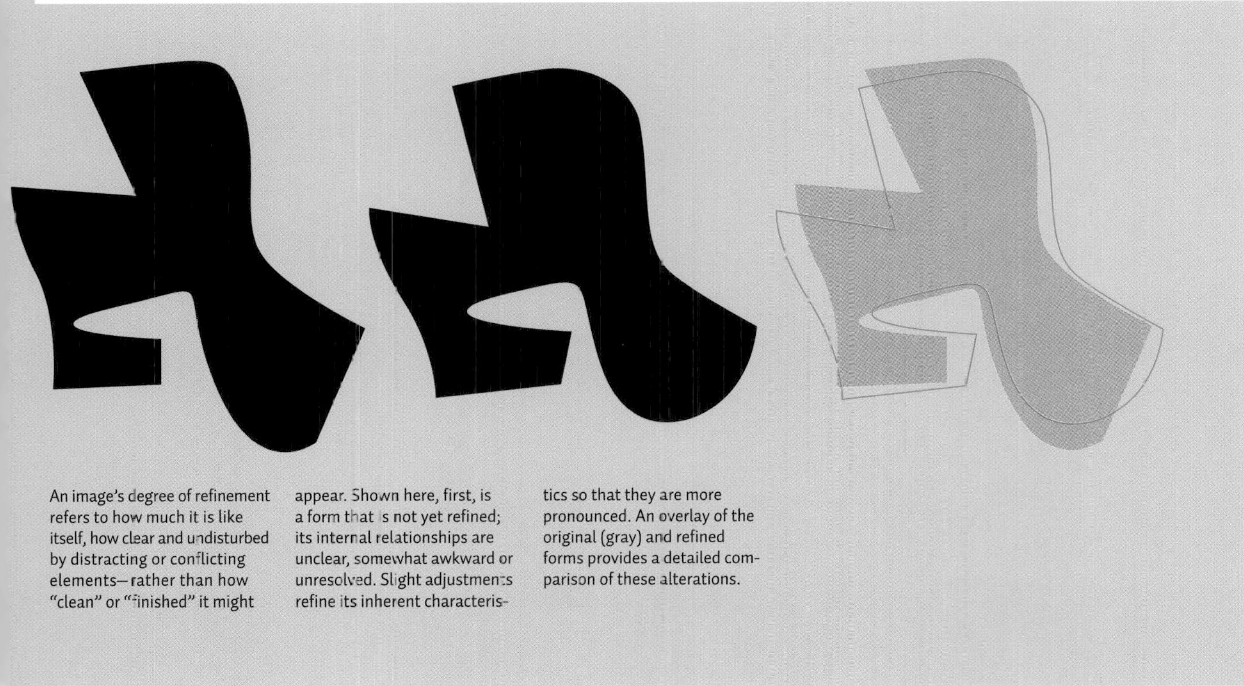

An image's degree of refinement refers to how much it is like itself, how clear and undisturbed by distracting or conflicting elements—rather than how "clean" or "finished" it might appear. Shown here, first, is a form that is not yet refined; its internal relationships are unclear, somewhat awkward or unresolved. Slight adjustments refine its inherent characteristics so that they are more pronounced. An overlay of the original (gray) and refined forms provides a detailed comparison of these alterations.

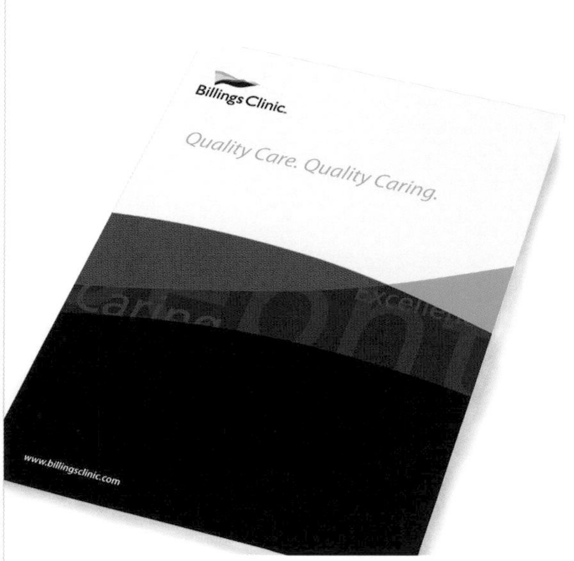

THE LOGO'S ABSTRACTION is expanded into a clearly branded graphic environment whose wave-like forms allude to the protective, organic, enveloping quality of health care. The lines created by the typography contrast the liquid plane forms, but respond to their lateral movement across the format.

Monigle Associates *United States*

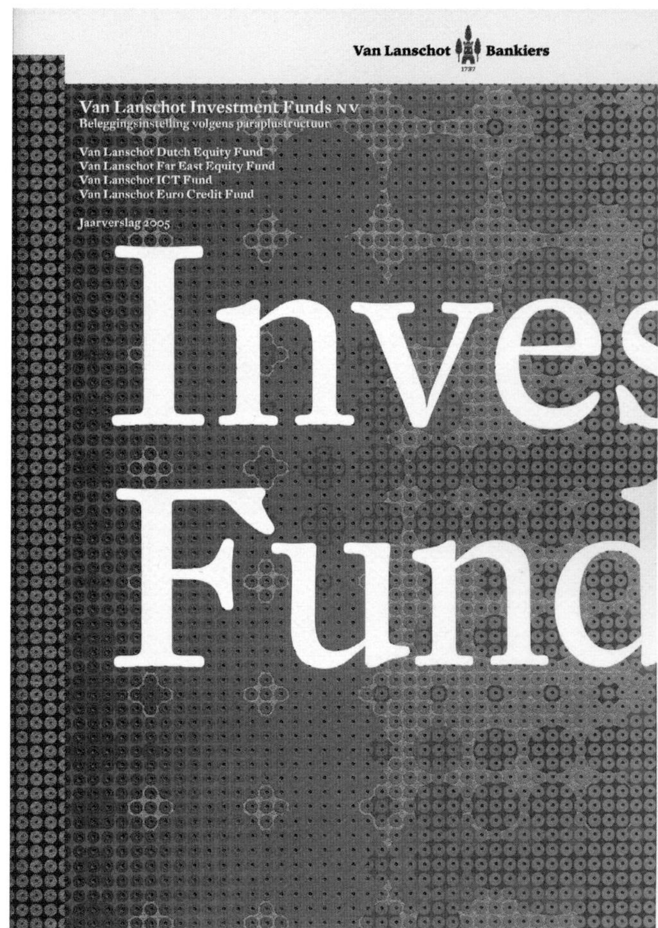

THE DOT PATTERN EMBODIES ideas related to financial investing, given context by the typography: graph-like organization, growth, merging and separating, networking, and so on.

UNA (Amsterdam) Designers *Netherlands*

LINE CONTRASTS with texture, organic cluster contrasts with geometric text, and large elements contrast with small in this promotional poster.

Munda Graphics *Australia*

Each of These Things Is Unlike the Other

There are several kinds of basic form, and each does something different. Rather, the eye and the brain perceive each kind of form as doing something different, as having its own kind of identity. The perception of these differences and how they affect the form's interaction with space and other forms around it, of differing identities, is what constitutes their perceived meaning. The context in which a given form appears—the space or ground it occupies and its relationship to adjacent forms—will change its perceived meaning, but its intrinsic identity and optical effect always remains an underlying truth. The most basic types of form are the dot, the line, and the plane. Of these, the line and the plane also can be categorized as geometric or organic; the plane can be either flat, textured, or appear to have three-dimensional volume or mass.

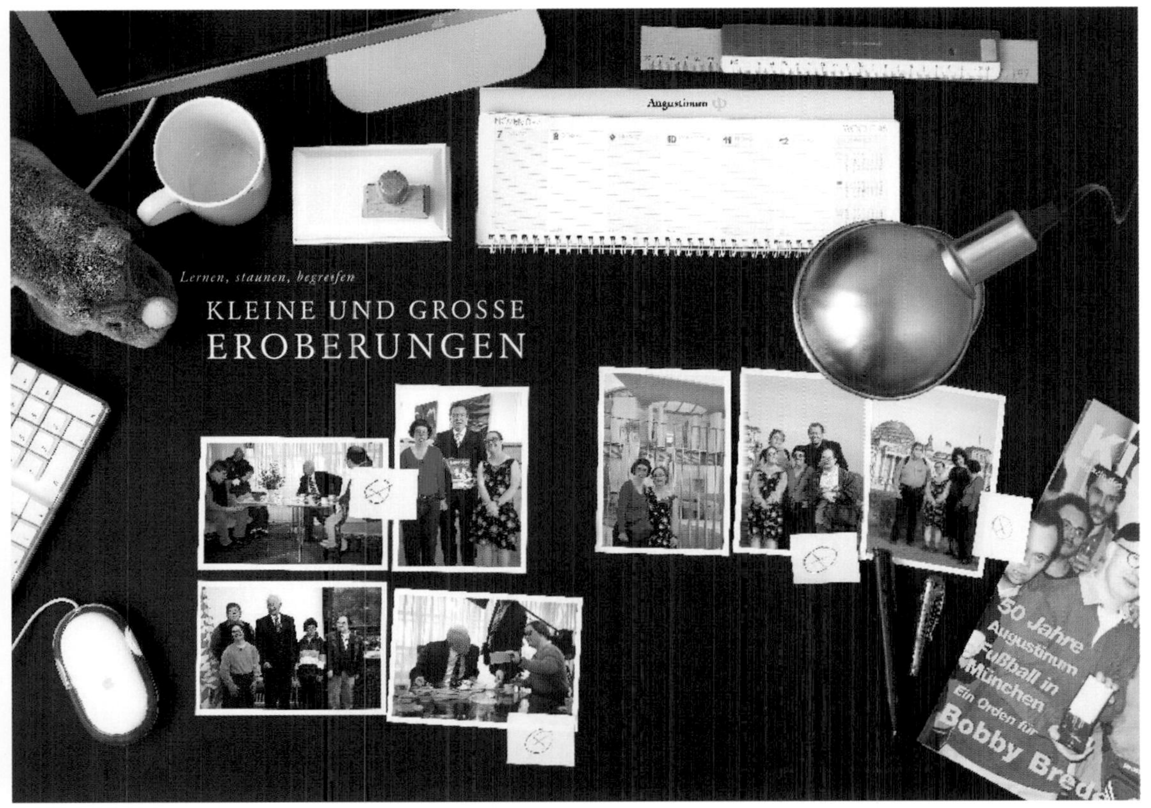

IT'S TRUE THAT THIS BOOK spread is a photograph of what appears to be a desktop. But it's actually a composition of dots, lines, rectangles, and negative spaces—all of different sizes and orientation, relative to each other.

Finest Magma *Germany*

ALTHOUGH THE JAZZ FIGURES are recognizable images, they behave nonetheless as a system of angled lines, interacting with a secondary system of hard- and soft-edged planes. In addition to considering the back-and-forth rhythm created by the geometry of all these angles, the designer has also carefully considered the forms' alternation between positive and negative to enhance their rhythmic quality and create a sense of changing position from foreground to background.

Niklaus Troxler *Switzerland*

MOST OF THE VISUAL elements in this brochure are dots; some are more clearly dots, such as the circular blobs and splotches, and some are less so, such as the letterforms and the little logo at the top. Despite not physically being dots, these elements exert the same kind of focused or radiating quality that dots do, and they react to each other in space like dots. In terms of a message, these dots are about gesture, primal thumping, and spontaneity… and, more concretely, about music.

Voice *Australia*

The Dot The identity of a dot is that of a point of focused attention; the dot simultaneously contracts inward and radiates outward. A dot anchors itself in any space into which it is introduced and provides a reference point for the eye relative to other forms surrounding it, including other dots, and its proximity to the edges of a format's space. As seemingly simple a form as it might appear, however, a dot is a complex object, the fundamental building block of all other forms. As a dot increases in size to cover a larger area, and its outer contour becomes noticeable, even differentiated, it still remains a dot. Every shape or mass with a recognizable center—a square, a trapezoid, a triangle, a blob—is a dot, no matter how big it is. True, such a shape's outer contour will interact with space around it more dramatically when it becomes bigger, but the shape is still essentially a dot. Even replacing a "flat" graphic shape with a photographic object, such as a silhouetted picture of a clock, will not change its fundamental identity as a dot. Recognizing this essential quality of the dot form, regardless of what other characteristics it takes on incidentally in specific occurrences, is crucial to understanding its visual effect in space and its relationship to adjacent forms.

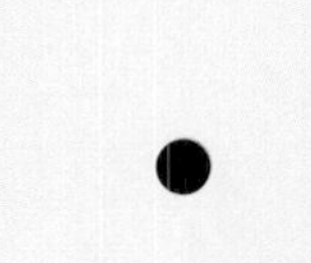

When a dot enters a space, it establishes an immediate relationship with the space; the proportion of the dot to its surrounding area is the most important consideration; second is its relative position to the edges of the space.

The dot breaks the space in a neutral way, being weightless and internally balanced, but it might already create noticeable differences in spatial areas if it is placed off center. The centrally located dot is settled, comfortable, and static, but it dominates the space around it; as it moves from the center, there is a shift in dominance—the background asserts itself and tension arises.

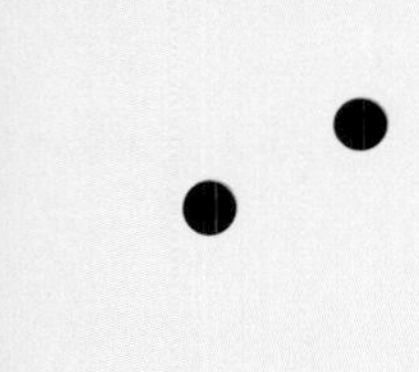

Introducing a second dot shifts attention away from the relationship of the space to the interaction of the two dots. They refer to each other and imply a structure—an invisible, connecting path that splits space apart.

As dots approach each other, the tension between them increases. If the space between dots is just about zero, its presence assumes more importance than the dots themselves, and even more importance relative to any other spatial interval. If the dots overlap, especially if they are different sizes, the tension created by their closeness is somewhat relieved. However, a new tension arises—the dichotomy of flat, graphic form and the appearance of three-dimensional depth as one dot seemingly inhabits a foreground, and the other, a background position.

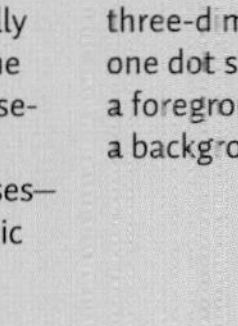

The flat dot and photographic images are all still dots.

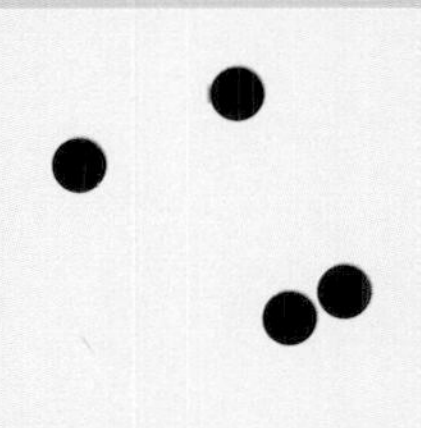

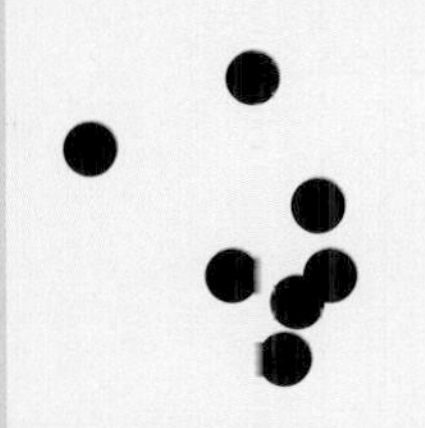

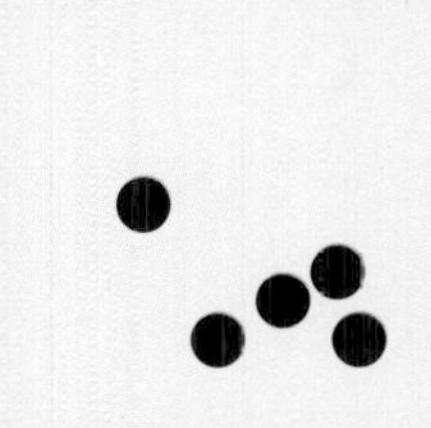

The closer the dots are to each other, the more powerful the sense of their unique identity as objects; the further apart, the more pronounced the sense of structure, induced by the invisible path between them.

Additional dots in close proximity to the pair, however, reduce the focus on identity and increase attention to their reciprocal relationship and thus, a sense of structure or meaning. How far are the dots from each other?

Is each dot the same distance from its counterparts? What is their configuration, and what outer shape does it make? What does this shape signify?

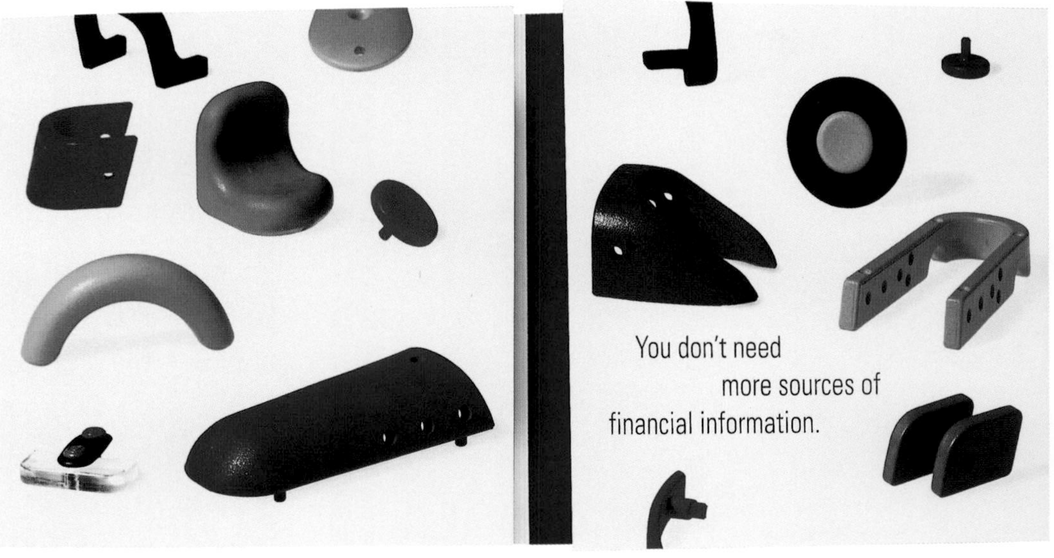
You don't need
more sources of
financial information.

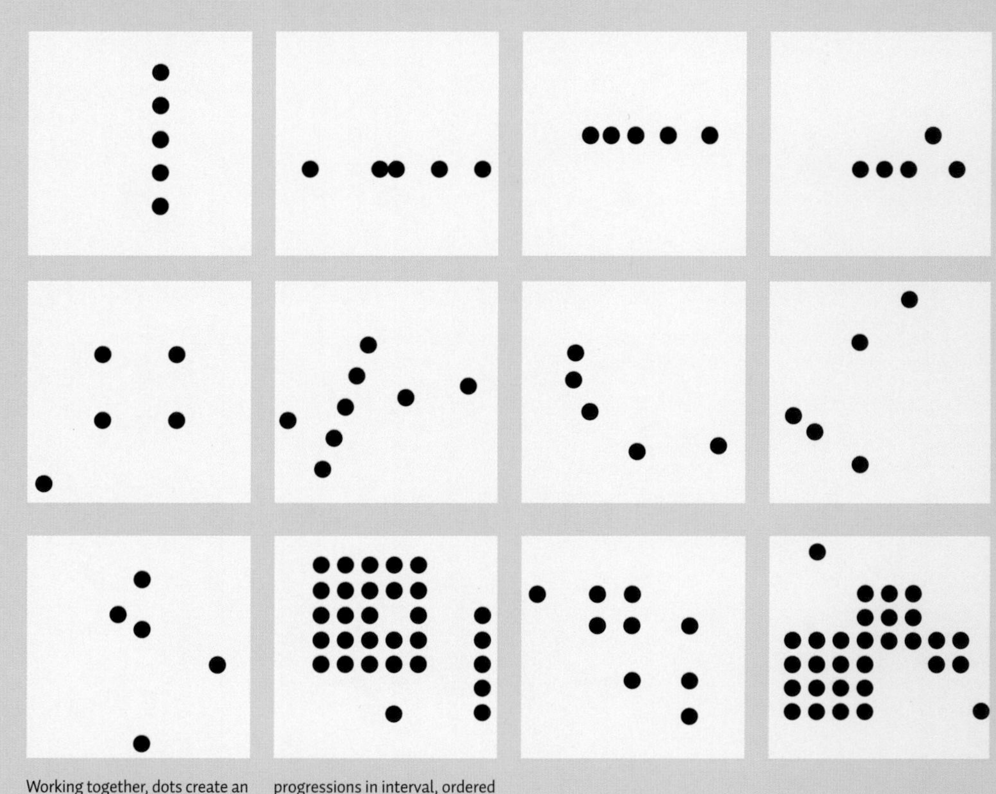

Working together, dots create an endless variety of arrangements and increasing complexity—a single vertical or horizontal row, rotated rows, an isolated dot in contrast to a group, progressions in interval, ordered rows in a grid structure, angles and geometric patterns, curves, and so on.

NOT ALL DOTS ARE CIRCULAR! Barring a few elements that are clearly lines, many of the dots on the gatefold pages of this brochure are something other than circular. However, they are still treated as dots for the purpose of composition, judging size change, proximity, tension, and negative spaces between as though they were flat, black, abstract dots. Note how the type's linear quality contrasts with the dots on the pages.

C+G Partners *United States*

The negative dot is created in reverse from the convergence of other forms.

Clustering dots of different sizes creates a more varied contour, but overall the cluster retains its identity as a dot.

The perception of spatial depth occurs among dots that are different sizes; a larger dot advances in front of a smaller one. Changing the relative tonal values of the dots, however, can create an ambiguous spatial tension among the dots, even though their relative sizes remain the same.

A

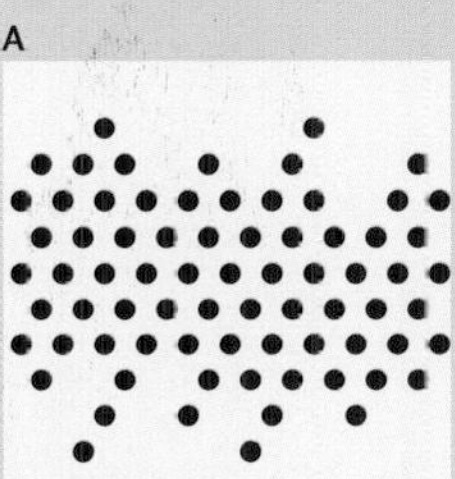

B

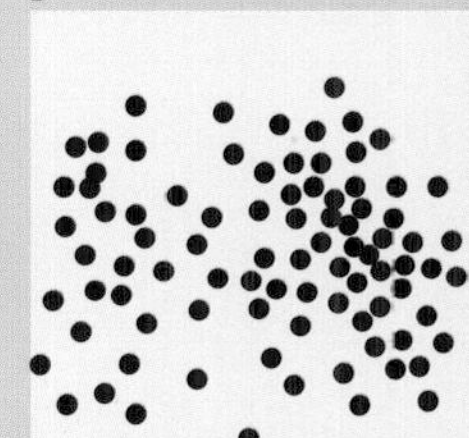

A tremendous number of small dots create (A) a regularized pattern or (B) a randomized texture. The darkness or lightness of these dots depends on density—how close the dots are to each other.

THE CLUSTER OF DOTS creates a kind of undulating mass. The outer contour of the cluster is very active, with differing proximity and tension to the format edges. The initial "b" offers a complement to the cluster and contrast in scale. The compositional logic is clear and decisive.

Leonardo Sonnoli *Italy*

The Line A line's essential character is one of connection; it unites areas within a composition. This connection may be invisible, defined by the pulling effect on space between two dots, or it may take on visible form as a concrete object, traveling back and forth between a starting point and an ending point. ■ Unlike a dot, therefore, the quality of linearity is one of movement and direction; a line is inherently dynamic, rather than static. The line might appear to start somewhere and continue indefinitely, or it might travel a finite distance. While dots create points of focus, lines perform other functions; they may separate spaces, join spaces or objects, create protective barriers, enclose or constrain, or intersect. Changing the size—the thickness—of a line relative to its length has a much greater impact on its quality as a line than does changing the size of a dot. As a line becomes thicker or heavier in weight, it gradually becomes perceived as a plane surface or mass; to maintain the line's identity, it must be proportionally lengthened.

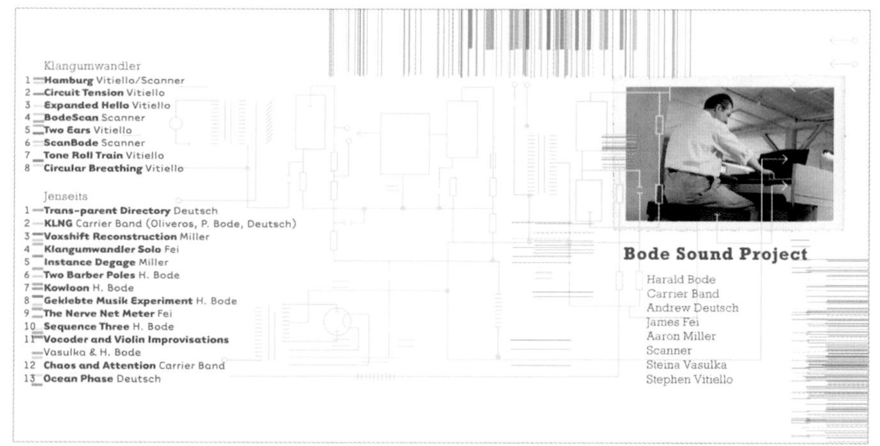

Klangumwandler
1 Hamburg Vitiello/Scanner
2 Circuit Tension Vitiello
3 Expanded Hello Vitiello
4 BodeScan Scanner
5 Two Ears Vitiello
6 ScanBode Scanner
7 Tone Roll Train Vitiello
8 Circular Breathing Vitiello
Jenseits
1 Trans-parent Directory Deutsch
2 KLNG Carrier Band (Oliveros, P. Bode, Deutsch)
3 Voxshift Reconstruction Miller
4 Klangumwandler Solo Fei
5 Instance Degage Miller
6 Two Barber Poles H. Bode
7 Kowloon H. Bode
8 Geklebte Musik Experiment H. Bode
9 The Nerve Net Meter Fei
10 Sequence Three H. Bode
11 Vocoder and Violin Improvisations Vasulka & H. Bode
12 Chaos and Attention Carrier Band
13 Ocean Phase Deutsch
Bode Sound Project
Harald Bode
Carrier Band
Andrew Deutsch
James Fei
Aaron Miller
Scanner
Steina Vasulka
Stephen Vitiello

LINES PLAY A DUAL ROLE on this CD-ROM cover. First, they create movement around the perimeter of the format, in contrast to the rectangular photograph. Other lines are more pictorial, and represent musical scoring and circuitry.

JRoss Design *United States*

Seeing Form and Space

Categories of Form

Putting Stuff Into Space

Compositional Strategies

A Foundation for Meaning

GAL NAUER ARCHITECTS
PAST PRESENT FUTURE

TOTAL COLLECTION OF 10 INTERNATIONAL PROJECTS DESIGNED BY GAL NAUER ARCHITECTS DURING THE YEARS 2000-2005. ••• EDITION NO. 1.0 •••••••••••••••••• WWW.GNARCHITECT.COM •••

AS LINES IN SEQUENCE change weight (thickness) and get closer and further apart, they create rhythms. On this cover, the rhythm is more open and expansive toward the bottom, tightens or quickens in the middle, opens slightly, wavers, and then tightens again. The rhythm between lines is made more complex by the color change from black to hot pink. Note that the typography participates in the composition; there's a reason why designers refer to "lines" of type.

Not From Here *United States*

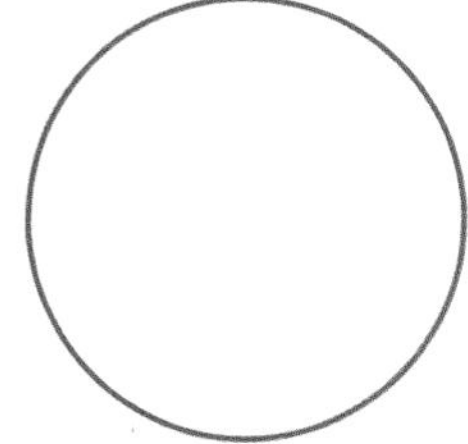

A line traveling around a fixed, invisible point at an unchanging distance becomes a circle. Note that a circle is a line, not a dot. If the line's weight is increased dramatically, a dot appears in the center of the circle, and eventually the form is perceived as a white (negative) dot on top of a larger, positive dot.

A spiraling line appears to move simultaneously inward and outward, re-creating the visual forces inherent in a single dot.

bossa:nova
global music : future tech clubbing
now at our new home in santa monica
zanzibar
thursday nights
from 10 to 2
with resident djs
jason bentley
jun
dave hernandez
allen voskanian

THREE STATIC LINES with minimal color difference form a backdrop to a fluctuating formation of wave-like lines; stasis and activity contrast with each other. The typography picks up on this movement in the flip of alignment from left to right.

344 **Design** *United States*

A thin, single line has no center and no mass, expressing only direction and an effect on the space surrounding it.

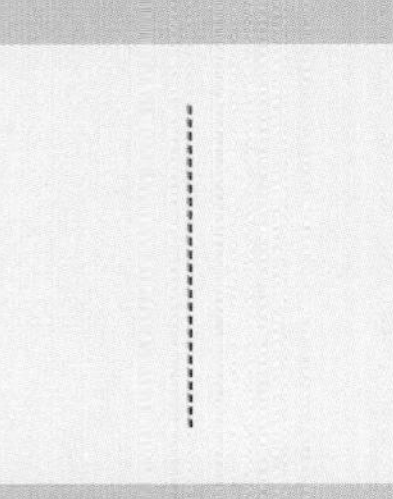

Breaking the line increases its surface activity without distracting from its movement and direction.

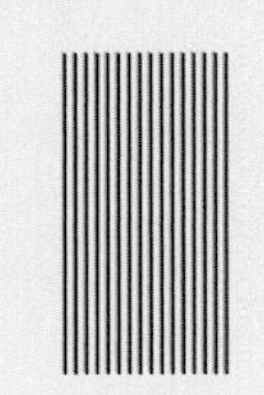

Several thin lines together create a texture, similar to that created by a dense grouping of similar-sized dots.

Separating the lines increases attention to their individual identities. It also calls attention to the intervals between them and what, if any, variation there might be.

A change in weight among a group of lines, as well as a change in the intervals between them, creates the illusion of spatial depth. Lines that are closer together exert tension on each other and advance

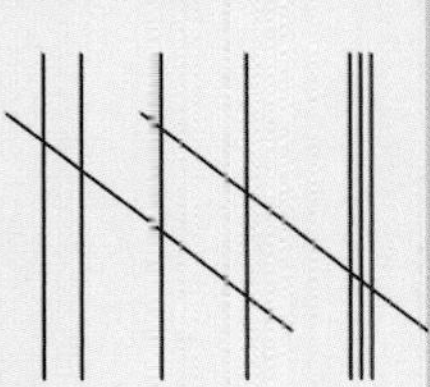

in space, while those further apart recede. If any of the lines are rotated to cross their counterparts, the perception of spatial depth is enhanced—and even more so if their weights also are differentiated.

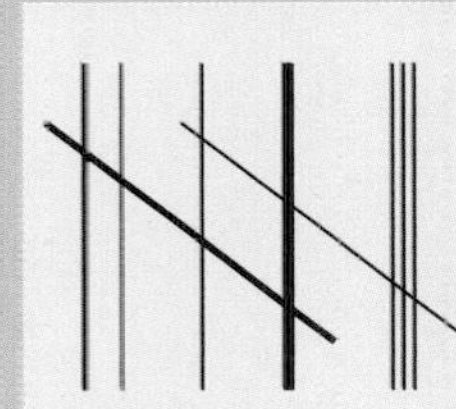

Although a thin line generally will appear to recede against a thicker line, the mind is capable of being convinced that the thin line is crossing in front of the thick line.

Two heavy lines that are very close together create a third—negative—line between them. The optical effect of the negative white line is that of a positive element on top of a single black element, even if the negative line joins open spaces at either end.

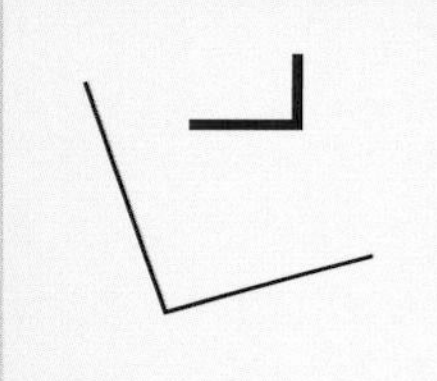

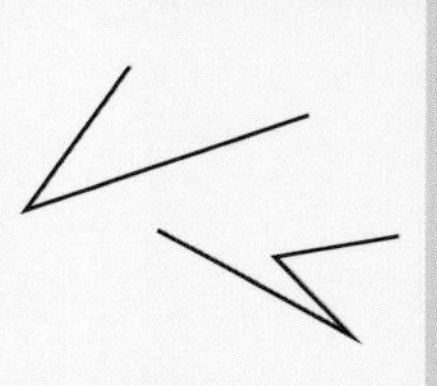

Two lines joining create an angle. The joint between two lines becomes a starting point for two directional movements; multiple joints between lines create a sense of altered direction in one movement. An extremely acute angle might also be perceived as a rapid movement from one direction to another.

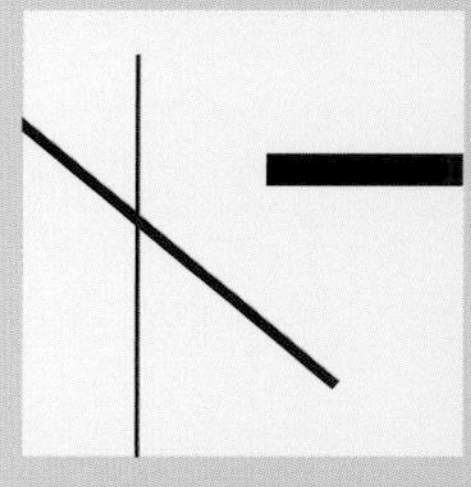

Lines that both enter and leave a format reinforce the sense of their movement along the direction in which they do so. If the beginning or ending points of the lines are contained within the format, their directional movement is changed from continuous to specific; the result is that their tension with surrounding space or forms is increased greatly as the eye is able to focus on the point at which they start or stop.

White (negative) lines crossing in front of (and behind) black (positive) lines create increasingly complex spatial relationships.

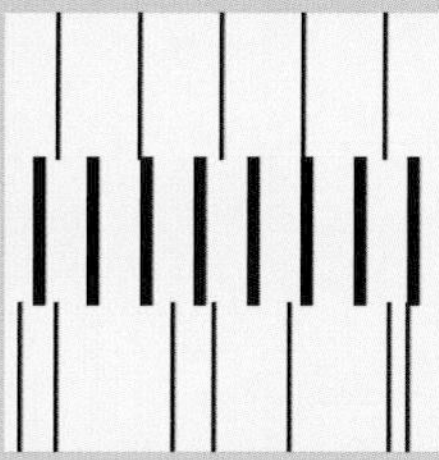

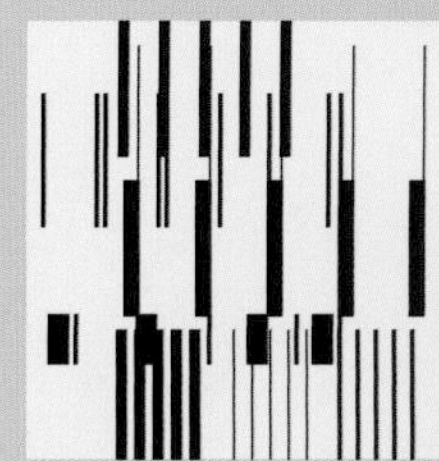

Lines together produce rhythm. Equally spaced, a set of lines produces an even, relatively static tempo; differences in space produce a dynamic, syncopated tempo. The kind of spatial difference introduced between lines affects the perceived rhythm, and might create meaning: progression, sequence, repetition, or system. Such rhythmic changes in interval create directional movement; the more complex the changes, and the more variation in line weights, the more complex the rhythm and movement become.

ON THIS PAGE SPREAD from a concert program, lines of different weights are used to separate horizontal channels of information. Varying the weights of the lines, along with the degree to which their values contrast with the background, not only adds visual interest but also enhances the informational hierarchy.

E-Types *Denmark*

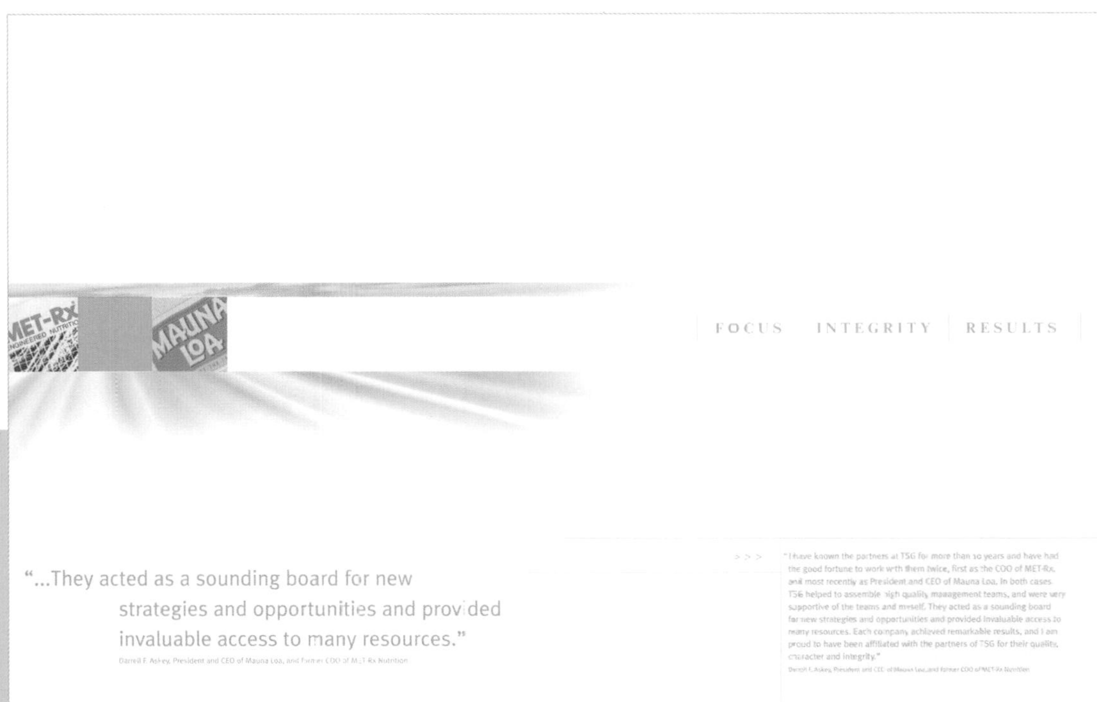

FOCUS
INTEGRITY
RESULTS
"...They acted as a sounding board for new strategies and opportunities and provided invaluable access to many resources."

ON THIS BROCHURE SPREAD, less-distinct blue lines form a channel around images at the left while sharper yellow lines draw attention to the text at the right and help to join the two pages into one composition. The staggered lines created by the text at the lower left, as well as the thin vertical lines used as dividers in the headline, bring type and image together with corresponding visual language.

C. Harvey Graphic Design
United States

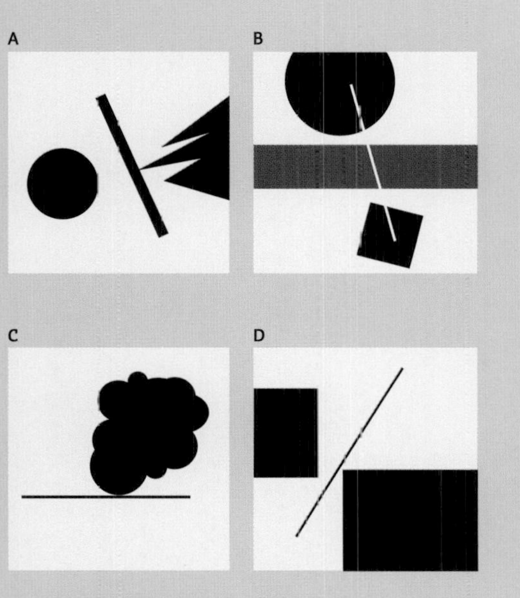

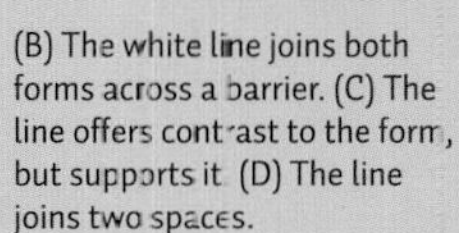

Lines might break or join spaces within a format. In breaking or joining these spaces, lines might perform additional functions relative to other forms within the same format. (A) The line protects the circular form. (B) The white line joins both forms across a barrier. (C) The line offers contrast to the form, but supports it. (D) The line joins two spaces.

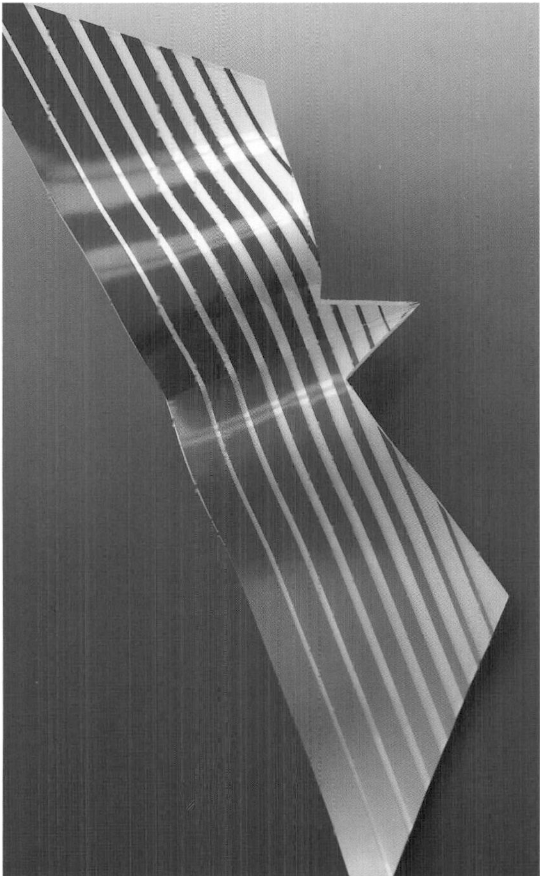

BECAUSE LINES ARE rhythmic, they can be used to create or enhance meaning in images or compositions. Here, the idea of movement is imparted to the abstract bird by the progression of line weights from "tail" end to front.

Studio International *Croatia*

Plane and Mass A plane is simply just a big dot whose outer contour–the sense of its shape–becomes an important attribute: for example, that it may be angular, rather than round. Its dotlike quality becomes secondary the larger the plane object becomes. This change depends on the size of the plane relative to the space in which it exists; in a large poster, even a relatively large plane object–a square or a triangle, for example–will still act as a dot if the volume of space surrounding it is much larger than the plane object itself. At the

As a dot increases in size, its outer contour becomes noticeable as an important aspect of its form; eventually, appreciation of this contour supercedes that of its dot-like focal power, and it becomes a shape or plane. Compare the sequences of forms, each increasing in size from left to right. At what point does each form become less a dot and more a plane?

ROTATING RECTANGULAR PLANES create movement–and mass as their densities build up toward the bottom–and an asymmetrical arrangement on this media kit folder. The planes in this case reflect a specific shape in the brand mark as well as refer to the idea of a screen.

Form *United Kingdom*

A plane surface will be more or less definable as a dot, depending on the volume of space surrounding it. The plane's angular shape in the first example is unimportant because its shape is overwhelmed by the larger space and thus remains a dot.

In the second example, the format's decrease in size, relative to the plane, causes its shape to become more important and thus is no longer simply a dot.

point where a plane object enlarges within a format so that its actual shape begins to affect the shapes of the negative space around it, the character of its outer contour, as well as its surface texture, come into question. ■ All such shapes appear first as flat surfaces; their external contour must be defined by the mind to identify it as being one kind of shape or another and, subsequently, what meaning that shape might have. The more active the plane's contour—and more so if the contour becomes concave, allowing surrounding negative space to enter into the dimensional surface defined by the shape—the more dynamic the shape will appear, and the less it will radiate and focus in the way a dot, with a simple, undifferentiated contour, does. ■ The relative size and simplicity of the shape has an impact on its perceived mass, or weight. A large form with a simple contour retains its dot-like quality and presents a heavy optical weight; a form with a complex contour, and a great deal of interaction between internal and external positive and negative areas, becomes weaker, more line-like, and exhibits a lighter mass. As soon as texture appears on the surface of a plane, its mass decreases and it becomes flatter—unless the texture emulates the effect of light and shade, creating a perceived three-dimensionality, or volume. Even though apparently three-dimensional, the plane or volume still retains its original identity as a dot.

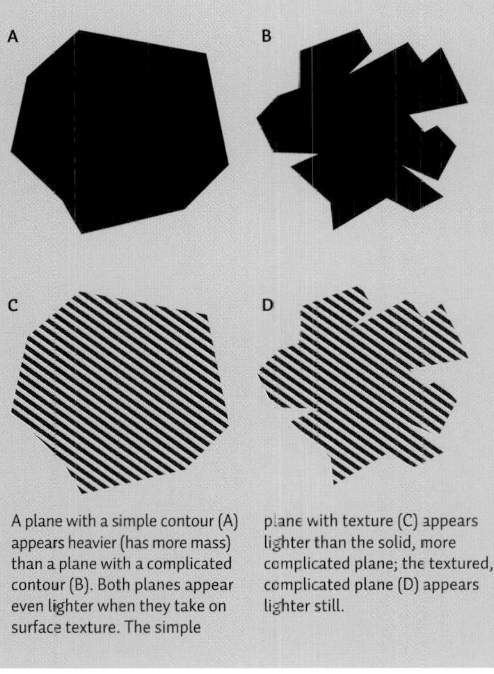

A plane with a simple contour (A) appears heavier (has more mass) than a plane with a complicated contour (B). Both planes appear even lighter when they take on surface texture. The simple plane with texture (C) appears lighter than the solid, more complicated plane; the textured, complicated plane (D) appears lighter still.

A plane whose mass is lightened by a consistent texture seems more active but appears flatter than an adjacent solid plane. The solid plane appears to advance, however, because of its perceived greater weight. Overlapping the solid plane with the textured plane creates an ambiguous tension between foreground and background. A plane whose texture emulates the effect of light and shade appears to have volume.

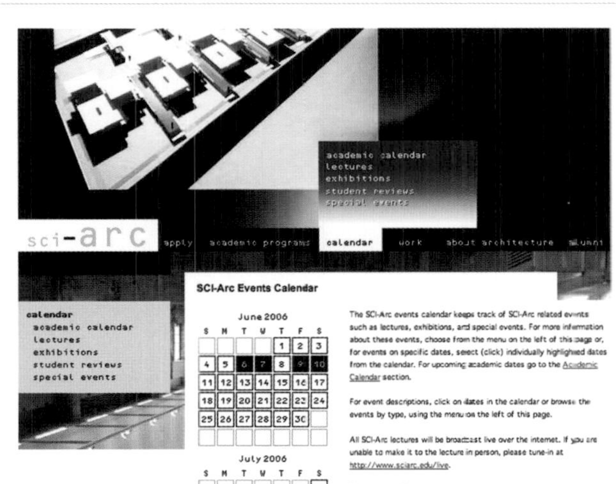

THE VARIOUS CONTENT AREAS of this website can be considered as a set of flat, rectangular planes in space. The images above and below the horizontal strip of navigation are two planes; the logo at the left is another; the navigation flyouts are additional planes; and the content area at the lower right is another. Color and textural changes help establish foreground and background presence, and affect the hierarchy of the page.

Made In Space, Inc. *United States*

Geometric Form As they do with all kinds of form, our brains try to establish meaning by identifying a shape's outer contour. There are two general categories of shape, each with its own formal and communicative characteristics that have an immediate effect on messaging: geometric form and organic form. A shape is considered geometric in nature if its contour is regularized—if its external measurements are mathematically similar in multiple directions—and, very generally, if it appears angular or hard-edged. It is essentially an ancient, ingrained expectation that anything irregular, soft, or textured is akin to things experienced in nature. Similarly, our expectation of geometry as unnatural is the result of learning that humans create it; hence, geometry must not be organic. The weird exception to this idea is the circle or dot, which, because of its elemental quality, might be recognized as either geometric or natural: earth, sun, moon, or pearl. Lines, too, might have a geometric or organic quality, depending on their specific qualities. Geometric forms might be arranged in extremely organic ways,

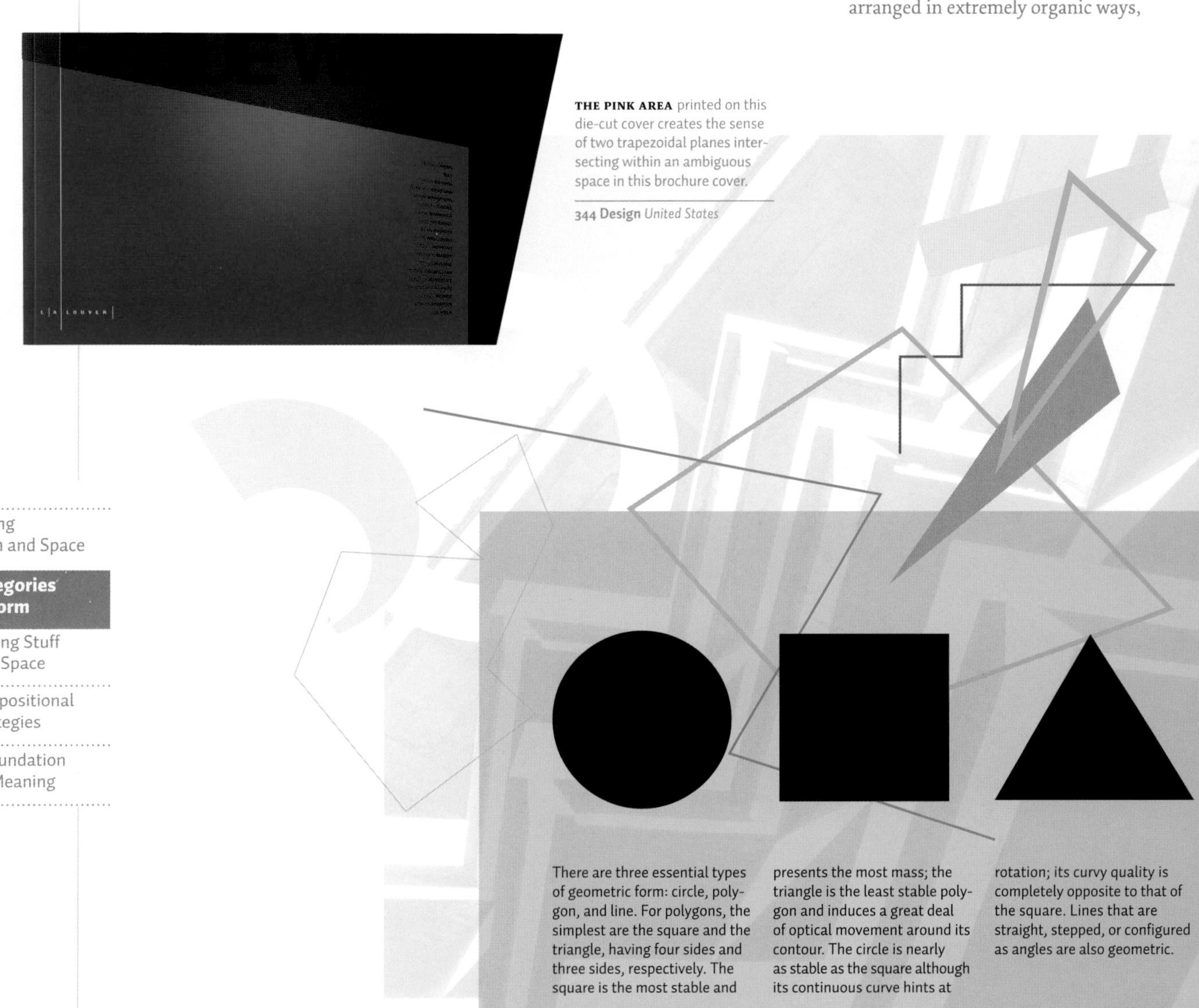

THE PINK AREA printed on this die-cut cover creates the sense of two trapezoidal planes intersecting within an ambiguous space in this brochure cover.

344 Design *United States*

There are three essential types of geometric form: circle, polygon, and line. For polygons, the simplest are the square and the triangle, having four sides and three sides, respectively. The square is the most stable and presents the most mass; the triangle is the least stable polygon and induces a great deal of optical movement around its contour. The circle is nearly as stable as the square although its continuous curve hints at rotation; its curvy quality is completely opposite to that of the square. Lines that are straight, stepped, or configured as angles are also geometric.

creating tension between their mathematical qualities and the irregularity of movement. Although geometric shapes and relationships clearly occur in nature, the message a geometric shape conveys is that of something artificial, contrived, or synthetic.

A1

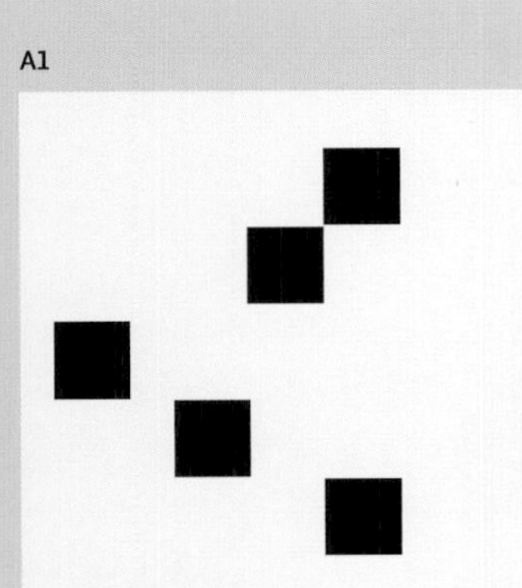

A2

B1

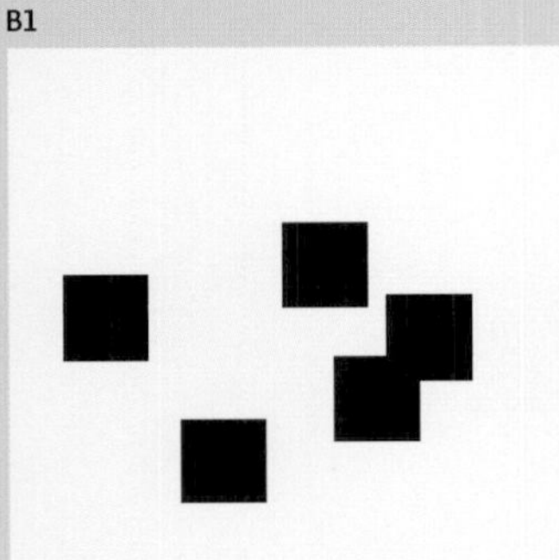

B2

Arrangements of geometric forms in geometric, or mathematical, spatial relationships (A1 and A2) are contrasted by the irregular, organic quality of their arrangements in irregular relationships (B1 and B2).

THE BLOCKS ON THIS poster are purely geometric. The lighting that is used to change their color also affects their apparent dimensionality; the blue areas at the upper left sometimes appear to be flat.

Studio International *Croatia*

BASIC GEOMETRIC FORMS— the rectangular plane of the photographs, the circle of the teacup, and the triangle of the potting marker—provide a simple counterpoint to the organic leaves and the scenes in the photographs themselves.

Red Canoe *United States*

THE IRREGULAR, UNSTUDIED, constantly changing outer contour of flowers is a hallmark of organic form. These qualities contrast dynamically with the linear elements—including type, both sans serif and script—and create striking negative forms.

Pamela Rouzer *Laguna College of Art, United States*

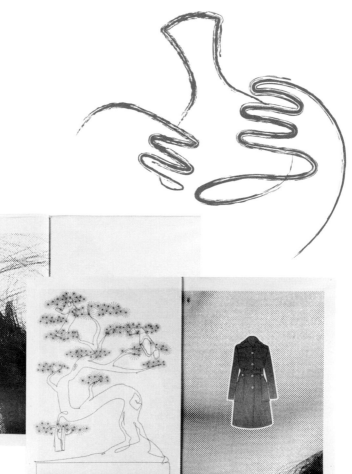

SOME LINES ARE ORGANIC rather than geometric. The linear brush drawing of this logo exaggerates the spontaneous motion of potting and alludes to its humanity and organic nature.

StressDesign *United States*

THE DRAWINGS AND TEXTURES that support the images of the dresses in this fashion catalog create a sense of the handmade, the delicate, and the personal.

Sagmeister *United States*

Organic Form Shapes that are irregular, complex, and highly differentiated are considered organic—this is what our brains tell us after millennia of seeing organic forms all around us in nature. As noted earlier, geometry exists in nature, but its occurrence happens in such a subtle way that it is generally overshadowed by our perception of overall irregularity. The structure of most branching plants, for example, is triangular and symmetric. In the context of the whole plant, whose branches may grow at different rates and at irregular intervals, this intrinsic geometry is obscured. Conveying an "organic" message, therefore, means reinforcing these irregular aspects in a form, despite the underlying truth of geometry that actually might exist. Nature presents itself in terms of variation on essential structure, so a shape might appear organic if its outer contour is varied along a simple logic—many changing varieties of curve, for example. Nature also appears highly irregular or unexpected (again, the plant analogy is useful) so irregularity in measurement or interval similarly conveys an organic identity. Nature is unrefined, unstudied, textural, and complicated. Thus shapes that exhibit these traits will also carry an organic message.

A CURLING, ORGANIC wave form integrates with the curved, yet geometric, letterform in this logo.

LSD *Spain*

Soft, textured forms appear organic compared to similar forms with hard edges, as do forms that are gestural, mostly curvilinear, or whose contours are constantly changing in rhythm, direction, and proportion.

Geometry exists as a building block of natural, organic forms. In the photograph of the leaf, above, lines and dots—the leaf's veins and holes from insect activity or fungal degradation—are clearly apparent. The outer contour of the leaf also presents a symmetrical structure.

Distilled and stylized (A), this form retains its pictorial identity but loses its organic quality. Enforcing differentiated measurements between internal components (B) enhances its organic quality, while retaining its stylization.

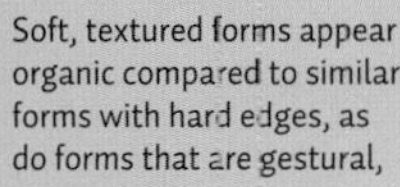

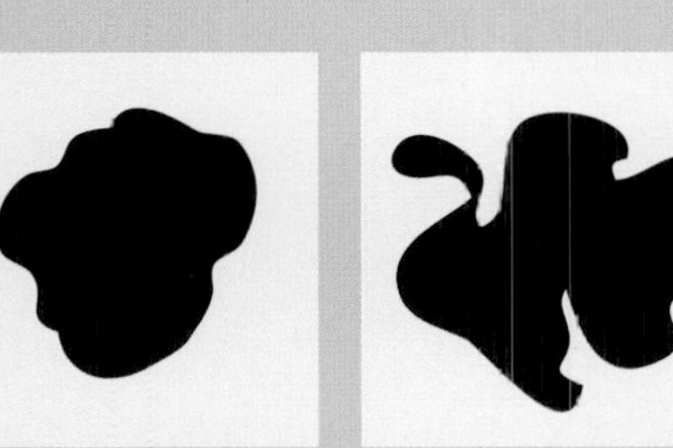

The shapes shown here—one, with a relatively simple contour (left), and the other, with a highly differentiated contour—are organic, but to lesser and greater degrees. The first shape, despite changes in contour, retains an intrinsically circular or dot-like—and therefore, more geometric—identity; the shape adjacent, with a complex contour that is ever-changing in measurement and directional movement, is dramatically more organic.

Variation is an inherent aspect of organic form in nature. All these essentially similar shapes are varied slightly relative to each other and transmit an overall organic message, despite their structural similarity.

Surface Activity The quality of surface activity helps in differentiating forms from each other, just as the identifiable contours of form itself does. Again, the dot is the building block of this formal quality. Groupings of dots, of varying sizes, shapes, and densities, create the perception of surface activity. There are two basic categories of surface activity: texture and pattern. ■ The term "texture" applies to surfaces having irregular activity without apparent repetition. The sizes of the elements creating surface activity might change; the distance between the components might change; the relative number of components might change from one part of the surface to another. Because of this inherent randomness, texture generally is perceived as organic or natural. Clusters and overlaps of lines—dots in specific alignments—are also textural, but only if they are relatively random, that is, they are not running parallel, or appearing with varying intervals between, or in random, crisscrossing directions. ■ "Pattern," however, has a geometric quality—it is a specific kind of texture in which the components are arranged on a recognizable and repeated structure—for example, a grid of dots. The existence of a planned structure within patterns means they are understood to

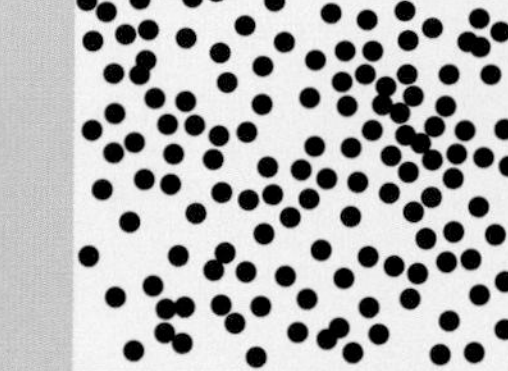

Visual activity on a plane surface is categorized as a texture if it appears random or if it changes in quality from one location to another. While most often organic in source (top), such textures may also be created from dot-based or linear form (bottom).

UPON CLOSER INSPECTION, the irregular texture around the numeral is revealed to be a flock of hummingbirds. Oddly enough, their apparently random placement is carefully studied to control the change in density.

Studio Works *United States*

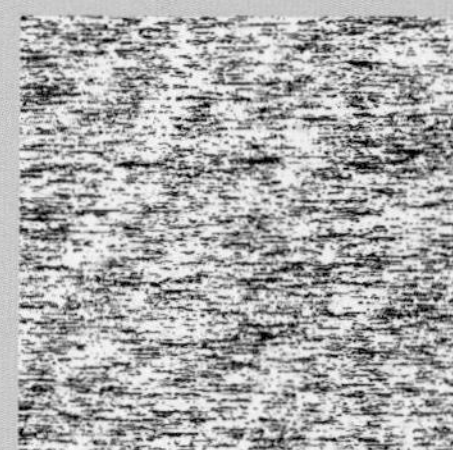

The more constantly irregular a texture's density is within a given area, the less overall contrast and, therefore, the flatter, or more two dimensional, the surface will appear—and the less organic or natural. Conversely, strong contrast in a texture's density within a given area, along with a certain randomness of distribution, increases the texture's dimensional quality as well as its inherent organic quality. An evenly continuous transition from lighter to darker within a given area will often be perceived as the play of light across a volume.

WARPING THE PROPORTIONS of a dot grid creates a dramatically three-dimensional pattern. This quality refers to the activity of the client, a medical imaging and networking organization.

LSD *Spain*

be something that is not organic: they are something synthetic, mechanical, mathematical, or mass produced. ■ When considering texture, it's important to not overlook the selection and manipulation of paper stock—this, too, creates surface activity in a layout. A coated paper might be glossy and reflective, or matte and relatively non-reflective. Coated stocks are excellent for reproducing color and detail because ink sits up on their surfaces, rather than being partly absorbed by the fibers of the paper. The relative slickness of coated sheets, however, might come across as cold or impersonal but also as refined, luxurious, or modern. Uncoated stocks, on the other hand, show a range of textural qualities, from relatively smooth to very rough. Sometimes, flecks of other materials, such as wood chips, threads, or other fibers, are included for added effect. Uncoated stocks tend to feel organic, more personal or hand-made, and warmer. The weight or transparency of a paper also will influence the overall feel of a project. ■ Exploiting a paper's physical properties through folding, cutting, short-sheeting, embossing, and tearing creates surface activity in a three dimensional way. Special printing techniques, such as varnishes, metallic and opaque inks, or foil stamping, increase

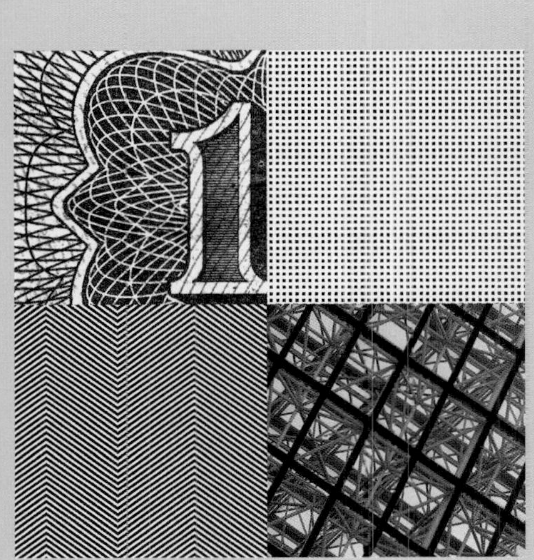

Visual activity on a plane surface should be categorized as pattern if it exhibits some repeated, consistent relationship, such as a grid structure, between its component elements. Shown clockwise from upper left are an engraving, a grid of square dots, pattern created by photographing architecture, and a simple herringbone.

A

Increasing the density of a pattern's components creates a change in darkness, or value. Changes in pattern density, or value, may be stepped, as in the example above (A), or continuous, as in the grid of dots, right (B).

B

While the continous transition from lighter to darker values in the dot grid is smooth, and less geometric in appearance, the pattern still retains its mechanical quality in contrast to texture.

In a patterned surface, creating the perception of three dimensionality and the play of light is also possible, but the geometric quality of the pattern presents a highly stylized version of volumetric appearance. Compare the patterned volume at top with the textured volume at bottom.

PATTERN IS CONSIDERED decorative and man-made, and too much usually is a bad thing. In the case of this book on a trend in design called *Maximalism* however, its use as an allover background treatment enhances the communication of excess.

Loewy *United Kingdom*

surface activity by changing the tactile qualities of a paper stock's surface. Opaque inks, for example, will appear matte and viscous on a gloss-coated stock, creating surface contrast between printed and unprinted areas. Metallic ink printed on a rough, uncoated stock will add an appreciable amount of sheen, but not as much as would occur if printed on a smooth stock. Foil stamping, available in matte, metallic, pearlescent, and iridescent patterns, produces a slick surface whether used on coated or uncoated stock and has a slightly raised texture.

PRINTING THIS POSTER ON a translucent, handmade paper stock presents unusual textural potential for the typography and adds a distinctly organic quality to the piece.

Made In Space, Inc. *United States*

A LEATHER-BOUND BOX contrasts texture and subdued, neutral color with vibrant, saturated hues and smooth surfaces in this promotional item from a design studio.

Roycroft Design *United States*

Seeing Form and Space

Categories of Form

Putting Stuff Into Space

Compositional Strategies

A Foundation for Meaning

THE DELICATE GLOSS VARNISH on the surface of this invitation creates just enough surface activity to be appreciated by the viewer, and its slight enlargement over the original insignia image creates a sense of expansion.

There *Australia*

DIE-CUTS ARE a popular way of engaging the paper stock in the design of a printed piece. Die-cut holes can reveal color or surprise images, or they can be used to orchestrate complex pop-ups that add dimensionality.

A C+G Partners *United States*

B Voice *Australia*

C, D Thomas Csano *Canada*

THIS SET OF INVITATIONS exploits the tactile surface quality of foil stamping and the interaction of colored ink. The foil stamp is pearlescent and somewhat transparent; its refractory effect changes in color depending on the color of the surface onto which it is stamped.

Form *United Kingdom*

EMBOSSING ADDS subtle visual activity and tactile quality to this cover while colored stickers, applied to the surface, introduce random variation to the layout of each copy, at the same time alluding to the subject matter.

Mutabor *Germany*

Breaking Space Space—the ground or field of a composition—is neutral and inactive until it is broken by form. But how does the designer break the space, and what happens as a result? Thoughtfully considering these fundamental questions gives the designer a powerful opportunity not only to engage a viewer but also to begin transmitting important messages, both literal and conceptual, before the viewer even gets the chance to assimilate the content. ■ Space is defined and given meaning the instant a form appears within it, no matter how simple. The resulting breach of emptiness creates new space—the areas surrounding the form. Each element brought into the space adds complexity but also decreases the literal amount of space—even as it creates new kinds of space, forcing it into distinct shapes that fit around the forms like the pieces of a puzzle. These spaces shouldn't be considered "empty" or "leftover;" they are integral to achieving flow around the form elements, as well as a sense of order and unity throughout the composition. When the shapes, sizes, proportions, and directional thrusts of these spaces

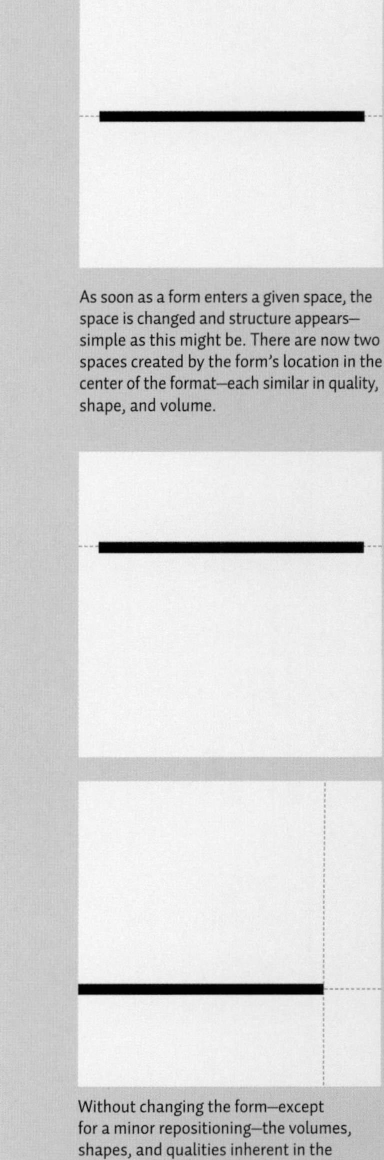

As soon as a form enters a given space, the space is changed and structure appears—simple as this might be. There are now two spaces created by the form's location in the center of the format—each similar in quality, shape, and volume.

Without changing the form—except for a minor repositioning—the volumes, shapes, and qualities inherent in the spaces surrounding the form are made different from each other.

THE FORMS ON THIS poster break the space decisively—meaning that the proportions of negative space have clear relationships to each other—and the locations of elements help to connect them optically across those spaces. The accompanying diagram notes these important aspects of the layout.

Leonardo Sonnoli *Italy*

exhibit clear relationships with the form elements they surround, they become resolved with the form and with the composition as a whole.

Static and Dynamic The proportions of positive and negative might be generally static or generally dynamic. Because the picture plane is already a flat environment where movement and depth must be created as an illusion, fighting the tendency of two-dimensional form to feel static is important. The spaces within a composition will generally appear static—in a state of rest or inertia—when they are optically equal to each other. Spaces need not be physically the same shape to appear equal in presence or "weight." The surest way of avoiding a static composition is to force the proportions of the spaces between forms (as well as between forms and the format edges) to be as different as possible.

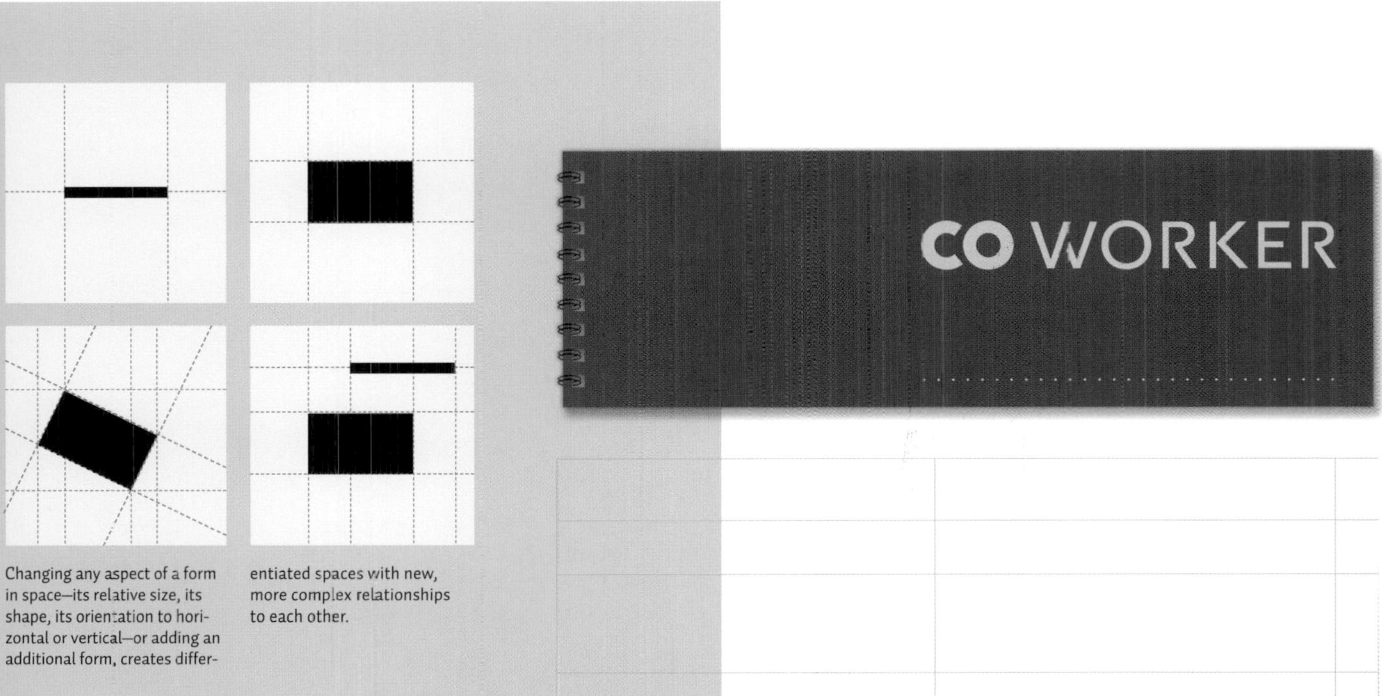

Changing any aspect of a form in space—its relative size, its shape, its orientation to horizontal or vertical—or adding an additional form, creates differentiated spaces with new, more complex relationships to each other.

DECISIVELY BROKEN SPACE can be restrained yet still have a visual richness to it. The placement of the type element and the dotted line create four horizontal channels of space and two vertical channels of space.

AdamsMorioka *United States*

Multiple forms situated around similar spatial intervals create static interaction. This composition—the arrangement of forms within space—seems restful, comfortable, and quiet, and exhibits a kind of stasis despite the irregularity and rotation of the forms.

Altering the intervals between form elements, or between elements and format edges, creates a dynamic composition. The movement of the eye is enhanced as these intervals exhibit more contrast with each other. Note the areas where the negative spaces become compressed or exhibit a directional thrust.

Arranging Form Within a compositional format, a designer can apply several basic strategies to organizing forms. Each strategy a designer employs will create distinctly different relationships among the forms themselves and between the forms and the surrounding space. Just as the identities of selected forms begin to generate messages for the viewer, their relative positions within the format, the spaces created between them, and their relationships to each other all will contribute additional messages. Forms that are clustered together, for example, will suggest that they are related to each other, as will forms that appear to align with one another. Forms separated by different spatial intervals will imply a distinction in meaning. **Near and Far** In addition to side-by-side, or lateral, arrangements at the picture plane, a designer may also organize form in illusory dimensional space—that is, by defining elements as existing in the foreground, in the background, or somewhere in between. Usually, the field or ground is considered to be a background space and forms automatically appear in the foreground. Overlapping forms, however, optically positions them nearer or further

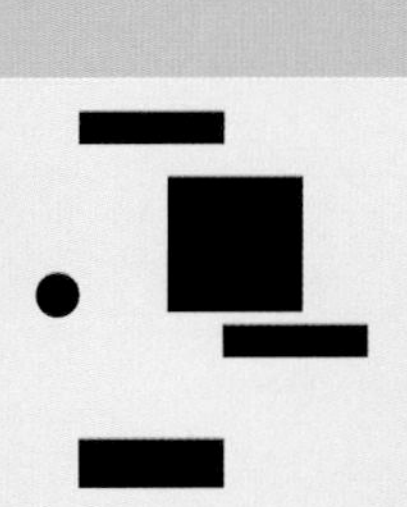

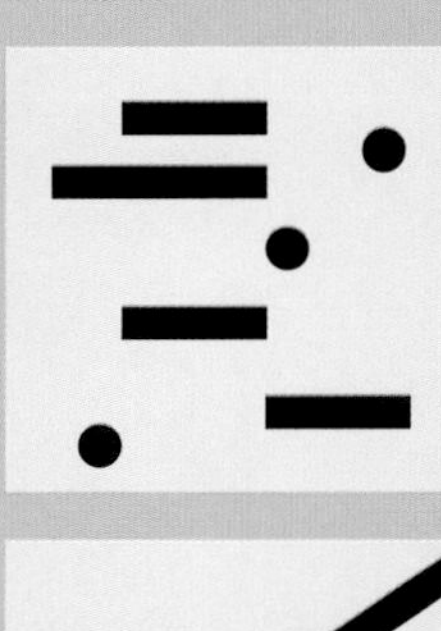

Distinguishing Forcing clear separation between individual formal elements—whether they have similar or different identities—enhances the sense of difference between them. Despite such distinction, forms that have similar identities will retain the sense that they are related. One result of distinguishing through spatial separation, however, is that intervals of negative space may become more regularized and, therefore, potentially static. Rotating elements to create directional movement will alleviate this quality somewhat.

Clustering Grouping form elements together may simplify a composition overall as well as create a sense of relationship between clustered elements—and of difference between a cluster and a separate element or between several clusters. As a result of clustering, where the forms do not necessarily overlap but come into close proximity, a contrast arises between the smaller, intricate spaces among the clustered forms, and larger, simpler contours around the outer contour of the cluster. The greater the proportional changes in the outer contour of the cluster, the more dynamic it will appear, along with the spaces around the cluster.

Aligning Creating edge relationships between form elements—aligning them to each other from top to bottom, left to right, making them parallel, and so on—might create geometric superstructures and rhythmic repetitions or systems.

Overlapping Allowing one form to cross in front of another, even if both are the same color, will create the illusion of foreground and background. Introducing size changes among forms that overlap, as well as changes in their relative values—or, for that matter, placing negative forms on top of positive—will greatly enhance the illusion that the forms exist within three dimensional space.

away from the viewer. The designer may increase this sense of depth by changing the relative values of the forms by making them transparent and increasing the differences in their sizes.Placing forms that are reversed—made negative, or the same value as the field or format space—on top of positive forms, will similarly exaggerate the sense of spatial depth, as well as potentially create interesting reversals of figure and ground. The seeming nearness or distance of each form will also contribute to the viewer's sense of its importance and, therefore, its meaning relative to other forms presented within the same space.

Movement Overlapping and bleeding, as well as the rotation of elements compared to others, may induce a feeling of kinetic movement. Elements perceived to occupy dimensional space often appear to be moving in one direction or another—receding or advancing. Juxtaposing a static form, such as a horizontal line, with a more active counterpart, such as a diagonal line, invites comparison and, oddly, the assumption that one is standing still while the other is moving. Changing the intervals between elements also invites comparison and, again, the odd conclusion that the changing spaces mean the forms are moving in relation to each other. The degree of motion created by such overlapping, bleeding, and rhythmic spatial separation will evoke varying degrees of energy or restfulness; the designer must control these messages as he or she does any other.

Layering The use of transparency in a cluster enhances the illusion of their apparent existence in three dimensional space. Carefully considering which elements appear solidly positive or negative—and which appear transparent—can result in startling conflicts in apparent spatial position.

Bleeding When forms within the compositional space appear to leave the format—that is, are cropped off by the edge of the format—they imply a much bigger composition extending outward into the "real" world.

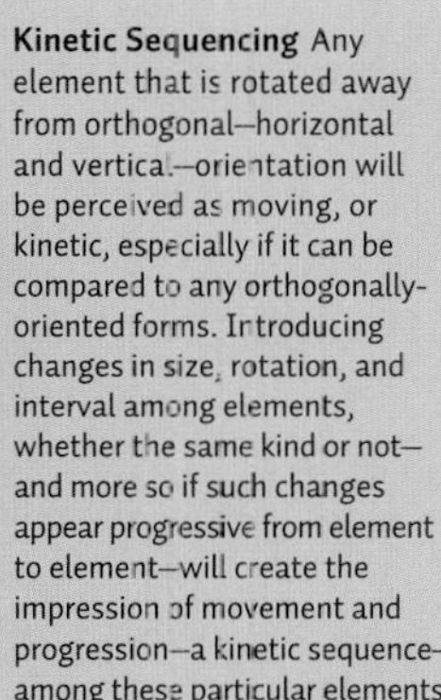

Kinetic Sequencing Any element that is rotated away from orthogonal—horizontal and vertical—orientation will be perceived as moving, or kinetic, especially if it can be compared to any orthogonally-oriented forms. Introducing changes in size, rotation, and interval among elements, whether the same kind or not—and more so if such changes appear progressive from element to element—will create the impression of movement and progression—a kinetic sequence—among these particular elements.

TYPE, GRID PATTERNS, and geometric blocks—some white—exhibit mostly clustering, aligning, and overlapping strategies.

STIM Visual Communication
United States

Conservatoire
National
Supérieur d'Art
Dramatique

Atelier de 3e année
dirigé par
Philippe Adrien

Eugène Ionesco
Jeux de massacre

Mardi 7, mercredi 8
et jeudi 9 février 2006
à 19h30

THIS POSTER PLAYS a dangerous game with symmetry. Without the dynamic optical "buzzing" and movement generated by the diagonal lines and their color relationships, the arrangement of the type would be quite static, and the proportions of all the spaces would be the same in all four directions.

Apeloig Design *France*

Department Store
on Broadway

Twentieth-century design cognoscente Dorian LaPadura has lived in architectural gems by Frank Lloyd Wright, Frank Gehry, and Gregory Ain since selling his mural business in 1995 and moving west from New York City. He was feeling the itch to move again in the late '90s when a friend told him about a loft with lots of space, reasonable rent, and an intriguing location.

When he saw the 1919 five-story Kress Building on Broadway in the Historic Theater District, LaPadura was as excited by the neighborhood as by the space. His fourth-floor loft, shared with Museum of Contemporary Art store manager Fran Vincent, overlooks the 1911 Orpheum Theater (now the Palace) and directly abuts the 1931 Los Angeles Theater. Iconic Clifton's Cafeteria, also established in 1931, is across the street. St. Vincent's Court, a colorful back alley lined with

CONTENT IS ALWAYS different and always changing, and an asymmetrical approach allows a designer to be flexible, to address the spatial needs of the content, and to create visual relationships between different items based on their spatial qualities. The horizon line in the room, the vertical column, the red headline, the text on the page, and the smaller inset photograph all respond to each other's sizes, color, and location; the negative spaces around them all talk to each other.

ThinkStudio *United States*

Symmetry and Asymmetry The result of making all the proportions between and around form elements in a composition different is that the possibility of symmetry is minimized. Symmetry is a compositional state in which the arrangement of forms responds to the central axis of the format (either the horizontal axis or the vertical axis); the forms might also be arranged in relation to each other's central axes. Symmetrical arrangements mean that some set of spaces around the forms—or the contours of the forms around the axis—will be equal, which means that they are also static, or restful. The restfulness inherent in symmetry can be problematic relative to the goals of designed communication. Without differences in proportion to compare, the viewer is likely to gloss over material and come to an intellectual rest quickly, rather than investigate a work more intently. If the viewer loses interest because the visual presentation of the design isn't challenging enough, the viewer's attention might shift elsewhere before he or she has acquired the content of the message. ■ A lack of visual, and thus cognitive, investigation is also likely to not make much of an impression on the viewer and, unfortunately, become difficult to recall later on. Asymmetrical arrangements provoke more rigorous involvement—they require the brain to assess differences in space and stimulate the eye to greater movement. From the standpoint of communication, asymmetrical arrangements might improve the ability to differentiate, catalog, and recall content because the viewer's investigation of spatial difference becomes tied to the ordering, or cognition, of the content itself.

Symmetrical spatial intervals are inherently static, and their static quality is greater the smaller (or fewer in number) the elements that separate them.

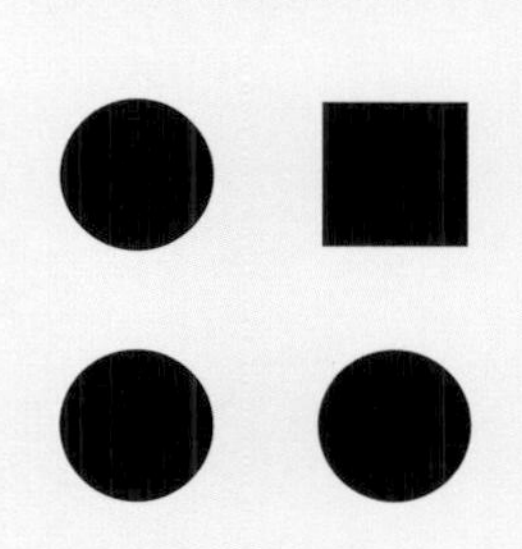

Form elements and spatial intervals that share a similar presence in volume or weight produce the most static configuration possible.

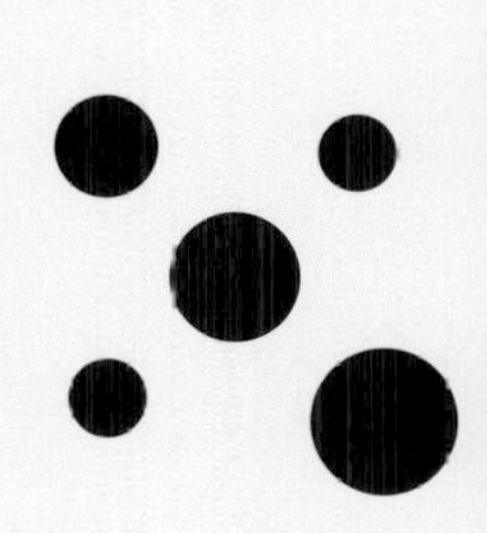

As the relative size or number of elements within a symmetrical arrangement increases, the static quality decreases but remains present.

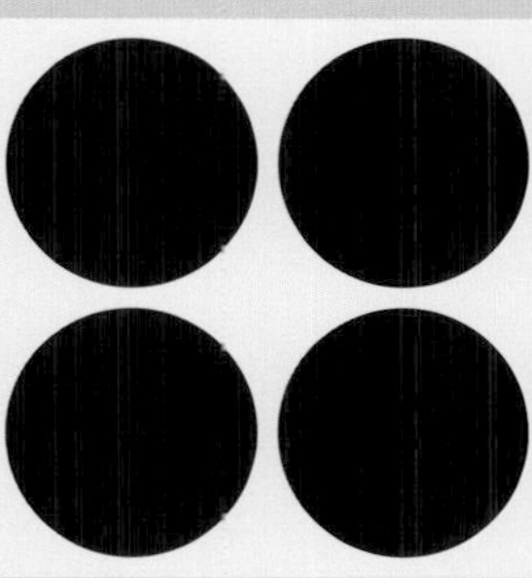

When symmetrically organized forms become so large that they are clearly bigger than the remaining symmetrical spaces, their confrontation with the format becomes very tense, and their static quality is greatly reduced.

ASYMMETRY IS INHERENTLY dynamic. The movement of the type, created by its repetition and rotation, creates strong diagonals and wildly varied triangular negative shapes. The movement is enhanced greatly by the rhythmic linearity of the ultra-condensed sans serif type.

Stereotype Design *United States*

Activating Space During the process of composing form within a given space, portions of space might become disconnected from other portions. A section might be separated physically or blocked off by a larger element that crosses from one edge of the format to the other; or, it might be optically separated because of a set of forms aligning in such a way that the eye is discouraged from traveling past the alignment and entering into the space beyond. Focusing the majority of visual activity into one area of a composition—for example, by clustering—is an excellent way of creating emphasis and a contrasting area for rest. But this strategy might also result in spaces that feel empty or isolated from this activity. In all such cases, the

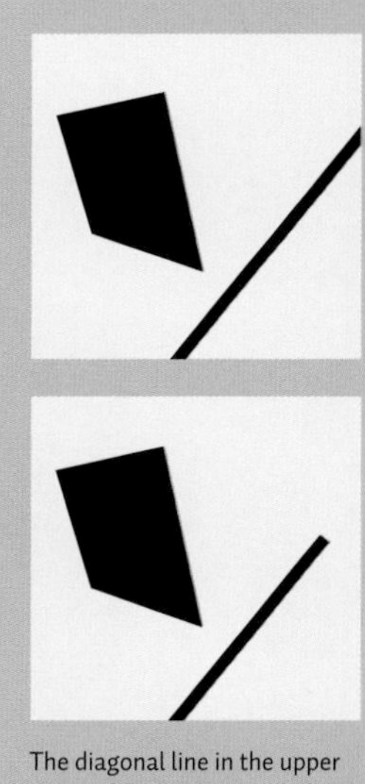

The diagonal line in the upper composition separates a triangular space from the remainder of the format; this space disconnects from the composition and is deactivated. By ending the line short of the format edge, even minimally, the eye is encouraged to travel optically around its ending point and join the two spaces together, activating and relating them to each other.

In this example, a line once again intersects the format, but, because there is an overlap of shape connecting the spaces on either side of the line, both spaces are activated.

Because the arrangement of these forms creates an optical alignment that, while open to the space at the top of the composition, stops the movement of the eye begun in the lower part, this same space now appears inert. In contrast, a simple shift of one element beyond this invisible alignment invigorates the formerly inactive space.

The degree of spatial activation in various parts of this composition differs because of the changing proximity and tension between forms… as well as from differences in how the various forms confront each other—some overlapping and decreasing tension, some aggressively opposing each other in direction or contrasting curve and angle.

ON THE TEXT SIDE of this business card, the spaces are all activated with content. On the "image" side, the light, transparent blue wave shape activates the space above the purple wave; the line of white type activates the spaces within the purple wave area.

Monigle Associates *United States*

space can be called "inert," or "inactive." An inert or inactive space will call attention to itself for this very reason: it doesn't communicate with the other spaces in the composition. To activate these spaces means to cause them to enter back into their dialogue with the other spaces in the composition.

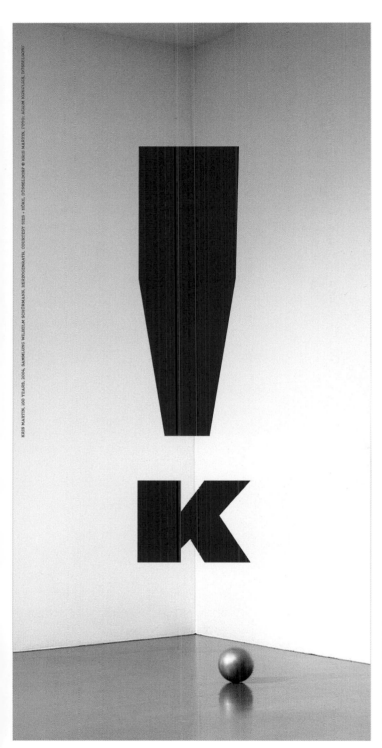

KRIS MARTIN, 100 YEARS, 2004, SAMMLUNG WILHELM SCHÜRMANN, HERZOGENRATH, COURTESY SIES + HÖKE, DÜSSELDORF © KRIS MARTIN, FOTO: ACHIM KUKULIES, DÜSSELDORF

AS THE LINES OF TYPE in the foreground shift left and right, they create movement, but they also create a separation of dead horizontal spaces above and below. The irregular contour of the background letterforms, however, breaks past the outer lines of type, activating both the upper and lower spaces.

C. Harvey Graphic Design
United States

ALTHOUGH THE GIGANTIC pink exclamation point—created by the line and the letter K—is strong, it is surrounded by relatively static spaces of the same interval, value, and color. This static quality is broken by the brass ball, a dot, which very decisively is not centered and activates the space defined by the floor.

Mutabor *Germany*

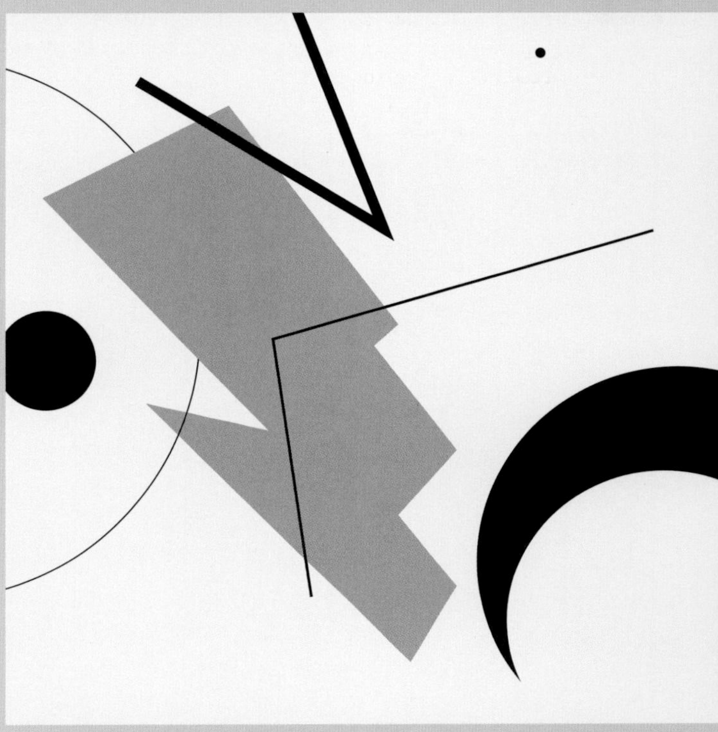

In this composition, the edge relationships offer one kind of tension within the space, some more aggressive and others less so. At the same time, the edge relationships of angular forms create tension relative to the open, sweeping forms of the curved elements; a similar change in tension occurs between the line elements—which are themselves angular, but in the foreground—and the angular plane surface—which appears as a background element. Both angled plane and lines contrast with each other in identity and apparent spatial position, but complement each other's sharp, geometric qualities. This attribute is yet another type of tension.

The sensual pleasures of warmth and cleanliness seem to bring out the best in people: the Japanese respond with happy chatter and contented sighs. The smooth floors and walls of tile magnify the din of spirited conversation punctuated by splashes and the high-pitched laughter of children. The sounds of the bathhouse change with the shifting cycle of the daily clock, beginning relatively quietly in the midafternoon, when the doors open to the first customers – generally, elderly

PLEASURES OF THE JAPANESE BATH

retired folk eager for the company of other senior citizens. Later in the afternoon, the decibel level rises as the bathhouse fills up with children home from school and young mothers bathing babies before going home to begin preparing the evening meal. The noise reaches its highest pitch during the evening hours when older children come for their baths, along with fathers and young single men and women, many of whom may have thrown back a drink or two on their way to the bathhouse. By ten-thirty or eleven at night, quiet begins to fall on the bathhouse again as weary shopkeepers or late-returning office workers enjoy a relaxing soak before drifting home to bed. The last sounds of the day are the gurgle of drains, the splashing of water, and the swishing of soapy brushes as the proprietors and staff scrub the floors and tubs and rinse away the aftermath of one long day and prepare the bathhouse for the next.

Women's tub
at the Hashidate-Yu

by Peter Grilli and Dana Levy

Men's tub
at the Hashidate-Yu

A BLACK LINE dividing the spread contrasts with the loose texture of the type; the white type in the line creates spatial tension as one word breaks out of the line and another appears to recede into it. The two photographs have very different edge relationships to the format.

Cheng Design *United States*

Compositional Contrast Creating areas of differing presence or quality—areas that contrast with each other—is inherent in designing a well-resolved, dynamic composition. While the term "contrast" applies to specific relationships (light versus dark, curve versus angle, and dynamic versus static), it also applies to the quality of difference in relationships among forms and spaces interacting within a format together. The confluence of varied states of contrast is sometimes referred to as "tension." A composition with strong contrast between round and sharp, angular forms in one area, opposed by another area where all the forms are similarly angular, could exhibit a tension in angularity; a composition that contrasts areas of dense, active line rhythms with areas that are generally more open and regular might be characterized as creating tension in rhythm. ■ The term tension can be substituted for contrast when describing individual forms or areas that focus on particular kinds of contrast—for example, in a situation in which the corner of an angular plane comes into close contact with a format edge at one location, but is relatively free of the edge in another; the first location could exhibit more tension than that of the second location.

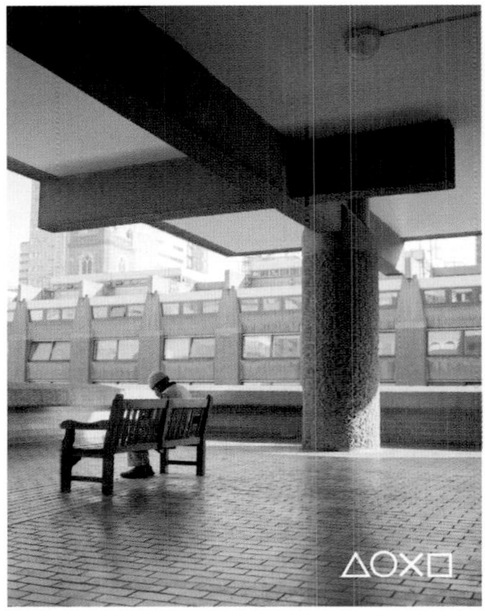

NEARLY DEVOID OF people and activity, these three photographic ads rely on compositional contrast (OK, and a little mystery!) to generate interest.

CHK Design *United Kingdom*

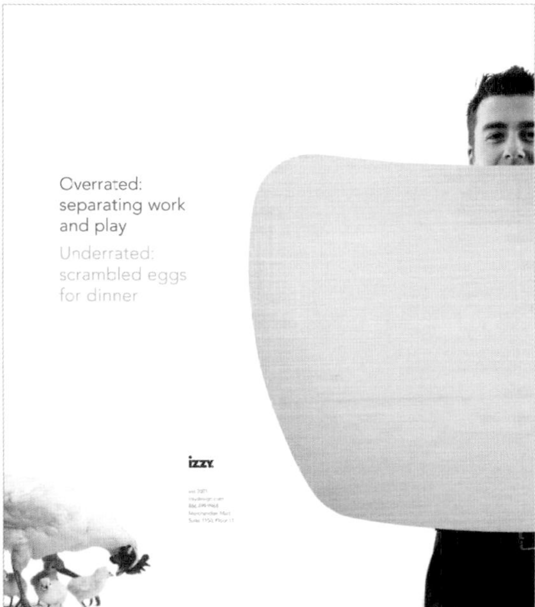

Overrated:
separating work
and play
Underrated:
scrambled eggs
for dinner
izzy

DRAMATIC SCALE CHANGE is instantly engaging because the optical effect is one of perceiving deep space; the brain wants to know why one item is so small and the other so large. In this particular ad, the foreground-to-background tension is intensified by making the figure and the chicken bleed out of the format.

BBK Studio *United States*

Proportional Systems Controlling the eye's movement through, and creating harmonic relationships among, form elements—whether pictorial or typographic (see page 202, Structure: The Grid System)—might be facilitated by creating a system of recognizable, repeated intervals to which both positive and negative elements adhere. A designer might approach devel-

THE BOTTOM LINE of the colored type occurs at the lower third of the format in this ad. The white tag line, at the bottom, occurs at the lower third of that third.

BBK Studio *United States*

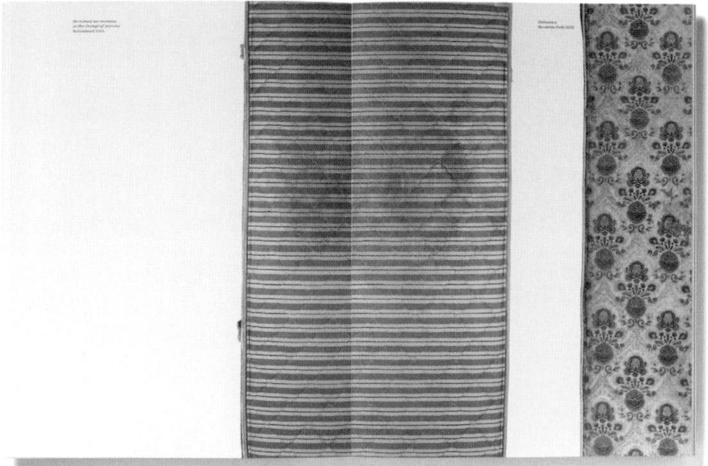

PATTERNED TEXTILES create a system of mathematical proportions on this brochure spread.

Voice *Australia*

THE BREAK BETWEEN the photograph and colored field at the right defines the right-hand third, but the first two thirds are a square, indicating that the Golden Section might be playing a role in defining the proportions.

AdamsMorioka *United States*

oping these proportions in an intuitive way—moving material around within the space of the format or changing their relative sizes—to see at what point the spaces between elements and their widths or heights suddenly correspond or refer to each other. After this discovery, analyzing the proportions might yield a system of repeated intervals that the designer can apply as needed. ■ Alternatively, the designer might begin with a mathematical, intellectualized approach that forces the material into particularly desirable relationships. The danger in this approach lies in the potential for some material to not fit so well—making it appear indecisive or disconnected from the remainder of the compositional logic—or, worse, creating static, rigid intervals between positive and negative that are too restful, stiff, awkward, or confining.

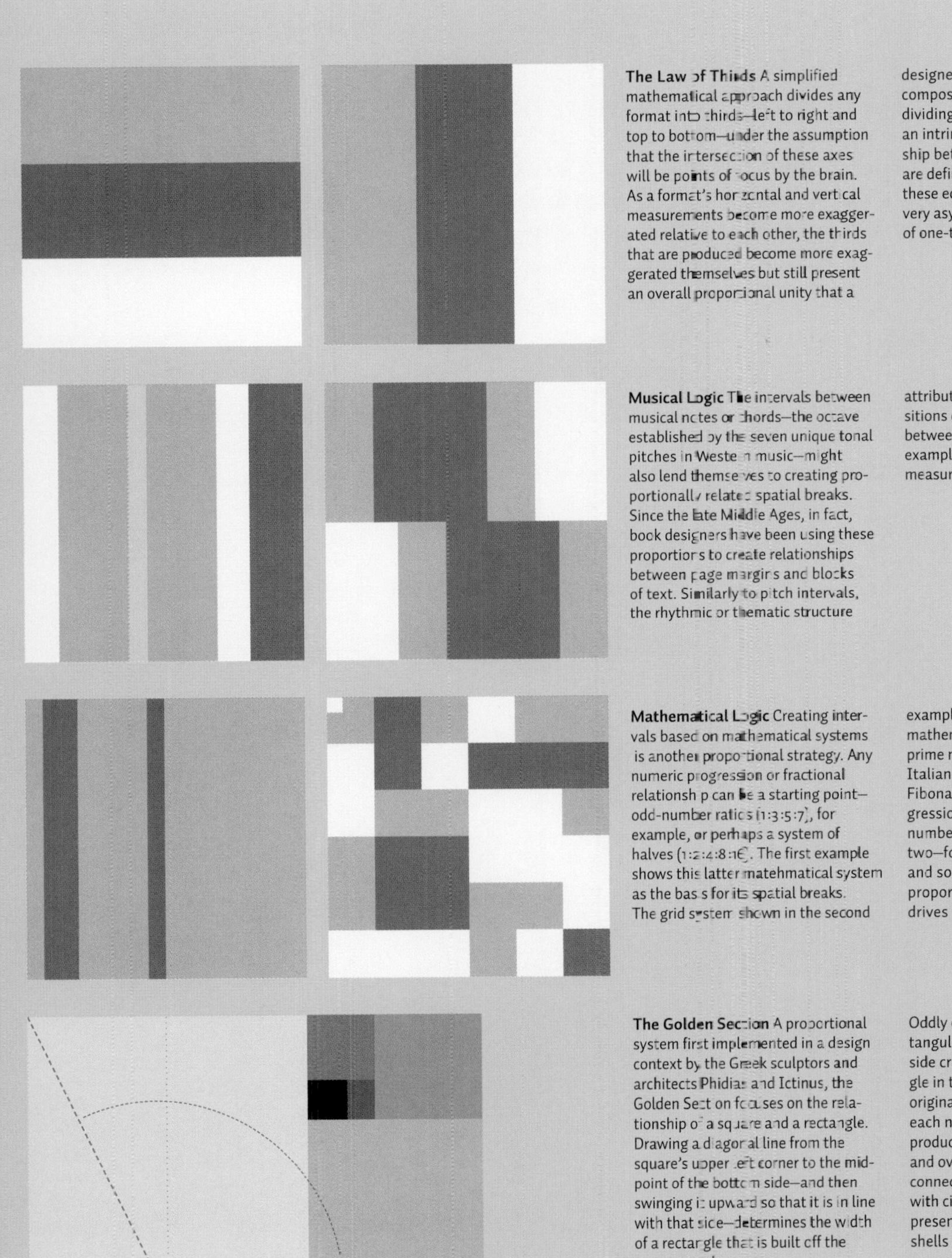

The Law of Thirds A simplified mathematical approach divides any format into thirds—left to right and top to bottom—under the assumption that the intersection of these axes will be points of focus by the brain. As a format's horizontal and vertical measurements become more exaggerated relative to each other, the thirds that are produced become more exaggerated themselves but still present an overall proportional unity that a designer can use to map out major compositional arrangements. While dividing a format into thirds presents an intrinsically symmetrical relationship between the three spaces that are defined, the two axes that define these equal intervals also provide a very asymmetrical proportional system of one-third relative to two-thirds.

Musical Logic The intervals between musical notes or chords—the octave established by the seven unique tonal pitches in Western music—might also lend themselves to creating proportionally related spatial breaks. Since the late Middle Ages, in fact, book designers have been using these proportions to create relationships between page margins and blocks of text. Similarly to pitch intervals, the rhythmic or thematic structure attributed to structure musical compositions can be applied to the distances between elements in a layout: ABA, for example, or ABAC, in which "A" is one measurement, "B" another, and so on.

Mathematical Logic Creating intervals based on mathematical systems is another proportional strategy. Any numeric progression or fractional relationship can be a starting point—odd-number ratios (1:3:5:7), for example, or perhaps a system of halves (1:2:4:8:16). The first example shows this latter matehmatical system as the basis for its spatial breaks. The grid system shown in the second example is a system based on repeated mathematical intervals with a common prime number, 3. A thirteenth-century Italian mathematician, Leonardo Fibonacci, discovered a natural progression of numbers in which each number is the sum of the preceding two—for example, 1:1:2:3:5:8:13:21, and so on. Coincidentally, this same proportional relationship is what drives the Golden Section.

The Golden Section A proportional system first implemented in a design context by the Greek sculptors and architects Phidias and Ictinus, the Golden Section focuses on the relationship of a square and a rectangle. Drawing a diagonal line from the square's upper left corner to the midpoint of the bottom side—and then swinging it upward so that it is in line with that side—determines the width of a rectangle that is built off the square as a base. Oddly enough, dividing this new rectangular area by the width of its short side creates a new square and rectangle in the same proportions as the original square and rectangle. Dividing each new rectangle in the same way produces the same relationship over and over again in decreasing size. By connecting the corners of the squares with circular arcs, the spiral that is present in the formation of nautilus shells is magically revealed.

Seeing Is Believing What is the result of all this form and space interacting? At this most fundamental level, the result is meaning. Abstract forms carry meaning because they are recognizably different from each other—whether line, dot, or plane (and, specifically, what kind of plane). As a beginning point in trying to understand what it's seeing, the mind makes comparisons between forms to see how they are different and whether this is important. Forms with similar shapes or sizes are linked by the mind as being related; if one form among a group is different, it must be unrelated, and the mind takes note.

Distance *Isolation*

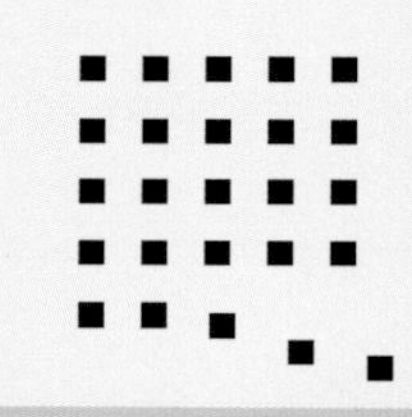

Progressive Separation *Breaking out or leaving*

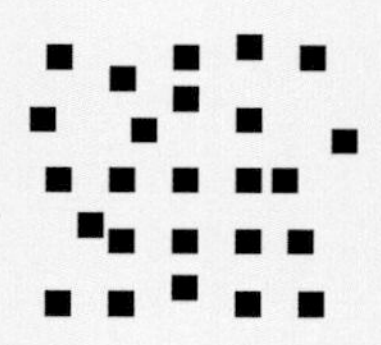

Reordering *Disharmony or disorder*

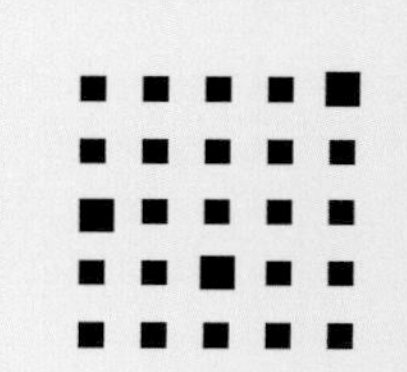

Size Change *Increased importance; implied relationship*

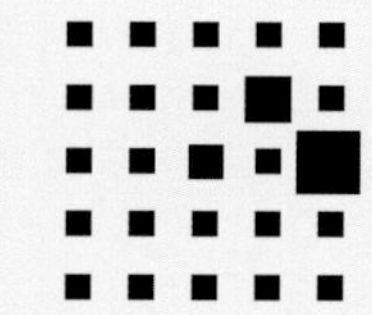

Progressive size change *Increased importance; growth*

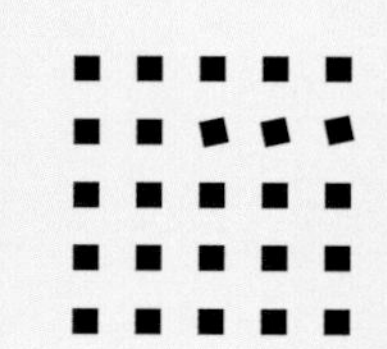

Direction *Movement or energy*

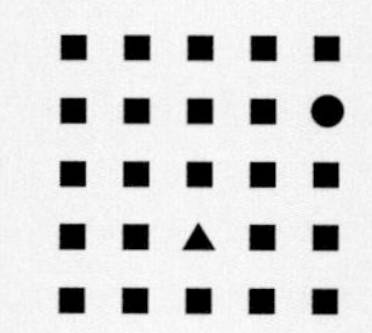

Differentiated Shape *Specificity*

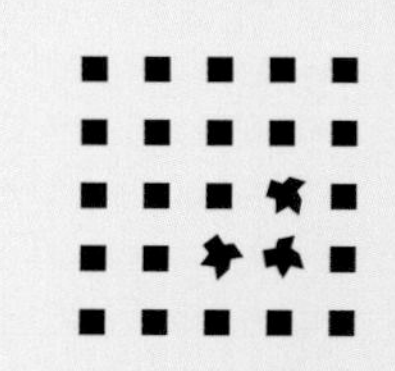

Contour complexity *Aggression or complication*

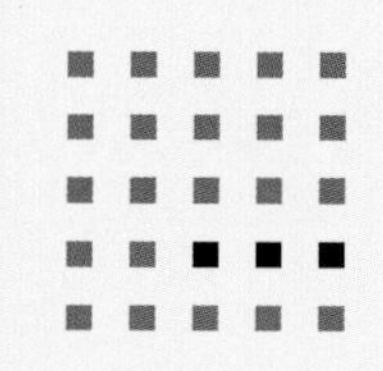

Value Change *Confrontation*

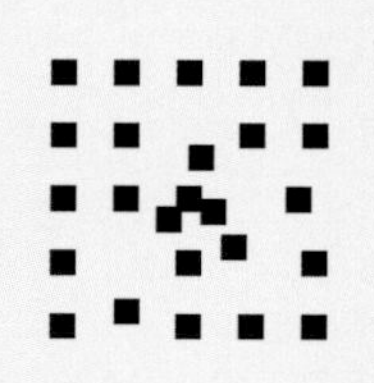

Movement Inward, Overlap *Interference; assembly*

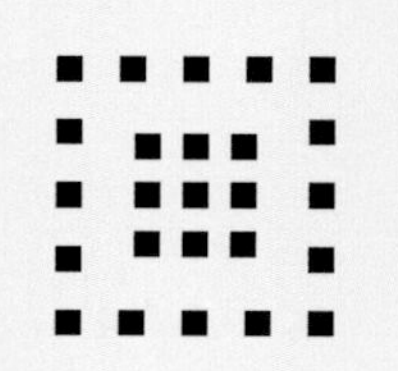

Interval change *Enclosure or protection*

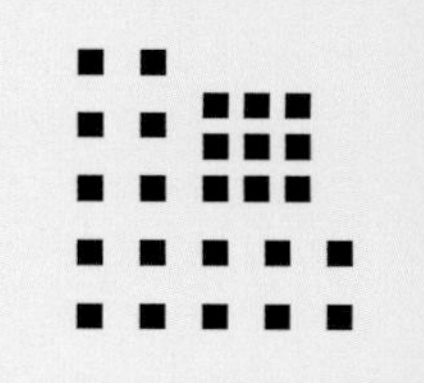

Interval change *Unity and opposition*

By differentiating elements from others within an overall grouping, a designer creates a focus for consideration, allowing the viewer to identify one set of elements and compare them to another.

This comparison elicits several questions: "What is the nature of each grouping? How are they different? What does this difference signify? Does the difference make one grouping clearly more important than the other?

Shown here are a number of potential strategies for visually distinguishing groups and, therefore, creating meaning.

Identity and Difference There are numerous strategies for creating comparisons between groupings of form or among parts within a group. The degree of difference between elements can be subtle or dramatic, and the designer can imply different degrees of meaning by isolating one group or part more subtly, while exaggerating the difference between others. Because tiny adjustments in form are easily perceived, the difference between each group can be very precisely controlled. Of course, which strategy to employ will depend heavily on the kind of message the designer must convey as a result of such distinction; he or she will trigger very different perceptions of meaning by separating components spatially, as opposed to creating a sense of movement in components by rotating them or changing their size. In the first instance, the difference may be perceived as a message about isolation and may introduce anxiety; in the second instance, the change may be perceived as an indication of growth, a change in energy, or a focusing of strength.

b a u s a u c
a b a c u s a
c a b s a u c
u c s a b a s
a b u c a s b
s u a b c b a

THIS LOGOTYPE USES color to distinguish the company name from within a cluster of letterforms (coincidentally arranged in a grid pattern). Within a grouping of varied elements, any elements that are made similar in even one aspect will separate optically from the others.

Monigle Associates *United States*

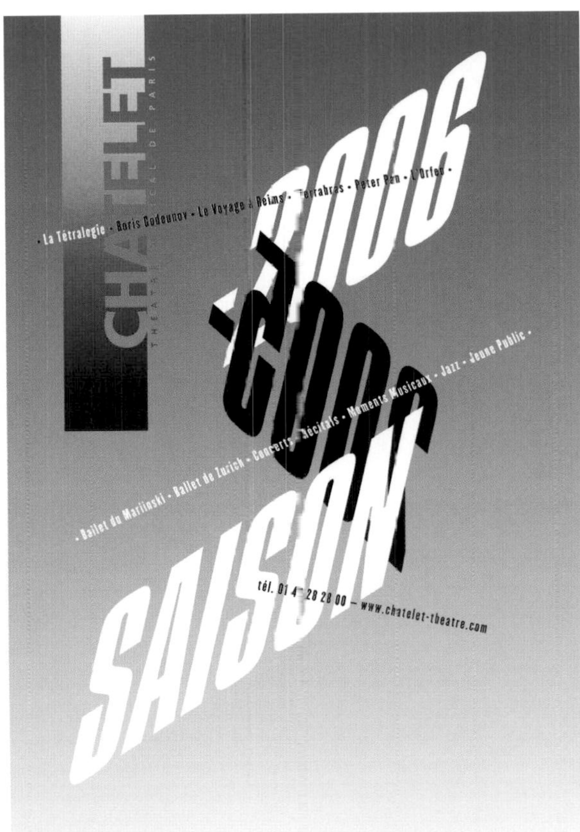

THE GROUPING OF four square dots creates a white cross element from the negative space between them, while the differentiation of one dot—as a punctuation element—evokes the idea of language in this medical newsletter logo.

LSD *Spain*

THE LINEAR, DIAGONAL, and multidirectional type forms create a kind of dance back and forth across the format of this theater poster. There are three groupings of line elements: the vertical logo band; the large, three-dimensional season type, and the three lines of smaller informational type. Each is differentiated from the other by direction, foreground-background relationship, and planar quality versus linear.

Design Fudi Meyer *France*

THIS BROCHURE USES very simple spatial and color interaction among dots and lines to communicate simple, but abstract, concepts expressed in large-size quotations. The first spread is about "delivering;" the concentric dots create a target, and their colors act to enhance the feeling that the blue dot at the center is further back in space than the others (see **Color: Form and Space** on page 102). The second spread is concerned with persuasion, and so the dots overlap to share a common spatial area. In the third spread, the issue is planning; the green dot is "captured" by the horizontal line and appears to be pulled from right to left.

And Partners *United States*

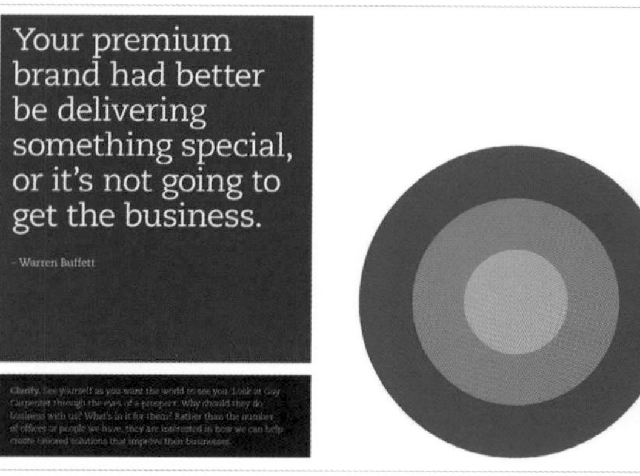

Your premium brand had better be delivering something special, or it's not going to get the business.
– Warren Buffett

If you wish to persuade me, you must think my thoughts, feel my feelings, and speak my words.
– Cicero

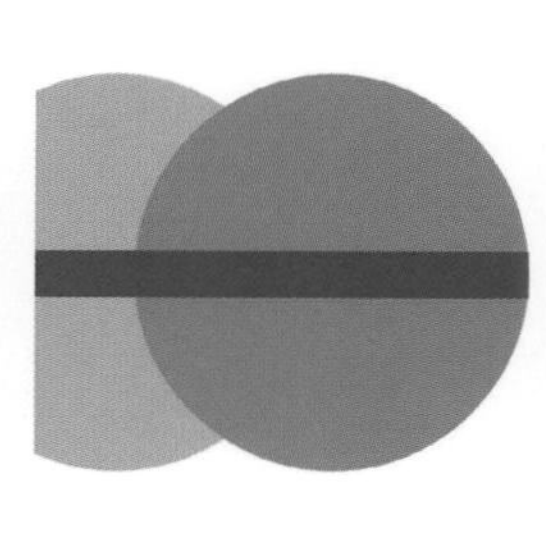

Planning is bringing the future into the present so that you can do something about it now.
– Alan Lakein

ECLIPSE

COMBINING LINES WITH DOTS offers a powerful visual contrast and, in this logo, creates meaning.

LSD *Spain*

THE REPETITION OF linear hand forms, rotated around the circular element, creates the sense of movement in DJ scratching. The pattern in the background seems to vibrate.

Thomas Csano *Canada*

Interplay Makes a Message Forms acquire new meanings when they participate in spatial relationships; when they share or oppose each other's mass or textural characteristics; and when they have relationships because of their rotation, singularity or repetition, alignment, clustering, or separation from each other. Each state tells the viewer something new about the forms, adding to the meaning that they already might have established. Forms that appear to be moving, or energetic, because of the way they are rotated or overlapped, for example, mean something very different from forms that are staggered in a static space. ■ The simplicity of abstraction belies its profound capacity to transmit messages on a perceptual level that is very rarely acknowledged by viewers intellectually—flying below their radar—but which they feel and understand nonetheless. Manipulating such base perceptions—in concert with whatever representational or pictorial content might be included—offers the designer a powerful medium for communication.

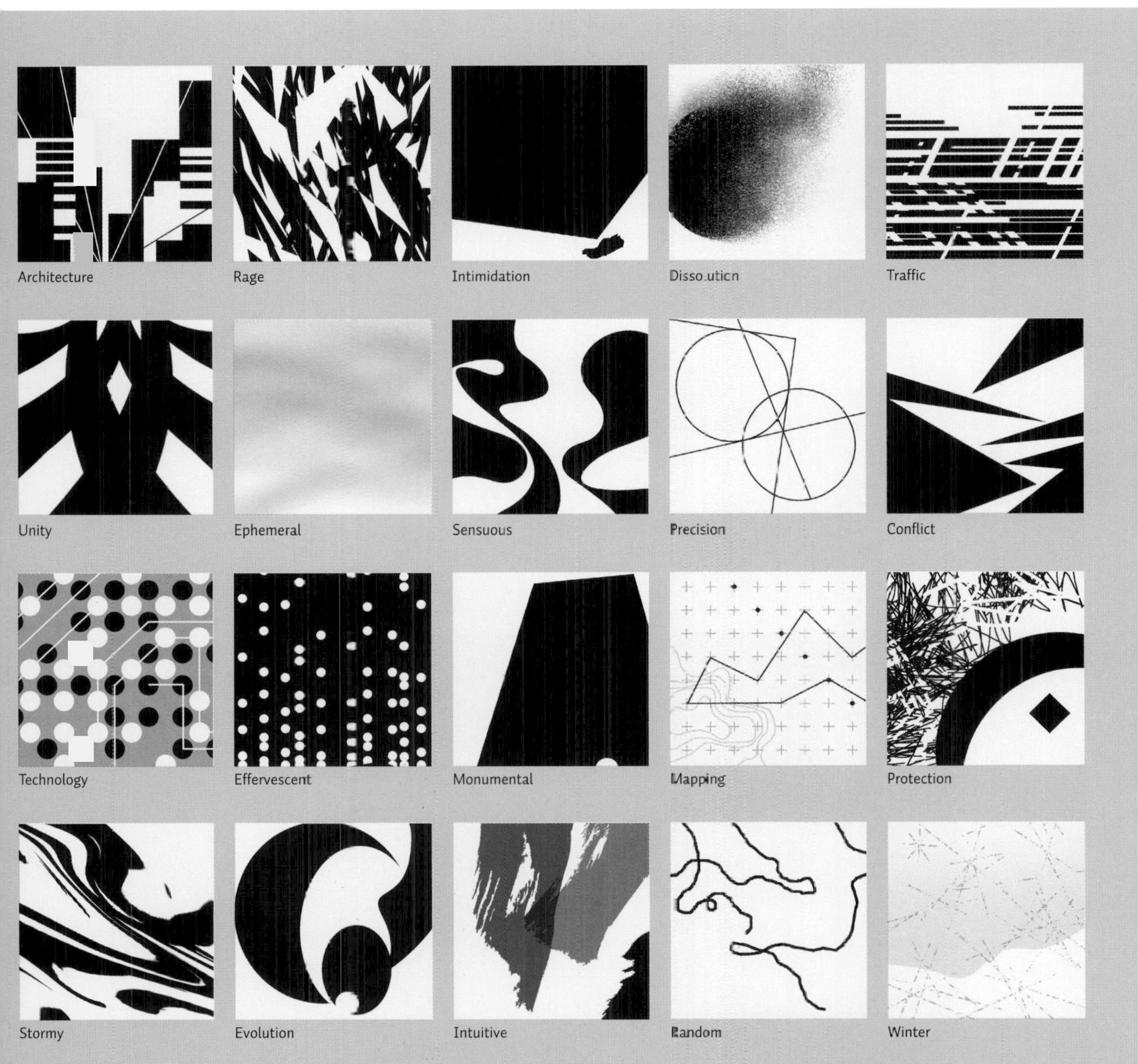

THE ARCING STROKE of the Euro character, as it crosses the linear boundary created by the horizontal stroke of the character, seems to shoot into the future.

Studio International *Croatia*

LINE ELEMENTS clustered in an orthogonal configuration, with emphasis along a horizon, allude to the idea of architecture, while their lateral rhythm and the blurring of particular components creates a sense of energy and movement.

Made in Space, Inc. *United States*

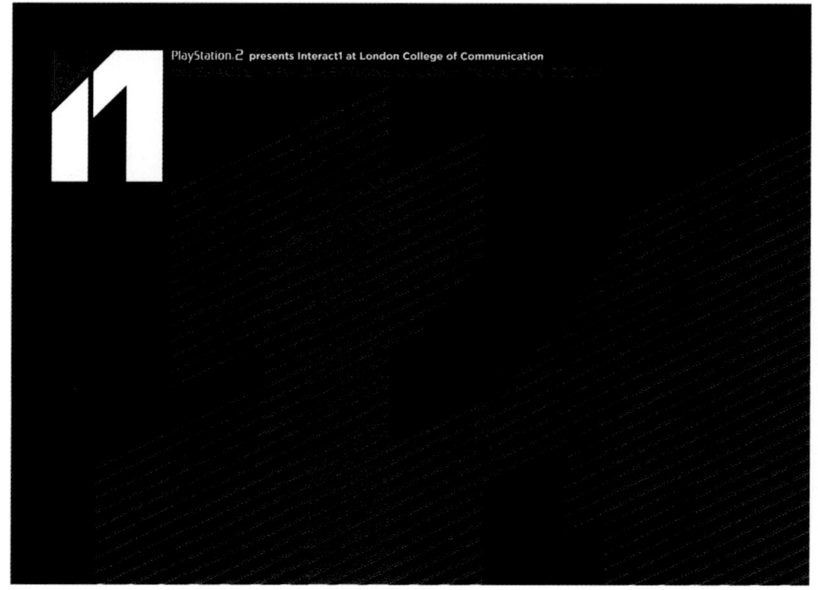

PlayStation.2 presents Interact1 at London College of Communication

REPEATED PATTERNS of lines create vibration and the illusion of three-dimensional planes which may be interpreted as printed surfaces, video texture, and ideas related to transmission associated with communication design.

Research Studios *United Kingdom*

PLANAR AND SPATIAL relationships between the images on this brochure cover create a rhythmic movement upward that helps convey the idea of achievement or personal improvement.

Metropolitan Group *United States*

NOT ONLY DO THE neon lines in this poster communicate the idea of industrial design and the British flag, but their extreme perspective also creates a sense of energy and expansion.

Form *United Kingdom*

ANGLED GEOMETRIC elements create a relatively literal representation of stairs; the progression in interval between the shapes expands, moves upward, and overall can be interpreted as the feathers on a wing.

Drotz Design *United States*

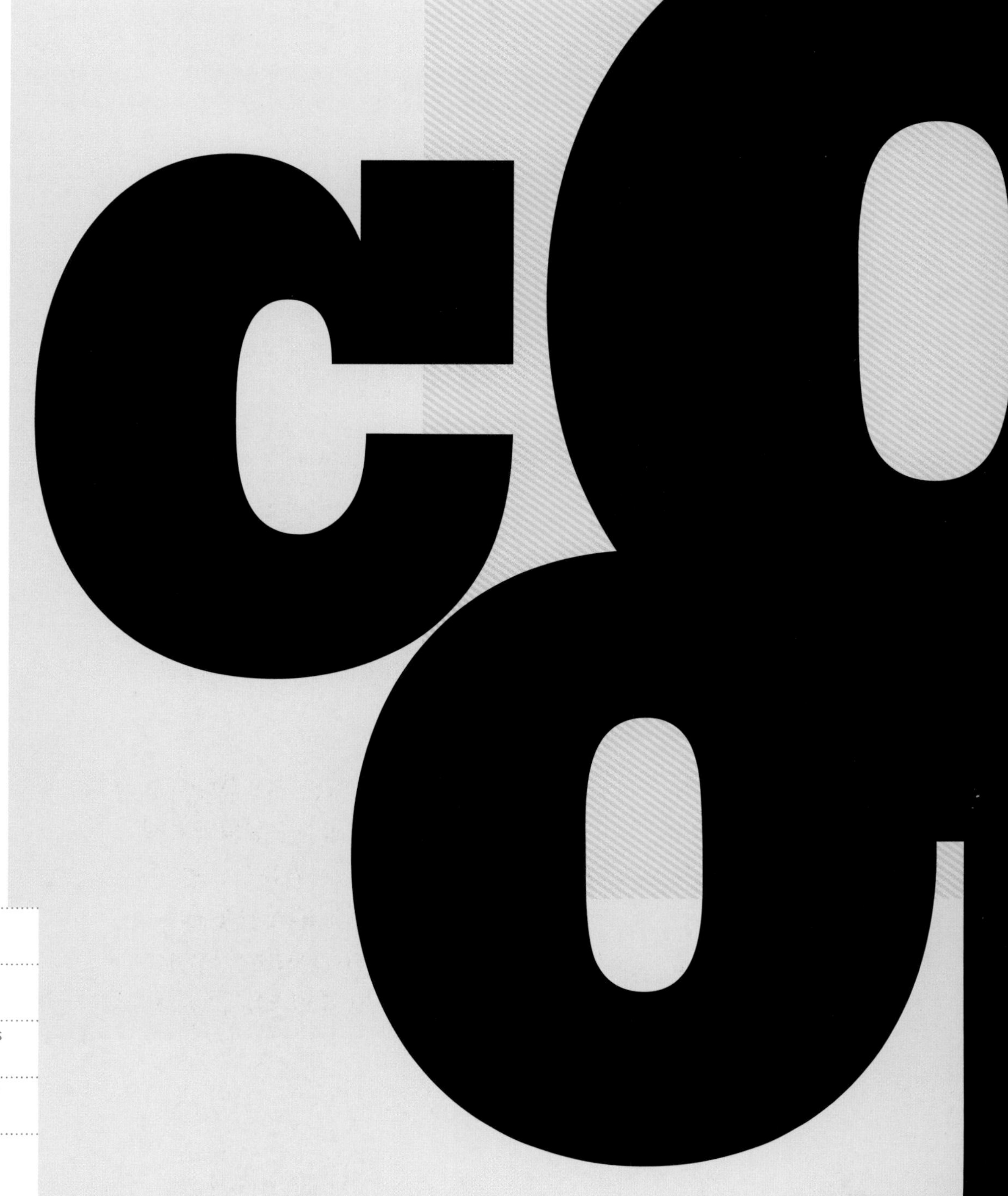

Chapter 2

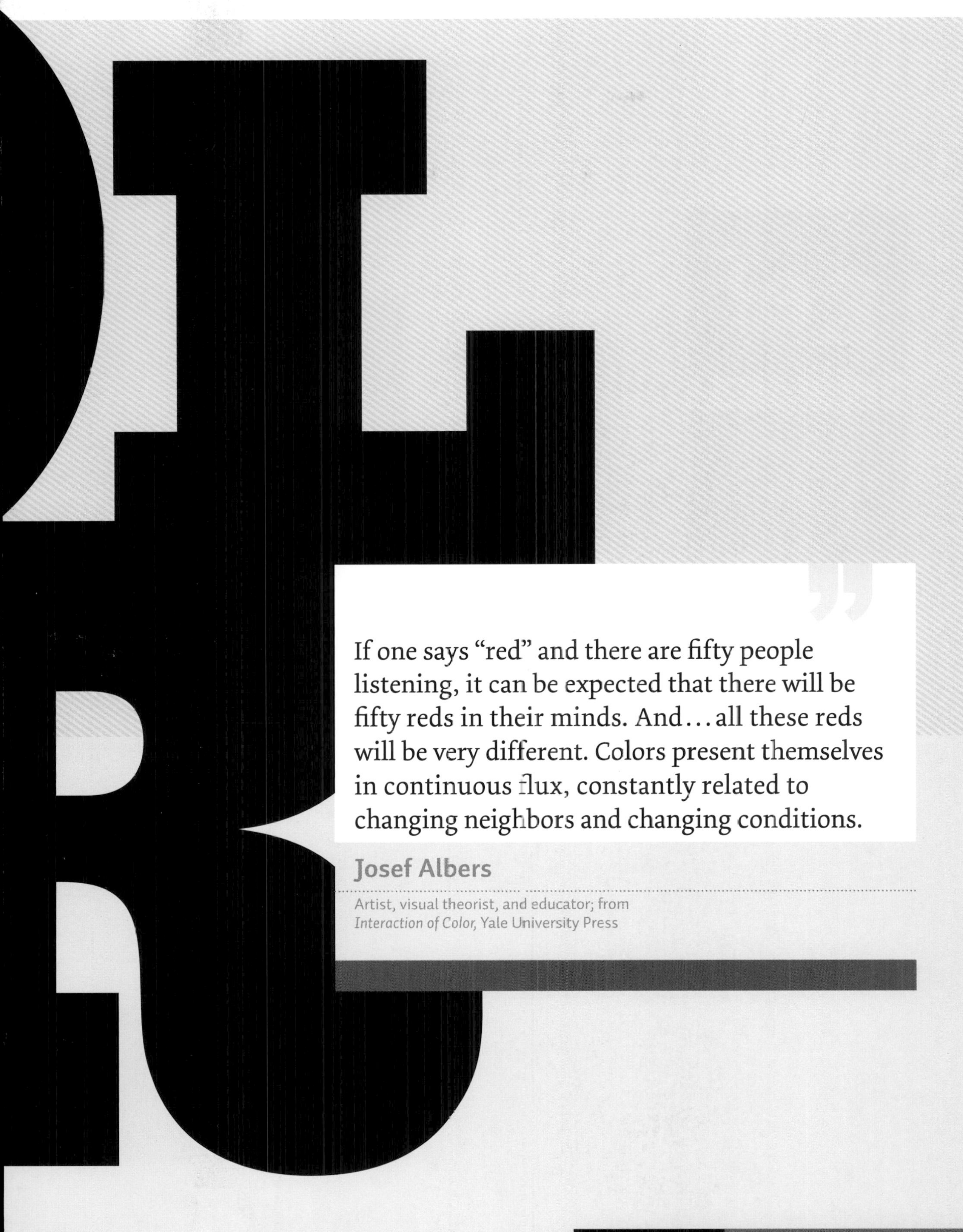

> If one says "red" and there are fifty people listening, it can be expected that there will be fifty reds in their minds. And... all these reds will be very different. Colors present themselves in continuous flux, constantly related to changing neighbors and changing conditions.

Josef Albers

Artist, visual theorist, and educator; from *Interaction of Color,* Yale University Press

A

B

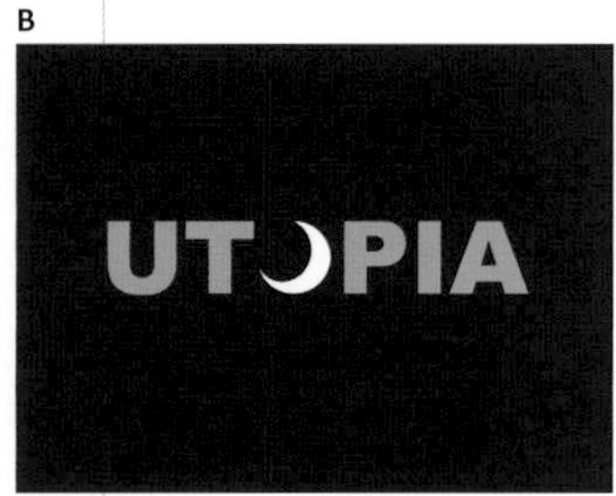

COLOR PLAYS IMPORTANT, yet very different, communicative roles in these two logotypes. In the **GEF** logo, the dark blue of the color field feels stable and personable; the more vivid, lighter blue field in the **Utopia** logo is energetic and cool. The color break in the **GEF** logo creates a recognizable flag; in the **Utopia** logo, the color break enhances the moon-like quality of the **O** form.

A Made In Space, Inc. *United States*

B Raidy Printing Group *Lebanon*

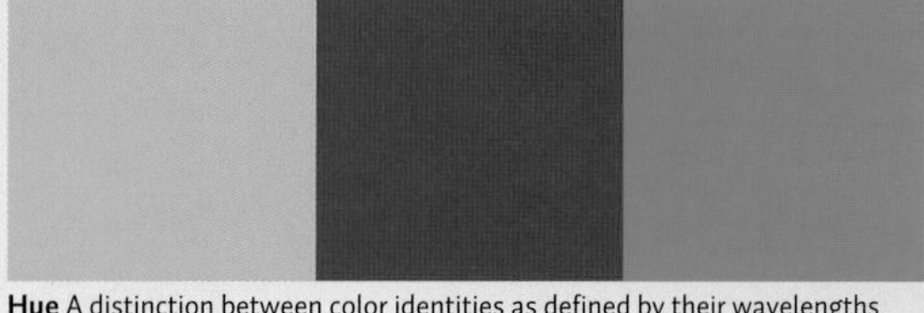

Hue A distinction between color identities as defined by their wavelengths

Saturation The relative dullness or brightness of a color

Temperature A color's perceived warmth or coolness

Value Whether a color appears light or dark

A single color is defined by four essential qualities related to our perception of its essential nature as waves of light.

There are few visual stimuli as powerful as color; it is a profoundly useful communication tool. But the meaning transmitted by color, because it results from reflected light waves transmitted through an imperfect organ—the eyes—to an imperfect interpreter—the brain—is also profoundly subjective. The mechanism of color perception is universal among humans. What we do with it once we see it is another thing altogether, and controlling it for the sake of communication depends on understanding how its optical qualities behave.

THESE TWO POSTERS exemplify the different characteristics that define a color's identity and quality. The red poster is warm in temperature, darker in value, and more intense or saturated than the violet poster—which is cool in temperature and lighter in value.

Paone Design Associates
United States

COLOR IN TYPOGRAPHY is highly effective in enhancing spatial relationships, as well as creating relationships between text and image. In this brochure spread, the warm golden type helps push the type closer to the spatial position of the mantis, but contrasts with the cool violet tones of the beetle, helping it to optically advance in space.

Carolyn Calles *The Art Institute, Orange County, United States*

Hue This term refers to the identity of a color—red, violet, orange, and so on. This identity is the result of how we perceive light being reflected from objects at particular frequencies. When we see a green car, what we're seeing isn't a car that is actually green; we're seeing light waves reflected off the car at a very specific frequency while all other frequencies are absorbed. Of color's four intrinsic attributes, the perception of hue is the

When light is split by a prism, the separate wavelengths are perceived as individual colors. The same is true of light that is reflected by an object: the material of the object absorbs some wavelengths and reflects others; the reflected wavelengths are what cause us to understand an object to have a particular hue.

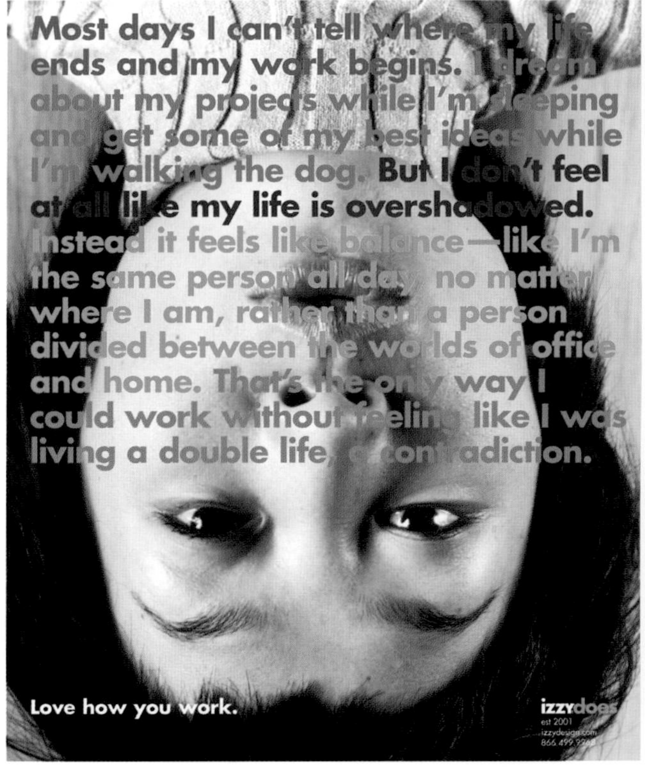

Most days I can't tell where my life ends and my work begins. I dream about my projects while I'm sleeping and get some of my best ideas while I'm walking the dog. But I don't feel at all like my life is overshadowed. Instead it feels like balance—like I'm the same person all day, no matter where I am, rather than a person divided between the worlds of office and home. That's the only way I could work without feeling like I was living a double life, a contradiction.
Love how you work.
est 2001

THE PRIMARY TEXT in this ad changes in hue but generally maintains similar value and intensity. Since hue is tied intrinsically to the perception of temperature, that variable also changes.

BBK Studio *United States*

most absolute: we see a color as red or blue, for example. But all color perception is relative, meaning that a color's identity is really knowable only when there's another color adjacent with which it can be compared. ■ Some hues we are able to perceive are absolutes of a sort, what we call the primary colors. These colors—red, blue, and yellow—are as different from each other in terms of their frequency as can be perceived by the human eye. Even a slight change in frequency in any one of the primary colors will cause the eye to perceive that it has shifted slightly toward one of the other primary colors.

■ When we are presented with a light frequency between those of two primary colors, we perceive a hue that evenly mixes them. These hues are the secondary colors: between red and yellow is the frequency perceived as orange; between yellow and blue, green; and between blue and red, violet. Further intermixing produces the tertiary hues: red orange, orange-yellow, yellow-green, blue-green, blue-violet, and violet-red.

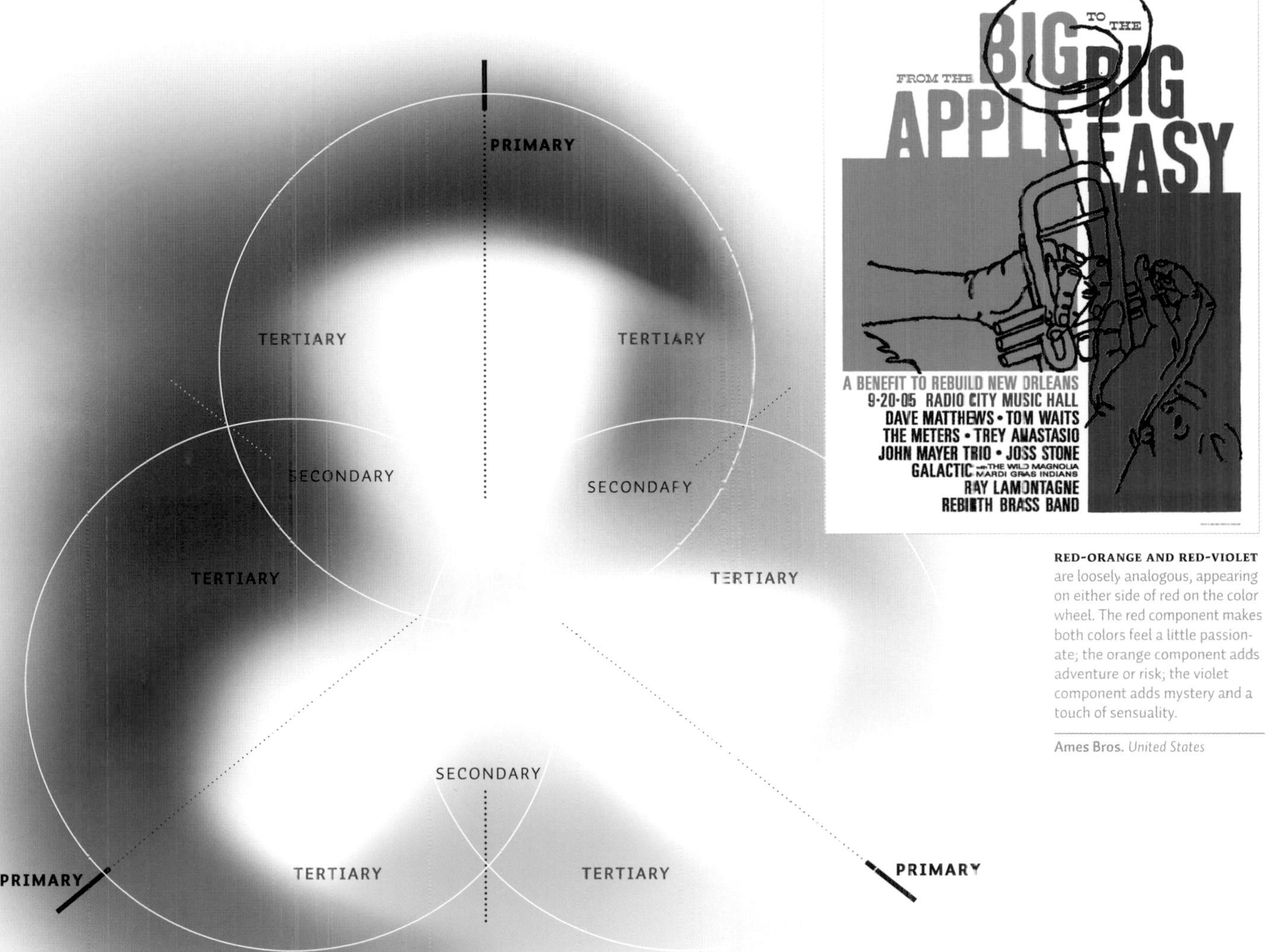

RED-ORANGE AND RED-VIOLET are loosely analogous, appearing on either side of red on the color wheel. The red component makes both colors feel a little passionate; the orange component adds adventure or risk; the violet component adds mystery and a touch of sensuality.

Ames Bros. *United States*

The primary colors of an additive system (in which all colors mix together to create white) are red, blue, and green. These wavelengths are as different from each other in frequency as can be discerned by the rods and cones in the human optical system. The secondary colors in an additive system—orange, green, and violet—represent shifts in frequency toward one primary color or another. The tertiary colors are still smaller shifts perceptible between the secondary colors and their parent primaries.

Saturation The color's saturation describes its intensity, or brilliance. A saturated color is very intense or vibrant. Colors that are dull are said to be desaturated; colors in which almost no hue is visible–such as a warm gray or a very dull brown–are said to be neutral. As with hue, the apparent saturation of a color will change if it can be compared to an adjacent color. ■ Bringing together hues that are as different from each other in frequency as possible, meaning closer to either of the opposing primaries, will cause the intensity of both colors to increase dramatically. This effect is even more pronounced if the amount of the two colors is very different; the color present in a smaller amount will become much more intense against a large field of the second color. Interestingly, a small amount of a desaturated–even neutral–color, presented against a large field of another color, will appear to gain in intensity and shift hue toward the opposite end of the spectrum.

FiscAlert

Bespaar op uw verzekeringen 13

Betaal minder belasting door slim te schuiven 14

Alles over de bijleenregeling 17

Hoe dichten we ons pensioengat? 22

Ontslagen. Wat nu!? 23

Geef lijfrentetermijnen aan uw kinderen 27

HIGHLY SATURATED bands of color help advance the idea of "alert" in this newsletter cover.

Martin Oostra *Netherlands*

On a white background, primary yellow will appear somewhat less intense—white is the ultimate in saturation—but on a black background, the same yellow will become extremely intense. Against a middle value of gray, the yellow decreases in saturation unless the surrounding value (darkness or lightness) is similar.

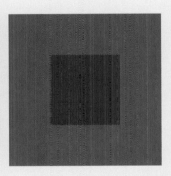

The same violet is presented against three fields of varied intensity. Against a similarly intense violet of slightly different hue, the base color appears desaturated. Against a neutral gray, the base violet appears moderately intense.

Juxtaposing the base violet with a field of a very different hue, but one that is of similar value, again increases the base violet's apparent saturation.

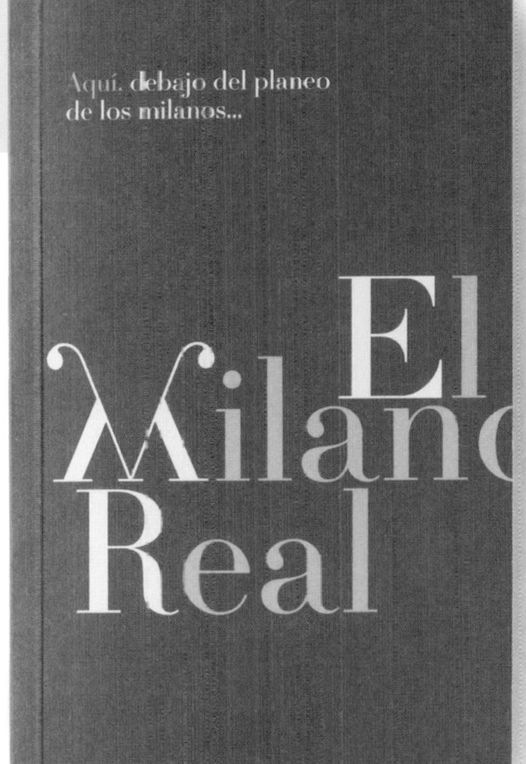

Aquí, debajo del planeo
de los milanos...
El
Milano
Real

THE BACKGROUND OF this book cover is darker but less saturated than the type, which is lighter and more saturated (intense or vibrant).

LSD *Spain*

DESATURATED colors, all of a similar temperature, create a feeling of sophistication and repose in the splash page of this website.

BBK Studio *United States*

LIKE A PHOTOGRAPH that is considered "good," this drawing exhibits a great deal of value change—a full range from deep shadows, through a generous number of middle tones, up through a bright highlight or white. However, the values are not distributed evenly across the format; they progress from one side to another, and they are concentrated in specific places to create contrast.

Raidy Printing Group *Lebanon*

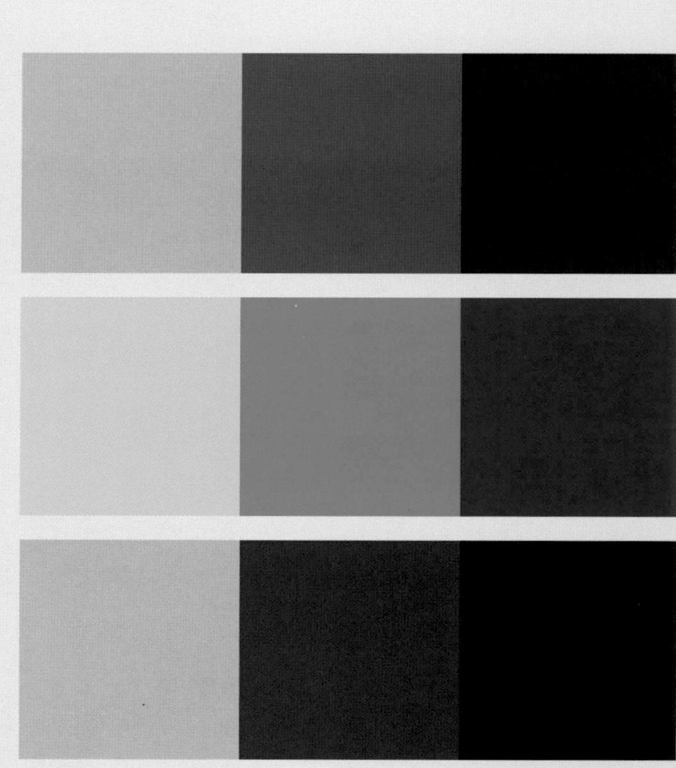

As the value of a single hue changes, either darker or lighter, its intensity decreases.

Value A color's value is its intrinsic darkness or lightness. Yellow is perceived as being light; violet is perceived as being dark. Again, it's all relative. One color can be considered darker or lighter only compared to another. Yellow, even, appears darker than white, which has the lightest possible value of any color. An extremely deep blue or violet appears quite luminous against a maximal black, which has the darkest value of any color (black being technically the absence of any reflected light). Lightening the value of an intensely saturated hue tends to desaturate it. Darkening the value of a moderately to intensely saturated hue will initially intensify its saturation, but if the value is darkened too much, the hue will become less vibrant. Placing any color on a darker color will make it seem lighter, as will increasing the amount of a color. If you've ever had the unfortunate experience of picking out a paint swatch for your living room only to find that it's three or four values too light once you paint an entire wall, you already know this to be true. Bringing two hues of the same value together, regardless of their relative intensities, creates an odd "bleeding" effect that messes with our ability to see a sharp, distinct boundary between the two. The more different the two hues, or the more similar they are in intensity, the more pronounced this effect becomes; at some magical intersection of hue and saturation, the boundary between two colors of the same value will be nearly impossible to see.

THE COLOR VALUES in this brochure spread affects the reading order, or hierarchy, of the text. The darkest elements read first because they have the most value contrast with the color of the background; middle-value and lighter elements read later because they have less value contrast against the background.

Research Studios *United Kingdom*

The effect of value relationships is shown here in a close-in comparison of two colors of relatively similar hue and intensity; the greater the difference in the value of either color—or of the color field on which it sits—the greater the effect on relative intensity. In the lower example, the deeper ochre becomes more intense as the yellow orange lightens.

The boundary between the blue-violet on the left and the blue-green on the right is easy to see in the top pair. Replace the darker color with a violet of similar value to the blue-green, however, and their boundary is more difficult to see and seems to vibrate.

Temperature The temperature of a color is a subjective quality that is related to experiences. Colors considered “warm,” such as red or orange, remind us of heat; cool colors, such as green or blue, remind us of cold objects or environments, such as ice. Colors of a particular temperature remind us of these specific kinds of objects or substances because those substances reflect similar wavelengths of light. The temperature of any color will be thrown in one direction or another if compared to any other color. Placing a hot red near an even hotter orange will make that red seem cool; conversely, placing a slightly cooler magenta next to the same hot red will simply enhance the perception of its intrinsic temperature.

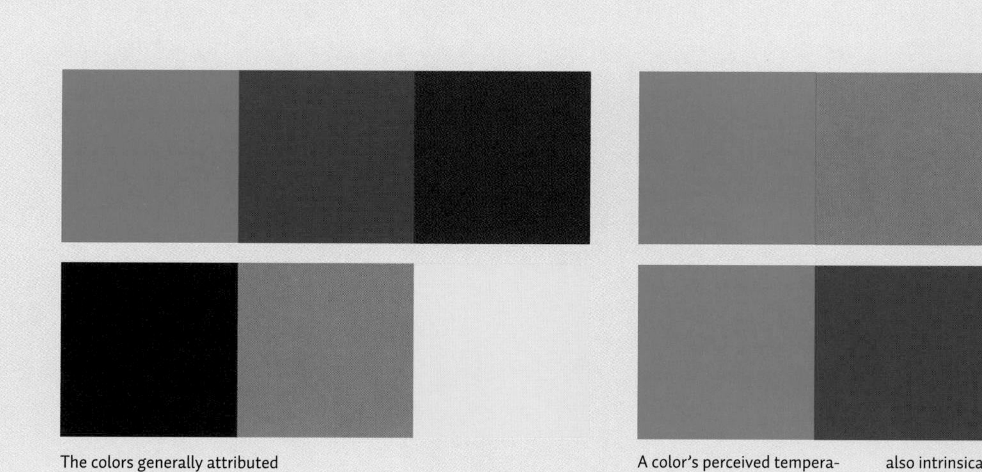

The colors generally attributed to be cool are green, blue, and violet. The colors usually perceived as warm are red, yellow, and orange.

A color’s perceived temperature is subject, like all color relationships, to relativity. Even colors that are commonly experienced as cool or warm will demonstrate a shift in temperature when placed adjacent to another, similar hue that is also intrinsically cool or warm—one will always appear cooler or warmer than the other. In this example, a very cool green—cool, that is, when next to a warm orange—becomes unusually hot when next to an icy cool blue.

THE WARM, SLIGHTLY desaturated orange square appears to advance, while the cool blue-green pattern appears to recede, enhancing the separation created by the translucent jacket.

Shinnoske, Inc. *Japan*

WARMER COLORS SEEM more aggressive and alive, while cooler colors seem more passive. In the right context, this contrast can convey a message that negates energy and, therefore, a sense of life. In this poster, the SOS in yellow-orange seems to call out urgently; the cooler blue overlapping the yellow-orange type quiets it down. This simple change alludes to flooding and, possibly, death.

Stereotype Design *United States*

A COOLER IMAGE on the left-hand page of this brochure spread—with blue-green and pale violet tones—contrasts with the warmth of the wood in the image on the right-hand page. The contrast is important to help add interest, as both images share a repeating pattern of linear, curving, and angular elements.

Not From Here *United States*

Color Relationships Since the fifteenth century, artists and scientists have been creating methods for organizing color perception in visual models. A color model helps a designer see these relationships for planning color ideas. Of these, the most common is the color wheel, developed by Albert Munsell, a British painter and scientist. Munsell's color wheel is a circular representation of hue—the differences in wavelength that distinguish blue from yellow from red—modified along two axes that describe the color's darkness or lightness (its value) and its relative brilliance (its saturation). Johannes Itten, a Bauhaus master at Weimar, Germany, in the 1920s, posited a color sphere—a three-dimensional model that integrates the value scale of Munsell's color wheel into a globe—in his landmark book *The Art of Color*, published

AN ABSTRACTED MODEL for additive, or light-based, color, forms the symbol for this media company's brand signature.

Paone Design Associates
United States

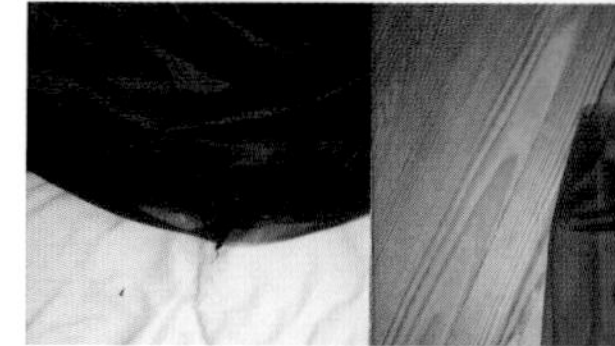

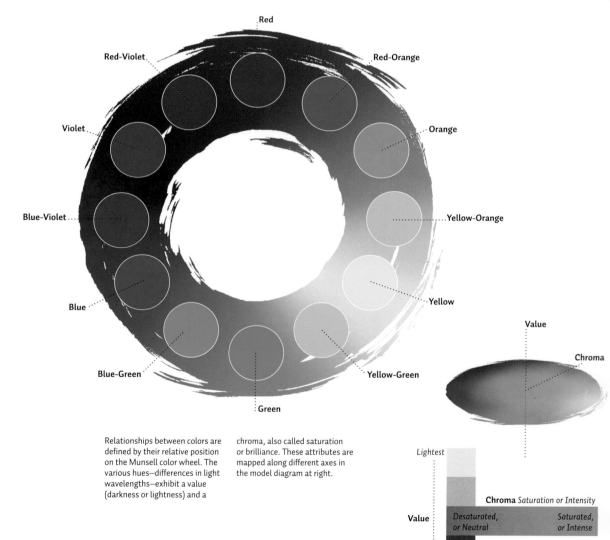

Relationships between colors are defined by their relative position on the Munsell color wheel. The various hues—differences in light wavelengths—exhibit a value (darkness or lightness) and a chroma, also called saturation or brilliance. These attributes are mapped along different axes in the model diagram at right.

in 1961. Both models focus on hue as color's defining aspect, radiating at full intensity around the outside of a circular form and decreasing in intensity toward the center. In Itten's sphere, the decrease in intensity toward the center of the solid globe is the result of mixing hues that are situated opposite each other (as they are on Munsell's color wheel) and results in a cancelling out toward a neutral. ■ These color models were developed to describe how color works with refracted light, but, for the most part, graphic designers work with color derived from mixing chemical pigments—paint or inks. The relative color relationships described by these models, however, work in much the same way with mixed pigments; the difference is simply how these relationships are achieved in a physical sense. When working with inks (see page 108), the type of ink being used contributes to the designer's consideration of color relationships. If the inks being combined are solids, the beginning color relationships are much more direct and have a more aggressive effect on each other when added together; they will define the secondary and tertiary colors by virtue of their printing on top of each other. If color is being produced by a buildup of primary colors—as in process, or CMYK printing—a wider range of colors is possible.

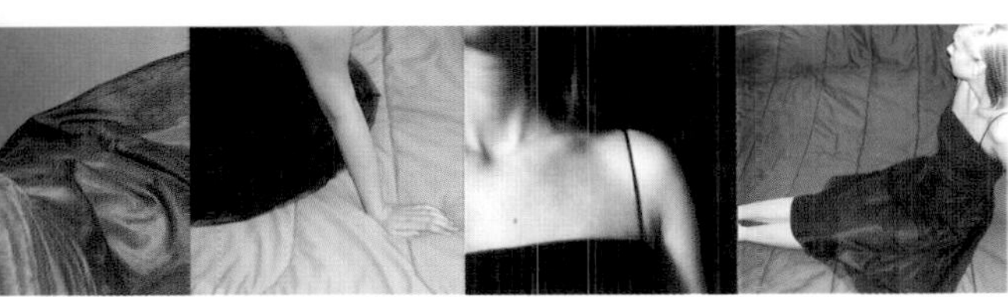

THIS COLOR STUDY is interesting for its examination of relationships between warmer and cooler colors as well as between analogous and complementary colors.

Diana Hurd *Carnegie Mellon University, United States*

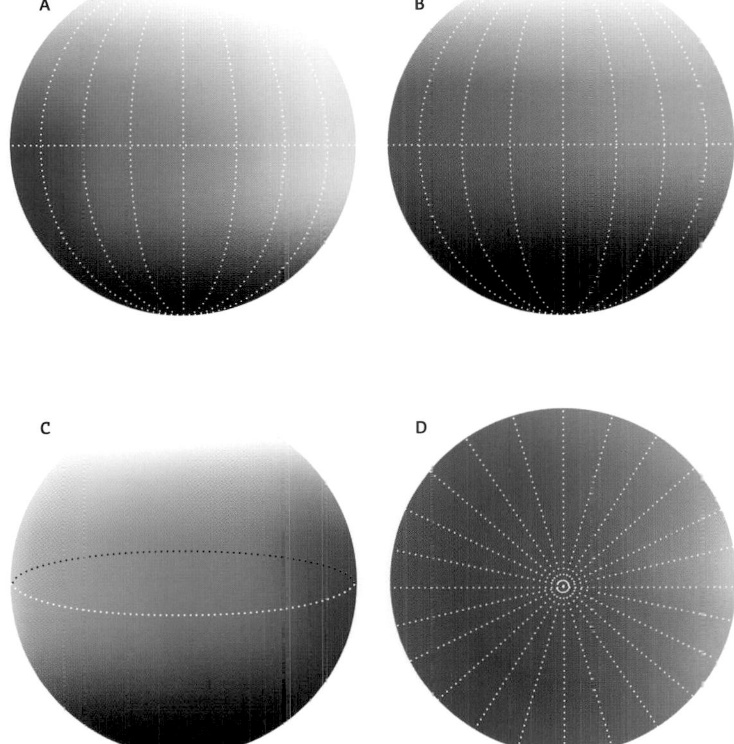

The color sphere, developed from earlier models by Swiss artist and theorist, Johannes Itten, extrapolates the color wheel into a three-dimensional model. Shown here are (A) the warm hemisphere of the sphere; (B) the cool hemisphere; (C) a cross-section of the sphere, cut vertically between warm and cool hemispheres; and (D) a cross-section cut horizontally, separating the top (lighter) half from the lower (darker) half—in this cross-section, we're looking down at the bottom half.

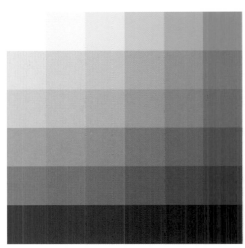

In a subtractive color model, such as that which defines ink mixtures for printing shown above, successive layers of ink result in darker, more saturated colors, to a point. Once the ink layers no longer permit a substantial amount of light to reflect from the printed surface, the combined colors become less saturated and eventually neutral and black. Subtractive color is also altered by the chemical makeup of the pigments used to color the inks.

Hue Relationships Designers can create interaction between different hues, independent of their saturation or value, according to where they lie on the color wheel. The closer together the colors appear on the wheel, the more similar their optical qualities and, hence, the more harmonious or related. The further apart colors are on the wheel, the more their optical qualities contrast.

THE YELLOW-ORANGE background of this Web page is complementary to the blue-violet inset images, and is analogous to the two colors wrapped around the central figure.

Sub Communication *Canada*

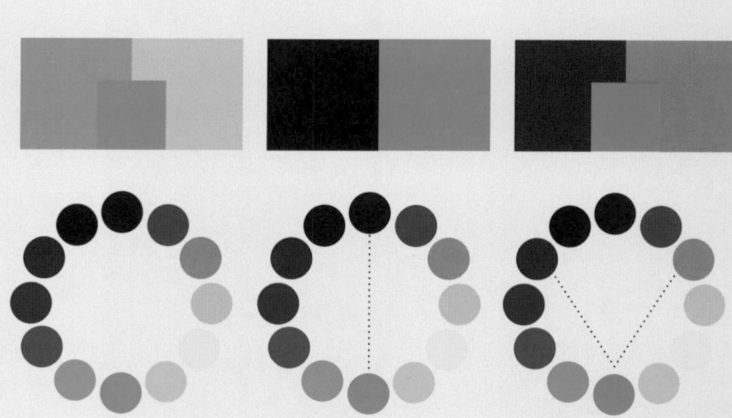

Analogous Colors adjacent to each other on the color wheel are said to be *analogous*. Although noticeably different from one another, the relationship becomes more about temperature difference. Above, for example, a viewer will note a collection of green hues of varying warmth.

Complementary Two colors appearing opposite each other on the color wheel are complements of each other. Their mixture results in a neutral tone, or *neutral*. With light, the neutral is a medium gray; with ink it's a dull brown.

Triadic Sometimes referred to as *split complements*, a color triad involves three colors at 120° intervals from each other on the color wheel. One color is complementing the two colors equidistant from its true complement.

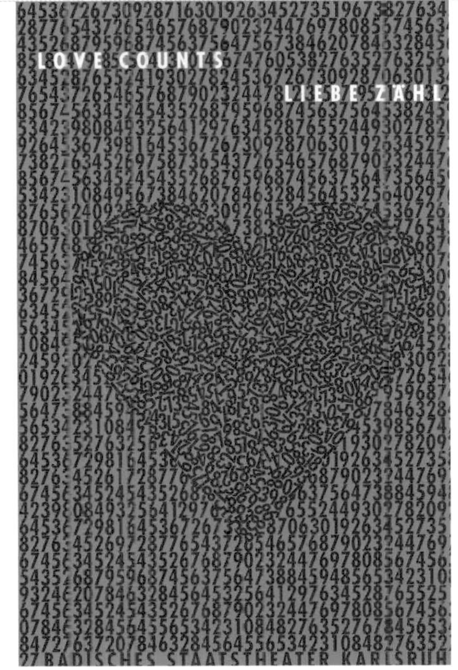

BLUE-GREEN AND VIOLET are loosely analogous, being separated by pure blue and blue-violet on the color wheel.

Templin Brink Design
United States

COMPLEMENTARY COLORS buzz when they get close to each other, and neutralize each other when mixed. If you cover up the heart and blur your vision, you'll perceive a less intense olive color where the pure red and green mix more evenly. The increase in red numbers in the heart area appropriately changes its relative intensity.

Gunter Rambow *Germany*

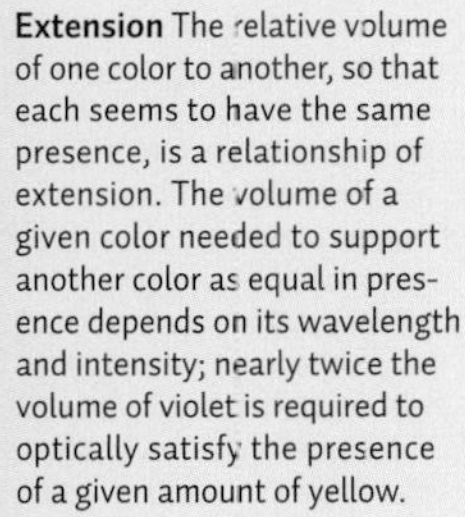

Extension The relative volume of one color to another, so that each seems to have the same presence, is a relationship of extension. The volume of a given color needed to support another color as equal in presence depends on its wavelength and intensity; nearly twice the volume of violet is required to optically satisfy the presence of a given amount of yellow.

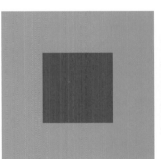

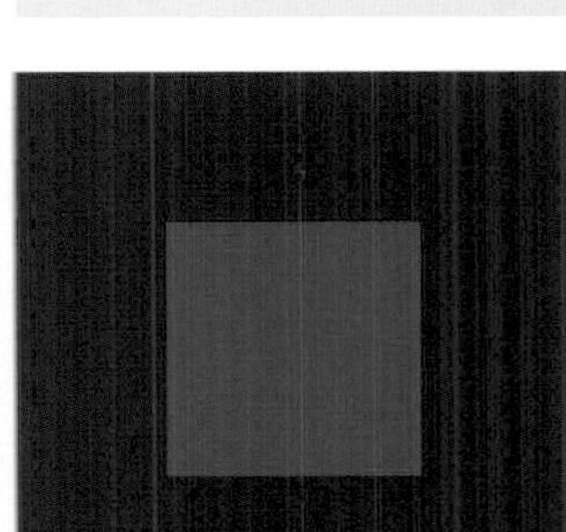

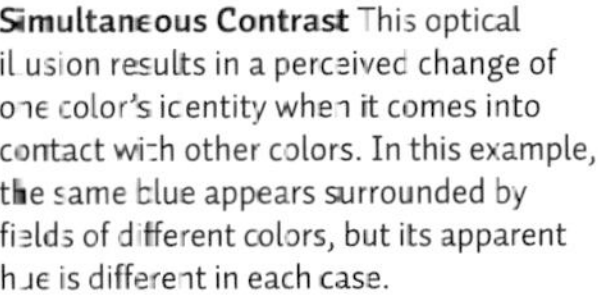

Simultaneous Contrast This optical illusion results in a perceived change of one color's identity when it comes into contact with other colors. In this example, the same blue appears surrounded by fields of different colors, but its apparent hue is different in each case.

A CHANGE IN VALUE from dark to light among the type elements, culminating in the reversed white title, correspond to the value changes in the woman's head in the photograph.

Research Studios *United Kingdom*

VALUE CHANGES IN the base blue are used to highlight important content and clarify navigation in this website.

Swim Design *United States*

Value Relationships Regardless of their specific hues, the colors selected for a palette will have relationships of darkness or lightness. By varying the number of jumps from value to value, or by how dramatically the values among the colors change, a designer can create contrast and rhythm among darker and lighter areas—even if the number of hues used, or how different they are, is limited.

Rhythmic Extension A series of values, lighter and darker, is considered rhythmic if there are recognizable jumps between shades, relative to the extension or volume of each shade. The result is an optical proportioning of value similar to a spatial proportion system, but dependent on dark-to-light difference.

Analogous In a scale from lightest to darkest, two colors are considered to have analogus value if they exhibit the same (or very similar) darkness or lightness, relative to each other—regardless of saturation or hue. As colors approach each other in value, the ability to distinguish their boundary is diminished.

USING A LIGHTER VALUE for the word "taxi" in this logo makes the image that it conjures feel lighter or have less impact, reinforcing the concept "eco," which appears in a deeper value.

Kropp Associates *United States*

Progressive A sequence of values among colors—in either optically even steps or optically geometric steps—is considered progressive if the overall effect is perceived as one of continual lightening or darkening within a given palette.

Simultaneous Contrast This optical illusion results in a perceived change of one color's value when it comes into contact with colors of differing value. The effect in this case is that one color appears to be lighter or darker depending on the values of colors surrounding it. In this example, a blue of the same value appears surrounded by fields of different value, causing it to appear lighter or darker in turn.

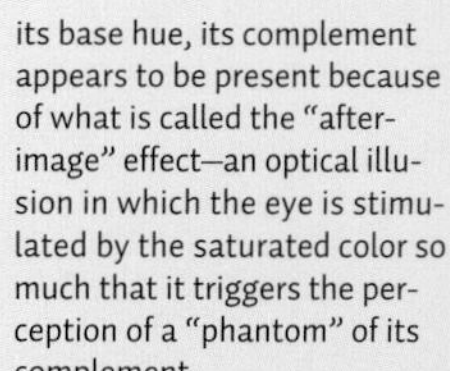

Analogous Any colors, regardless of hue, temperature, or value, that exhibit the same intensity or brilliance, are said to exhibit analogous saturation.

Diametric Opposition Similar to hue complements, but expressed in terms of saturation, this relationship concerns the juxtaposition of the most intense and almost completely desaturated versions of the same hue. The result of this kind of pairing is that while the desaturated component retains its base hue, its complement appears to be present because of what is called the "after-image" effect—an optical illusion in which the eye is stimulated by the saturated color so much that it triggers the perception of a "phantom" of its complement.

THE PINK OF THE letterform, whose value is also lighter, is less saturated than the red droplet, enhancing its vitality and symbolic quality.

LSD *Spain*

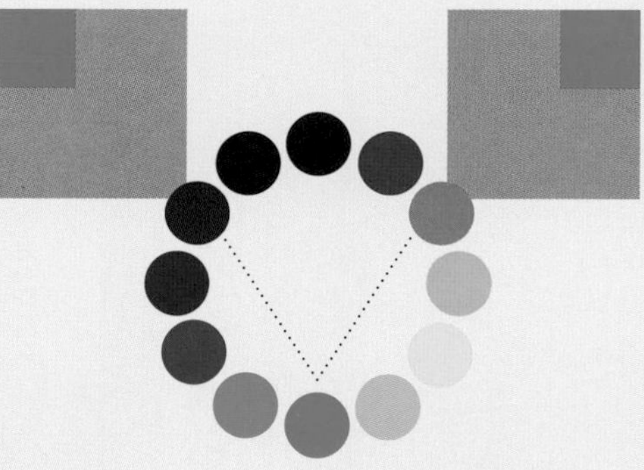

Split Opposition The most intense version of a given color in relation to the nearly desaturated versions of its split complements creates a relationship of split opposition.

The split relationship can also occur between the desaturated hue and the most intense versions of its split complements.

Extension Juxtapositions of two or more colors of similar intensity, but in different volumes, create effects of simultaneous contrast and after-image. Juxtaposing a small volume of a desaturated color with a large volume of an intensely saturated color creates hue-shifting; the intense volume acts on the desaturated color to skew it toward the intense color's complement.

THE IDEA OF EXTENSION is manipulated for this book cover. The background yellow is relatively intense, more so than the medium gray of the title type; the effect of extension renders the type slightly bluish or violet, the complement of yellow. At the same time, the red elements are intensified through their analogous relationship—in hue and saturation—with the background.

Red Canoe *United States*

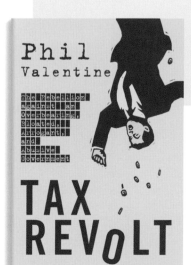

Saturation Relationships Saturation relationships may occur independently of hue relationships, but will usually have an effect on value or temperature. As a hue is desaturated, it may appear to become darker adjacent to a different hue of greater saturation, but it may also appear to become cooler if the adjacent hue is a warm color. Grouping analogous hues of similar intensity, but changing the intensity of one, will create a rich, intimately harmonious palette. Grouping complementary hues, or split complements, all with similar values but different saturations, will create a rich color experience.

A PROGRESSION IN VALUE and saturation from less intense to more intense imparts rhythm and movement to the rigidly grid-shaped typography.

Voice *Australia*

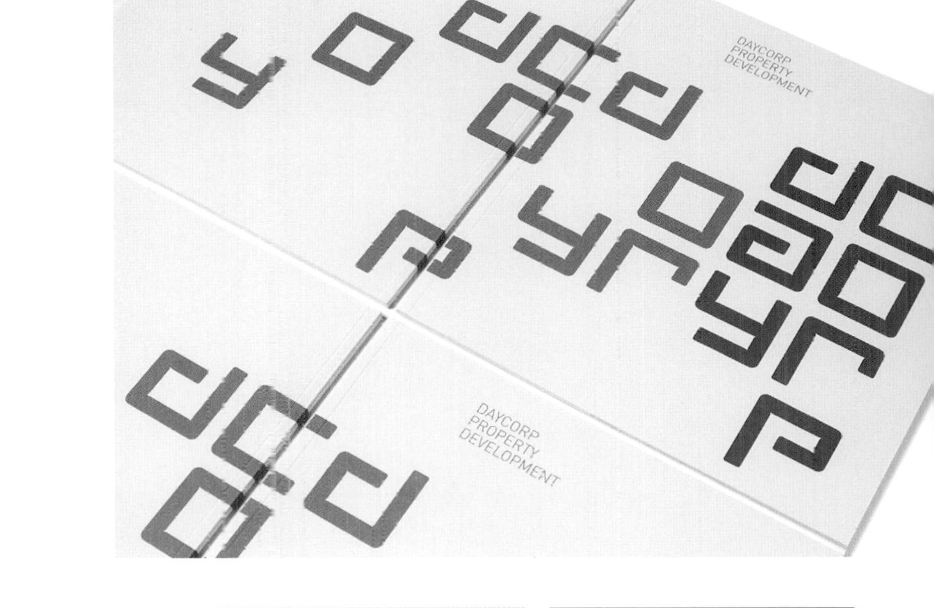

THE EFFECT OF DIAMETRIC opposition occurs here; the more intense squares in this logo (T, E) cause the viewer to see the complement in the desaturated squares. Looking at the T and E tiles will cause the others to appear greenish.

Drotz Design *United States*

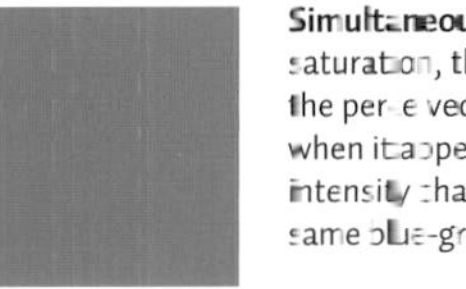

Simultaneous Contrast With regard to saturation, this optical illusion results in the perceived change of a color's intensity when it appears adjacent to colors whose intensity changes. In this example, the same blue-green appears surrounded by fields of different saturation, appearing more saturated in some contexts and less saturated in others.

Looks
Living
Moving
Feeling
Flavor

Looks

Under the sun? Chill out

There's a new reason to relax when the heat is on.

Next time a deadline's looming or the kids have just emptied the cat's litter box on the floor, take note: you may want to stay out of the sun. A report published in the *Journal of the American Academy of Dermatology* shows there may be a connection between stress and skin cancer, similar to the link that's already been established between stress and many other ailments.

To evaluate the effects that high anxiety and sun exposure can have on skin, scientists at The Sidney Kimmel Comprehensive Cancer Center at Johns Hopkins University

July/August 2005 Health TK

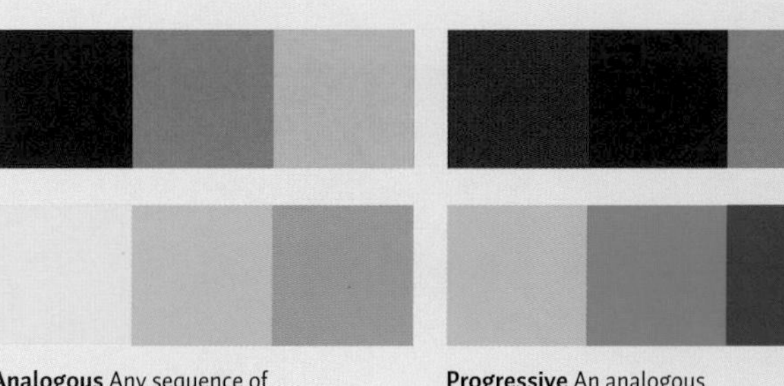

Analogous Any sequence of colors that are adjacent on the color wheel so long as they are similarly warm or cool: red/orange/yellow, for example, or yellow/yellow-green/green, but not orange/yellow/green.

Progressive An analogous grouping in which temperature makes a transition, color by color, from cooler to warmer or vice versa.

THE ANALOGOUS shift in temperature—added warmth that transforms a blue-green into green—not only adds visual interest, but evokes a sense of sky and landscape.

Cobra *Norway*

Temperature Relationships Designers can establish relationships within a color palette based on relative temperature. Grouping colors with similar temperature, together with one or two variations on the same hues that are warmer or cooler—for example, a cool green, blue, and violet with a warmer green—can generate enormous possibilities for combining the colors while maintaining a tightly-controlled color environment.

TEMPERATURE RELATIONSHIPS tie together each page of this magazine spread (note the locations of the warmer green elements) and separate elements in the hierarchy.

AdamsMorioka *United States*

Extension Between two colors sharing intensity and value, differences in volume will have the effect of changing the perception of their relative temperature. If two colors are both relatively close to each other in temperature, the one given in smaller volume will appear to shift temperature away from that given in greater volume.

A CLOSE-IN PROGRESSION in temperature is the most important aspect of this logo, although value also plays a role. The light element in the M symbol is the warmest, being closer to the yellow range of greens. Each stroke of the M becomes progressively cooler; the full logotype is the coolest. As green becomes cooler and deeper, it communicates less about refreshment and more about economic growth and stability.

Jelena Drobac *Serbia*

Simultaneous Contrast This optical illusion affects the apparent temperature of a color in much the same way it affects its hue, value, or saturation. A given color will appear warmer when situated against cooler colors, but cooler when against warmer colors. In this example, the same green appears surrounded by fields of different warmth and coolness; the result is a corresponding change in the green's perceived warmth or coolness in turn.

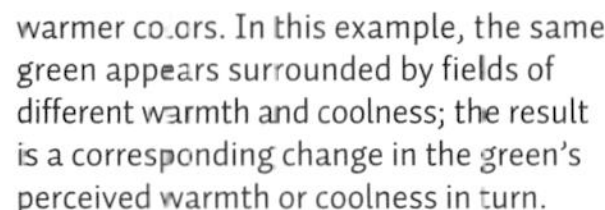

Color: Form and Space Color exhibits a number of spatial properties. Cool colors appear to recede while warm colors appear to advance. Of the primary colors, blue appears to recede and yellow to advance, but red appears to sit statically at a middle depth within space. ■ Applying color to a composition will have an immediate effect on hierarchy, the relative order of importance of the forms in space. The intrinsic relationships in a black-and-white composition might be exaggerated through the application of chromatic color, or made purposely ambiguous. Color distinctions can greatly enhance the perception of spatial depth and force greater separation between the hierarchic levels. For example, if an element at the top of a hierarchy is set in a deep, vibrant orange-red, while secondary forms are colored a cool gray, these two levels of the hierarchy will be separated visually to a much greater degree. Although the values of the colors are similar, the saturated orange form will advance in space, and the cool gray one will recede. ■ The application of color to

EACH COLOR—blue, red, and yellow—assumes a place in space: blue recedes, red stays in the middle, and yellow advances. In this case, the application of color enhances the desired spatial location of each element.

Thomas Csano *Canada*

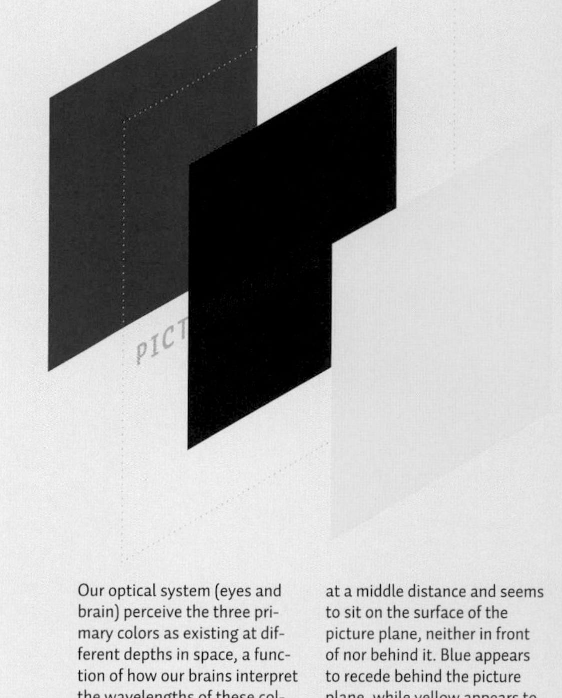

Our optical system (eyes and brain) perceive the three primary colors as existing at different depths in space, a function of how our brains interpret the wavelengths of these colors. Red appears stationary at a middle distance and seems to sit on the surface of the picture plane, neither in front of nor behind it. Blue appears to recede behind the picture plane, while yellow appears to advance.

COLORS OF SIMILAR VALUE will appear to cluster together into one form, as do the grayish and olive green areas at the upper left of this study. Because their values are similar, the boundary between them appears less pronounced than those between other areas whose values are much different, even if their intensities are also very different. Note the relative lack of separation between the desaturated orange and light gray at the lower right.

JRoss Design *United States*

the ground within a composition can further enhance the hierarchy. A form in one color, set on a field of another color, will join closely with it or separate aggressively, depending on their color relationship. If the colors of foreground and background elements are related, the elements will occupy a similar spatial depth. If they are complementary in nature, the two will occupy very different spatial depths.

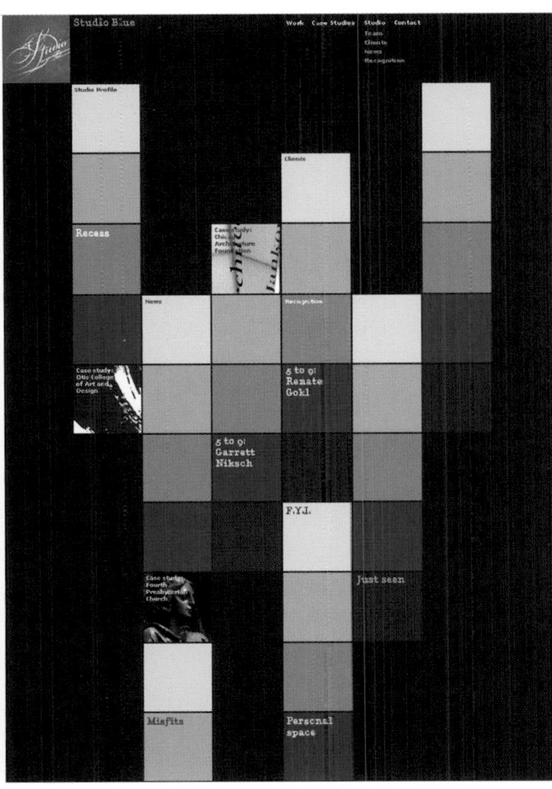

THE SPATIAL DIFFERENCE between the squares in this website creates hierarchy: the lighter squares advance and so become the more important, or sequentially primary elements in the navigation.

Studio Blue *United States*

The result of color's appearance at different planar locations can have a tremendous impact on the perceived depth of forms in space and, consequently, on the order in which each form presents itself: the visual hierarchy. In this study, each form element—regardless of size or arrangement—is made to register in the foreground, then the middle ground, and then the background of the composition, merely by alternating the element to which each color is applied. The effect becomes even more dramatic when the background also participates in the color swap.

The amount of color that can be perceived—and its intensity and value—are all affected by volume. The orange of the narrow line appears darker and less intense against the white field of the page than either the thicker line or the larger square. The opposite is true when the same elements cross over a dark field.

Color Stories: Coding with Color Within a complex visual environment, color can help distinguish different kinds of information, as well as create relationships among components or editions of a publication. A designer might develop, for example, a palette for graphic and typographic elements that helps readers distinguish between specific text components (headlines, subheads, and body) or between sections of information. Or, a designer might use a general palette for all elements that is based on the color or thematic content of photographs. Perhaps this palette has a consistent base, like a selection of warm neutrals that remains constant, while accent colors change. ■ The use of colors can be coded—assigning colors to identify sections or components—or not. Color coding is one option for using color as a system. To be effective, color coding must be relatively simple and must

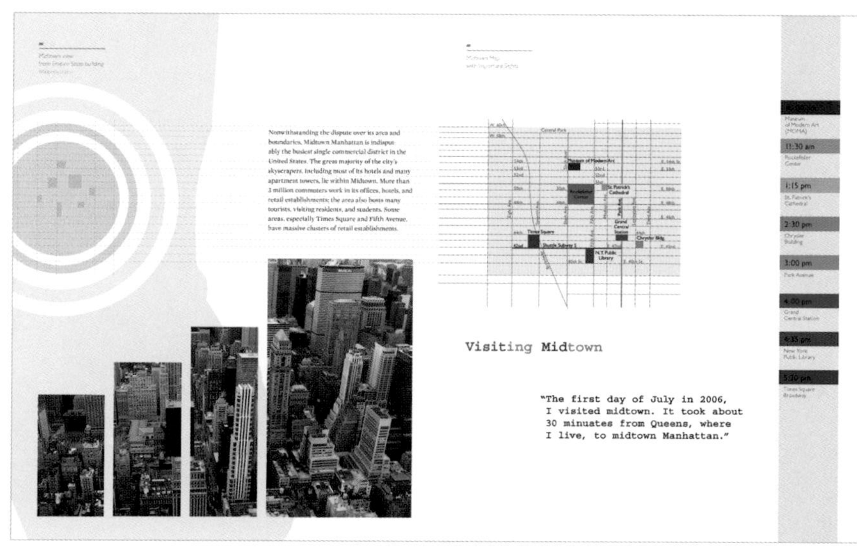

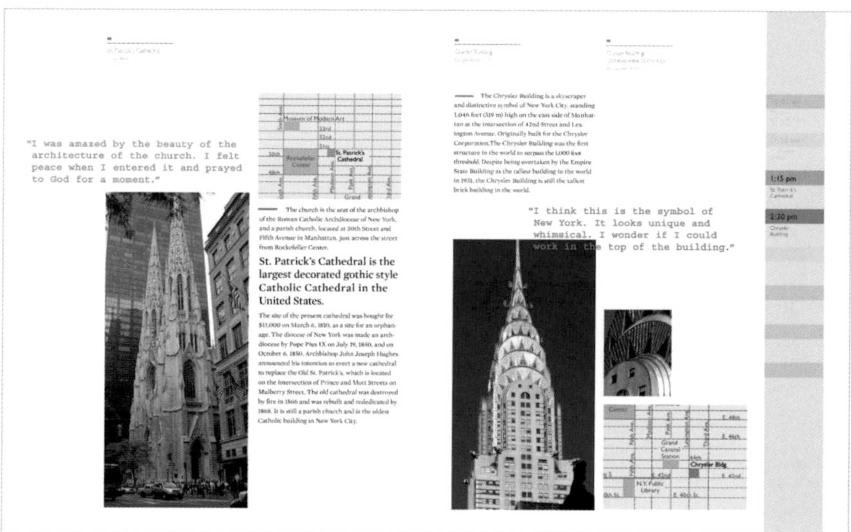

COLOR ACTS AS INFORMATION in these book spreads about New York City neighborhoods. In the overview map, each location's color is made different enough to clearly separate them; in subsequent detail maps, the specific coloration of a location indicates that this is the subject currently in focus. Color connects map locations with associated text, as well as the time of a visit to that location displayed in the chronological list at the right.

Myung Ha Chang *School of Visual Arts, United States*

be easily identifiable. Using more colors for coding creates confusion, as the viewer is forced to try to remember which color relates to which information. Color coding within a related set of hues—a deep blue, an aqua blue, and a green, for example—can help distinguish subcategories of information within an overall grouping, but ensure that the viewer is able to perceive the differences between the colors. Pushing the colors further apart in relation to each other might help—for example, the deep blue might be skewed toward the violet while yellow is added to the green.

IN ADDITION TO the optical game created by the super-coarse dot screen, color relationships are used as part of the identity system in these business cards.

Sagmeister *United States*

EACH SERIES OF BOOKLETS is grouped in terms of a color relationship. At the upper left, the grouping is by intensity and temperature; at the right, by value and temperature; and in the foreground, as complements.

Leonardo Sonnoli *Italy*

THIS SERIES DISTINGUISHES products with a hue change but maintains a similar saturation among the colors.

AdamsMorioka *United States*

Color Proportioning Establishing some flexibility in a system is always important. For one thing, the components in a system—such as a family of brochures—might change over time, or new ones might be added to the system that weren't accounted for during initial planning. ■ Furthermore, the various parts of the system need to be distinguishable from each other while maintaining a clear family appearance; in this way, the color coding not only helps a viewer separate the components from each other quickly, but also continues to enhance the unity of the system. One possibility to investigate is to develop a family of a few colors, along with several formal elements, and swap the colors among those elements. The colors could all be the same hue but occur in differing values and intensities; or, there could be a selection of intense hues that are split complements of each other. The number of colors selected, and how closely they are related, will have to be determined by evaluating how many components within the system must be delineated.

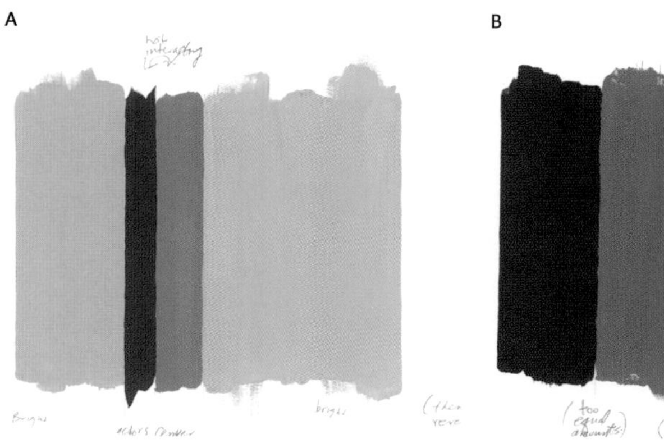

COLOR STUDIES improve understanding of color in a deeper way than simply selecting colors strictly for a project. Each study pits relationships of value (A) or intensity (B) against the extension of colors of varying temperatures.

JRoss Design *United States*

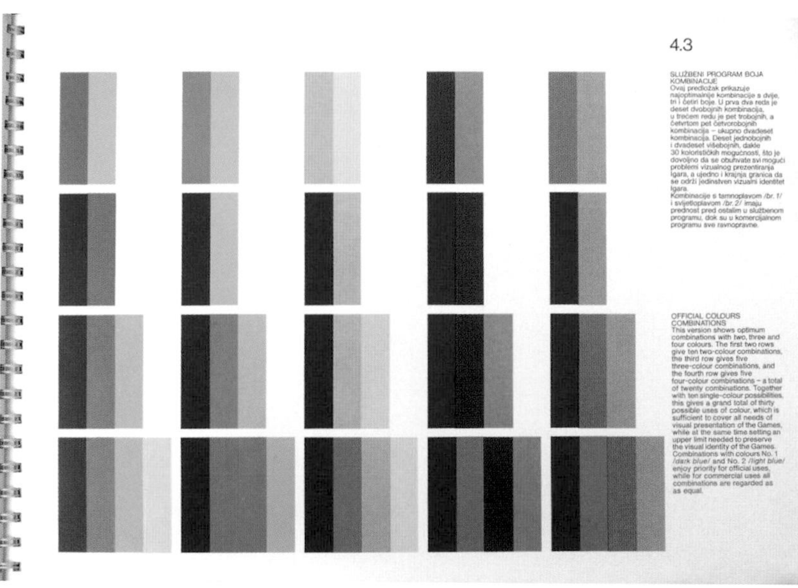

4.3

SLUŽBENI PROGRAM BOJA KOMBINACIJE
Ovaj predložak prikazuje najoptimalnije kombinacije s dvije, tri i četiri boje. U prva dva reda je deset dvobojnih kombinacija, u trećem redu je pet trobojnih, a četvrtom pet četvorobojnih kombinacija – ukupno dvadeset kombinacija. Deset jednobojnih i dvadeset višebojnih, dakle 30 kolorističkih mogućnosti, što je dovoljno da se obuhvate svi mogući problemi vizualnog prezentiranja Igara, a ujedno i krajnja granica da se održi jedinstven vizualni identitet Igara.
Kombinacije s tamnoplavom */br. 1/* i svijetloplavom */br. 2/* imaju prednost pred ostalim u službenom programu, dok su u komercijalnom programu sve ravnopravne.

OFFICIAL COLOURS COMBINATIONS
This version shows optimum combinations with two, three and four colours. The first two rows give ten two-colour combinations, the third row gives five three-colour combinations, and the fourth row gives five four-colour combinations – a total of twenty combinations. Together with ten single-colour possibilities, this gives a grand total of thirty possible uses of colour, which is sufficient to cover all needs of visual presentation of the Games, while at the same time setting an upper limit needed to preserve the visual identity of the Games. Combinations with colours No. 1 */dark blue/* and No. 2 */light blue/* enjoy priority for official uses, while for commercial uses all combinations are regarded as as equal.

THIS PAGE FROM an identity manual shows how colors from the supporting color palette can be combined with the primary corporate color in the system, the medium-value blue. The supporting colors are strictly controlled for their value and intensity relationships so that the corporate blue is always the deepest and most intense.

Studio International *Croatia*

GROUPINGS OF ANALOGOUS colors can provide a very flexible, yet very consistent, system for color coding, as seen in this packaging system. Each wrapper uses two analogous colors to identify its specific product in the system—blue-violet and aqua, red and yellow-orange, violet-red and orange—and each item's base color is also analogous in relation to each other.

A10 Design *Brazil*

SINGLE VARIABLE SYSTEMS

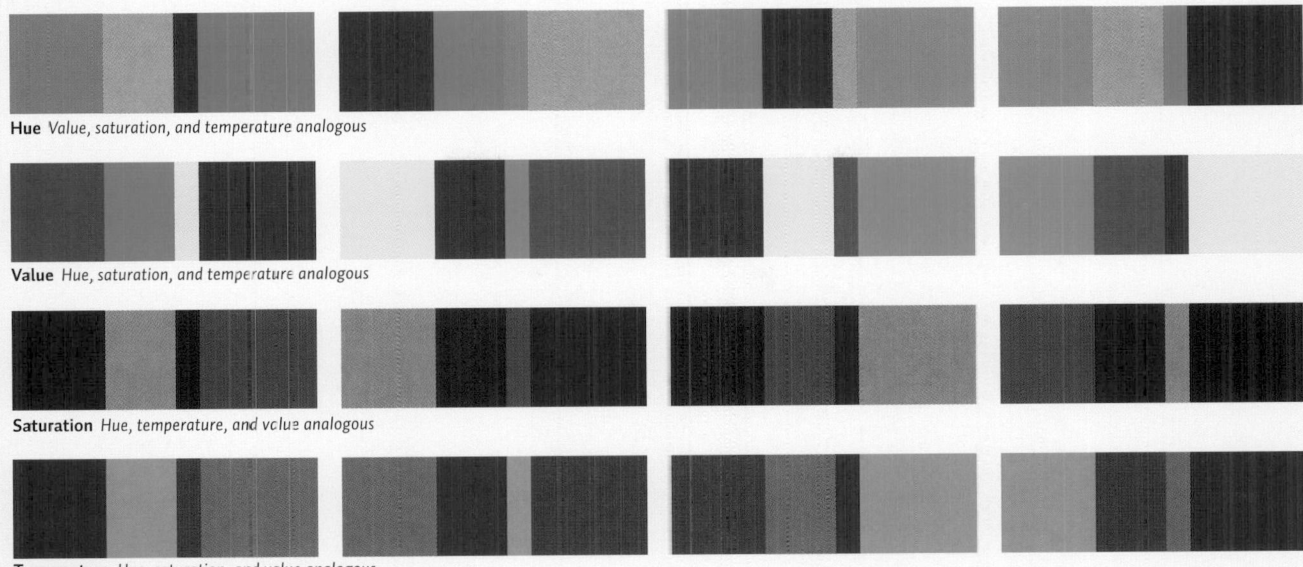

Hue *Value, saturation, and temperature analogous*

Value *Hue, saturation, and temperature analogous*

Saturation *Hue, temperature, and value analogous*

Temperature *Hue, saturation, and value analogous*

MULTIPLE VARIABLE SYSTEMS

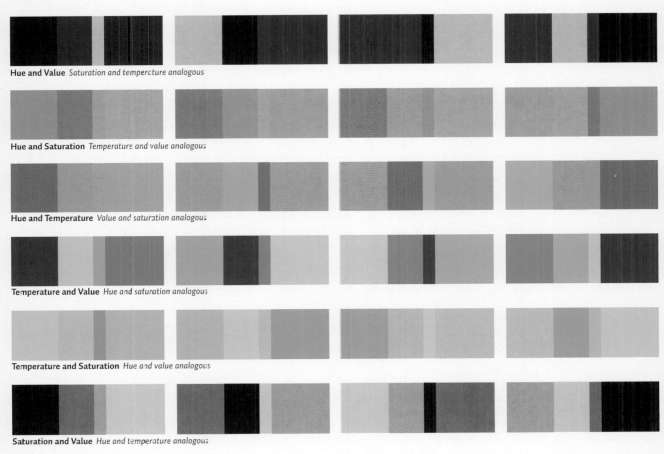

Hue and Value *Saturation and temperature analogous*

Hue and Saturation *Temperature and value analogous*

Hue and Temperature *Value and saturation analogous*

Temperature and Value *Hue and saturation analogous*

Temperature and Saturation *Hue and value analogous*

Saturation and Value *Hue and temperature analogous*

A simple proportional system is shown here as the basis for different color-coding relationships. The intervals within the composition remain the same throughout; the criteria for the coding system changes from series to series while, within a single series, the color components alternate position among the proportional intervals.

Limited Color Systems While a great number of projects call for full-color—process, or CMYK—imagery, choosing to use specific colored inks instead—called "spot" color—offers exciting possibilities. Spot color need not be limited to small-run or low-budget projects; a palette of even two thoughtfully-selected colors may communicate just as powerfully and further unify materials. This approach is particularly useful for branding, where the interrelation of inks can be used to clarify different publications in a literature system while reinforcing the identity of the brand. ■ When a designer is working with only two or three ink colors, choosing colors with dynamic chromatic interaction is of greatest concern. Printing a job with

Simply replacing black ink with ink of another color—even in a one-color job—can give an extra punch to an otherwise mundane project.

Choose two (or three) colors with value and saturation as considerations. The deeper, overall, and the closer the inks are in value, as well as saturation, the wider the range of possible combinations, and the greater their potential contrast.

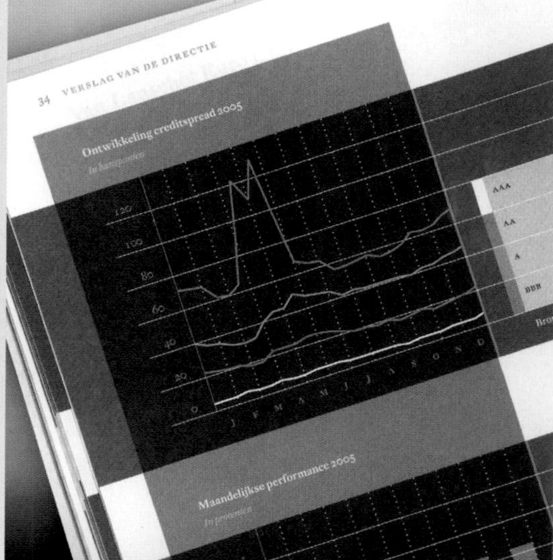

OVERLAPPING SPOT COLORS create rich color interaction among typographic and graphic elements in this detail of a financial report.

UNA (Amsterdam) Designers
Netherlands

Strict Complement

Near Complement
Cool

Near Complement
Warm

Split Complement

Analogous
Same Saturation

Analogous
Different Saturation

Analogous
Temperature Shift

Strict Complement
Same Value
Saturation Shift

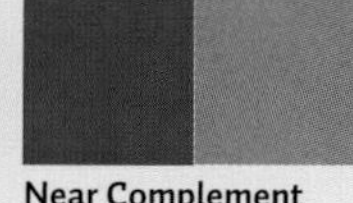

Near Complement
Different Value
Same Saturation

With a particular blue as a starting point, different combinations with a succession of ink colors as counterparts create a variety of possibilities.

Two different combinations of orange with another color create different tinting and surprinting possibilities. Remember that ink is a subtractive color system; the darker or greater the density of ink combinations, the darker and less saturated the resulting surprints will be.

two complements as counterparts, for example, is an intuitive first possibility. Their complementary nature need not be exact, that is, as with blue and orange; skewing this relationship can create interesting combinations but retain their inherent contrast: a blue-violet and orange, for example. ■ Most printing inks are translucent, so a designer has the option not only to print each ink at full strength–or "tinting" them to lighten their values–but also to print the inks on top of each other, either at full strength or in combinations of tints. Printing one ink on top of another is called "surprinting," and creates new colors because of their overlap. Such new colors will vary in hue, saturation, and value, depending on the base ink colors selected; usually the resulting third color (and tinted variations) will be darker and less saturated. If the base inks are very intense or pure, however, the surprint color will also be relatively intense. ■ Photographic images, or illustrations with varied tonality, are excellent material with which to explore ink coloration: an image might be printed in one, two, three, or more spot colors, with different portions of the image's tonal range acted upon by the inks at different levels. Such options give the designer an opportunity to customize images for a client, enrich the dialogue of color among images, type, and other graphic elements, and to bring images into closer visual alignment with brand-related color messages.

Be careful when tinting a color that is being used for type, especially if it's relatively light to begin with. Getting a printer to run a press proof to test the effect of tinting on type and images will be an additional cost, but in the end it's worth it to see exactly what's going to happen in the actual press run.

Color Halftone Also called a monotone, an image printed using a single ink color is called a color halftone. The top image is printed directly on a white field; in the bottom image, the color halftone is shown crossing over a supporting color, which changes the appearance of the halftone's color.

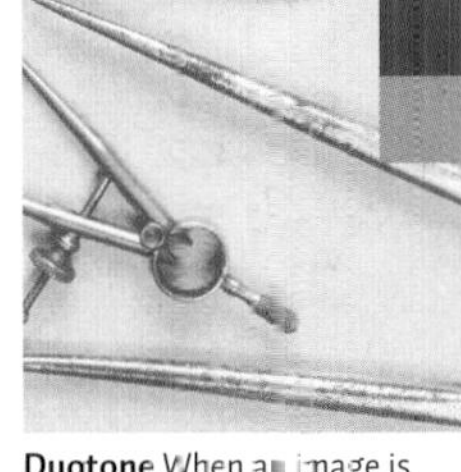

Duotone When an image is printed using two ink colors, the result is a duotone. The image at the top is printed using two similar color inks to enhance its overall tonal range; in the lower example, the image is printed using two ink colors that are very different.

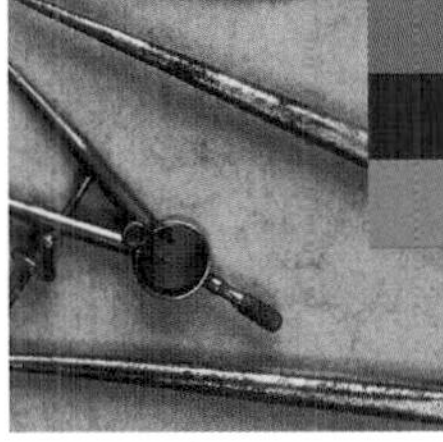

Tritone Similar to a duotone, a tritone results from printing an image using three different ink colors. Both tritones above share two ink colors, but differ in their use of a third ink color.

By using image-manipulation software, the amount of a given ink color applied to specific tonal ranges in an image can be adjusted. In this example, the two colors used in the duotone are distributed differently. In the top image, color 1 has been pushed toward the shadow range; in the bottom image, color 1 has been pushed toward the highlight range

A THREE-COLOR PALETTE not only unifies the components in this literature system, it allows the designer to diferentiate different product offerings and still reinforce the core identity of the brand. The signature (logo) retains its color identity, and the components all seem intrinsically related to it, as well as to each other.

STIM Visual Communication *United States*

SURPRINTING A FIELD of red ink on top of found, make-ready sheets means budget-conscious production with interesting visual effects in this detail of a poster. The ink's transparency allows a haze of the surprinted image to show through.

Brett Yasko *United States*

Color Psychology With color comes a variety of psychological messages that can be used to influence content—both imagery and the verbal meaning of typography. This emotional component of color is deeply connected to human experience at an instinctual and biological level. Colors of varying wavelengths have different effects on the autonomic nervous system—warmer colors, such as red and yellows, have long wavelengths, and so more energy is needed to process them as they enter the eye and brain. The accompanying rise in energy level and metabolic rate translates as arousal. Conversely, the shorter wavelengths of cooler colors—such as blue, green, and violet—require far less energy to process, resulting in the slowing

DEEP OLIVES AND BROWNS evoke a sense of history, especially in the context of photographs, which were tinted brownish and sometimes olive in the early stages of photography.

Studio Blue *United States*

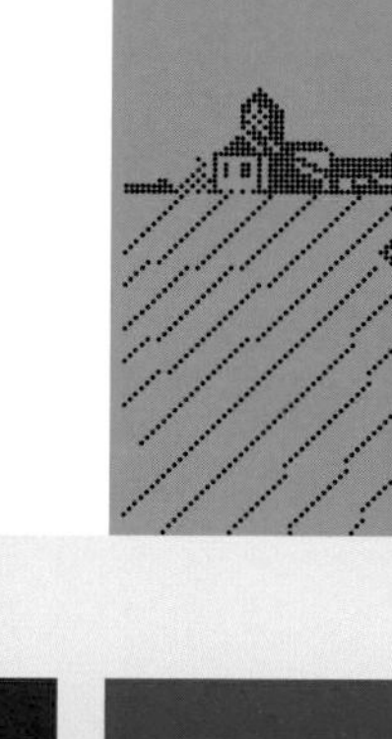

THE ROOSTER appears in a field of friendly, dynamic orange.

Apeloig Design *France*

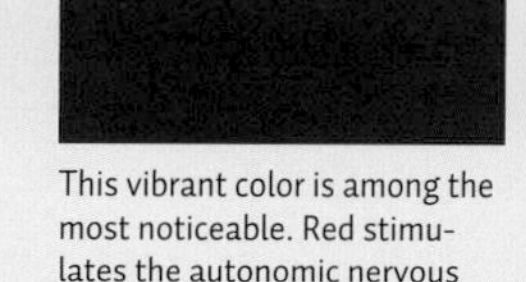

This vibrant color is among the most noticeable. Red stimulates the autonomic nervous system to the highest degree, invoking the "fight or flight" adrenaline response, causing us to salivate with hunger, or causing us to feel impulsive. Red evokes feelings of passion and arousal.

The power of blue to calm and create a sense of protection or safety results from its short wavelength; its association with the ocean and sky account for its perception as solid and dependable. Statistically, blue is the best-liked of all the colors.

Associated with the sun and warmth, yellow stimulates a sense of happiness. It appears to advance spatially in relation to other colors and also helps to enliven surrounding colors. Yellow encourages clear thinking and memory retention. A brighter, greener yellow can cause anxiety; deeper yellows evoke wealth.

The association of brown with earth and wood creates a sense of comfort and safety. The solidity of the color, because of its organic connotation, evokes feelings of timelessness and lasting value. Brown's natural qualities are perceived as rugged, ecological, and hardworking; its earthy connection connotes trustworthiness and durability.

Violet is sometimes perceived as compromising—but also as mysterious and elusive. The value and hue of violet greatly affect its communication: deep violets, approaching black, connote death; pale, cooler violets, such as lavender, are dreamy and nostalgic; red-hued violets, such as fuchsia, are dramatic and energetic; plum-like hues are magical.

With the shortest wavelength, green is the most relaxing color of the spectrum. Its association with nature and vegetation makes it feel safe. The brighter the green, the more youthful and energetic. Deeper greens suggest reliable economic growth. More neutral greens, such as olive, evoke earthiness. However, green, in the right context, can connote illness or decay.

A mixture of red and yellow, orange engenders feelings similar to that of its parent colors—vitality and arousal (red) and warmth and friendliness (yellow). Orange appears outgoing and adventurous but may be perceived as slightly irresponsible. Deeper orange induces salivation and a feeling of luxury. Brighter orange connotes health, freshness, quality, and strength. As orange becomes more neutral, its activity decreases, but it retains a certain sophistication, becoming exotic.

The ultimate neutral, gray may be perceived as noncommittal, but can be formal, dignified, and authoritative. Lacking the emotion that chroma carries, it may seem aloof or suggest untouchable wealth. Gray may be associated with technology, especially when presented as silver. It suggests precision, control, competence, sophistication, and industry.

of our metabolic rate and a soothing, calming effect. ■ The psychological properties of color, however, also depend highly on a viewer's culture and personal experience. Many cultures equate red with feelings of hunger, anger, or energy because red is closely associated with meat, blood, and violence. By contrast, vegetarians might associate the color green with hunger. In Western cultures, which are predominantly Christian, black is associated with death and mourning, but Hindus associate the color white with death. Christians associate white with purity or cleanliness. Because of the history of Western civilization, violet conveys authority, status, and luxury to members of that culture. Most cultures respond to blue with an association of water and, therefore, of life. Blue is also often perceived as deeply spiritual or contemplative, perhaps because of this particular association. ■ Clearly, selecting a color for specific words in a composition can add meaning by linking its associations to the verbal message. A headline or title set in one color might take on additional, or completely different, meaning when set in another color. Comparing color options for type simultaneously helps determine which color may be the most appropriate for a given communication.

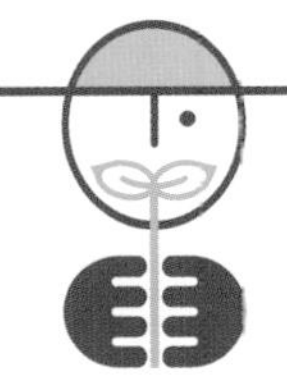

THE RELIABILITY and strength of brown protect the growing green plant.

Sohyun Kim *Iowa State University, United States*

Unknowable and extreme, black is the strongest color in the visible spectrum. Its density and contrast are dominant, but it seems neither to recede nor to advance in space. Its indeterminate quality reminds viewers of nothingness, outer space, and, in Western culture, death. Its mystery is perceived as formal and exclusive, suggesting authority, superiority, and dignity.

In a subtractive color model, white represents the presence of all color wavelengths; in an additive model, it is the absence of color. Both of these models help form the basis for white's authoritative, pure, and all-encompassing power. As the mixture of all colors of light, it connotes spiritual wholeness and power. Around areas of color activity in a composition—especially around black, its ultimate contrast—white appears restful, stately, and pure.

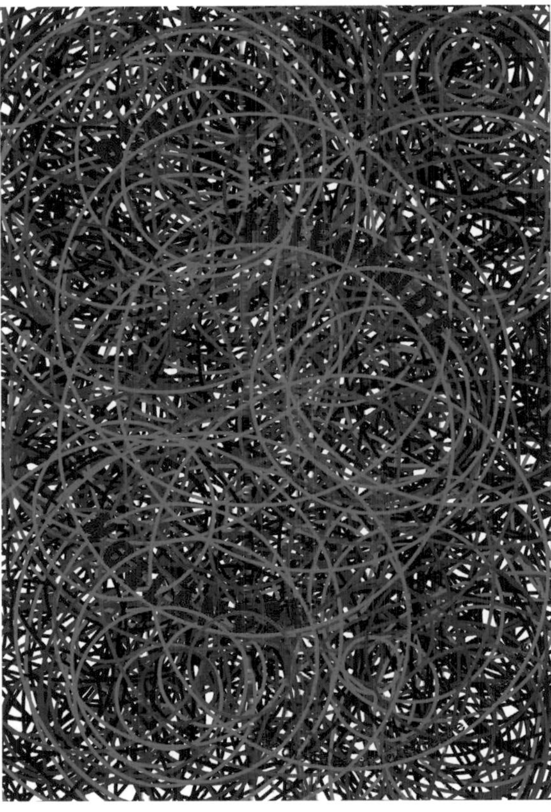

BLUE AND BLUE-VIOLET are cool and waterlike. In this poster, their calming quality represents the ocean as a contrast to the hectic movement of the red title.

Gunter Rambow *Germany*

IN WESTERN CULTURE, groupings of reds, golds, and deeper green evoke the winter holiday season.

BBK Studio *United States*

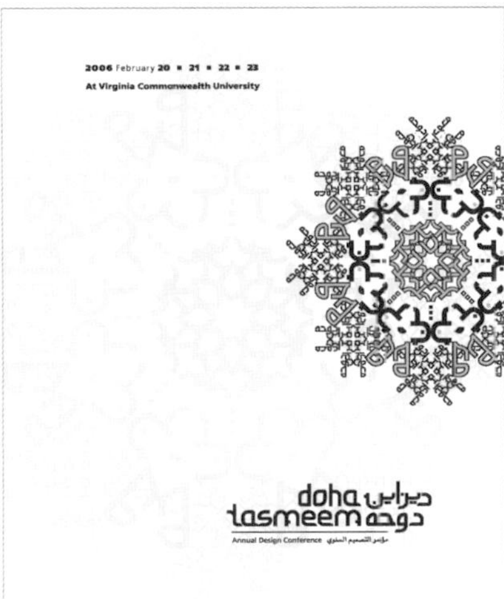

PALE YELLOW, YELLOW-ORANGE, and fuchsia make reference to the cultural environment of Qatar but also evoke the sun, energy, and happiness.

VCU Qatar *Qatar*

Changing Color, Changing Meaning

Because color so strongly evokes emotional response, its effect on imagery—both abstract and representational—is of great concern to the designer. ■ First, the issue of "local color" in subject matter—the empirical color of objects—comes into play, influencing emotional responses in the viewer. For example, a corporate executive in a blue suit is approachable, but in a dark gray suit, possibly arrogant or shady; wearing a striped green tie, inexperienced, but wearing a solid red one, commanding and assured. Second, manipulation of the overall tonal balance of an image—warm or cool, intense or dull, greenish or blueish—will usually skew an image's feeling in one direction or another. Last, in considering color application to typography or abstract form elements, the designer must anticipate the powerful directness of any associations created as the color is embodied by forms that the mind is attempting to interpret.

RICH SEPIA COLORATION augments the fragmented, historical quality of this treated photograph; the deeper values add a somber, reflective note.

Thomas Csano *Canada*

quiet

quiet

quiet

Color forcefully changes the feeling of words, sometimes enhancing their meaning and sometimes opposing the meaning or altering it. Subdued colors, especially those that are cool or desaturated, enhance the meaning of the word "quiet;" interestingly, the word's meaning is intensely appreciated when set in a vibrant color.

In attempting to identify a form and thereby assign it some meaning, viewers will focus on color after they appreicate the form's shape—but the two messages are nearly simultaneous. As a result, the color message will exert tremendous force on perception. Comparing the dots above, guess which is being presented as a sun, and which the earth.

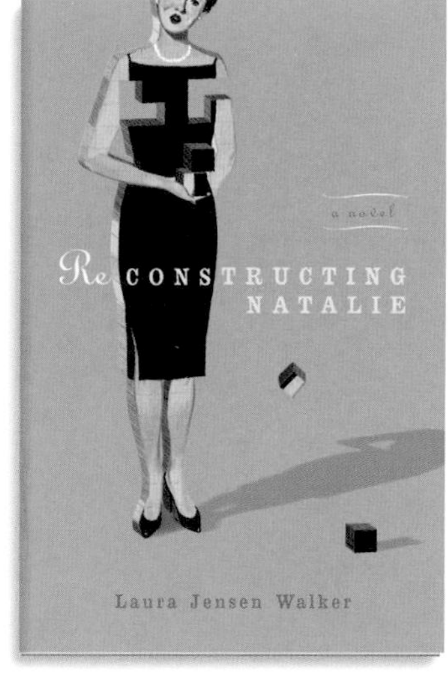

PINK WAS ONCE associated strictly with femininity. This book uses that color to evoke the time period in which that idea was prevalent.

Red Canoe *United States*

A

B

C

D

E

Manipulating the overall color or color balance of an image will change a viewer's feeling about the image's content. When the original image (A) is presented in black and white (B), it becomes more documentary; printed in a duotone of intense colors (C), the image takes on a surreal and illustrative quality; skewing the image's color balance makes it refreshing (D) or somber (E).

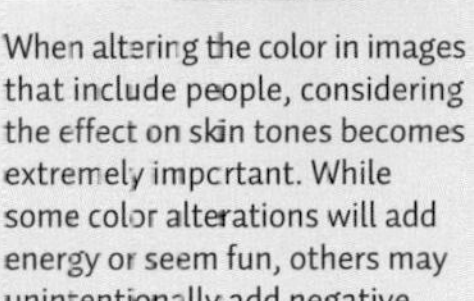

When altering the color in images that include people, considering the effect on skin tones becomes extremely important. While some color alterations will add energy or seem fun, others may unintentionally add negative connotations; in this example, the greenish toning produces a sickly feeling, while the blueish toning makes the people seem cold and dead.

This image has been manipulated on press by raising and lowering the density of the four process inks to correct and enhance the color balance and saturation: original image; cyan decreased and yellow increased; cyan increased again, yellow decreased, and magenta increased; yellow increased slightly, black increased.

Similar to duotoning or tritoning in spot color printing, an image might be colorized or toned overall in four-color process, or CMYK, printing—called quadtoning. Because the image is being produced using the four process colors (cyan, magenta, yellow, and black), the possible color variation within a single image is endless, as indicated in this example. Further, different images within the same project can be quadtoned in different ways.

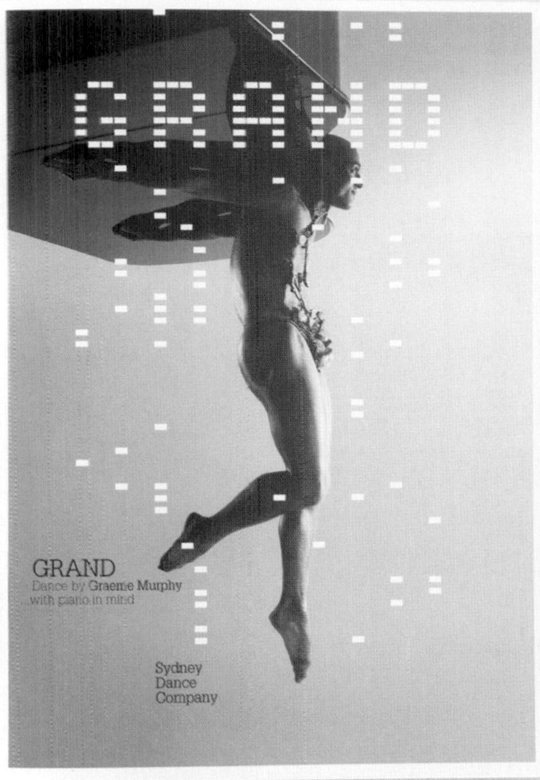

A GREENISH-BLUE HAZE transforms the upside-down figure into one that appears to be floating in water.

Frost Design *Australia*

CHOOSING AND USING T

> Typography is what language looks like.

Ellen Lupton

Graphic designer and director of the MFA program in design at Maryland State University

Chapter 3

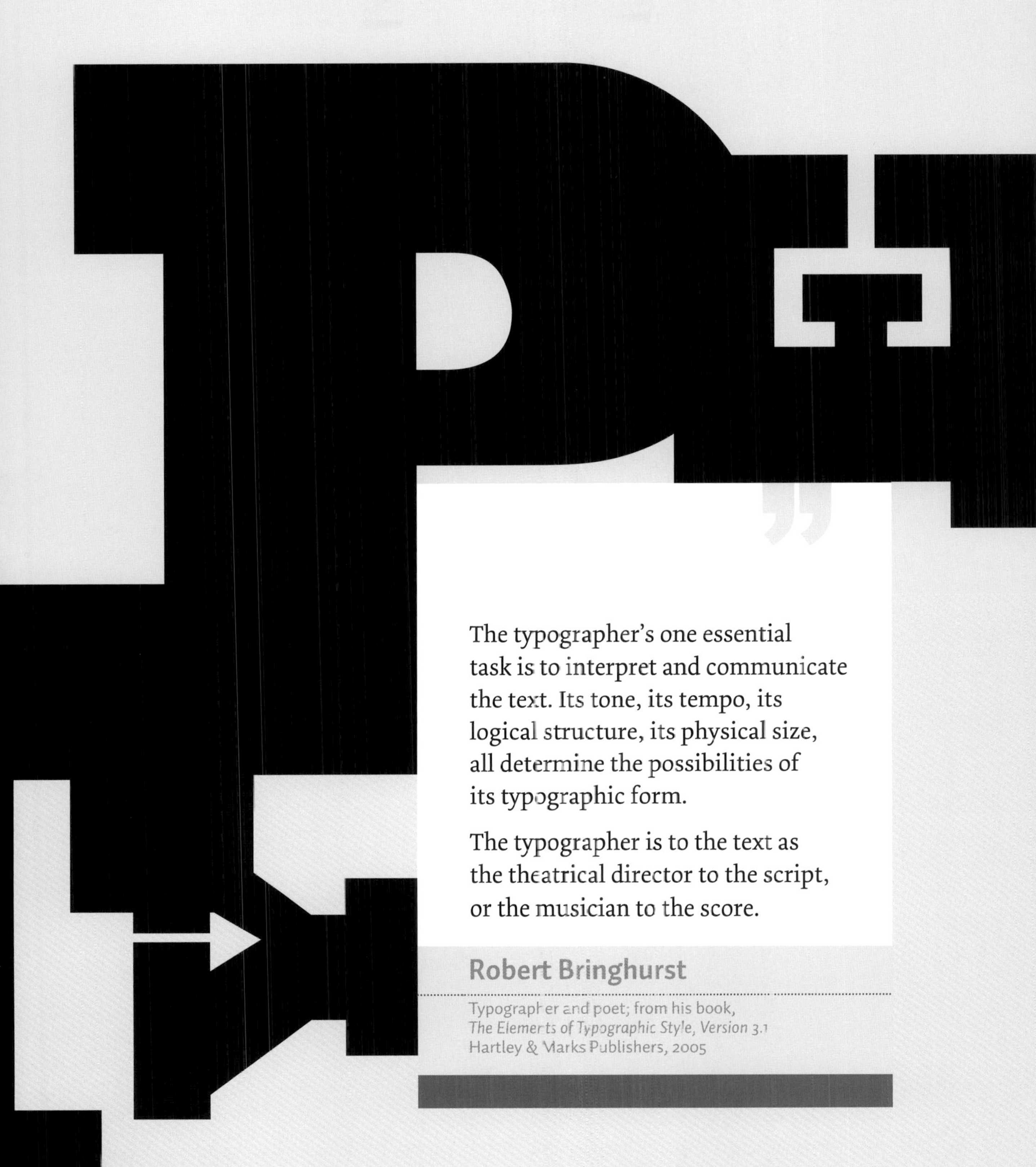

The typographer's one essential task is to interpret and communicate the text. Its tone, its tempo, its logical structure, its physical size, all determine the possibilities of its typographic form.

The typographer is to the text as the theatrical director to the script, or the musician to the score.

Robert Bringhurst

Typographer and poet; from his book, *The Elements of Typographic Style, Version 3.1* Hartley & Marks Publishers, 2005

The Nuts and Bolts The letters of the Western alphabet are built from a system of lines with intricate visual relationships that are nearly invisible. With letters at a standard reading size, the eye perceives letters to be all the same weight, height, and width. This is the most critical aspect of type: stylistic uniformity discourages distraction during the reading process. When the same type is enlarged, minute changes in character height, stroke width, and shape become apparent. Becoming sensitive to these optical issues and understanding their effect on spacing, organization, stylistic communication, legibility, and composition is crucial.

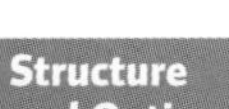

Enlarging letters reveals the tiny adjustments made by their designer to overcome optical characteristics and unify them. Differing angles, stroke shapes, and overall size changes, evident in a large setting, disappear in a text-sized setting. The same is true of corrections for weight and width in a family of typefaces.

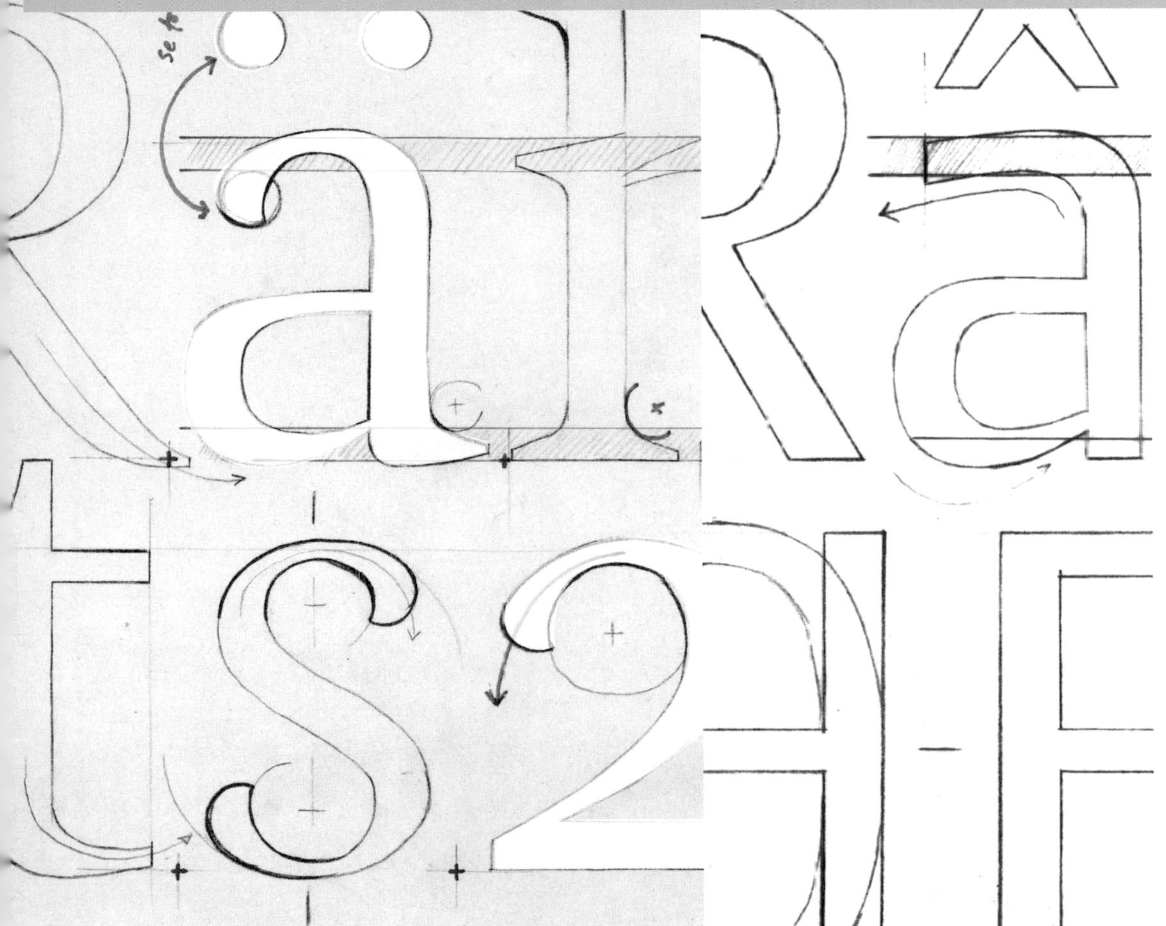

THE INTERRELATIONSHIP of detail is apparent in these letterform studies for a custom, corporate typeface. Note the comparisons of crossbars, letter widths, and terminal shapes.

E-Types *Denmark*

Form and Counterform: The Optics of Spacing The spacing of letters in words, sentences, and paragraphs is vital to create a uniform gray value for minimal reader distraction. Every typeface has a distinct rhythm of strokes and spaces. This relationship between form and counterform defines the optimal spacing of that particular typeface and therefore of the overall spacing between words, between lines of type, and among paragraphs. ■ Looking at letters set together as a word offers a clue as to how they should be spaced in that particular typeface and size. Creating a consistent gray value in text depends on setting the letters so that there is even alternation of solid and void–within and between the letters. A series of letters that are set too tightly, so that the counterforms within the letters are optically bigger than those between letters, creates noticeable dark spots in the line: the exterior strokes of the letters bond to each other visually where they come together.

XPRESS FUNDING
Capital for Growing Companies

IN THIS LOGOTYPE, loose letter spacing makes a more distinct rhythm, improves the legibility of the all-uppercase setting, and obviates spacing problems that might have occurred among certain letter combinations (for example, **X** and **P**) if they had been spaced normally.

Paone Design Associates
United States

words
words
MATHEMATICAL SPACING

words
words
OPTICALLY NORMAL SPACING

words
OVERLY TIGHT SPACING

words
A

words
OVERLY LOOSE SPACING

words
B

words
C

Optical spacing for the Univers regular weight is shown, compared to mathematically spaced or overly tight or loose spacing. The optimally spaced lines (second line) show a consistent rhythmic alternation between dark (the strokes) and light (the counterforms), both within characters and between them. Dark spots are evident in the examples spaced too tightly, where the strokes are closer together between letters than within them. Compare the normal spacing of these faces to those of the bold condensed style of Univers (A), the italic serif (B), and the high-contrast modern serif (C); note how the internal logic of the stroke-to-counter relationship in each provides the clues to their optimal spacing.

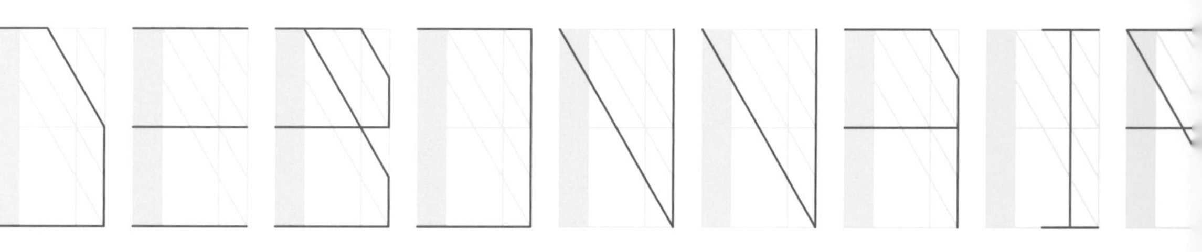

At the other extreme, letters that are set too loosely become singular elements, divorced from the line and recognizable as individual forms, making the appraisal of words difficult. Evenly set sequences of letters show a consistent, rhythmic alternation of black and white—form and counterform repeating at the same rate from left to right. ■ The primary difficulty in achieving evenly spaced type is that the letters are of different densities. Some letters are lighter or darker than others. Added to this phenomenon are the directional thrusts of different strokes and the varied sizes and shapes of the counterforms. Some are very open, some are closed, and some are decidedly uneven in relation to the distribution of strokes in a given letter. To correct for these disparities, digital typefaces are programmed to add and subtract space from between different pairs of letters, depending on what the combinations are. These sets of letters, called "kerning pairs," provide for most circumstances of letterform combination, but not all. Invariably, a designer will need to correct unusual spacing that the computer's software is unable to address.

LIQUID

LIQUID

Always evaluate the spacing needs of a type component on a case-by-case basis. Some letters in a particular word are going to cause unresolvable problems, either because of their dramatic asymmetry, deep counters, or overall density. When presented with a word (or phrase of reasonable length), take time to correct the spacing throughout based on this worst-case scenario. In this word, nothing really can be done about the enormous counter following the **L**. To make sure it doesn't make more of itself than it needs to, the remainder of the line was spaced more loosely (still in the "normal" range) to minimize the effect of the **L** counter.

TYPOGRAPHY
The art of designing with words and letters

TYPOGRAPHY
The art of designing with words and letters

Uppercase letters are more uniform in width and shape than lowercase letters, as well as optically more dense; to enhance their look and legibility, all-uppercase setting must always be spaced a little more loosely than normal.

To To
Ty Ty
Tr Tr
We We
Wo Wo
Ae Ae
Pe Pe

Tightening or loosening the spacing between these pairs of letters corrects for the awkward counterspaces inherent in their forms. Shifting the lowercase **y** to the right, under the right crossbar of the **T**, for example, allows the spacing between them to become optically similar to that of subsequent letters.

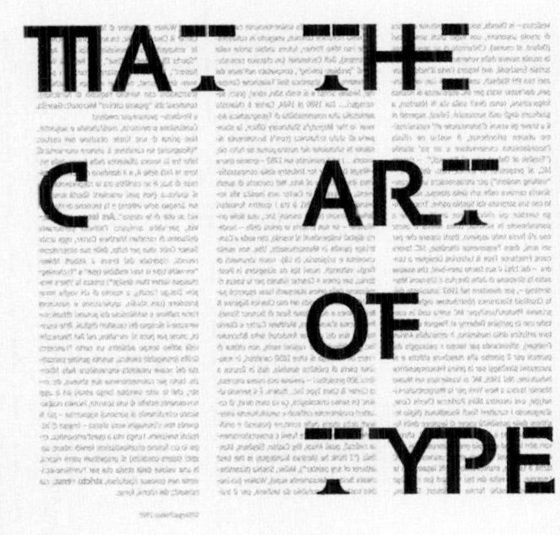

BY PURPOSELY ALTERING the spacing of the title text, the designer is able to merge two separate thoughts—a speaker's name and a lecture title—into one structure.

Leonardo Sonnoli *Italy*

THE YELLOW VERTICAL STROKES in this logotype create a more consistent rhythm of stroke and counter alternation behind the hairline blue strokes, which change in shape and rhythm.

Thomas Csano *Canada*

Trips Trips Trips

The same word is set here in three faces at 36 points. The oldstyle serif appears smallest; its lowercase letters have a proportionally small x-height. Because the sans-serif lowercase letters are larger in proportion to the cap height, they appear larger; the same is true of the modern serif to the right.

Spacing must change at different sizes.

Spacing must change at different sizes.

Spacing must change at different sizes.

The same words, set first at 14 points in size and again at 6 points. Uncorrected, the spacing in the smaller type is inadequate for good character recognition. Adding space between letters greatly improves their legibility and their look.

Type changes when printed positive or reversed from color.	Type changes when printed positive or reversed from color.
Use a face with uniform stroke weights for knockouts if possible.	Use a face with uniform stroke weights for knockouts if possible.
Especially if it's small! You might also want to **beef up the weight of small, knockout text elements.**	Especially if it's small! You might also want to **beef up the weight of small, knockout text elements.**

The strength of a typeface's stroke weights, at any size, will present optical size disparities between type printed positive, on a light background, and in reverse, on a dark background. Generally, a typeface will appear smaller and denser if reversed from a solid field. Typefaces with small x-heights, extreme contrast, or extremely thin strokes overall usually need to be enlarged slightly to ensure their strokes are robust enough to hold up against ink gain that might threaten their legibility.

t

...vated associatio...
...approach fro...

Printing exacerbates the issue of space between letters, especially at smaller sizes. Ink bleeds when it hits paper; as a result, the space between and within letters is made smaller.

Trying to judge proper spacing on a monitor, with its coarse resolution, is nearly impossible; a laser printer or an inkjet printer creates some bloating in the type but not nearly as much as will happen on press. A designer's prior printing experience will help him or her judge these spacing issues.

72 M

60 M

48 M

36 M

30 M

24 M

18 M

14 M

12 M

10 M

9 M

7 M

Historically standard type-size measurements use the point measuring system, based roughly on the height of the capital M. Sizes above 14 points are considered display sizes, to be used for such items as headlines or callouts; sizes between 14 points and 9 points are considered text sizes; and sizes smaller than 9 points are considered caption sizes.

M	72
M	60
M	48
M	36
M	30
M	24
M	18
M	14
M	12
M	10
M	9
M	7

Note the disparity in size between sans-serif examples (left column) and serif examples (right column) of the same point size. Always evaluate the appearance of type, set in a particular typeface, to determine whether it's set at an appropriate size, rather than assuming that a 9-point "text size" will be legible. The oldstyle face Garamond, for example, will be difficult to read when set at 9 points, while the sans serif Helvetica will seem gigantic.

Type Sizes and Spacing The drawing of a typeface has an impact on the perception of its size. A sentence set in an oldstyle serif and a similar-weight sans serif at the same point size will appear to be two different sizes. The discrepancy results from the sans serif's larger x-height: its lowercase letters are larger in relation to the cap height than those of the serif. The difference in set size and apparent size can vary as much as two or three points, depending on the face. A sans-serif face such as Univers might be perfectly comfortable to read at a size of 9 points, but an oldstyle such as Garamond Three at that size will appear tiny and difficult to read. Setting the Garamond at 11 or 12 points will make it more legible as well as make it appear the same size as the Univers. ■ Setting type smaller or larger than the optimal reading size for text also has an impact on spacing. Comfortable and efficient reading of long texts, such as books, newspapers, or journals, takes place when the type size ranges between 9 points and 14 points—the texture of the type is a uniform gray and the letterforms are small enough that their details are not perceived as distinct visual elements. Optimal spacing at reading size means that the strokes and counterforms are evenly alternating. As type is decreased in size, the letterspace must be increased to allow the eye to separate the letters for clarity. At the other extreme, the space between letters must be decreased as the type size increases beyond reading size.

THE LARGER TYPE on this brochure spread needs to be set a little tighter than normal to account for the apparent size of the counters as it increases in point size; the tighter spacing compensates for the spread of ink that will very, very slightly decrease the thickness of the reversed white strokes. The smaller caption type, however, has been set more loosely.

And Partners *United States*

TO OUR STOCKHOLDERS:

Last year at this time, we talked about our expectations for another record year in 2004, and projected a 5% increase in both sales and earnings. I'm pleased to report that we had a banner year, substantially exceeding those projections. In 2004 sales jumped 16%, topping the $6 billion mark for the first time in VF's history. Earnings increased 17% to a record $4.21 per share. Sales benefited from growth across most of our core businesses, plus the addition of three terrific new brands: *Vans*®, *Napapijri*® and *Kipling*®.

37
"Be open to change — it's another word for innovation."

MACKEY J. MCDONALD *Chairman, President and Chief Executive Officer*

THE "CHATTERING MEN" THE VOLATILE FIREPLACE FIREPROOF GHOSTS TWO THOUSAND PHENOMENA

E N G A G I N G T E X T U A L S P E C T R E S

Harry Price's The End of Borley Rectory

An essay by — Peter Sachin

A "DESPERATE DAY" THE "ETERNAL EVASION" AN INVISIBLE WALKER NUN-GHOST SEEN

THE DEGREE OF STYLIZATION or neutrality in any typeface is relative, much like the relativity of color: any typeface becomes more neutral when something more stylized appears next to it. These two faces share contrast in stroke thickness but are completely opposed in terminal shape, ductus, width, and posture. Both faces are generally considered somewhat stylized, but the script is more stylized than the all-uppercase serif.

CHK Design *United Kingdom*

Aa Bb Cc Dd
Ee Ff Gg Hh
Jj Ll Mm Nn
Oo Pp Qq Rr
Ss Uu Xx Yy

Case Every letter in the Western alphabet occurs in a large form—the capitals, or uppercase—and a small, more casual form—lowercase. The uppercase requires added space between letters to permit easier reading. The lowercase is more varied and more quickly recognized in text.

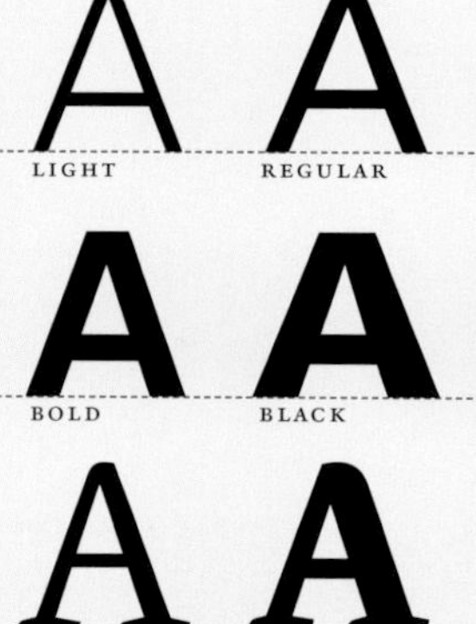

Weight The overall thickness of the strokes, relative to the height of the uppercase, might change. Light, regular, bold, and black weights—increasing in stroke thickness—for a single type style define a type family. Variation in weight helps to add visual contrast as well as to distinguish between informational components within a hierarchy.

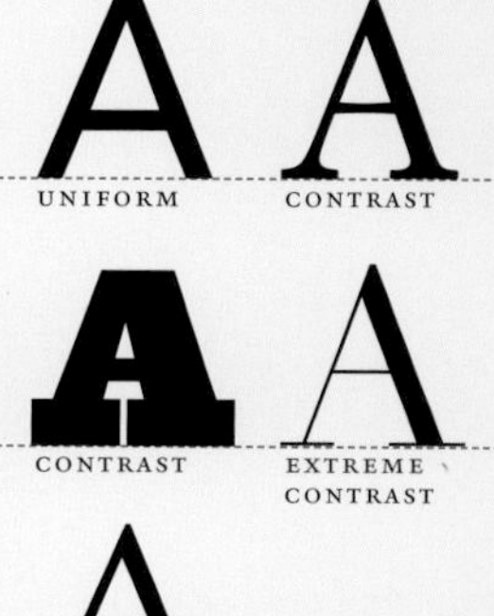

Contrast The strokes within the letters of a typeface may be uniform in weight or may vary significantly; the more they do so, the more contrast the face is said to exhibit. Contrast within a stroke—such as flaring from thin to thick—is called modulation; the rate at which this occurs is referred to as the typeface's ductus.

Visual Variations The letterforms in all typefaces vary from their archetypes in only six aspects: case, weight, contrast, width, posture, and style. Type designers, referring to historical models, subtly alter and combine the variables in these six aspects to create individual type styles that, although appearing remarkably different, all convey the same information about the letterforms in the alphabet. Different approaches to the drawing of typefaces have evolved, become popular, or been discarded over time; as a result, the formal aspects of particular typefaces often carry associations with specific periods in history, cultural movements, and geographic location—some typefaces feel "modern" or "classical," while others feel "French" or "English." More important, the drawing of a typeface will often exhibit a particular kind of rhythm, or cadence, as well as provide a distinct physical presence in a design that may connote feelings—fast or slow, aggressive or elegant, cheap or reliable. ■ Consider that not all viewers will perceive the same associations in a given typeface; the designer must carefully evaluate his or her typeface selection in the context of the audience for a particular piece. Additionally, mixing typefaces that are incongruous with the subject matter—for example, using an archaic Roman capital in a flyer promoting a concert of Electronica—will often add surprising layers of communication. Further, the drawing characteristics of typefaces affect their functional qualities, making some more legible at certain sizes, or affected by color in particular ways. Recognizing and understanding the six fundamental aspects of alphabet variation is an important first step in being able to select and combine appropriate typefaces for a project.

A MIXTURE OF CLASSICAL, decorative script and neutral serif makes a stylistic connection with the subject matter without sacrificing legibility in the navigation and informational text.

Swim Design *United States*

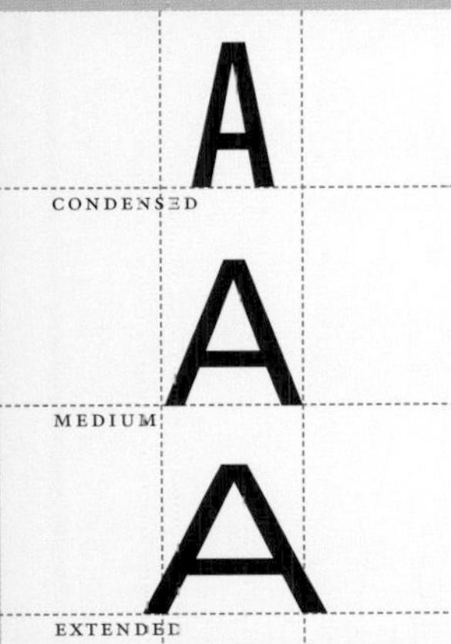

Width The proportional width of the letters in a typeface is based on the width of the uppercase M. Faces that are narrower are said to be condensed, while wider ones are said to be extended or expanded.

ROMAN ITALIC

REVERSE OBLIQUE

Posture Roman letters are those whose vertical axis is 90° to the baseline; they stand upright. Italic letters, developed by humanist scholars during the Renaissance, slant 12° to 15° to the right, mimicking the slant of handwriting.

1 2 3

NEUTRAL STYLIZED

Style This term is used to describe (1) the two major classes of type—serif (having little feet at the ends of the strokes) and sans serif (having no such feet); (2) the historical period in which the typeface was drawn; and (3) the relative neutrality or decorative quality of a typeface. Typefaces that are neutral are closest to the basic structure while those with exaggerated characteristics are said to be stylized, idiosyncratic, or decorative.

Detail of serif shape
Terminals
Oldstyle x-height for comparison with later typefaces
HRMafgo
Leg and joint shapes
Degree of axis
HRMafgo
HRMafgo
HRMafgo
HRMafgo
HRMafgo

Style Classifications Classifying type helps a designer grasp the subtle differences among styles, organizing them in a general way and further helping to select an appropriate typeface for a particular project; sometimes the historical or cultural context of a particular style will add relevant communication to a typographic design. ■ Classification is by no means easy, however, especially as our typographic tradition becomes increasingly self-referential and incorporates historical formal ideas into modern ones. The typeface Meta, for example, drawn in 1994 by the German designer Erik Spiekermann, is a modern sans-serif face sharing characteristics associated with oldstyle serif types: contrast in the stroke weights, modulation of weight within major strokes, an oblique axis, and a bowl-formed lowercase **g.** A number of systems for classifying type have been developed during the past several decades. Today, as then, these classifications often change—but a few basic categories remain constant.

Oldstyle Characterized by organic contrast of weight in the strokes—from brush or pen drawing; an angled, or oblique, axis in the curved forms; and a notably small x-height defining the lowercase letters. The terminals are pear-shaped and the apertures in the lowercase letters are small.

Transitional These types show an evolution in structure. Stroke contrast is greatly increased and more rationally applied—its rhythm is greatly pronounced. The x-height of the lowercase is larger; the axis is more upright; and the serifs are sharper and more defined, their brackets curving quickly into the stems.

Modern Stroke contrast is extreme—the thin strokes are reduced to hairlines, and the thick strokes made bolder. The axis of the curved forms is completely upright, and the brackets connecting the serifs to the stems have been removed, creating a stark and elegant juncture. The serifs in a number of the lowercase characters have become completely rounded, reflecting the logic of contrast and circularity.

Sans Serif These typefaces are an outgrowth of "display types" of the nineteenth century, designed to be bold and stripped of nonessential details. They are defined by a lack of serifs; the terminals end sharply without adornment. Their stroke weight is uniform, and their axis is completely upright. Sans-serif types set tighter in text and are legible at small sizes; during the past fifty years, they have become acceptable for extended reading.

Slab Serif Another outgrowth of display types, slab serif faces hybridize the bold presentation of a sans-serif and the horizontal stress of a serif face, characterized by an overall consistency in stroke weight. The serifs are the same weight as the stems, hence "slabs;" the body of the slab serif is often wider than what is considered normal.

Graphic These typefaces are the experimental, decorative, children of the display types. Their visual qualities are expressive but not conducive to reading in a long text This category includes specimens such as script faces, fancy and complex faces inspired by handwriting, and idiosyncratic faces that are illustrative or conceptual.

One of the most damaging scourges in a vineyard is small birds which peck at the fruit, leaving them to rot. We control these birds by deterring, rather than destroying them. Scraps of offal littered around the vineyard during the ripening season attract a family of hawks, whose menacing presence deters the smaller birds. The shadowy spectre of these hawks, eerily floating over the vines, lends its name to this fine range of varietal wines – Sparkling Chardonnay Pinot Noir, Chardonnay, Shiraz and Merlot.
BLACKWING
These are wines where oak and extreme winemaking influences are kept to a minimum, to ensure all you see is the epitome of varietal character. The wines are deliberately selected to be rich, full flavoured, and yet round and soft, leaving a most memorable lingering impression on the back palate. They are classy, rich and sophisticated but always approachable and arguably represent the best value for money.

THE ICONIC BIRD DRAWING, which refers to a specific time and place, has its very own language of line and mass. The inline capitals used for the page title echo these linear qualities, but they also are classical capitals with their own history. The supporting text is a sans serif with similar width proportions as the capitals, but it contrasts their thins and thicks with a uniform weight that is clearly modern.

Voice *Australia*

THE WORD "ARROGANTLY" APPEARS HERE and on the next page spread, set in selected faces to compare the effect of particular details on meaning. Large-scale letter details are highlighted as illustration of the subtle changes in the various attributes being described. Take a look, too, at the selection of logos shown to see how decisions in typeface selection—based on such details—affects their meanings or emotional qualities.

Body Width and X-Height Variation away from the regular proportional width established by the uppercase M results in a perceived change in rhythm. The counters in condensed typefaces become similar to the weight of the strokes as the overall letter width decreases, creating a more rapid alternation of positive and negative that may seem to "speed up" the reading rhythm or add a perception of increased energy or tension. Conversely, the counters in extended faces tend to slow the reading rhythm. The ratio of the lowercase letters to the uppercase letters—the x-height—is an important factor in considering not only feeling but also legibility. The larger the x-height is in relation to the cap-height, the more open and inviting the counters of the lowercase letters will be, increasing their legibility, as well as the density of the line, and affecting the face's apparent size. An oldstyle serif set at 14 points, for example, will appear much smaller than a sans serif set at the same size, simply because its lowercase letters are much smaller compared to the uppercase letters.

Stroke Contrast, Modulation, and Ductus The amount of contrast between thicks and thins, or the lack thereof, also contributes to the rhythmic motion of a typeface. A line of type whose letters have strokes of the same weight produces an even, regular rhythm that remains consistent, while a face whose strokes vary in weight will seem to pulse or move across the line. Some faces show contrast within a single stroke—usually a flaring in thickness from the midpoint of the stem outward to the terminals. This feature, called "modulation," usually is indicative of older type styles, referring to the changes in pressure of a brush in delivering ink to the drawing surface. The degree of modulation, or the "speed" of the transitions between thicker and thinner strokes, is called the face's "ductus." The slower such transitions are—the more passive the ductus—the less vigorous or energetic the face will feel. As the ductus becomes more aggressive, the face will begin to feel more active. The same is true with modulation and contrast in general.

Terminals, Spurs, and Serifs The shapes that the terminals of the letters within a typeface exhibit contribute to the typeface's apparent sharpness and rigidity, which may have implications for its perception as being more casual or rigorous, older or newer, or more comforting or more austere. Terminals might end in a cut-off that is perpendicular to the angle of the stroke, or the cut-off itself might be angled against it. As the angle between cut-off and stroke becomes more acute, the terminal becomes sharper; in the curved forms of sans serif faces, this sharpness is especially pronounced, while in serif forms, the terminal's serif hides this sharpness to some degree. Among serif faces, the serifs themselves might be angled or more perpendicular, softer or more geometrically cut, and sometimes even round, as in the ball serif of a neoclassical lowercase A. Spurs—terminals that extend away from a stroke's expected cut-off near a baseline to form a kind of "kickstand" for the letter—are more evidence of the brush, being the point where the bristles lift off the drawing surface and leave a short mark in doing so. Spurs are often found in sans serif faces, even though they are less derivative of brush-drawn letters. The lowercase A, again, is often the site of a spur, as is the lowercase G—the spur in this case is the "ear."

Know What and Why: The Details Selecting a typeface for its feeling or mood is a tricky endeavor that often comes down to a designer's gut reaction to the rhythm or shapes inherent in a particular style. Some typefaces, for example, feel fast or slow, heavy or light; these qualities can be quickly attributed to the interplay of counterspaces, stroke weights and contrasts, joints, and so on. ■ Many typefaces also conjure associations with cultural motifs because of their common use in advertising or other pop-culture venues for specific kinds of subject matter: gothic blackletters or textura faces, for example, commonly evoke horror or fantasy because they are tied to certain historical time periods and because they have been used widely in posters and advertising for movies and books in this genre. However, the intrinsic drawing of a typeface may involve shapes that can be read as other shapes that are found in our environments. Sinewy, curved shoulders that seem to sprout from the vertical stems of letters, or leafy terminals, allude clearly to natural forms such as plants or animals. ■ When thinking about choosing an appropriate typeface, look at the images that accompany the text or think about objects or places related to the subject matter of the text as inspiration.

gantly

gantly

gantly

Logo development often demands that the structural and stylistic details of the type forms in the client's corporate name be altered—sometimes to visually correspond better with a symbol and sometimes simply to make the letters more custom or more specific. Pay close attention to the various details in each example, and try to describe what alteration has been made.

MAQUillAGE A

gorenje B

C

pearlsoft D

E

F

A Helmut Schmid *Japan*

B Jelena Drobac *Serbia*

C, D Made In Space, Inc. *United States*

E Apeloig Design *France*

F Grapefruit *Romania*

Bowls, Shoulders, Apertures, and Eyes The characteristics of these details vary tremendously among typefaces. Bowls—the lower part of the large circular forms O, Q, D, G, and so on—and shoulders—the upper part of such curves, as well as the upper curves on forms such as the uppercase R, the lowercase P, F, and G—might be rounder or more elliptical, fluid, or somewhat squared-off. Looking closely at these forms within a single typeface will reveal some variation as well, optical compensations the designer has made in response to how they join with other strokes. But they will share a basic logic in their curves that will be very different compared to another typeface, even within the same class or style. The axis of the curved forms changes also, being slanted in older styles and completely upright in more modern ones. Apertures, the entry into the counters of letters such as the lowercase E and A, for example, may be tight or more open. Small, closed-off counters, called "eyes," appearing in letters such as the lowercase E and G, also vary considerably in shape and proportion in relation to the lower counters of these letters among typefaces.

Joints, Branches, Ascenders, and Descenders A great deal of a typeface's character is found where the strokes come together—the joints. Sometimes these joints are smooth, with curves flowing into the stems with slow ductus; in other cases, the transition is more abrupt. Looking at the insides of the strokes in forms where bowls meet stems to see how the joint varies is an excellent way to compare typefaces. Where the joints and branches are abrupt, the typeface might feel more geometric, more energetic or more formal; where they are softer, the face might correspondingly feel more organic, more relaxed, or more casual. In addition, the movement and height or depth of the ascenders and descenders above and below the body of the lowercase, respectively, are details worth considering. Some ascenders strike the capline, while others extend above it; similarly, the descenders might be deep or shallow compared to the body of the text. The larger the x-height, usually, the more shallow the ascenders and descenders are, meaning those characters will be more dense in a given typeface than in others. The height and depth of these strokes have an impact on how tightly lines of a given typeface might be leaded, as well as the character of the face.

Graphic Details Many faces are easily distinguished by the existence of stylistic or decorative details that might be strictly textural or might carry very specific associations. There's no way to compare these typefaces since they vary so much, other than to appraise the effect of the graphic details, in combination with other attributes—overall weight, width, contrast, and posture—on legibility and rhythm. The degree to which graphic inclusions, such as inlines or textures, interfere with character recognition, is an issue that must be addressed in the context of the face's use. If the interference is extreme in most of the characters, the face is likely useful only for larger-sized display applications, rather than in running text. It's important to judge such faces, however, on their ability to visually relate to other kinds of elements in a layout, such as subject matter in photographs, illustrative textures, or abstract forms.

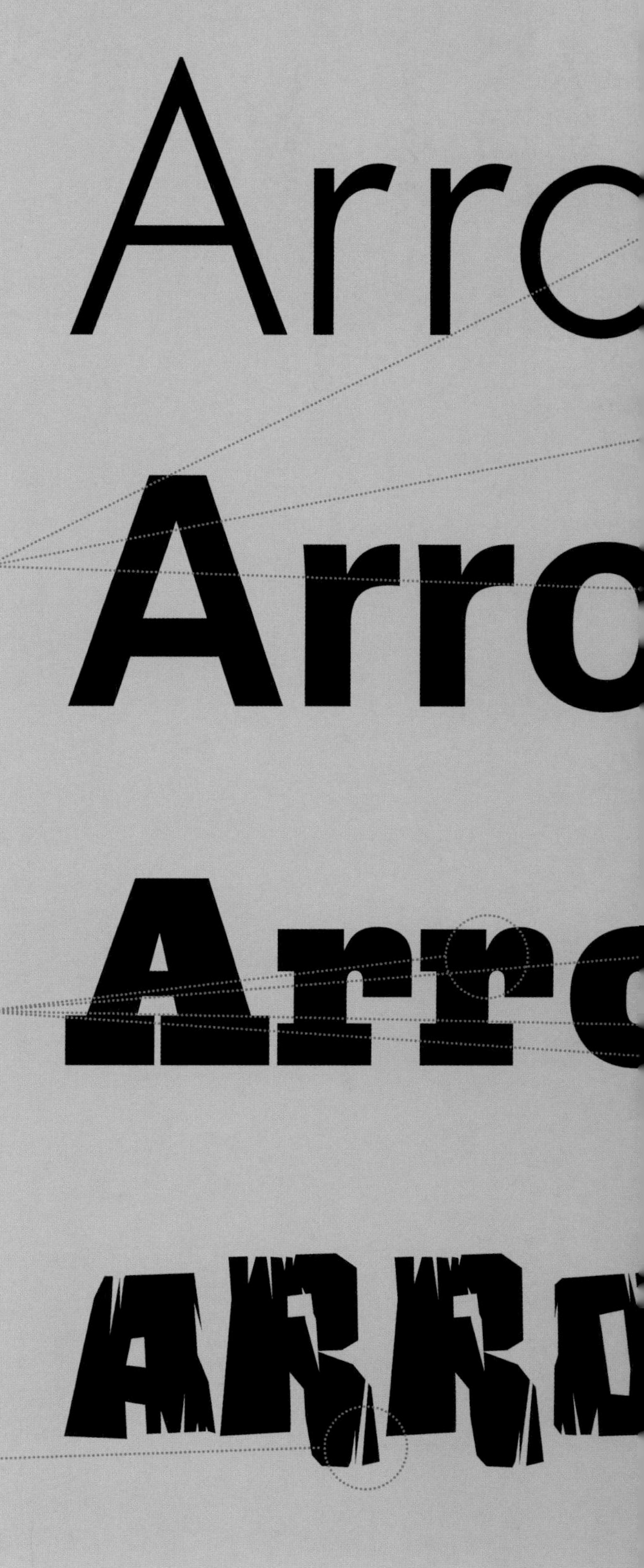

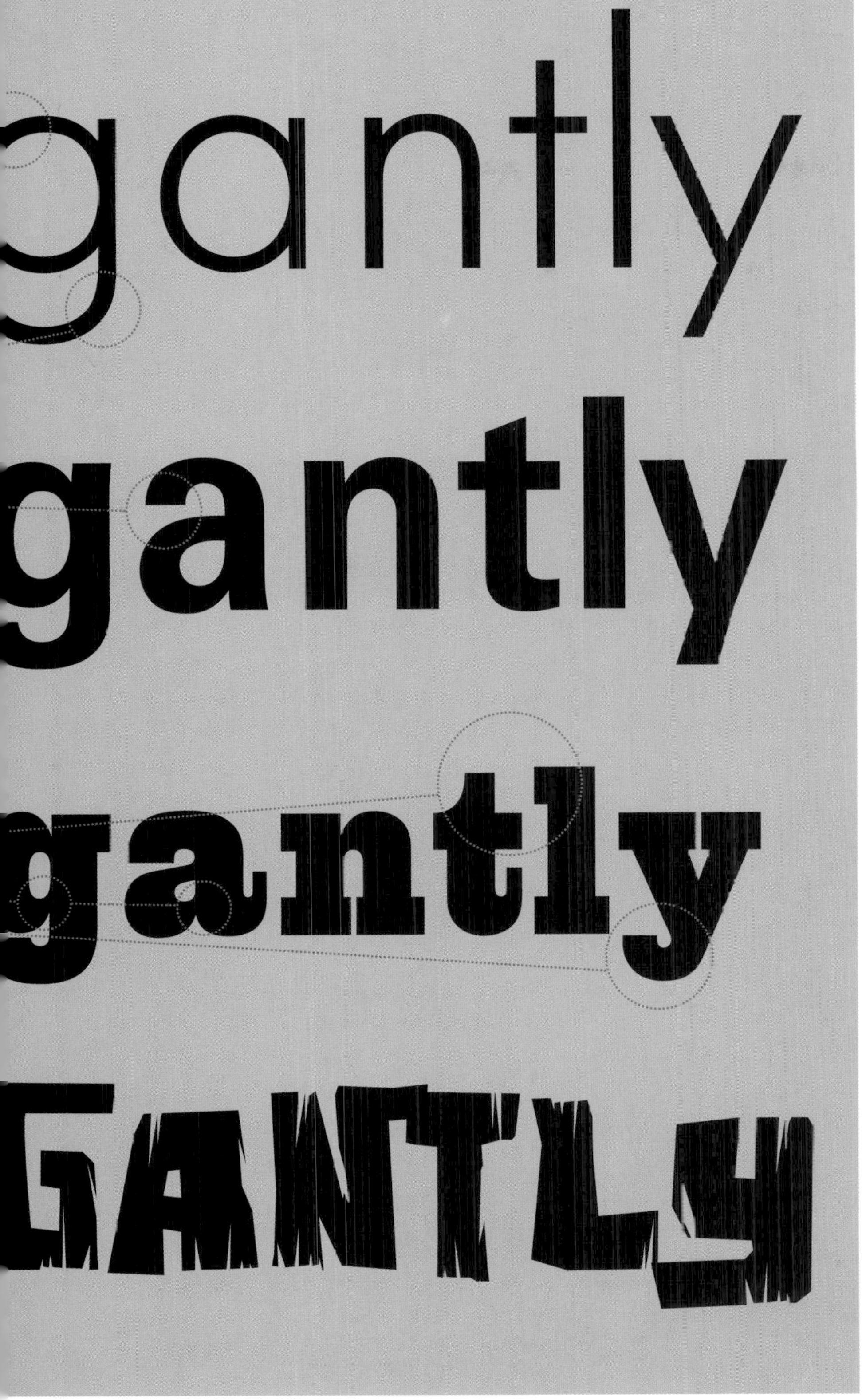

gantly

gantly

gantly

GANTLY

A

B

C

D

E

F

A Grapefruit *Romania*

B C. Harvey Graphic Design *United States*

C I Just Might *United States*

D Igawa Design *United States*

E Raidy Printing Group *Lebanon*

F Michelle Pinkston *Iowa State University, United States*

Combining Type Styles The conventional wisdom for mixing typefaces is to select two type families for a given job. As a basic bit of advice, this is a good start; it provides a framework for finding a maximum amount of contrast, and it forces a designer to exercise some restraint. In one sense, this rule is predicated on the notion of establishing clear hierarchy; the greater the variety of typefaces, it is reasoned, the more difficult it will be for a reader to categorize and remember the meanings of different treatments among informational components. ■ As with all typographic rules, of course, context plays an important role in deciding whether or not to adhere to such a limitation. The complexity of the information being presented is one variable; the overall neutrality, consistency, and expressiveness are others to consider. If a job requires seven or eight typefaces to communicate the appropriate message, so be it—but choose wisely. ■ Contrast among typefaces that are juxtaposed is critical. The only reason to change a typeface is to gain an effect of contrast, and so the contrast achieved by the combination should be clearly recognizable. Otherwise, why bother? Opposing the extremes of weight (light against bold), of width (regular against condensed or expanded), or style (neutral sans serif against slab serif or script) is a natural starting point. ■ But somewhere in the mix, even among extremes of this nature, some formal relationship must exist between the selected fonts to enrich their visual dialogue. ■ Choosing a sans serif and a serif that are about the same weight or width, for example, creates a tension of similarity and difference that can be quite sophisticated. Selecting two serif faces that are similar in weight, but very different in width or contrast, achieves a similar tension. Sometimes this choice is functional; for example, if the difference between the face selected for text and its bold counterpart in the same family is not particularly pronounced (meaning the use of the bold doesn't achieve the desired emphasis), a similarly shaped bold style

each incidenc BbAaOoSs

each incidenc BbAaOoSs

The bold weight of this text face isn't much different from the regular weight; a bold face from an alternate, yet similar, family can be substituted.

Note the similarity of the spurs, terminals, and other details between the two faces.

In choosing to mix typefaces, select counterparts with enough contrast, but be aware of their similarities as well. In this example, the serif and the sans serif are radically different in stroke contrast and detail, but their construction is similar—take note of the slight angularity of the curves; the oblique emphasis in the **O**s; the joint angle in the lowercase **a;** the abrupt joint in the lowercase **b.**

dynamic dynamic *dynamic*
dynamic *dynamic* dynamic
dynamic ***dynamic*** dynamic
dynamic dynamic *dynamic*

Within a single family, variations on weight, width, and posture lend an extraordinary range of textural and rhythmic changes that might have an effect on communication. Note how the word—set in members of the Univers family—changes in presence, cadence, and spatial location (foreground or background) as width, weight, and posture are changed in each.

MIXING TOGETHER MANY typefaces in one logo, headline, or other composition is perfectly fine as long as the typefaces chosen have a relationship in weight, width, texture, or contrast, as is the case in this logotype.

Raidy Printing Group *Lebanon*

may be substituted. Recognizing the differences in the details among a selection of faces from which to choose is an important step in making a choice for a clear combination. Generally, avoid combing two faces of a similar style unless the difference is pronounced enough for the average reader to notice. Combining Caslon and Baskerville, for example—two transitional serifs with similar axis, weight, width, and terminal shapes—isn't such a great idea. But combining Bodoni—a modern serif of extreme contrast—with Glypha—a slab serif of uniform stroke weight but similar width and axis—might be effective. ■ As another possibility, similar faces set at dramatically different scales might be unified by the weight of their strokes at these different sizes. For example, 7-point Futura Heavy capitals, which are very dot-like, might correspond in overall weight to the strokes of Univers 45 set at 13 points in size on the same page. Both are sans serif; their different sizes create contrast in their counters and linearity even as the overall weight of the smaller Futura begins to approach the stroke weight of the larger Univers 45. ■ The historical quality of typefaces may also play a role in how they are combined. Since the average reader usually associates certain qualities with a given typeface because of its classical or modern drawing qualities, mixing typefaces from related—or dramatically different—periods might help generate additional messages. A Roman capital, such as Trajan, in combination with a geometric sans serif, such as Futura, not only might present a great deal of contrasting typographic color but also might allude to a historical association: old and new, continuum, evolution, innovation, and so on. In this particular case, both Trajan and Futura are based on Roman geometric proportion, despite being separated by 2,000 years of history.

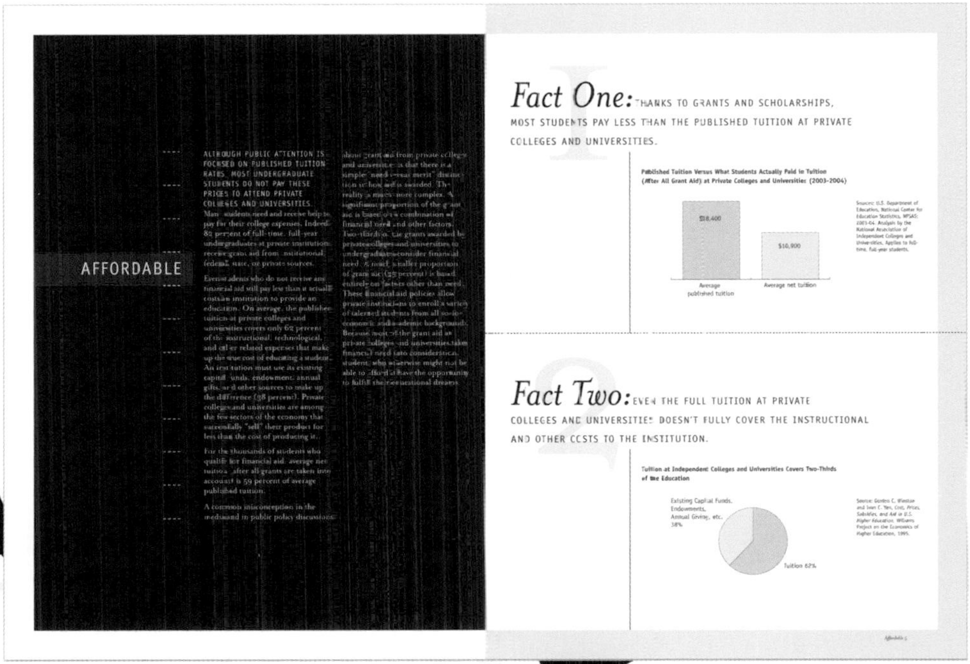

THE MAJORITY OF the text in this brochure is set in a sans serif face with a uniform stroke weight and mostly all uppercase. The result is austere and direct, but the addition of the italic serif face adds some warmth and contrast to the sans serif face's regularity.

Robert Rytter & Associates
United States

AT LEAST FIVE different display typefaces, all typical of early twentieth-century newspaper and advertising design, rhythmically contrast each other in weight, stroke contrast, width, and style. The size and spacing changes between each item allow each face to be appreciated and create rhythmic linear intervals.

AdamsMorioka *United States*

Assessing Character Count, Leading, and Paragraph Width The width of a paragraph depends heavily on the size of type being used and therefore how many characters can be fit onto a single line. Regardless of the type size or the reader's maturity, between fifty and eighty characters (including spaces) can be processed before a line return. With words averaging between five and ten letters, that means approximately eight to twelve words per line. Achieving this character count determines the width of a paragraph. The proportions of the page format—and how much text must be made to fit overall—might affect paragraph width, but character count is the best starting point for defining an optimal width. ■ The leading of the lines, as noted, depends somewhat on the width of the paragraph, the type size, and its spacing. The space between lines should be noticeably larger than the optical height of the lines, but not so much that it becomes pronounced. Similarly, the leading must not be so tight that the reader locates the beginning of the same line after the return and begins reading it again. As paragraph width increases, so must the leading, so that the beginnings of the lines are more easily distinguished. ■ Oddly, as the width of a paragraph narrows, the leading must also be increased: otherwise, the reader might grab several lines together because the snapshots he or she takes while scanning encompass the full paragraph width.

IN THIS PAGE SPREAD from a brochure, the designer uses larger type in the vertical column but smaller type in the wide paragraph at the left; in both cases the leading remains constant. This causes the vertical column to read more quickly (having optimal qualities of character count and spacing), which increases its vertical pull in the format. The smaller type at the left reads more slowly because the line length of the paragraph is far wider than optimal, and the leading appears greater between the lines; the slower, horizontal emphasis of this text is a visual contrast to the vertical column.

Paone Design Associates
United States

In The School of Design's graduate program in Fine Arts, motivated and promising artists work in a range of styles and approaches while immersing themselves in a curriculum that nurtures their technical skills and allows them the freedom to pursue ideas and develop their personal visions. Students benefit from spending two years in a cultural environment dedicated to recognizing the diversity and complexity of today's visual arts world.

Graduate students in Fine Arts work in the disciplines of painting, photography, printmaking, sculpture, and combined media/newer technologies. They are challenged to consider the wider implications of their work and respond to the constantly expanding requirements and responsibilities of artists. Emphasis is placed on individual studio work, supported by a rigorous examination of critical and conceptual issues. Students participate in individual critiques, intensive group critiques, critical and professional seminars, and work with visiting critics on contemporary issues. The MFA program offers opportunities to study abroad, with summer residencies, and an exchange program with the Royal Academy and Royal College in London. Students also pursue the interdisciplinary opportunities available within the school, as well as the exceptional resources of a world class urban university.

John Moore
Monroe and Edna Gutman
Professor of Fine Arts
Chair, Department of Fine Arts

9 POINTS

50

Lorem ipsum dolor sit amet consectitur adipscing elit in nonum erat summa es

50

Lorem ipsum dolor sit amet consectitur adipscing elit in nonum erat summ

50

Lorem ipsum dolor sit amet consectitur adipscing elit in nonum est

50

Lorem ipsum dolor sit amet consectitur adipscing elit in nonum erat summa est nunc

11 POINTS

50

Lorem ipsum dolor sit amet consectitur adipscing elit in nonum

50

Lorem ipsum dolor sit amet consectitur adipscing elit in nonu

50

Lorem ipsum dolor sit amet consectitur adipscing elit i

50

Lorem ipsum dolor sit amet consectitur adipscing elit in nonum erat s

13 POINTS

50

Lorem ipsum dolor sit amet consectitur adipscing elit i

Lorem ipsum dolor sit amet consectitur adipscing el

Lorem ipsum dolor sit amet consectitur adipsc

50

Lorem ipsum dolor sit amet consectitur adipscing elit in no

A comparison of character count for a selection of typefaces, at varying sizes, is shown set on the same paragraph width. As with all typographic "rules," there is a range to what is comfortable for the average reader. Given a fifty- to eighty-character comfort range, it is easy to see that a paragraph must widen as the type size increases and narrow as it decreases, to maintain the optimal number of characters on a line.

Lorem ipsum dolor sit amet consectitur adipscing elit in nonum erat summa es nunc et semper quam gloriosa de duis autem velure quod vam uns erat lorem ipsum dolore sit amet consectitur adipscit

Lorem ip consectit nonum e et sempe

Lorem ipsum dolor sit amet consectitur adipscing elit in nonum erat summa es nunc et semper quam gloriosa de duis autem velure quod vam uns erat lorem ipsum dolore sit amet consectitur adipscit

Lorem ip consectit nonum e et sempe

Lorem ipsum dolor sit ame consectitur adipscing elitin nonum erat summa es nun cet semper quam gloriosa e deduis autem velure cuod vamuns erat lorem ipsum doloresit amet consectitura

Lorem ip consecti nonum e cet semp

Comfortable interline space, or leading, varies according to several characteristics in typeface style and size; but generally, the interline space should seem a point or two larger than the height of the lowercase running as text. Because the x-height varies so much among faces, a designer will need to judge the leading appropriate to the appearance of the lower case, rather than try to assign a leading to a point size by way of a specific formula.

Une pièce gentille sur des gens sympathiques

(Een vriendelijk stuk over aardige mensen)

Personnages
SOFIA
MICHAEL
GABRIËL

Résumé

Commentaires de la presse

Extrait de Une pièce gentille sur des gens sympathiques / 1

THE OPTIMAL QUALITY of the column widths for the running text in this page spread is evident in lines of relatively consistent length, a comfortable rag, and notably few occurrences of hyphenated line breaks. This column width also appears to accommodate heads and subheads of different sizes.

Martin Oostra *Netherlands*

Alignment Logic Type can be set in several different configurations called alignments. It can be set so that every line begins at the same left-hand starting point (flush-left) or right-hand starting point (flush-right), or with an axis centered on the paragraph width (centered). In this case, there are two options: in centered type, the lines are different lengths and are centered over each other on the width's vertical axis; in justified type, the lines are the same length, aligning on both the left and the right sides. Justified text is the only setting in which the lines are the same length. In text set to align left, right, or centered, the uneven lengths of the lines create a soft shape on the nonaligned side that is called a "rag." ■ The alignment of text has an effect on the spacing within it and, therefore, on the search for a desirable text setting. In a paragraph set flush-left, ragged right (FLRR), the word spaces are uniform. This is also true in a paragraph set flush-right, ragged left (FRRL) and in a centered paragraph. The word space in a justified paragraph, however, varies because the width of the paragraph is mathematically fixed, and the words on any given line

Alignment structures *Text excerpted from* The Elements of Typographic Style *by Robert Bringhurst*

FLUSH-LEFT/RAGGED RIGHT

Think of the blank page as alpine meadow, or as the purity of undifferentiated being. The typographer enters this space and must change it. The reader will enter itlater, to see what the typographer has done there. The underlying truth of the blank page must be infringed, but it must never altogether disappear.

FLUSH-RIGHT/RAGGED LEFT

Think of the blank page as alpine meadow, or as the purity of undifferentiated being. The typographer enters this space and must change it. The reader will enter itlater, to see what the typographer has done there. The underlying truth of the blank page must be infringed, but it must never altogether disappear.

CENTERED AXIS

Think of the blank page as alpine meadow, or as the purity of undifferentiated being. The typographer enters this space and must change it. The reader will enter itlater, to see what the typographer has done there. The underlying truth of the blank page must be infringed, but it must never altogether disappear.

JUSTIFIED

Think of the blank page as alpine meadow, or as the purity of undifferentiated being. The typographer enters this space and must change it. The reader will enter it later, to see what the typographer has done there. The underlying truth of the blank page must be infringed, but it must never altogether disappear.

CENTERED-AXIS AND flush-left alignments are mixed to great effect in this classically influenced page spread design. The margins of the flush-left, asymmetrical text set on the right-hand page are symmetrical and optically balanced with the material on the left.

CHK Design *United Kingdom*

THE TIGHTLY JUSTIFIED columns of text in this asymmetrical layout reinforce the geometry of the page. Weight changes within the text add contrast, and the spacing is consistent.

Brett Yasko *United States*

must align on both sides—no matter how many words or how long they are. In justified text, wordspacing variation is the single most difficult issue to overcome. The result of poorly justified text in which the wordspace constantly changes is a preponderance of rivers—chains of white negative space that visually join each other from line to line. In particularly bad justified setting, the rivers are even more apparent than the interline space, causing the paragraph to become a jumble of strange word clusters. ■ One method of minimizing this problem is to find the optimal flush-left paragraph width for the size of the type before justifying—and then to widen the paragraph slightly or shrink the type size by a half-point or a point. This adjustment can result in an optimal number of characters and words that comfortably fit upon justification and can compensate for the potential of long words to create undesirable spacing. A slightly wider paragraph also allows some flexibility in how words are broken from line to line and gives the designer more options for re-breaking text to make it fit with good spacing. ■ Ragged paragraphs offer the opportunity to avoid the spacing issues inherent in justified text. The word spaces in these kinds of paragraphs remain constant. Ragged setting also introduces the pronounced textural effect of an organic edge whose opposition to the hard edge of the alignment imparts an immediate visual contrast to the page, as well as provides optical separation between horizontally arranged paragraphs. Changing line lengths within the ragged edge helps the reader establish breaks more easily and therefore differentiate individual lines on the return.

EVERY DAY IS
VIA DAY

THIS JUSTIFIED SETTING uses wide margins to create focus on the text block. The internal spacing of the text is relatively consistent.

AdamsMorioka *United States*

A Centered-Axis

Think of the blank page as alpine meadow, or as the purity of undifferentiated being. The typographer enters this space and must change it. The reader will enter it later, to see what the typographer has done there. The underlying truth of the blank page must be infringed, but it must never altogether disappear.

B Justified

Think of the blank page as alpine meadow, or as the purity of undifferentiated being. The typographer enters this space and must change it. The reader will enter it later, to see what the typographer has done there. The underlying truth of the blank page must be infringed, but it must never altogether disappear.

Symmetrical text arrangements—type centered on an axis with rags both left and right (series A), as well as justified blocks (series B)—are intrinsically difficult to work with.

Center-axis text logically implies a symmetrical, and therefore static, relationship with the surrounding space of the format. To create tension and contrast, the designer is left to consider only the relative size of the overall text mass and its internal spacing and color. Additionally, the exterior shape of center-axis configurations dominates the linearity of the lines and impairs readability. In this study, these issues are addressed sequentially.

Poorly justified text displays wildly varied word spaces and rivers, as well as extensive hyphenation. To justify text on optimal width—and avoid rivers and hyphens—first find "optimal" in a flush-left setting and then widen the text box slightly or scale the type down a half-point upon justifying. Correcting spacing and hyphenation line by line creates other worries—lines that are exceptionally open and others that are extremely dense. The variations in width and size here show gains and losses in desirable spacing, text size, and hyphenation.

Think of the blank page as alpine meadow, or as the purity of undifferentiated being. The typographer enters this space and must change it. The reader will enter it later, to see what the typographer has done. The underlying truth of the blank page must be infringed, but it must never altogether disappear—and whatever displaces it might well aim to be as lively and peaceful as it is. It is not enough, when building a title page, merely to unload some big, prefabricated letters into the center of the space, nor to dig a few holes in the silence with typographic heavy machinery and move on. Big type, even huge type, can be beautiful and useful.

Think of the blank page as alpine meadow, or as the purity of undifferentiated being. The typographer enters this space and must change it. The reader will enter it later, to see what the typographer has done. The underlying truth of the blank page must be infringed, but it must never altogether disappear—and whatever displaces it might well aim to be as lively and peaceful as it is. It is not enough, when building a title page, merely to unload some big, prefabricated letters into the center of the space, nor to dig a few holes in the silence with typographic heavy machinery and move on. Big type, even huge type, can be beautiful and useful.

Think of the blank page as alpine meadow, or as the purity of undifferentiated being. The typographer enters this space and must change it. The reader will enter it later, to see what the typographer has done. The underlying truth of the blank page must be infringed, but it must never altogether disappear—and whatever displaces it might well aim to be as lively and peaceful as it is. It is not enough, when building a title page, merely to unload some big, prefabricated letters into the center of the space, nor to dig a few holes in the silence with typographic heavy machinery and move on. Big type, even huge type, can be beautiful and useful.

Example of a paragraph showing a desirable rag (left), and two paragraphs whose rags are frought with problems: the rag is either too deep or active; shows sharp inclusions of negative space and protrusions of long lines; a contour with a noticeable shape; or irregular width overall from top to bottom.

Think of the blank page as alpine meadow, or as the purity of undifferentiated being. The typographer enters this space and must change it. The reader will enter it later, to see what the typographer has done. The underlying truth of the blank page must be infringed, but it must never altogether disappear—and whatever displaces it might well aim to be as lively and peaceful as it is. It is not enough, when building a title page, merely to unload some big, prefabricated letters into the center of the space, nor to dig a few holes in the silence with typographic heavy machinery and move on. Big type, even huge type, can be beautiful and useful.

Think of the blank page as alpine meadow, or as the purity of undifferentiated being. The typographer enters this space and must change it. The reader will enter it later, to see what the typographer has done. The underlying truth of the blank page must be infringed, but it must never altogether disappear—and whatever displaces it might well aim to be as lively and peaceful as it is. It is not enough, when building a title page, merely to unload some big, prefabricated letters into the center of the space, nor to dig a few holes in the silence with typographic heavy machinery and move on. Big type, even huge type, can be beautiful and useful.

Think of the blank page as alpine meadow, or as the purity of undifferentiated being. The typographer enters this space and must change it. The reader will enter it later, to see what the typographer has done. The underlying truth of the blank page must be infringed, but it must never altogether disappear—and whatever displaces it might well aim to be as lively and peaceful as it is. It is not enough, when building a title page, merely to unload some big, prefabricated letters into the center of the space, nor to dig a few holes in the silence with typographic heavy machinery and move on. Big type, even huge type, can be beautiful and useful.

A ragged edge is considered appropriate for a given paragraph setting if it varies within a fifth to a seventh of the paragraph's width. A much more active rag, however, also is visually interesting; the designer must, however, ensure that the rag throughout the project remains consistent in its activity, rather than changing from page to page or even from column to column. The more active the rag—meaning, the greater the difference between short and long lines—the more attention is due the rag of both the exterior edge formed by the long lines and the interior edge formed by the short lines.

Natural bathing facilities are highly valued by the Japanese for their healing capabilities. At right, the women's bath at Makiba-no-ie Ryokan in Yufuin, Japan, 2000.

The Hashidate-Yu operated out of the basement of the Panama Hotel, a single room occupancy (SRO) hotel in what is now known as Seattle's International District, for more than 50 years — from 1910 until the mid-1960s — closing only during the evacuation and relocation period associated with Japanese internment during the Second World War. All indications are that the bathhouse was built at the time of the hotel's construction in 1910 by the first Japanese architect to practice in the city, Saburo Ozasa. The location of the Hashidate-Yu bathhouse at Sixth and South Main put it at the heart of Seattle's Nihonmachi, which served as a regional draw for Japanese immigrants who had settled on the urban periphery, as well as a residential center in its own right.

Immigrants came to soak at the sentos because life was hard, the hot water was relaxing, bathing facilities were scarce in prewar housing, and it was a traditional cultural activity. Japanese bathing traditions are at least twelve centuries old and have taken many forms. Bathhouses have existed in Japan since the eighth century, when they were a central feature of Buddhist temples. The earliest public bathhouses were connected with temples and monasteries, such as the one in the Second Month Hall of the Todai-Ji Temple in Nara. Built on a natural spring, the temple served as a bathhouse for the monks as well as a site of Buddhist purification rites.

Buddhist temples provided baths as resources for the general public, who lacked private facilities.[1] Although its religious connotations eventually faded, the act of bathing persisted in Japan. Bathhouses became social gathering places for urban dwellers. The first sento was established in Osaka in 1590; and by the mid 1800s there were 550 bathhouses in Tokyo alone. Neighborhood bathhouses in the eighteenth century were often two-story structures, with a room (or rooms) on the second level for relaxing, chatting, eating, drinking, and playing games.

Natural bathing facilities such as hot springs or onsen have been highly valued by Japanese for their healing capabilities. Bathing is still a valued tradition in Japan and was among the most significant traditional cultural practices to be brought over to the United States by the first Japanese immigrants. The furos, or soaking tubs, that Japanese immigrants constructed in American Nihonmachis are among the few surviving elements of the built environment that reflect a distinctively Japanese American heritage.

Several Japanese bathhouses were located within Seattle's Nihonmachi. Those who lived outside of the city frequently would visit Japantown on the weekend to do shopping and attend events at

ALTHOUGH THE DESIGNER has set this book text on a wide paragraph, she has decided to limit the rag activity. The soft rag keeps the page quiet in general, and it strives not to detract from the indents that define the beginnings of paragraphs.

Cheng Design *United States*

Exploring the Ragged Edge The rag of a paragraph might range from deep to shallow and active to subtle, but its uniformity and consistency from the top of a paragraph down to the bottom are what make it desirable. The ragged line endings are considered optimal if they create an organic, unforced "ripple" down the edge of the paragraph, without pronounced indents or bulges. In an optimally ragged paragraph, the rag becomes invisible: the reader is never aware that the lines are ending at their natural conclusion. If the alternating lines end short and very long, the rag becomes active and calls attention to itself, distracting the reader from following the content of the text. That said, a deep rag is acceptable if it remains consistent throughout the text. A designer might opt to mitigate a deep rag by introducing more interline space. ■ What is never desirable, however, is a rag that begins at the outset of a paragraph guided by one kind of logic but transforms into another kind of logic as the paragraph progresses in depth; a rag that shows excessive indenting from the right; or sharp, angular inclusions of space created by lines that become sequentially shorter. The overall unity of a rag can be easily compromised by the single occurrence of two short lines that create a boxy hole. In an optimal rag, the depth hovers between one-fifth and one-seventh of the paragraph's width. ■ Word order and word breaks across lines also affect the rag. Problems in ragged-right setting commonly arise when a series of short words—of, at, it, to, we, us—are broken to align at the left edge, creating a vertical river running parallel to the aligned edge; and when short words appear at the end of a long line between two shorter lines, appearing to break off and float. In such cases, the designer must weigh the consequences of re-breaking the lines to prevent these problems against their effect on the rag as a whole. ■ Similarly, the breaking of words across lines by using a hyphen can also be problematic if left untreated. From an editorial perspective, two successive lines ending with hyphens is undesirable. If a text is hyphenating excessively—more than once every ten lines or so—the problem lies in the relationship between the text's point size and the width of the paragraph; one or the other must be adjusted to correct the problem. Although a text free of hyphens would be best, this state of perfection is rarely possible; indeed, some designers argue that hyphenating words here and there helps contribute to the uniformity of the rag by allowing lines to remain similar in length.

Think of the blank page as alpine meadow, or as the purity of undifferentiated being. The typographer enters this space and must change it. The reader will enter it later, to see what the typographer has done. The underlying truth of the blank page must be infringed, but it must never altogether disappear—and whatever displaces it might well aim to be as lively and peaceful as it is. It is not enough, when building a title page, merely to unload some big, prefabricated letters into the center of the space, nor to dig a few holes in the silence with typographic heavy machinery and move on. Big type, even huge type, can be beautiful and useful.

Think of the blank page as alpine meadow, or as the purity of undifferentiated being. The typographer enters this space and must change it. The reader will enter it later, to see what the typographer has done. The underlying truth of the blank page must be infringed, but it must never altogether disappear—and whatever displaces it might well aim to be as lively and peaceful as it is. It is not enough, when building a title page, merely to unload some big prefabricated letters into the center of the space, nor to dig a few holes in the silence with typographic heavy machinery and move on. Big type, even huge type, can be beautiful and useful.

Think of the blank page as alpine meadow, or as the purity of undifferentiated being. The typographer enters this space and must change it. The reader will enter it later, to see what the typographer has done. The underlying truth of the blank page must be infringed, but it must never altogether disappear—and whatever displaces it might well aim to be as lively and peaceful as it is. It is not enough, when building a title page, merely to unload some big, prefabricated letters into the center of the space, nor to dig a few holes in the silence with typographic heavy machinery and move on. Big type, even huge type, can be beautiful and useful.

Hyphenated word breaks are a constant source of frustration for a designer. Too many hyphens in a row are considered undesirable, and a slight adjustment in text size or paragraph width might correct the problem. The three paragraphs shown here are set in the same size text, with subtle differences. The first paragraph shows uncorrected hyphenation and rag. The second shows a more active rag but no hyphens—a toss-up between desired goals. The third shows a slightly wider paragraph and a more even rag; the only hyphen appears in the second line. One hyphen every ten lines or so is optimal.

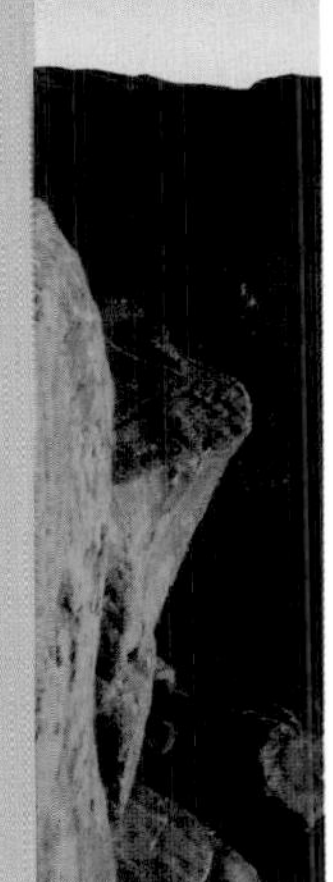

Präambel

THE EVEN, UNFORCED RIPPLE in the rags of these text columns is considered desirable in text that is lengthy and intended to be read continuously. The rag in the caption has also been thoughtfully considered to minimize activity despite the narrow caption width.

Andreas Ortag *Austria*

The Optimal Paragraph A desirable paragraph setting is one in which a constellation of variables achieves a harmonic balance. Since extended running text is such an important consideration for a publication, finding the optimal paragraph is one way to begin developing overall typographic structure. ■ A designer might first make some assumptions about the text typeface, based on his or her sense of its appropriateness from a conceptual standpoint and in consideration of its visual attributes—the relative height of the lowercase letters, the general weight of the strokes and any contrast within them, the height of the ascenders and descenders—and set a text paragraph at an arbitrary width and arbitrary text size. Judging from this first attempt, a designer might opt to adjust the size of the text, loosen or tighten its overall spacing, open and close up the leading, and change the width in successive studies. ■ By comparing the results of these variations, a designer will be able to determine the most comfortable text setting for extended reading. At what point is the type size too small—or uncomfortably large? Are the lines relatively even in length or varying a lot? Is excessive hyphenation occurring, meaning that the paragraph is too narrow to allow a useful character count? Is the leading creating too dense a field of text to feel comfortable? During this study, it might become clear that several options for width and leading are optimal, but a designer will need to choose one as a standard for the publication. ■ The choice that the designer makes has implications for the page size, the number of columns of text that might fit on it, and optimal sizes for other text groupings, such as captions, callouts, introductory paragraphs, and so on.

A "what if" book, *The Switch* is inspired by the blood-boiling enmity of polar opposites found in all spheres of life: families, shared living spaces, war-zones, ideological divides, and places of work. *What if* there was a compulsory shoe-swopping day? *What if* flashes of light lit up dark pockets of hate and misunderstanding all over the world, even for only a moment? Can empathy be cajoled or would it make no difference at all?

The Switch was published by Jewel Weed Press, Middletown NY, a garage-based small press owned by a former High School of Printing classmate, Ronald Hodamarsky. Although Jewel Weed's list focused mainly on books written by Ronald's wife Pat Hodamarsky, Ronald really dug the premise of *The Switch* when I pitched it to him over the phone. He agreed to publish the book if I would pay for all the printing and binding expenses including the costs of having their small second-hand offset press fixed. Published in an edition of 400 copies, my first novel was reviewed in two obscure literary journals—favorably in one and very unfavorably in the other. The reviewer of the pan was particularly irritated by the book's structure: "It is dizzying enough slogging through

46

THE SWITCH

A NOVEL BY BLEU MOBLEY

The Switch *a novel*

One morning, a woman wakes to find she's living the life of her number one nemesis. Her nemesis has become her as well, at least for the day. They witness themselves in each other. It seems, on this one day at least, these switches have occurred all over the world. ***The Switch*** chronicles the day in the lives of six sets of switched enemies: three pairs who are face to face enemies, and three pairs who never even met but despise the very thought of the other.

1978, Jewel Weed Press, Middletown, NY

THE SWITCH

excerpt

Joanne, in the person of Carlotta, feeling the weight of a body sixteen pounds heavier than her own, sees herself coming down the hallway and wants to duck into the bathroom or turn around and head the other way. Carlotta feels so much revulsion associated with this person walking towards her, the feeling is physical. Her neurons hurl frantically over synapses in search of a means of escape, her stomach knots, her fingers and toes tremor. She recalls a dream where Joanne is nice to her, confides in her. In the dream, the two of them were singing a song together and embraced each other in the way old friends do. Whose dream was that? Joanne's? Carlotta's? Both? Neither? Carlotta decides to keep walking, say good morning, maybe ask Joanne how her dad is doing or something about the Anderson case.

Carlotta, in the person of Joanne, decides not to go into the mailroom after all. Instead she ducks into a stairwell. Joanne despises the way Carlotta tries to engage her in small talk. *It's so dishonest. We both detest each other, why bother acting like it's any different.* Joanne will take truth over niceness any day of the week.

Two people disliking each other, even with great intensity, is not a serious problem in and of itself. It is a serious problem for Joanne and Carlotta because they are both intellectual property lawyers at Bennett and Bennett and have no choice but to work together on at least one third of their cases. Truth is, Joanne doesn't care for 90% of her colleagues at Bennett and Bennett. She considers most of them immoral, shiftless hypocrites. She hates working there but would never leave the firm because it's pretty much her whole life. Carlotta dreamed of working at Bennett and Bennett ever since she was a pre-law student reading about the firm's landmark class-action suits against big pharmaceutical companies. It's not a huge firm but it has an excellent reputation and they let her take on a lot of pro bono cases. Still, she often considers leaving, primarily because of Joanne. As a lawyer, Carlotta prides herself in finding solutions that avoid having to go to court. She's a mediator by nature and considers it a personal failure that she's never been able to reach some kind of common ground with Joanne. She loses sleep over the conflict and has named a deepening worry line in her forehead after her nemesis.

Carlotta believes that Joanne is not, deep down, a bad person. She is just severely fucked up, clinically depressed, and probably had a very difficult

a book where every character is simultaneously someone else, but then halfway through *The Switch*, the reading orientation flips 180 degrees forcing the reader to physically turn the book upside down. Once vertigo sets in you realize this device is nothing but a trick to get you to notice the book's palindromic cover design which forms a face from both orientations. Cute, but it doesn't make up for the preposterous premise and the altogether convoluted read. Switch it off!"

47

THREE STYLES OF TEXT set on different widths are also set in three different sizes to achieve as near to optimal relationship between type size and column width as possible—approximately 30 characters per line for short bursts of reading, 50 to 70 characters for extended reading. The wide, primary text column is likely too wide to be optimal, but the designer has increased the leading, relative to the point size, to make it more comfortable.

EarSay *United States*

Think of the blank page as alpine meadow, or as the purity of undifferentiated being. The typographer enters this space and must change it. The reader will enter it later, to see what the typographer has done. The underlying truth of the blank page must be infringed, but it must never altogether disappear—and whatever displaces it might well aim to be as lively and peaceful as it is. It is not enough, when building a title page, merely to unload some big, prefabricated letters into the center of the space, nor to dig a few holes in the silence with typographic heavy machinery and move on. Big type, even huge type, can be beautiful and useful.

Initial setting Set solid; the activity of the ascenders and descenders, and a relatively large x-height, create an uncomfortably dense setting. Furthermore, the rag shows indecisive lengths, as well as inclusions, and there are two hyphenated breaks in sequence.

Think of the blank page as alpine meadow, or as the purity of undifferentiated being. The typographer enters this space and must change it. The reader will enter it later, to see what the typographer has done. The underlying truth of the blank page must be infringed, but it must never altogether disappear—and whatever displaces it might well aim to be as lively and peaceful as it is. It is not enough, when building a title page, merely to unload some big, prefabricated letters into the center of the space, nor to dig a few holes in the silence with typographic heavy machinery and move on. Big type, even huge type, can be beautiful and useful.

Second Setting Same leading; adjusting the size to 8 points alleviates the density and somewhat improves the rag shape; however, the size is too small for the width of the paragraph to be optimal (50–70 characters on each line).

Think of the blank page as alpine meadow, or as the purity of undifferentiated being. The typographer enters this space and must change it. The reader will enter it later, to see what the typographer has done. The underlying truth of the blank page must be infringed, but it must never altogether disappear—and whatever displaces it might well aim to be as lively and peaceful as it is. It is not enough, when building a title page, merely to unload some big, prefabricated letters into the center of the space, nor to dig a few holes in the silence with typographic heavy machinery and move on. Big type, even huge type, can be beautiful and useful.

Third Setting Same size and leading, but substitution of a face with a smaller x-height. This face appears to small to be comfortable, however, and the width is still too wide for an optimal character count.

Think of the blank page as alpine meadow, or as the purity of undifferentiated being. The typographer enters this space and must change it. The reader will enter it later, to see what the typographer has done. The underlying truth of the blank page must be infringed, but it must never altogether disappear—and whatever displaces it might well aim to be as lively and peaceful as it is. It is not enough, when building a title page, merely to unload some big, prefabricated letters into the center of the space, nor to dig a few holes in the silence with typographic heavy machinery and move on. Big type, even huge type, can be beautiful and useful.

Fourth Setting A return to the typeface of the initial settings, but narrowing the paragraph, retains legibility, optimizes the character count (to 65 per line) and creates a more active rag. The leading still seems a bit dense, and there are problems with the rag and excessive hypehnation that are yet to be addressed.

Think of the blank page as alpine meadow, or as the purity of undifferentiated being. The typographer enters this space and must change it. The reader will enter it later, to see what the typographer has done. The underlying truth of the blank page must be infringed, but it must never altogether disappear—and whatever displaces it might well aim to be as lively and peaceful as it is. It is not enough, when building a title page, merely to unload some big, prefabricated letters into the center of the space, nor to dig a few holes in the silence with typographic heavy machinery and move on. Big type, even huge type, can be beautiful and useful.

Final Setting Another slight decrease in the paragraph width, an added point of leading, and decisive re-breaking of the lines yields a paragraph with a comfortable texture, an optimal line count, minimal hyphenation, and a beautiful rag. From this ultimate paragraph, the typographer is ready to consider how to structure columns and supporting treatments for elements such as captions, subheads, and so on.

In this study of a paragraph, the variables of type size, spacing, leading, and paragraph width are tested to arrive at a text setting that results in the most comfortable spacing, the least hyphenation, and a decisive rag.

Text excerpted from The Elements of Typographic Style *by Robert Bringhurst*

heavy machinery and move on. Big ty
Think of the blank page as alpin
or as the purity of undifferentiated b
The typographer enters this space an
change it. The reader will enter it lat
see what the typographer has done.
underlying truth of the blank page m
infringed, but it must never altoget
and whatever displaces it might wel

heavy machinery and move on. Big ty
Think of the blank page
or as the purity of undifferentiated b
The typographer enters this space an
change it. The reader will enter it lat
see what the typographer has done.
underlying truth of the blank page m
infringed, but it must never altoget
and whatever displaces it might wel

heavy machinery and move on. Big ty
■ Think of the blank page as alpin
or as the purity of undifferentiated b
The typographer enters this space an
change it. The reader will enter it lat
see what the typographer has done.
underlying truth of the blank page m
infringed, but it must never altoget
and whatever displaces it might wel

Examples of various indenting approaches hint at the possibilities of this simple kind of paragraph break.

a few holes in the silence with typog
heavy machinery and move on. Big ty
huge type, can be beautiful and use

Introducing the Space
Think of the blank page as alpine me
or as the purity of undifferentiated b
The typographer enters this space an
change it. The reader will enter it lat
see what the typographer has done. T
underlying truth of the blank page m
infringed, but it must never altoget

a few holes in the silence with typog
heavy machinery and move on. Big ty
huge type, can be beautiful and use

Introducing the Space

Think of the blank page as alpine me
or as the purity of undifferentiated b
The typographer enters this space an
change it. The reader will enter it lat
see what the typographer has done. T
underlying truth of the blank page m

Subheads are sometimes included as separators. (A) The subhead may follow a hard or proportional return, and the first line of the paragraph might follow the same leading, baseline to baseline, from the subhead as its subsequent lines do. (B) Or the subhead might have a distinct space before and after.

Think of the blank page as alpine me
or as the purity of undifferentiated b
The typographer enters this space an
change it. The reader will enter it lat

The underlying truth of the blank pa
but it must never altogether disapp
ever displaces it might well aim to be
is. It is not enough, when building a t

A single hard return between paragraphs is a common approach to separating paragraphs by using space.

Think of the blank page as alpine me
or as the purity of undifferentiated b
The typographer enters this space an
change it. The reader will enter it lat

The underlying truth of the blank pa
but it must never altogether disapp
ever displaces it might well aim to be
is. It is not enough, when building a t

Using a half-measure of leading to follow a paragraph is another way of separating paragraphs.

Think of the blank page as alpin
or as the purity of undiffer
The typographer enters thi
change it. The reader will

The underlying truth of the blan
infringed, but it must nev
disappear—and whatever di
well aim to be as lively and

The hanging indent of starting lines of paragraphs in this example creates a beautiful, as well as informational, detail that will influence the structure of the page, requiring larger gutter spaces between columns.

Think of the blank page
as alpin
or as the purity of undifferentiated b
The typographer enters this space an
change it. The reader will enter it lat
see what the typographer has done. T
underlying truth of the blank page m
infringed, but it must never altoget

Shown here is an interesting approach in which the first few words of the paragraph are shifted above the baseline and set in a style that contrasts with the text.

FACTSET

To enhance your investment performance, you need an information resource that's more than the sum of its parts. Many services offer a wide array of databases. But only the FactSet online service offers you the tools to integrate this global information totally and seamlessly, turning raw data from more than 50 different databases into usable, actionable investment intelligence.

FactSet has been helping institutional investors make information meaningful since 1978. Our proprietary software is the result of over 15 years of dialogue between FactSet and thousands of FactSet clients—from investment bankers to research analysts to portfolio managers. Using FactSet software, you can easily cull information from multiple databases into a single report. Or set up multi-database screening systems. Or integrate your own proprietary data into our system. In short, you can custom-tailor vast amounts of financial data to meet your personal information needs 24 hours a day, 365 days a year.

To learn more about how you can integrate a world of investment information, and turn financial information into financial intelligence, please call Philip Hadley at 203.863.1500.

Visit us on the World Wide Web at
http://www.factset.com

THE BEGINNING OF each paragraph, in addition to a proportional return, is indicated by a bold lead line.

C+G Partners *United States*

Separating Paragraphs As recently as the fifteenth century, text was set continuously without breaks; the definition of the paragraph as an informational nugget emerged in the 1500s as a way of helping readers navigate text. Initially, a paragraph change was indicated by a larger space after the period following the last sentence of one paragraph; a later evolution introduced graphic elements, such as squares or bullets, as paragraph separators—but still there was no break in the text, such as a line return. ■ Eventually, columns were set with a line return, but without space between paragraphs; instead, the beginning of a new paragraph was indicated by an indent—where the first line of a new paragraph starts a few character-widths in from the left alignment. This treatment works particularly well in justified setting. The depth of the indent is subjective but must be noticeable. The indent must be deeper if the leading is loose; more interline space normalizes the perception of the column's width and a bigger "hole" must be cut into the paragraph. ■ Sometimes a designer will exaggerate the indent for visual effect. If the paragraphs are long and set in relatively wide columns, this treatment often will help to break up the wall of text by introducing a rhythm of cuts into the columns. Indents are usually not a great idea if the text is set ragged right. Since the rag is already changing the line lengths on the right edge of the column, the indent on the left side loses some of its visual power, appearing somewhat sloppy or causing the top lines of the columns to appear as though they are changing alignment.

Erhard Juritsch
Vorstand des Kärntner Wirtschaftsförderungs Fonds und Geschäftsführer der Lakeside Science & Technology Park GmbH

» Damit Menschen maximal produktiv sind, braucht es Räume für Zusammenarbeit, Räume, in denen schnelle, informelle Entscheidungen getroffen werden können. Denn ich glaube nicht, dass der einzelne Programmierer in seiner Wohnung die gleiche Dynamik entwickelt wie zwanzig Kollegen, die sich in einem Team gegenseitig anstecken. «

Sechs neue Professuren
Für einen technischen Fachbereich – der sich inhaltlich an Themen der technischen Informatik und den damit verbundenen Technologien orientiert – werden an der Universität Klagenfurt in den nächsten Jahren sechs Lehrstühle neu geschaffen: Mobile Systeme, Verkehrsinformatik, Embedded Systems, Pervasive Computing, Media Engineering und Servicerobotik.

Fachhochschule Kärnten
Fünfzehn Studiengänge an vier Fachhochschulstandorten (Spittal an der Drau, Villach, Klagenfurt und Feldkirchen) bieten maßgeschneiderte akademische Berufsausbildungen. Im Bereich Informationstechnologie & Elektronik umfasst das Angebot Telematik | Netzwerktechnik, Communication Engineering for IT, Medizinische Informationstechnik, Health Care IT, Elektronik, Integrated Systems and Circuit Design, Equipment Engineering, Geoinformation und Elektronik berufsbegleitend.

Lakeside
PARK

BOLD SUBHEADS WITH a slight indent, along with a proportional return, distinguish the paragraphs within the columns of this layout.

Clemens Théobert Schedler
Austria

M

mother often asks 'Why don't you take photographs of normal things?'

And it has taken me some time to realise that's exactly what I do – as a photographer, I document everyday life. I attempt to find extraordinary beauty and interest in everyday objects, my camera allows me to uncover the stories/messages these objects possess.

Recently this desire has seen me documenting councils' Hard Waste collections. I have become increasingly interested in documenting individual remnants of everyday life, particularly people's discarded mattresses. These objects bear the traces of intensive use, they show the imprints and marks of the life in which they had a function. They are individually stained with their owners' sweat and urine, each mattress has its own unique signature that distinguishes it from any other mattress.

Along with these objects are the intensely personal words from their previous owners. This is what intrigues me, these records of everyday living.

This is about more than the aestheticisation of waste, it questions our awareness of environmental issues and challenges our obsessive consumerism. It's about infinitely more than just waste.

I hope this work persuades you to question our obsessive nature as humans, and tempts you to engage in voyeuristic behaviour.

Toby Richardson
Lecturer of Photography
South Australian School of Art

A PROPORTIONAL RETURN separates the paragraphs in the text column.

Voice *Australia*

OK, Now Deal With It: The Finer Points of Text Typography Very little attention is paid to the crafting of type beyond composition and style. The tiny details of text setting are equally, if not more, important to ensure smooth reading and grammatical correctness, and are often overlooked. Knowing these fundamental rules for clean text setting keeps the designer alert to potential spacing problems and helps improve the look and readability of running text.

"Hey!" Dad's
“Hey!” Dad’s

HEY! YEAH, YOU! USE THE RIGHT MARKS! There is no quicker giveaway that the designer of a text is a total amateur than the use of prime marks (or “hatch marks” as they’re sometimes called) in place of the punctuation that’s supposed to be there. Prime marks are used to indicate foot and inch measures. The most egregious error—and, oddly, the most ubiquitous—is the substitution of a prime mark for an apostrophe. Just don’t do it. Second in line: substituting prime marks for quotation marks. There are two versions of quotation marks: an open quote and a closed quote. One is used to indicate the beginning of a quotation (the ones called “66” because of their shape), and the other is used to end a quotation (the ones called “99”). Please use accordingly.

ize; however these
ize ; however these
you say? That’s pr
you say ? That’s pr

PUSH AND PULL. Colons and semicolons need additional space preceding them and less space following them. Exclamation points and question marks often benefit from being separated from their sentences by an extra bit of space. A full word space is too much, as is half a word space; but 20/100 of an em (set-em), or +20 tracking, is usually sufficient.

in the year 1254 before moving on to
in the year 1254 before moving on to
in the year 1254 before moving on t
in the year 1254 before moving on t

10,336.00 10,336.00
135.36 135.36

LOOK AT THE FIGURES. Numerals always need spacing adjustments, especially in sequences. Lining numerals, which extend from baseline to cap height, usually require extra letter space, even though they’re more varied in form than uppercase letters. Numerals in complex arrangements, such as tables, are generally tabulated—arranged flush right or around a decimal point in vertical arrangements of figures. In such situations, the lining figures are preferred to ensure vertical alignment for making calculations.

(f) [f] {f} *(f) [f] {f}*
(f) [f] {f} *(f) [f] {f}*

AVOID A SERIOUS CRASH. The content within parentheses and brackets usually will benefit from additional space to separate it from these marks, especially italic forms with ascenders that are likely to crash into the marks if left at the default spacing. In particular, lowercase italic f, l, k, h, and many of the uppercase letters will need this adjustment.

(by listening to the sea) will c
determined, and thought it
“Think carefully,” he said, ag
foremost a kind of singular

- Optional leather seats and dash board
- Five-speed transmission
- ABS breaking system with titatnium discs
- Power steering and automatic mirrors

HANG YOUR PUNCTUATION. Most punctuation marks—especially quotations—should hang outside the aligned text if they occur at the beginning of a line. This rule sometimes applies to bullets as well; a designer might opt to maintain the alignment of the bulleted text and hang the bullets in the margin or gutter.

as Thoreau² said, the

arently CH_2O_3 will ca

FIND A FORMULA FOR SUPERS AND SUBS. The size and spacing of subscript and superscript characters, which are used to indicate footnotes or in chemical formulas, must be determined in relation to a given font size and the leading within paragraphs. Typically, the subscript or superscript character is just shy of the x-height in size, although, in an oldstyle face with a small x-height, this measure might prove too small. The subscript character should be set shifted below the baseline so that it rests on the descent line but does not extend upward to the mean-line; a superscript character should hang from the cap-line and rest marginally below the mean-line. In terms of letter spacing, the subscript or superscript character should be set to follow the same optical rhythm of the surrounding characters. With an uppercase A, a following superscript character might benefit from being tucked a little closer to compensate for the A's inward diagonal thrust and therefore, intrusive counterspace.

the final chap

the final cha

the final ch

A CLUE TO OPTIMAL: THE LIGATURES. Ligatures—specially drawn characters that optically correct for spacing difficulties in particular combinations of letters—provide a clue to the optimal spacing of a given font. Since ligatures are drawn with a fixed space between the characters (for example, an "fi"), a designer can assume that the font's creator determined this fixed space as optimal for the ligated pair based on his or her appraisal of what optimal spacing for the entire font should be. If the ligatures within running text appear more tightly—or more loosely—spaced than the non-fixed characters around them, it means either the font either needs to be re-spaced accordingly or the designer needs to replace the ligature with the two independent characters instead.

ina@rockpub.com

ina@rockpub.com

earing and/or verti

earing and/or verti

SO IT'S NOT A LETTER. The appearance of analphabetic symbols, such as the @, #, $, and %, and some linear punctuation marks, such as the forward slash "/," are improved by slight spatial adjustments. The @ usually appears too high on the line; a slight shift below the baseline causes the character to center optically on the line of text. The # and % display a diagonal thrust akin to italic forms, and decreasing the space preceding them—but increasing the space following them—helps them participate in the overall rhythm of the letter spaces and word spaces. The "/" tends to benefit from additional space on either side, although a full word space is far too much; +20 to +30 tracking is comfortable.

The new AIGA building

The new AIGA building

The new AIGA building

UH-OH ... SMALL CAPS! Small caps used for acronyms, although smaller than uppercase letters, still need additional space around them to improve their recognition. The small caps of many fonts are too small and appear lighter in weight than surrounding text. Adjust their point size up by as much as a point or two to achieve uniform weight and spacing, but not so much as to confuse them with the uppercase.

erview Terrace • Luna Park, New Jerse

erview Terrace • Luna Park, New Jerse

erview Terrace • Luna Park, New Jerse

erview Terrace • Luna Park, New Jerse

erview Terrace • Luna Park, New Jerse

STYLE YOUR BULLETS. The default bullet is usually enormous and distracting compared to the typeface in which it appears. The bullet needs to be noticeable but not stick out; slightly heavier than the text's vertical stroke weight is enough. Feel free to change the bullet's typeface—or use a dingbat or even a period, shifted off the baseline—to bring it stylistically closer to the surrounding text.

122 Interview

www.borsellino.net

Piero Borsellino wird 1975 als Sohn sizilianischer Eltern in Frankfurt geboren. Mit 14 beginnt er sich sein Taschengeld mit dem Organisieren von Parties, dem Schreiben von Sponsoring Konzepten für Markenartikler sowie dem Entwerfen von Logos zu verdienen. Mit 16 macht er sich selbständig, wechselt jedoch mit 17 zur PR Agentur Leipziger & Partner und wird mit 18 Art Director der Plattenfirma des damaligen Nano und Bodesol Managers. Mit 21 gründet er sein eigenes Designbüro und arbeitet fortan für Kunden aus Musik, Mode und Kultur. 1999 gründet er sein erstes Modemagazin. 2001 folgt sein zweites Magazin namens T4X, welches 2002 in M Publication umbenannt wird. Für sein Design – zuvor für Kunden als auch aktuell für M – erhielt er mehrfach Auszeichnungen.

10.2/Piero Borsellino

Sex, Drugs and Rock'n'Roll.

01 \5 **Was gefällt dir an deinem Beruf?**
Sex, Drugs and Rock'n'Roll: Seine eigenen Ideen zu entwickeln und umzusetzen ist wie ein Orgasmus, ein süchtigmachender Rausch und ein gutes Konzert zugleich. Wer das nicht verspürt, sollte den Beruf wechseln.

02 \5 **Wer waren bzw. sind deine Vorbilder?**
Früher: Adriano Celentano, heute: Renzo Rosso (Diesel Chef).

03 \5 **Machst du freie Projekte?**
Freie Projekte? Hört sich absurd an. Auch wenn ich weiss was mit der Frage beabsichtigt ist, wundere ich mich über diese Bezeichnung. Kreative schaffen sich sogenannte "freelance projects", damit sie ganz ohne Vorgaben und Kundenwünsche Schalten und Walten können – sich „selbst-verwirklichen" können. Hört sich sehr arty an. Und vor allem so, als würden sie in der anderen Zeit nur "unfreie" Projekte verwirklichen. Was bin ich Dienstleister oder Künstler? Das zeigt, dass die kreativen Berufe, sei es Designer, Photograph, Illustrator, Texter oder Regisseur, immer nach größtmöglicher Freiheit (ja einem "Director's Cut") heischen. Der Idealfall: Versuchen Kunden zu finden, die von einem den Director's Cut und nicht das Gegenteil verlangen. Wie war noch mal die Frage? Aaah, ja ich mache freie Projekte!

04 \5 **Was sind Computer für dich?**
Moderne Mittel zum Zweck.

05 \5 **Mit was spielst du?**
Mit dem Feuer.

06 \5 **Wie bringst du Familie, Freizeit und Beruf unter einen Hut?**
Momentan in der genau umgekehrten Reihenfolge: Erst der Beruf, dann die Freizeit und dann die Familie. Kann sein, dass sich die Reihenfolge in einigen Jahren ändert. Und zwar wenn ich Papa werde.

07 \5 **Was magst du an deinen Arbeiten, was nicht?**
Die Freude ist meistens nur von kurzer Dauer, weil ich mit getaner Arbeit das Kapitel beendet habe. Umso mehr freue ich mich über Arbeiten, die noch nach Jahren wirken.

08 \5 **Dein Lieblingsfluch?**
Minghia! (Sizilianisch für "Schwanz", wie Fuck!).

09 \5 **Was machst du nachdem du aufgestanden bist?**
Meistens urinieren.

10 \5 **Empfehle drei Feinde:**
Die Ablenkung, den Perfektionismus und die Müdigkeit. Alle drei Kosten Zeit. Dies fordert wiederum die Disziplin.

11 \5 **Wo würdest du gerne leben, wo arbeiten?**
Beides in New York, Sizilien oder in der Renaissance.

12 \5 **Design und Politik – ist das ein Thema für dich?**
Nicht direkt. Beides ist abstrahiert gesehen ein Gestaltungsprozess. Gute Gestaltung gibt eine Richtung vor. Leitet die Massen. Dies wiederum verleiht Macht. Manifestiert eine Aussage. Kommt nur, wie immer, darauf an, welche Interessen(gemeinschaften) sich dahinter verbergen.

13 \5 **Wiedergeboren werden als?**
Wind. Mal ist man da, mal nicht. Mal stärker, mal schwächer.

14 \5 **Was sammelst du?**
Erfahrungen aller Art.

15 \5 **Wie findest du Prince, Prince Charles, Charles Bronson?**
Überragender Geist, geisttötend, tötender Mundharmonikaspieler.

16 \5 **Was würdest du gerne erfinden?**
Das Glücksrezept.

17 \5 **Wobei kannst du am besten entspannen?**
In der Sauna und beim Sex.

18 \5 **Die größte Revolution war/ist:**
Der Mikrochip.

19 \5 **Wen würdest du gerne einmal treffen?**
Denjenigen, dessen Idee "Adam & Eva" war.

20 \5 **Dein Lieblings-Buchstabe in deiner Lieblings-Schrift?** *Mir gefällt das grosse "S" in der Akzidenz Grotesk Black ganz gut.*

\5.30.06.THEMEN ..... Schriften\DigiBo Text\Monopoint\Gringo Tuscon\Copy

THE DESIGNER OF this page has carefully considered the editorial and visual qualities of the text components. List numbers hang outside the columns to maintain the clarity of alignment; the title is distinguished by its italic setting; callouts are pronounced in a bolder weight; and each different kind of text content is given a distinct stylistic treatment.

Finest Magna *Germany*

THE TEXT AND TABULAR data in this spread from a financial report have been carefully and clearly styled to impart a sense of credibility and attention to detail, appropriate to the sober, accurate nature of the material. Clear hanging indents, comfortable spacing for figures, and easily distinguished alignments all contribute to the report's exquisite craftsmanship.

UNA (Amsterdam) Designers
Netherlands

6 VAN LANSCHOT INVESTMENT FUNDS NV

Bedragen in duizenden euro's

Van Lanschot Investment Funds NV (Totaal)	2005	2004	2003	2002	2001
Resultaten					
Som der bedrijfsopbrengsten	29.290	21.773	13.968	– 59.267	– 83.661
Som der bedrijfslasten	3.271	3.236	2.410	1.678	3.620
Resultaat	26.019	18.537	11.558	– 60.945	– 87.281
Balansgegevens, ultimo boekjaar					
Financiële beleggingen	286.874	304.760	305.238	85.483	16.525
Vorderingen en overige activa	6.150	9.279	6.575	2.879	11.670
Eigen vermogen	292.846	313.878	311.655	88.235	179.075
Kortlopende schulden	178	161	158	127	120
Per aandeel van € 1,– nominaal, ultimo boekjaar					
Beurskoers (x € 1)	n.v.t.	n.v.t.	n.v.t.	n.v.t.	n.v.t.
Intrinsieke waarde (inclusief dividend) (x € 1)	n.v.t.	n.v.t.	n.v.t.	n.v.t.	n.v.t.
Dividend over boekjaar (x € 1)	n.v.t.	n.v.t.	n.v.t.	n.v.t.	n.v.t.
Aantal uitstaande gewone aandelen	7.878.446	9.421.697	10.274.914	6.642.644	7.924.894

De in de kerngegevens opgenomen resultaten zijn inclusief waardeveranderingen van beleggingen en exclusief de (variabele) kosten van uitgifte van aandelen conform de in het boekjaar 2003 gewijzigde grondslagen voor resultaatbepaling. Voor wat betreft de (variabele) kosten van uitgifte van aandelen zijn de kerncijfers voor 2001 niet herrekend.

7

Structuur

Algemene informatie

Van Lanschot Investment Funds NV is een beleggingsmaatschappij met veranderlijk kapitaal. De vennootschap is opgezet volgens een zogenaamde paraplu-structuur. Dit betekent dat het gewone aandelenkapitaal is verdeeld in verschillende series van gewone aandelen, Fondsen genaamd, waarin het vermogen van de beleggingsmaatschappij is belichaamd. De Fondsen als zodanig hebben geen rechtskarakter; zij vallen onder één en dezelfde rechtspersoon: Van Lanschot Investment Funds NV. Het geplaatste kapitaal van iedere serie vormt een Fonds, met een eigen beleggingsbeleid, risicoprofiel en koersvorming. Ook de administratie van elk Fonds is gescheiden door het gebruik van separate rekeningen. Het op een afzonderlijke serie (Fonds) gestort kapitaal wordt afzonderlijk belegd. Zowel de kosten als de opbrengsten worden per Fonds afzonderlijk verantwoord. Waardestijgingen en waardedalingen in de portefeuille van een Fonds komen uitsluitend ten goede aan of ten laste van de houders van de desbetreffende serie. Hoewel sprake is van (administratief) afgescheiden vermogens blijven de Fondsen in juridische zin deel uitmaken van Van Lanschot Investment Funds NV.

Binnen Van Lanschot Investment Funds NV bestaan per 31 december 2005 vier van dergelijke Fondsen, te weten:

Fonds A	Van Lanschot Dutch Equity Fund;
Fonds C	Van Lanschot Far East Equity Fund;
Fonds D	Van Lanschot ICT Fund;
Fonds E	Van Lanschot Euro Credit Fund.

De verschillende Fondsen hebben, zoals gezegd, alle ook hun eigen aspecten van het beleggingsbeleid, welke onder 'Kenschetsen afzonderlijke Fondsen' nader worden toegelicht.

Verhandelbaarheid

De afzonderlijke Fondsen zijn aan de effectenbeurs van Euronext Amsterdam NV genoteerde beleggingsinstellingen met een (semi) open-end structuur. De beurskoers volgt de intrinsieke waarde van de aandelen binnen nauwe grenzen. Behoudens wettelijke bepalingen en uitzonderlijke situaties is de directie met inachtneming van het navolgende verplicht aandelen af te geven en in te kopen. Deze afgifte en inkoop geschieden uitsluitend via

	Aankoop	*Verkoop*	*Maximale spread*
Fonds A	+ 0,50%	– 0,50%	0,70%
Fonds C	+ 0,75%	– 0,50%	1,25%
Fonds D	+ 0,50%	– 0,50%	1,00%
Fonds E	+ 0,50%	– 0,50%	0,50%

F. van Lanschot Bankiers NV, waarmee een contractuele verbintenis is aangegaan als liquiditeitsverschaffer in de aandelen van de afzonderlijke Fondsen. Met deze verbintenis wordt, voor zover mogelijk binnen het handelssysteem van Euronext Amsterdam, bewerkstelligd dat interventie in de markt door inkoop of uitgifte zodanig plaatsvindt dat de prijs inclusief kosten van de aandelen op de effectenbeurs van Euronext Amsterdam zich in principe steeds beweegt tussen intrinsieke waarde plus of min een maximaal bepaalde bandbreedte. Onderstaand wordt een actueel overzicht van de gehanteerde spreads ten opzichte van de intrinsieke waarde bij aan- en verkoop van aandelen voor de diverse Fondsen weergegeven.

In het algemeen zal een deel van de gehanteerde op- en afslagen ten goede komen aan de liquiditeitsverschaffer en een deel aan het Fonds (met uitzondering van Fonds E, Van Lanschot Euro Credit Fund, 0,1%) ter dekking van transactiekosten bij de belegging van verkregen middelen dan wel bij de verkoop van bestaande beleggingen. Onder omstandigheden kan besloten worden de inkoop van aandelen op te schorten.

Risicoprofiel

Aan een belegging in een van de Fondsen zijn risico's verbonden, welke in het algemeen gepaard gaan met het beleggen in aandelen en/of obligaties. De koersvorming van aandelen wordt beïnvloed door de resultaten van de individuele ondernemingen waarin belegd wordt, de verwachtingen hieromtrent en het beursklimaat in het algemeen. Het beleggen op basis van een thema brengt specifieke risico's met zich mee. Voor obligaties is de waarde-ontwikkeling in de eerste plaats afhankelijk van de ontwikkeling van de kapitaalmarktrente. In de tweede plaats is aan een belegging in obligaties debiteurenrisico verbonden. Verder bestaat er, indien van toepassing, het risico van valutaschommelingen. Voor een uitgebreide risicoparagraaf en het door de directie van de vennoot-

dolor sit amet, consetetur sadipscing.

Elitr, sed diam nonumy eirmod tempor invidunt ut labore et dolore magna aliquyam erat, sediam volu ptua. At vero eos et accusam et justo duo dolores et ea rebum. Stet clita kasd gubergren, no sea takim ata sanctus est Lorem ipsum dolor sit amet. Lorem ipsum dolor sit amet, consetetur sadipscing elitr, sed diam nonumy eirmod tempor invidunt ut labo re et dolore magna aliquyam erat.

At vero eos et accusam et justo duo dolores et ea rebum. Stet clita kasd gubergren, no sea takim ata sanctus est Lorem ipsum dolor sit amet. Lorem ipsum dolor sit amet, consetetur sadipscing elitr,

Lorem ipsum
elitr, sed diar
labore et dolo
ptua. At vero
ea rebum. St
ata sanctus e
ipsum dolors
sed diam nor
re et dolore n
duo dolores e
no sea takim
amet. Lorem
sadipscing el
invidunt ut la

SAVE THE ORPHANS. Don't allow the last line of a paragraph to begin the top of a column. This "orphan" is especially distracting if there is a space separating the paragraph that follows and really irritating if it occurs at the very beginning of the left-hand page. Run the text back so that the new page starts a paragraph, or space out the preceding text so that the paragraph continues with at least three lines after the page break.

whenever possible. A special

whenever possible. A special

not always, however, because

not always, however, because

MIND THE GAPS. A single word space, never two, follows a period before the initial cap of the next sentence. Furthermore, the space before a comma or a quotation mark should be reduced; these marks "carry" additional space above or below them. Similarly, the word space following a comma, apostrophe, or quotation mark should also be slightly reduced.

in-depth look

Hyphen Combines words or breaks them between lines.

100–200 pages
6:00–9:00pm

En-Dash Separates ranges of figures or durations in time

beware—it is the

Em-Dash Separates evolutionary phrases within text.

KNOW YOUR DASHES. There are three horizontal punctuation lines—the hyphen, the en dash, and the em dash. Use the correct one for its intended function, and adjust the spaces around them so that they flow optically within text. A full word space on either side is too much, although there are times when this might be appropriate. The default lengths and baseline orientation of each mark might need to be altered to improve their relationship to surrounding text; the hyphen often sits low, and the em dash is sometimes too long.

The Page Begins Here

A New Sequence Begins

TO INDENT OR NOT TO INDENT? In setting text in which paragraphs run together, separated by indenting the first line, the first paragraph on the page should have no indent. Every paragraph thereafter is then indented—until the next major sequential break or subheaded paragraph, which should not be indented.

When the editor and designer pay careful attention, bad
line-breaking will be radically reduced. It's always best
to break a word to leave a desirable syllable of four letters.

will be presided over by Ellen Mac-
Murray and her partner, Roberto M.
Castiglioni, along with Joy Adams.

WATCH THE BREAKS! Avoid breaking words across lines (hyphenating) so that short or incomplete stubs begin the line following: -ed, -er, -ing, -tion, -al, -ly. Make sure there are at least four letters in the word ending the line before the break. Try to avoid breaking names from one line to another. If absolutely necessary, however, break right before the last name—never in the middle of a name and never before an initial.

DUIS AUTEM VEL eumriure dolorame in hendrerit in vulputate velit esseracl molestie consequat, vel illum dolore eu feugiat nulla facilisis at vero eros et accu san et iusto odio dignissiquit blandit praesenta luptatum zzril delenit augue duis do.

Nalora ipsum dolor sitamet, consetetur sadipscing elitr, sed diam nonumy eirmo tempor invidunt ut labore et doloret magna aliquyam erat sediam volup tua. At vero eos et accusam et justivi duo dolores et ea rebum. Stet clita kasd gubergren, no sea takimata san ctus est Lorem ipsum dolor sit ame. Lorem ipsum dolor sitamet, consec tetur sadipscing elitr diam nonumy

LOREM IPSUM DOLOR sit amet, consec tetur sadipscing elitr, sed diam non my eirmod tempor invidunt ut labore et dolore magna aliquyam eratse dia volu ptua. At vero eos et accusam et justo duo dolores et ea rebum. Steclita kasd gubergren, no sea takimata san ctus est Lorem ipsum dolora sit amet. Lorem ipsum dolor sit amet, consec etur sadipscing elitr diam nonum sui eirmod tempor invidunt ea reabum

Subheading

INCLUDE WITH CLARITY. Text inclusions, such as drop caps, lead lines, and subheads, should exhibit some clear logic in their appearance. Drop caps should sit on a baseline three, four, five, or more lines from the top of the column. A lead line should be a consistent number of words in the first line or, alternatively, used to treat complete introductory phrases in a consistent way. A subhead, when appearing at the top of one column, should be consistently aligned with the text in columns preceding or following—optically.

DON'T CROSS THE CHANNELS. When possible, avoid hard returns between paragraphs aligning (or nearly aligning) between adjacent columns. As the horizontal negative channels created by the returns approach each other, not only do they become distracting, but they also tend to redirect the eye across the columns and break reading sequence.

nost *delicious* cakes fo

nost *delicious* cakes f

ITALIC TYPE NEEDS SPACING, TOO. Italic used for emphasis within text sometimes appears smaller and tighter than its roman counterpart. Always evaluate the italic and adjust its size or spacing to fit most seamlessly with its surrounding text.

Think of the blank page as alpine meadow, or as the purity of undifferentiated being. The typographer enters this space and must change it. The reader will enter it later, to see what the typographer has done. The underlying truth of the blank page must be infringed, but it must never altogether disappear—and whatever displaces it might well aim to be as lively and peaceful as it is. It is not enough, when building

TOO MUCH IS JUST TOO MUCH. In justified setting, adjusting the letter spacing to avoid rivers is inevitable, but don't adjust too much. Like rivers, overly tight—and therefore very dark—lines of text are distracting.

whenever she seems ti
period (let's face it) org

whenever she seems ti
period (*let's face it*) *org*

KEEP 'EM UPRIGHT. Use upright parentheses and brackets, even if the text in which they appear is italic. These marks, in their sloped versions, appear weak and usually exacerbate the spacing problems associated with them.

and whatever displaces it might well aim to be as lively and peaceful as it is. It is not enough, when building a title page, merely to unload some big, prefabricated letters into the center of the space, nor to dig a few holes in the silence with typographic heavy machinery and move on. Big type, even huge type, can be beautiful and useful.

CARE FOR THE WIDOWS. Never allow a single word (a widow) to end a paragraph. If widows constantly appear in the rough setting of a body of text, the column width should be adjusted. Ideally, the last line of a paragraph should be more than half the paragraph's width, but three words (no matter their length) are acceptable.

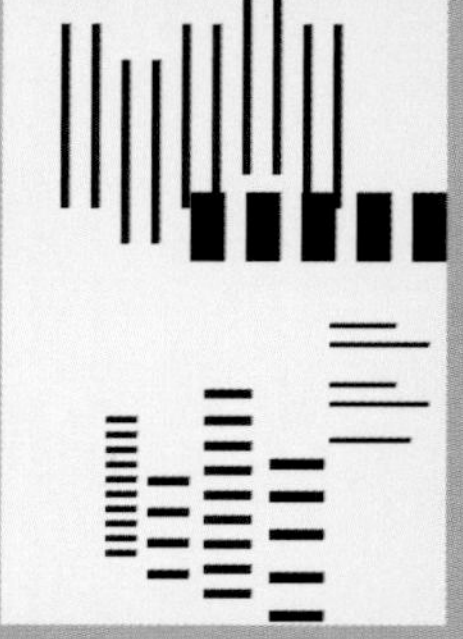

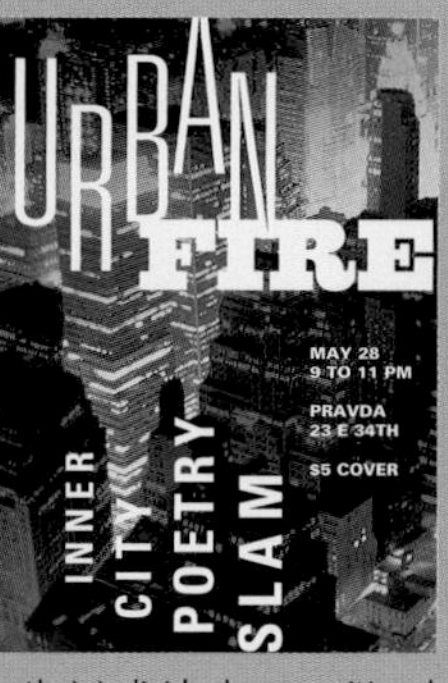

The visual quality of type is recognizable when it's further abstracted into its base components: dots, lines, planes, and masses. The freedom that simplicity implies—the liberty to move type around as freely as one might move the lines of a drawing around—becomes even more dramatic in the example in which type is related to image: see how each pictorial element and each type element plays off the other, responding to their individual compositional qualities. The type isn't on top of the layout or next to the picture. The picture and the type take on the same value.

The new time sense
of typographic man
is cinematic, sequential,
pictorial.

Marshal McLuhan
The Medium is the Massage
Publisher Name, 1967

THE NEW TIME SENSE
OF TYPOGRAPHIC MAN

Marshal McLuhan *The Medium is the Massage* Publisher Name, 1967

IS CINEMATIC
SEQUEN
TIAL
AND **PICTORIAL**

The same text information is treated differently in each composition—first, in a static and relatively neutral way, without much color; and second, with great variation in letter spacing, line spacing, width, size, and weight. Note how the negative spaces created by the type participate in the composition—some engaged as active players in the type treatments themselves, and others creating a proportional counterpoint to the type's rhythm and texture.

Structure and Optics
Issues Related to Style
Mechanics of Text
Texture and Space
Type as Information
How Color Changes Type

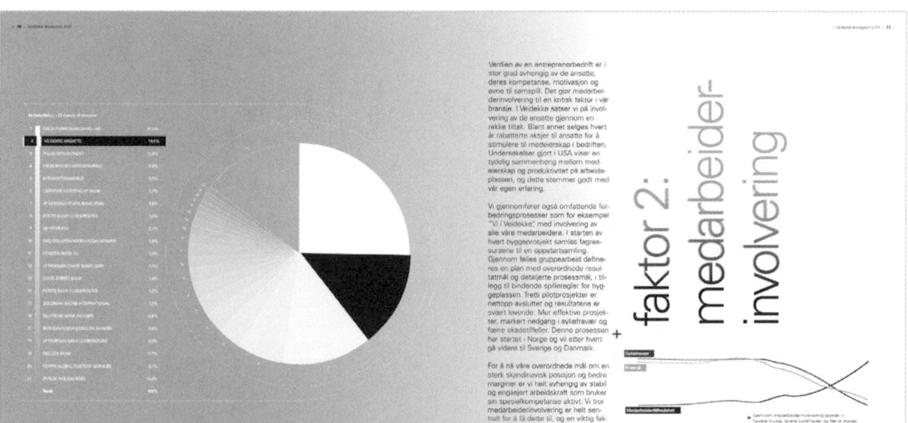

EVERY TYPE ELEMENT in this page spread participates in visually resolving the composition and activating space. The size of the dot-like chart weights it in relation to the texture of the column and the vertical motion of the large, rotated headline; the rhythm of positive and negative from left to right uses repetitions of specific intervals; and the type elements have a decisive up-and-down motion relative to each other.

Cobra *Norway*

Type Is Visual, Too Design students and novices often make the mistake of ignoring the abstract visual nature of type and, as a result, use type in a heavy-handed way that doesn't correspond with image material—in effect, separating the two things completely. Type is visual; in space, it acts the same way that dots, lines, squares, fields of texture, and patterns do in any composition. ■ Recognizing this truth about type, understanding it and feeling it intuitively, gives the designer a tremendous advantage in being able to make type and pictures become equal players.

Typographic Color In addition to how type is placed within a format, its rhythmic, spatial, and textural qualities are important considerations. The term for these qualities, as a whole, is "typographic color." Typographic color is similar to chromatic color—like red, blue, or orange—but deals only with changes in lightness and darkness, or value. ■ Moreover, it is different from the qualities of chromatic color in that it describes changes in rhythm and texture. Changing the typographic color of typographic components separates them from the surface and introduces the illusion of spatial depth and a sense of changing rhythm. A larger chunk of type, for example, appears closer than a smaller one, while a lighter element appears to recede into the distance. A texture appears to flatten out because perception of its shape and uniform value determine its spatial depth more so than its components. A line appears to come forward regardless of its weight, although a heavier line comes farther forward than a narrow line.

ABOUT THE CAMPAIGN | EVENTS | PARTNERS | PRESS ROOM | TAKE ACTION

ONE.

THE ONE CAMPAIGN IS A NEW EFFORT TO RALLY AMERICANS TO FIGHT THE EMERGENCY OF GLOBAL AIDS AND EXTREME POVERTY. THROUGH THE ONE CAMPAIGN, EACH ONE OF US CAN MAKE A DIFFERENCE. TOGETHER AS ONE WE CAN CHANGE THE WORLD.

SIMPLY SIGN UP TO ADD YOUR VOICE TO SUPPORT THE ONE CAMPAIGN DECLARATION. YOU WILL JOIN THE GROWING NUMBER OF AMERICANS WHO ARE GETTING INVOLVED ONLINE AND IN COMMUNITIES ACROSS THE COUNTRY.

SEE THE VIDEO HERE

ADD YOUR SIGNATURE TO THE ONE DECLARATION

FIRST NAME | LAST NAME
ZIP/POSTAL CODE
EMAIL ADDRESS
COUNTRY
HOW DID YOU HEAR ABOUT THE ONE CAMPAIGN? SELECT ONE

THE CAMPAIGN TO MAKE POVERTY HISTORY. SUBMIT

WE BELIEVE THAT IN THE BEST AMERICAN TRADITION OF HELPING OTHERS HELP THEMSELVES, NOW IS THE TIME TO JOIN WITH OTHER COUNTRIES IN A HISTORIC PACT FOR COMPASSION AND JUSTICE TO HELP THE POOREST PEOPLE OF THE WORLD OVERCOME AIDS AND EXTREME POVERTY.

WE RECOGNIZE THAT A PACT INCLUDING SUCH MEASURES AS FAIR TRADE, DEBT RELIEF, FIGHTING CORRUPTION AND DIRECTING AN ADDITIONAL ONE PERCENT OF THE U.S. BUDGET TOWARD MEETING BASIC NEEDS – EDUCATION, HEALTH, CLEAN WATER, FOOD, AND CARE FOR ORPHANS – WOULD TRANSFORM THE FUTURES AND HOPES OF AN ENTIRE GENERATION IN THE POOREST COUNTRIES.

WE COMMIT OURSELVES – ONE PERSON, ONE VOICE, ONE VOTE AT A TIME – TO MAKE A BETTER, SAFER WORLD

THIS WEB PAGE is typographically very colorful, even though it uses only black and tints of gray. The callout of the word "One," by setting it in solid black, reinforces the brand image and idea of singularity. The deeper density of the second paragraph makes the call to action more pronounced; secondary information is set smaller and in lighter tints of gray to help clarify the hierarchy.

Research Studios *United Kingdom*

ALTHOUGH ALL OF the typographic elements on this poster are printed in the same ink color, changes in size, weight, density, and spacing create what is considered a very "colorful" example of typographic composition.

Voice *Australia*

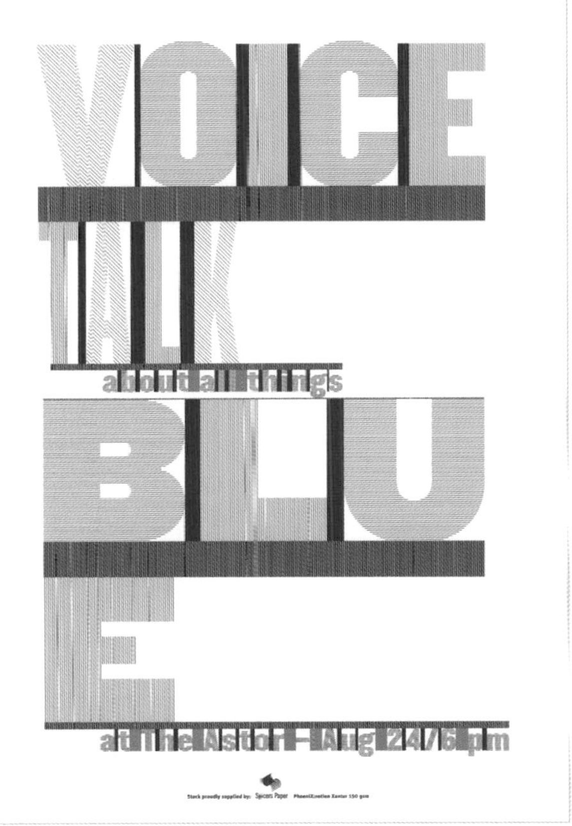

Because the continuous value of text has the potential to be overwhelming—creating a kind of gray "wall" that can be very daunting to look at (never mind dull and lifeless)—and because each specific thought, or informational component, within a text will benefit from a visual change, typographic color, composition, and verbal clarity are inseparable: a change of color automatically alters not only the spatial and textural quality of the type, but its meaning. A typographic color change allows a designer to highlight structure and invigorate a page.

THE DESIGNERS OF this foldout brochure use dramatic change in scale, spacing, and paragraph width to increase the textural activity of the type elements and their rhythmic up-and-down movement. The linearity and textural qualities of the text are a stark contrast to the giant image dots.

LSD *Spain*

THE CHANGING ALIGNMENTS of the paragraphs, along with small text details and complex negative spaces, creates a geometric and rhythmic color in this page from a book spread.

EarSay *United States*

DINU

"Communism with a human face." The Russians didn't like it, but after Czechoslovakia and Hungary, they didn't want another war. So Ceausescu opened things up for us enough to get passports.

Seen by the West as a "reformer," Nicholae Ceausescu was eventually toppled and murdered by a popular revolt in 1989. Among other crimes, he was accused of embezzling hundreds of millions of dollars from state coffers and overseeing the murder of thousands of his countrymen.

Marta and I met as music students and we both ended up assistant professors at the conservatory in Bucharest. After first semester, I said to Marta, "If we ever get a passport, I want to get out." And she said, "Yes." We were both bonkers to go. So we bit our tongues and joined the Communist Party to get our passports, but we still couldn't go anywhere other than Bulgaria, Hungary or Russia. Until one day in 1968, I saw

CHRISTINE

I thought hmm, what an interesting parallel. I'd put on a mask and all of a sudden borderline aspects of my personality would come out. Then I started researching what masks were all about — Venetian and Japanese and then the Romanian masks. Put on the old man mask or the goat or the demon elk and it's like we're reclaiming all the characters from Romanian folk heritage. And when we perform, each mask is tied into the songs. There are so many songs about goats and sheep and all the other mountain gods. I'm interested in how through these songs, ancient practices can be carried into the present. My father respects all my digging around in a scholarly way, but when it comes to actually putting it into practice, that's another thing. Looking at it as myths is fine — looking at it as an alternative reality is something very difficult for him because he is Greek Orthodox and my mom is Roman Catholic. Their religions are ritualistic, but in a very different way.

222

Scale, Weight, and Value

A

Jakarta
2 0 0 7
Indonesia
POST 75

B

Jakarta
2 0 0 7
Indonesia
POST 75

C

Jakarta
2 0 0 7
Indonesia
POST 75

D

Jakarta
2 0 0 7
Indonesia
POST 75

A Changes in size among type elements create differences in perceived density (larger forms are more open, smaller forms seem to cluster together more tightly)—as well as the perception of weight change within the composition, even though all the elements are the same, regular weight.

B The same size change strategy is enhanced by changing the weights of selected type elements as well.

C While the size of each element remains the same, the application of bold weight has been swapped among the various components to produce a different spatial effect.

D The same composition as **C,** but further changed using tints.

Interline Spacing (Leading)

A

Nam liber tempor cum soluta nc
bisar eleifend option congue nih
im perdieti domine id quod maz
imerti placerat facer possimsum
Loremipsum dolorsit amet cons
ectetuer adipiscing elit sed diam
nonum nibu reuismodi tincidunt
summa nunci et sem per dierae

B

Nam liber tempor cum soluta nc
bisar eleifend option congue nih
im perdieti domine id quod maz
imerti placerat facer possimsum
Loremipsum dolorsit amet cons
ectetuer adipiscing elit sed diam
nonum nibu reuismodi tincidunt

C

Nam liber tempor cum soluta nc
bisar eleifend option congue nih
im perdieti domine id quod maz
imerti placerat facer possimsum
Loremipsum dolorsit amet cons

D

Nam liber tempor cum solu ta
no bisar eleifend option cong
ue nihi ima perdieti domine ic
quod maz imerti placerat facei
pos asim sumte Loremipsum
dolorsit amet cons ectetue ad
piscing elit sed diame nonum
nibu rebar et uis odi tincidun

E

Nam liber tempor cum solu ta
no bisar eleifend option cong
ue nihi ima perdieti domine ic
quod maz imerti placerat facei
pos asim sumte Loremipsum
dolorsit amet cons ectetue ad
piscing elit sed diame nonum

F

Nam liber tempor cum solu ta
no bisar eleifend option cong
ue nihi ima perdieti domine ic
quod maz imerti placerat facei
pos asim sumte Loremipsum

A This example shows very tight leading; the space between lines appears the same as the spaces between words. The type is more texture than line, and appears optically the darkest of the examples.

B This example shows normal leading. Its texture and linearity are evenly balanced, and it appears lighter than the previous example, receding slightly in space.

C In this example of loose leading, linearity dominates; the text has the lightest value.

D, E, F The same treatments as above are repeated in bold weight.

Letterspacing

A

COMPRESSION

B

COMPRESSION

C

C O M
P R E S S
I O N

A Extremely tight spacing, and the resulting overlap of strokes, creates pronounced dark spots; the individuality of the letters is compromised in favor of overall linearity and mass.

B In normal spacing, the linearity of the word dominates the individuality of the letters, but the alternation of stroke and counter is more regular.

C Loose letter spacing causes the dot-like individuality of the letters to dominate.

Text Width

A

Lorem ipsum dolor sit amet, conetetur adipscing elit sed diam nonumy eirmod tempor invidunt ut labore et dolore magna aliquyam erat, sediam volup tua. At vero eos et accusam et justo duo dolores et. Stet clita kasd gubergren, no sea takimata sanctus est Lorem ipsum color sit amet.

B

Lorem ipsum dolor sit amet, consetetur sadipscing elitr, sed diam nonumeirmod tempor invidunt ut labore et dolore mag na aliquyam erat, sediam volup tua. At vero eos et accusam et justo duo dolores et ea rebum. Stet clita kasd gubergren, no sea takim ata sanctus est Lorem ipsum dolor sit amet. Diam nonum eirmod tem por invidunt ut labore et dolore magna aliquyam erat, sediam volup.

C

Lorem ipusum dolor sit amet, consetetur sadipscing elitar, sed diam nonum eirmo d tempor invidunt ut labore et dolore mag na aliquyam erat, se diam volup tua. Vero eos et accusam et jus to duo dolores et ea rebum. Stet clita kasd gubergren, no sea ta im ata sanctus. Lorem ipsum dolor sit amet.

A In a wide paragraph, horizontal emphasis, or movement, dominates the vertical.

B Although physically wider than deep, the optimal paragraph's width-to-depth ratio results in a type of comfortable stasis.

C In this deep, extremely narrow paragraph, the vertical emphasis dominates the horizontal. Consequently, the paragraph takes on a linear quality, as opposed to that of a mass.

Character Width and Weight

A

COMPRESSION

B

COMPRESSION
COMPRESSION

C

He ran **quickly,**
fast as he could —
but the distance
seemed to
stretch out
and he **could** not escape!

A The word, set all in a condensed face, contracts inward.

B The same word, now set in an extended face of the same weight, expands outward—and more so when set in a bold extended face.

C Dramatic compression and expansion in visual density (and enhanced communication!) are achieved by combining varying widths and weights of text within the same line.

The Texture of Language More than simply a tool for clarifying hierarchy, the variation of typographic texture–changes in boldness, size, linearity, texture, and rhythm–is an outgrowth of the way we speak or write… and the way we speak or write is a source for typographic color. Slowly spoken phrases contrast with sharp, abrupt outbursts. Long, contemplative soliloquies provide rest against erratic, fractured thoughts. ■ These qualities of spoken and written language can be made visual, not just to provide intriguing eye-candy, but to help an audience feel the author and the emotional import of his or her words. Changing sizes, weight, or posture within lines of running text, even within individual words, can make a dramatic, evocative statement without sacrificing clarity. It might even improve readability–the quality of and the degree to which the type engages its readers and leads them through the experience of the content. Bolding a subhead that begins a paragraph accomplishes this–making it seem louder and, therefore, a point of focus–but in an almost

Text excerpted from The Medium is the Massage *by Marshal McLuhan*

Our time
is a time for crossing barriers,
for erasing old categories—
for probing around.
When two seemingly disparate elements
are imaginatively poised,
put in apposition in new
and unique ways…
… startling
discoveries
often result.

Our time is a time for
crossing
barriers… for e r a s i n g
o l d c a t e g o r i e s —
for probing around.
When two seemingly disparate elements
a r e i m a g i n a t i v e l y p o i s e d ,
put in apposition
in new and unique ways…
startling discoveries
often result.

The text in these examples is powerfully altered by changing the typographic color of its internal parts. In the first version, a strategy of overall size change affects the sense of the text's loudness, creating a crescendo. In the second version, calling out specific parts through changes in weight, posture, width, and spacing produces a rhythmic journey—slowing down, speeding up—for the reader. In the third version, color changes are applied to distinguish linguistic and conceptual relationships among different

A

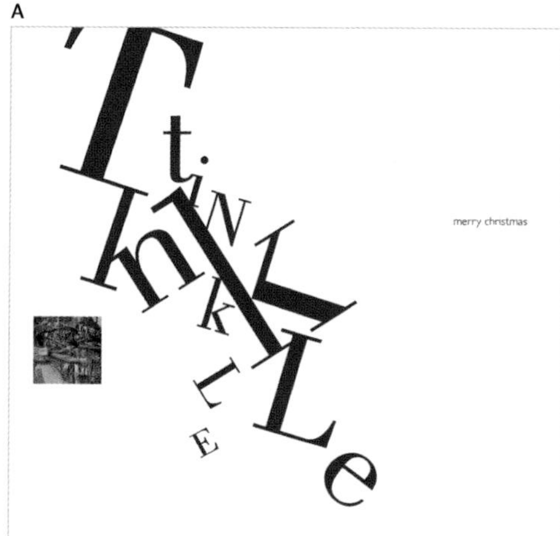

B

totally neutral, objective way. It's about giving the reader the chance to find something of interest or heightened importance. ■ But strategically approaching typographic material in a sensory way, giving it the visual quality of its sounds and cadence, is a powerful method designers can employ in creating a more vivid verbal experience.

Our time is **a time**
for crossing barriers,
for erasing old categories—
for probing around.

When two seemingly
disparate elements are imaginatively poised,
put in **apposition**
in new and unique ways,
startling discoveries
often result.

parts of the text; the result is rhythmically dynamic and supports the interrelationships of the author's ideas. This approach provides the added bonus of giving the reader a "snapshot" of the content before fully engaging the text.

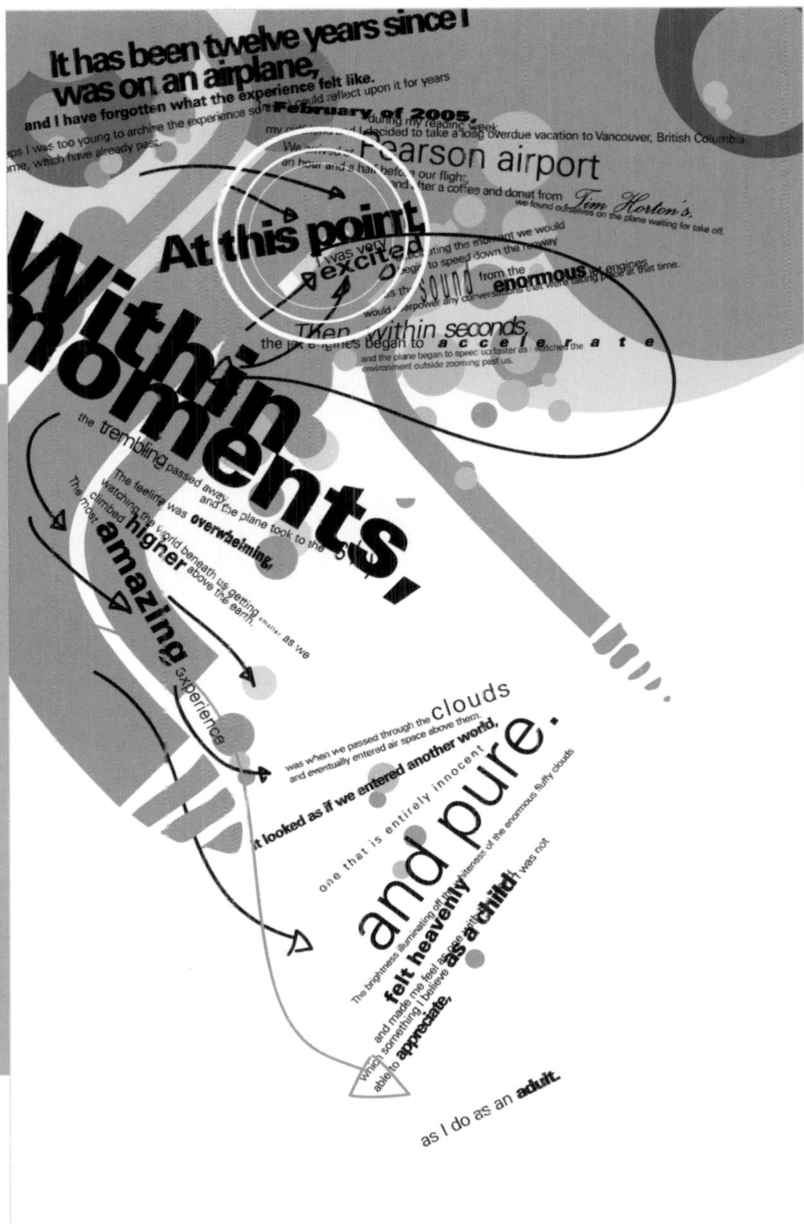

THE PERFORMATIVE quality of a text—its assumed volume and cadence changes—is a great source for typographic style. In this example, weight and size change reflect changes in volume and emphasis in the text.

Marek Okon *Canada*

C

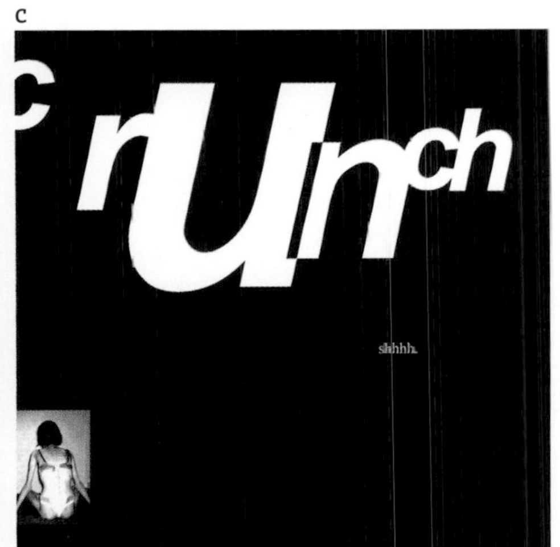

THE SOUND AND the meaning of words are often connected; in these examples, sound and meaning are linked through visual expression.

A Christine Chuo *Carnegie Mellon University, United States*

B Michael Sui *Carnegie Mellon University, United States*

C Tammy Chang *Carnegie Mellon University, United States*

Alignments, Masses, and Voids Dividing space creates structure, which unifies disparate elements in a composition. Several lines of type together create a different kind of structural relationship to the format than a single line of type; the grouping relates to the single line but visually contrasts with it. This mass of texture further defines the space around it into channels that correspond to its height and depth and between itself and the format in all directions. ■ Separating elements within a group maintains a sense of the mass; it also introduces a greater complexity of structure by further subdividing the space. ■ Visual structure must evolve out of the verbal structure of language. The verbal sense helps define what material within it might be mass or line. A continuous sequence of thoughts likely will be clarified if they cluster together; a distinct thought might benefit from being separated from the others. Both kinds of type elements are positive forms: the figures within the composition. They are in contrast with each other, as well as to the spaces, or voids, around them. ■ The relationship of the typographic mass to the voids within the format is essential to defining typographic space in composition, just

THE INTERACTION OF positive and negative drives the dynamic composition of type and image in this brochure spread. The type breaks the space into decisively different intervals; in addition, the shifting negative spaces and the rotation of some type elements restate the structural qualities of the photograph.

Research Studios *United Kingdom*

Design Elements

Design Elements

Design Elements

A passive composition of one line of type, centered within a format, is activated by shifting the line off center, both vertically and horizontally. Each space is altered in relation to the other.

Design Elements
Understanding the
rules and knowing
when to break them
Timothy Samara
Form; Color ; Type
Image; Layout
Rockport Publishers
Gloucester, MA

In this raw composition, the elements are clustered together in a passive relationship with the format. No relationship exists between type and space nor, indeed, among the informational components—except an arbitrary sequence.

Design Elements
Understanding the
rules and knowing
when to break them
Timothy Samara
Form; Color ; Type
Image; Layout
Rockport Publishers
Gloucester, MA

Visual structure, relative to the format, is created when the elements are positioned decisively to subdivide it and, thereby, create differentiated shapes of negative space. Still, the type elements exhibit no structural difference to help distinguish them.

Design Elements
Understanding the
rules and knowing
when to break them
Form
Color
Type
Image
Layout
Timothy Samara
Rockport Publishers
Gloucester, MA

Massing some elements and separating others creates focus and movement. The alignment of particular elements establishes a similarity of meaning among them; separating an element from the primary alignment creates distinction or emphasis.

as it is in defining the rhythm of letter spacing and the space within a paragraph. Regular intervals between masses and voids—unlike in letter spacing, word spacing, and leading—are undesirable because regularity implies sameness, and not all the type elements are the same: they mean different things. Smaller spaces between masses of text help improve the understanding that they are related, while greater spaces between or within typographic masses indicate that the masses are different in meaning. On a visual level, the designer creates contrast and rhythm within the composition by changing the proportional relationships between solids and voids. ■ As type elements divide space in proximity, their points of alignment become important. Aligning elements augments the sense of a relationship between them. Further, alignments between elements help create directional movement through the elements in the format.

The tension between positive and negative space—and the invisible linear connections between elements—is what drives typography. Here, the proportions of the negative spaces are created by the positive type elements, alternately contrasting and restating them. Alignments between the edges of positive forms establish potentially meaningful relationships and help activate spaces across the composition.

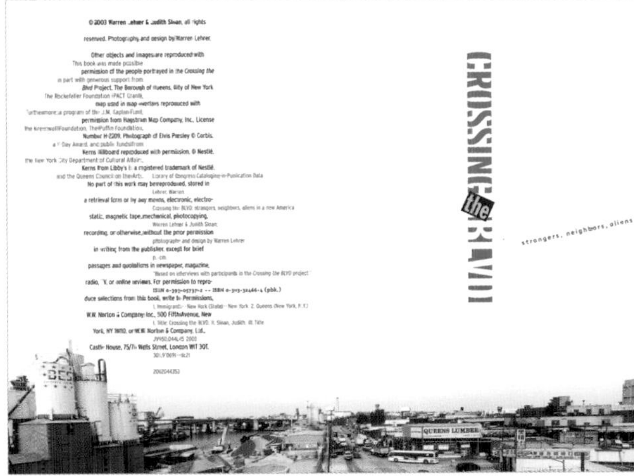

THE DESIGNER PLAYS with alignment and layering in this page spread; two paragraphs, aligned differently along the center axis of a tall column, appear to occupy an ambiguous, transparent space.

Earsay / W.W. Norton *United States*

Perhaps the best-known car designer of his generation, Chris Bangle is known as much for his divisive designs as his visionary approach. Jonathan Bell takes time out to meet BMW's controversial Director of Design.

Christopher E. Bangle is in an animated mood. Ensconced with tea and biscuits in the cosy Georgian sitting room of Hazlitt's Hotel in Soho, BMW's Director of Design is enthusing about work in progress at the company's DesignworksUSA outpost in California. The designer is en-route from the US to his Munich office, temporarily swapping BMW's sleek 1970s HQ for Hazlitt's squishy sofas before he faces tonight's D&AD-invited audience. Bangle is one of the best-known car designers of his generation, despite the fact that his current role involves very little hands-on design work. His is also a peculiar type of fame, the kind that arises off the back of controversy. His name evokes fierce emotions amongst car enthusiasts; to listen to his detractors you'd think he was responsible for heinous crimes against good taste. Typically, he is accused of turning BMW from a sober purveyor of Teutonic excellence into a brash, attention-seeking brand that's aesthetically all at sea.

"To listen to his detractors you'd think he was responsible for heinous crimes against good taste"

Born in 1956, Christopher Edward Bangle began his higher education with a Liberal Arts degree at the University of Wisconsin, and had a vague idea of becoming a Methodist preacher. By 1977 he was enrolled at Pasadena's celebrated Art Centre College of Design, and graduated just as the automobile industry was bottoming out at the end of an economically tough decade. Toying with Hollywood as a career, he instead joined GM, travelling to Germany for four years at Opel. This was followed by seven years at Fiat's Centro Stile, where he eventually became Director. From there, he joined BMW in 1992 as Head of Design Development. His current role is that of design steward, steering BMW and its sub-brands and ensuring the company's long-term design strategy is coherent. As someone who rarely wields a pen, pushes a mouse or sculpts clay, he admits it's been a long time since he was personally responsible for "every single line" on an automobile. That car was Fiat's elegant little coupé of 1994, which arose from Bangle's stint as head of the company's internal design team, a frustrating period during which he went head to head with all the iconic Italian design houses and usually lost. That the Fiat was

THE EDGES OF letter strokes in the gigantic title are used as alignment points for text and for intrusions of geometric negative space into the column; this spatial area is activated by the large red callout.

Frost Design *Australia*

Establishing Hierarchy Information is systematic. Most often, it appears as a collection of parts, each having a different function: for example, callouts, captions, and sidebars in magazine articles; or primary content, supporting content, and menus on a Web page. These various parts often repeat, appear within the same space, and support each other. ■ One of the designer's most important tasks is to give information an order that allows the viewer to navigate it. This order, called the information's "hierarchy," is based on the level of importance the designer assigns to each part of the text. "Importance" means "the part that should be read first, second, third…" and so on; it also refers to the "distinction of function" among the parts: running text (the body of a writing), as measured against other elements such as page folios, titles and subheads, captions, and similar items. ■ Determining hierarchy results from reading the text and asking some simple questions: What are the distinguishable parts of the information to be designed? What should be the main focus of the reader's attention? How do the parts that are not the main focus relate to each other? Does the viewer need to see a certain grouping of words before they begin to focus on the main part? ■ The answers to these questions are often common sense. On a publication's cover, for example, the masthead or title is most

MAJOR SECTIONS of information are indicated by large-scale headlines; distinctions between subcomponents are established by a change in weight and size, with bolder elements reading first. The top of the hierarchy, however, is defined by the vivid pink letterhead and asterisk, focusing attention on the overview of "contents" because of their intense contrast in value.

Stereotype Design *United States*

THE GEORGE ARENTS PIONEER MEDAL

The late George Arents made many notable contributions to Syracuse University. He served with distinction on the Board of Trustees from 1930 until his death in 1960; he was elected vice chairman in 1933, chairman in 1950, and chairman emeritus in 1953. His contributions to the University, its faculty, and students include the Lena R. Arents Rare Book Room, exceptional book collections, and the establishment of an annual award for the member of the graduating class who has assembled the most interesting collection of books.

In 1939, George Arents endowed a fund to provide annually the Arents Pioneer Medals. Only alumni of Syracuse University are eligible for the award, which is based on excellence in their field of endeavor. Those to be honored are selected by a committee of the Alumni Board of Director and approved by the Chancellor and the Executive Committee of the Board of Trustees. The first presentation of the medals was made at in 1939; since that date, 225 alumni have received the award. This is the occasion on which Syracuse University honors its alumni for extraordinary achievement.

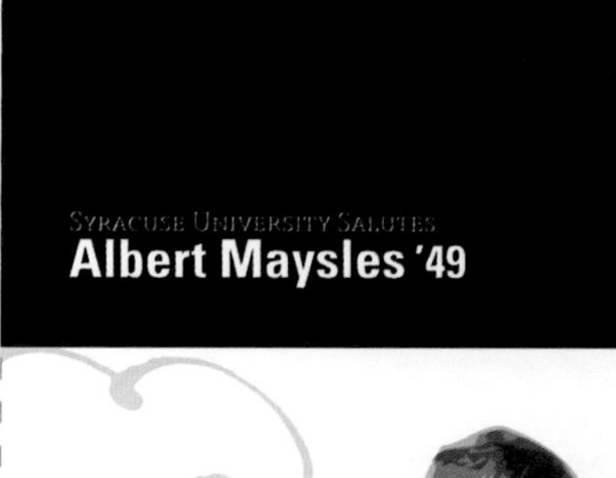

Syracuse University Salutes
Albert Maysles '49

THE PLACEMENT OF the heavy black field and reversed-out title on the right upsets our usual expectation of reading order, but the hierarchy is unquestionable nonetheless.

StressDesign *United States*

important, so it makes sense that it should be the first type the viewer sees. In a table of financial information, the viewer needs to understand the context of figures being presented, so the headers, which describe the meaning of the figures, need to be located easily. Within a publication's pages, where running text may interact with captions, callouts, and other details, the running text needs to occupy a consistent area and be visually noted as different from these other elements. The effect of these decisions becomes simultaneously verbal and visual. ■ All text looks equally important in raw form. If placed within a format as is, the words form a uniform field of texture. By manipulating the spaces around and between text, the designer's first option is to create levels of importance through spatial distinction. The designer might group the majority of elements together, for example, but separate a specific element—maybe a title—and give it more space. The uniformity that is usually desirable to keep the reader moving is thereby purposely broken, creating a fixation point that will be interpreted as deserving attention and, therefore, more important than the other elements. ■ Enhancing such spatial separations by changing the typographic color of separated elements will further distinguish each from the other. Similar to the way that viewers rely on visual comparisons of form to help identify their meaning, so too do they make assumptions about the roles of informational components because of their appearance. More than simply establishing a level of importance, creating

this text is less important
most important
this is not important
other text is more important
some text is important

Change in Size

this text is less important
this is not important
some text is less important
most important text
some is not as important

Change in Weight

less important
somewhat
important much
less important
most important

Change in Alignment

this text is more important than other text that is less important
some text is less important
than other text that is more
important more important
some text is less important

Change in Rhythm

this text is less important
this is not important
some text is important
i m p o r t a n t
this text is less important
this is not important

Change in Spacing

som text is less important than other text that is more important and other text is more *important* than other text and some is less

Change in Width or Posture

this text is most important
some text is less important
this is the most important
this text is more important than the other text this is much more important than

Change in Orientation

this text is less important
some text is less important
this is the most important
some text is less important

Change in Gray Value

some text is less important
this is the most important
some is less important
this is the most important
or maybe this?

Change in Background Contrast

The designer has, at his or her disposal, a great variety of approaches for establishing the relative importance of typographic elements to each other. As can be seen here, even type that is all one color—and even the same weight or size—can be effectively differentiated using extremely simple means.

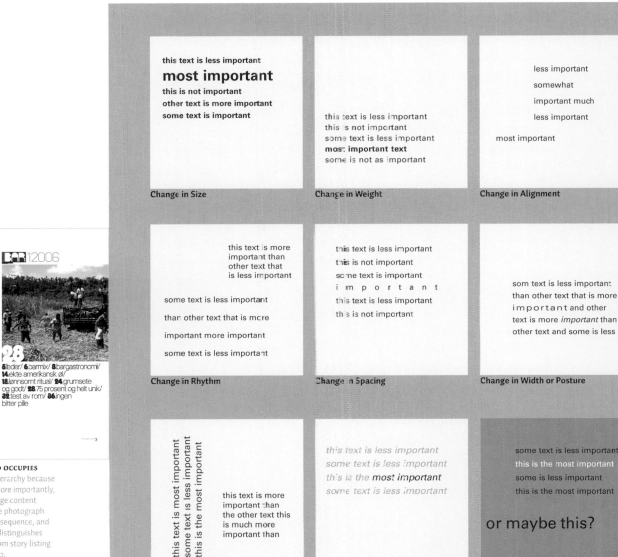

THE MASTHEAD OCCUPIES the top of the hierarchy because of its size but, more importantly, its color. The large content listing below the photograph reads second in sequence, and weight change distinguishes page number from story listing within this group.

Cobra Norway

hierarchy also means clarifying the function of informational components through their formal relationships: whether they are grouped together or separated; whether they appear in a consistent location; and how they are treated with regard to typeface, size, spacing, and so on. Blocks of information that are treated similarly will be assumed to mean similar things, or be closely related in function—captions in this book, for instance, are assumed to function differently (or carry a different kind of content) than the running text because of a difference in treatment.

The captions are no less important than the running text, but both play important roles, which the viewer learns by seeing how they behave in the page layouts and associating this behavior with each of their roles. ■ The designer, in effect, must visually categorize each kind of information for the viewer to identify and, most importantly, learn how to associate each identified kind of information with every other.

Es geht um ganz einfache Dinge,
wie etwa Zuhören,
verstehen lernen
was mein Gesprächspartner
am Herzen hat
und erkennen, wo ich ihm
einen Nutzen bringen kann.
Es geht um die persönliche,
gefühlvolle Auseinandersetzung
mit Menschen.

Es braucht jemanden,
der im Team immer wieder auf die Zielerreichung schaut,
dann wieder andere, die darauf achten,
dass kein Spieler verloren geht,
zwei die bereit sind, zu riskieren,
einer, der warnt,
und zum Schluss jemanden,
der das Resultat
– auch wenn es nicht sensationell ist –
verkaufen kann.
Das hat mit fachlichen Fähigkeiten
noch gar nichts zu tun,
ist aber für den Erfolg eines Teams
und für die Zufriedenheit seiner Mitglieder entscheidend.
Monika Kircher-Kohl

Ich will Kooperationspartner haben
und selber einer sein,
der mutig die Verantwortung für das Projekt mit übernimmt
und im Guten etwas beenden kann,
was nicht funktioniert hat,
oder auch dankbar die Früchte genießt,
wenn's erfolgreich gelaufen ist.
Lojze Wieser

Man glaubt, Kooperation ergibt sich von selbst,
wenn man sich nur halbwegs sympathisch ist.
Das ist vollkommen falsch.
Peter Heintel

ISBN 3 85129 4963

AS DIFFERENT AS EACH of the two text columns clearly is, their hierarchy is visually ambiguous. The larger, bright green text seems to advance because of its intensity, but it is obviously behind the darker blue text. At the same time, the blue text also appears more solid, drawing the viewer's attention, but its smaller size causes it to recede. Despite the strength of this darker blue text, the green paragraph wins out in the hierarchy because of its positioning at the natural, upper-left entry-point for reading.

Clemens Théobert Schedler
Austria

isang yun
(1917–1995)

	41' 58"	naui dang, naui minjokiyo! my land, my people! for soloists, chorus and orchestra (1987)	chorus and state symphony orchestra of the democratic peoples republic of korea conducted by byung-hwa kim
1	07' 42"	rjoksa (history)	cpo 999 047-2
2	14' 26"	hyon-shil I (presence I)	
3	06' 17"	hyon-shil II (presence II)	
4	13' 26"	mi-rae (future)	
myung-sil kim soprano	young-ok kim alto	sun-chai pak tenor	yong-yin han bass

isang yun
(1917–1995)

	41' 58"	naui dang, naui minjokiyo! my land, my people! for soloists, chorus and orchestra (1987)	
1	07' 42"	rjoksa (history)	myung-sil kim soprano
2	14' 26"	hyon-shil I (presence I)	young-ok kim alto
3	06' 17"	hyon-shil II (presence II)	sun-chai pak tenor
4	13' 26"	mi-rae (future)	yong-yin han bass
			chorus and state symphony orchestra of the democratic peoples republic of korea conducted by byung-hwa kim
			cpo 999 047-2

isang yun
(1917–1995)

	naui dang, naui minjokiyo! my land, my people! for soloists, chorus and orchestra (1987)	41' 58"
1	rjoksa (history)	07' 42"
2	hyon-shil I (presence I)	14' 26"
3	hyon-shil II (presence II)	06' 17"
4	mi-rae (future)	13' 26"

chorus and state symphony orchestra
of the democratic peoples republic of korea
conducted by byung-hwa kim

myung-sil kim, soprano
young-ok kim, alto
sun-chai pak, tenor
yong-yin han, bass

cpo
999 047-2

DIFFERENTIATING spaces between columns with similar proportions, and between informational components within columns—as well as changing vertical positioning—keeps positive and negative areas proportionally unified but easily distinguishable from each other.

Helmut Schmid *Japan*

Distinction and Unity The visual and perceptual aspects of grouping and differentiating, discussed in a formal context in Chapter 1 (page 74), are therefore extremely important considerations when developing a typographic hierarchy. Just as viewers will assume that abstract shapes that share similar attributes are related to each other, viewers will also assume text elements with similar treatment to be related. At the same time, all the components within a hierarchy must respond to each other's visual qualities. ■ Readers acknowledge minute changes in typographic quality—hence, the focus on achieving a uniform texture in running text to avoid optical fixation—but too much difference among hierarchic levels creates a visual disconnect: the danger of pushing stylistic differences between informational components is that, as a totality the typography—indeed, the entire project—will appear busy and lack a fundamental cohesion or "visual voice." ■ This is one reason why designers are admonished to employ only two or three type styles in a project and, as often as possible, to combine styles that share qualities such as proportion, weight, terminal shape, and so on. The reader need not be hit over the head with an optical baseball bat every time the content requires differentiation. Because minute changes in type quality are so easily recognized, the reader need only be shown an appreciable yet decisive, difference among hierarchic components to clue them in. Limiting the degree of stylistic difference to just what is needed to signal a change in information allows the reader to understand such changes while maintaining visual unity and more clearly creating interrelationships within the content.

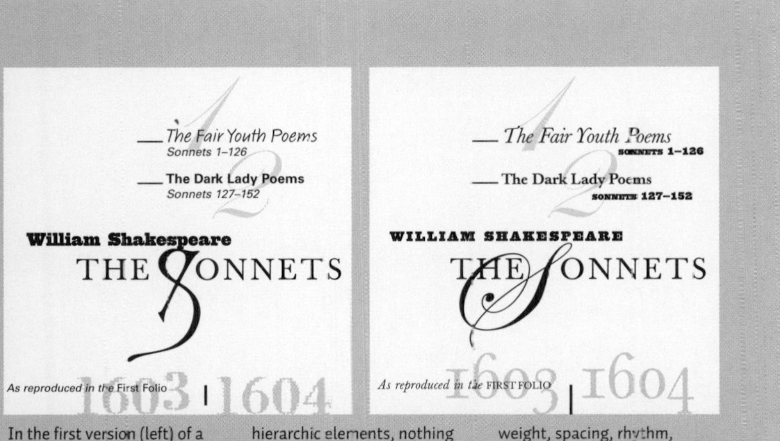

In the first version (left) of a composition, informational components are distinguished through radically different treatments. While this makes for very clear recognition of the hierarchic elements, nothing unifies them stylistically—each element has its own quality. In the second version, the treatments are stylistically related—through proportion, style, weight, spacing, rhythm, and so on—without losing the basic visual qualities that helped distinguish the type elements in the first place.

Historica
The Seeds c
ury, the design indus
teadily increasing in
its development or

A New Visual Reality Thes
began as reactions to World
strange, new language of vis
Dadaists applied it to verbal
their horror over the war.
In 1914, the poet Hugo Ball o
Voltaire in Zurich as a meeti
writers, musicians, and artist

EACH TYPE OF informational component—headline, subhead, deck, text, caption, and subcaption—is given its own unique style, but all the styles are selected from related families: a sans serif and a serif that have been designed to work with each other.

STIM Visual Communication
United States

BOTH SERIF AND SANS SERIF faces used in this brochure spread have similar overall weight (despite the stroke contrast in the serif face) and a similar body width. Note the slight squaring of the curved forms that appears in both faces.

Voice *Australia*

FOUR STUDIES FOR a book cover (below) demonstrate how dramatic changes in spacing can completely alter the reading order—and meaningful interrelationships—of informational components. In the second study, for example, the reader will move from the title down to the three last names of the artists, directly linking their last names with the subject matter. In the last study, the title (and therefore subject matter, of the book becomes secondary as a result of its position, emphasizing the identities of the artists.

JRoss Design *United States*

Structure, Detail, and Navigation

As noted previously, horizontal and vertical type alignments create channels of positive and negative space that the designer can use to create hierarchic interrelationships—helping readers locate, separate, or connect pieces of information… or, more simply, to "navigate" them. ■ Aligning shallow columns of text horizontally across a format, for example, will indicate that they share some verbal relationship and may indicate a temporal sequence—a series of steps that builds in meaning. Creating a band of space between one horizontal text alignment and another will keep the two sequences clearly defined, but the fact of their similar horizontal structure may indicate that they are interrelated—or perhaps they communicate two sequential processes for launching a software program. Running text vertically in columns enhances the sense of continuity between paragraphs. Grouping several vertical columns together, while introducing a space to separate this grouping from another, may imply that the two groups are unrelated, or it may signal a pause for the reader to assimilate the content of one grouping before proceeding to the next. ■ Keeping consistent spaces between groups that are related in meaning, and increasing the space between groups

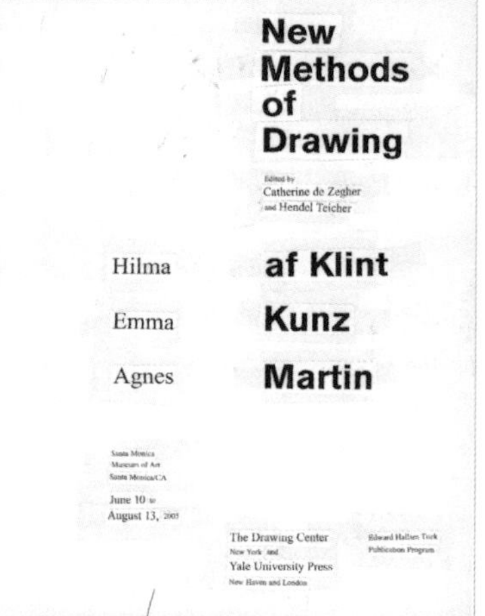

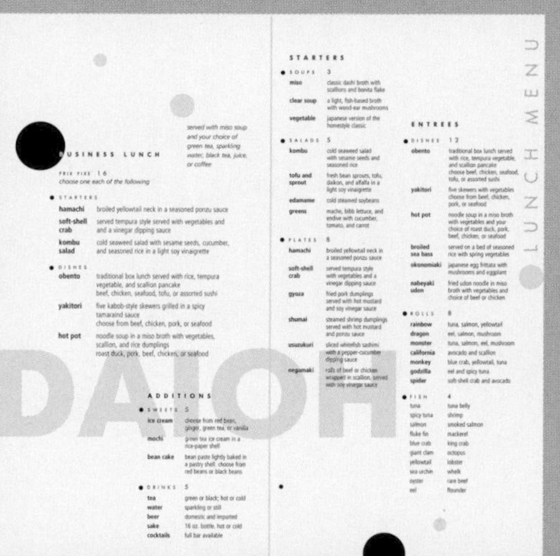

In this version of a menu, dots perform a variety of functions. The large dot acts as a focal point, bringing its associated type element to the top of the hierarchy. A system of smaller dots is used to highlight structural alignments and to denote a specific sublevel in the hierarchy. Still other dots activate negative spaces in the format.

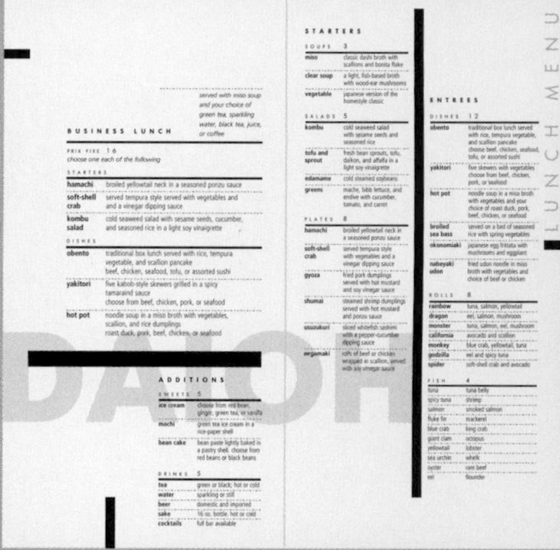

Lines, which share an inherent visual quality with typography, offer an immediate formal relationship in addition to whatever functions they serve. In this version of the menu, heavy lines separate clusters of information that are unrelated, while lighter lines help distinguish clusters that share a relationship. In addition, the lines also activate space and help add movement to the composition.

that are unrelated in meaning, is an easy way of helping readers navigate among more general sections of information and among subgroups of information within those sections. ■ Sometimes it is difficult to remember that type is just a collection of lines, dots and shapes, and that they behave in the same way their simplified components do. Integrating such visual forms can also enhance hierarchy and clarify navigation through text. The focal power of a dot, which defines a location in space, can indicate the beginning or ending point of a text element (for example, using bullets to call out items in a list), correspond to alignments, activate spaces within a composition, and separate informational material linguistically, like an exaggerated form of punctuation. Lines, too, can perform a variety of useful functions to enhance hierarchy and navigation: separating, enclosing, emphasizing, creating, or augmenting structural relationships, and activating space. Lines themselves are visually similar to lines of type, and relationships of contrast—in weight, solidity, relative length, and so on—operate the same way between them as they do among lines of type. Horizontal and vertical line configurations visually correspond to this intrinsic quality of text. Lines that are angled, curved, or wavy starkly contrast this "orthogonal" logic. Geometric shapes, whose hard-edged quality can be visually similar to that of letters, can act as inclusions or details among letters or words—as well as supports for clusters of text, operating as fields upon which the type lies or passes between. Because geometric shapes integrate so well with type forms, but retain their identity as images, they can also be used to create visual links between type and other pictorial elements.

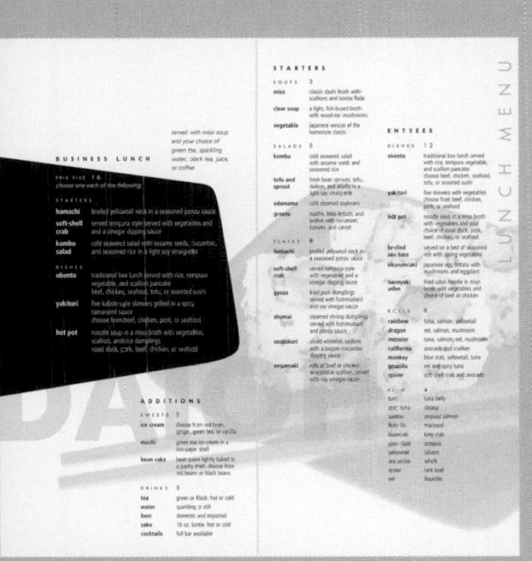

Planar geometric forms relate visually to the geometry of letterforms, but contrast with the texture and linearity of type. As fields or containers for informational elements, they can help reinforce hierarchic distinctions among groupings of content; in this particular case, they also create a visual link between the type and the imagery while honoring the layout structure.

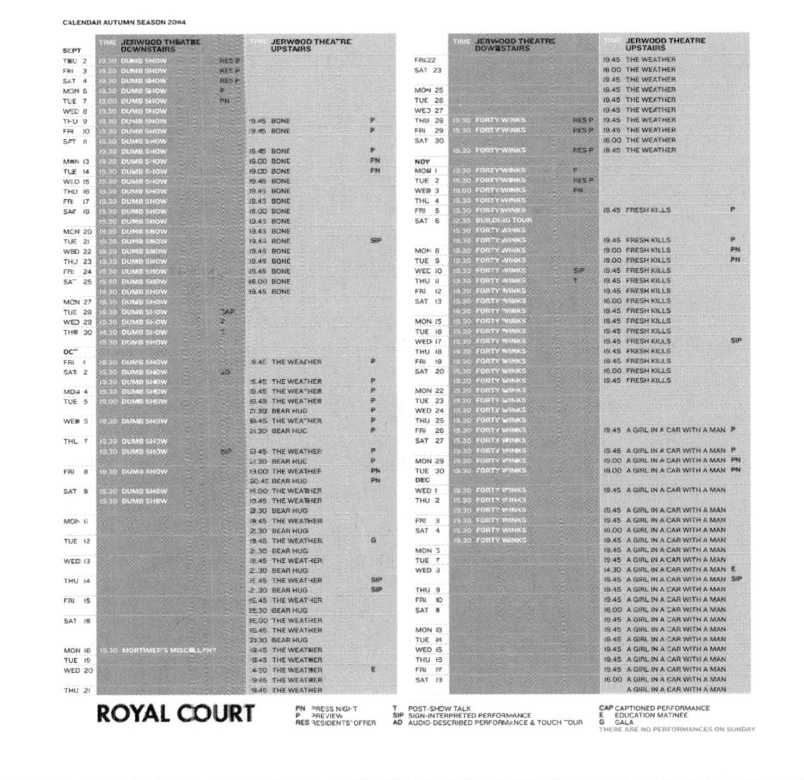

ALTHOUGH COLOR AND value changes clarify the hierarchy of information vertically, thin horizontal lines create connections between informational components from left to right.

Research Studios *United Kingdom*

As the relative color attributes of type and background change, so do their apparent spatial relationships, along with legibility. Contrast in hue and temperature help create clear separation, as does a strong contrast in value. As the value of a background's color comes closer to that of the type sitting on top of it, there is a loss of visual separation and, therefore, of legibility.

Itanium 2 presents lucrative opportunities for those organisations that offer it, but as with any new technology, customers will have questions and even objections. Here we give you the answers – and the chance to take advantage of the surging momentum in this market.

We bring you a clear view of Itanium 2 today, what's on the horizon and what the analysts are saying.

METROLOGIE

A SUBTLE VALUE CHANGE between text and background color forces the text into a secondary relationship to the spread's title. The large size of the text ensures that it remains legible despite its low value contrast with the background.

Loewy *United Kingdom*

DEPARTMENT OF FINE ARTS
MASTER OF FINE ARTS PROGRAM

2004/05

PennDesign
THE SCHOOL OF DESIGN
OF THE UNIVERSITY OF PENNSYLVANIA

PAINTING
PRINTMAKING
SCULPTURE
PHOTOGRAPHY
NEW MEDIA

DRAMATIC CHANGES in intensity and value create dynamic—and somewhat ambiguous—spatial interaction among the elements, although the hierarchy is clear.

Paone Design Associates
United States

What Happens Now? Type in Color

Chromatic color—differences in hues, such as red, orange, and violet—has a dynamic effect on typography. Chromatic color can greatly enhance the textural qualities of type—its boldness, lightness, openness, density, and apparent location in "three-dimensional" space (called "typographic color")—reinforcing these qualities as they already exist in black and white by adding the optical effect of a true color. ■ As we have seen, different hues appear at different locations in space; cool colors appear to recede, while warmer colors appear to advance. Applying a warm color to a type element that is large and important will enhance its contrast against other type elements. ■ The relative value of colors, their darkness or lightness, is an aspect of chromatic color that demands great care in regard to how it affects type—especially its legibility—for example, when colored type sits on a colored background. As their values approach each other, the contrast between type and background diminishes, and the type becomes less legible. All the qualities of chromatic color have a pronounced effect on hierarchy because of the way they affect the apparent spatial depth and prominence of the typographic elements to which colors are applied. Color presents the possibility of altering the meaning or psychological effect of words by introducing a layer of meaning that is independent of—yet becomes integral to—the words themselves.

THE COMPLEX SPATIAL changes created by the colored type forms—blues and violets receding, reds and yellows advancing—is further complicated and enriched by the use of transparency.

Leonardo Sonnoli *Italy*

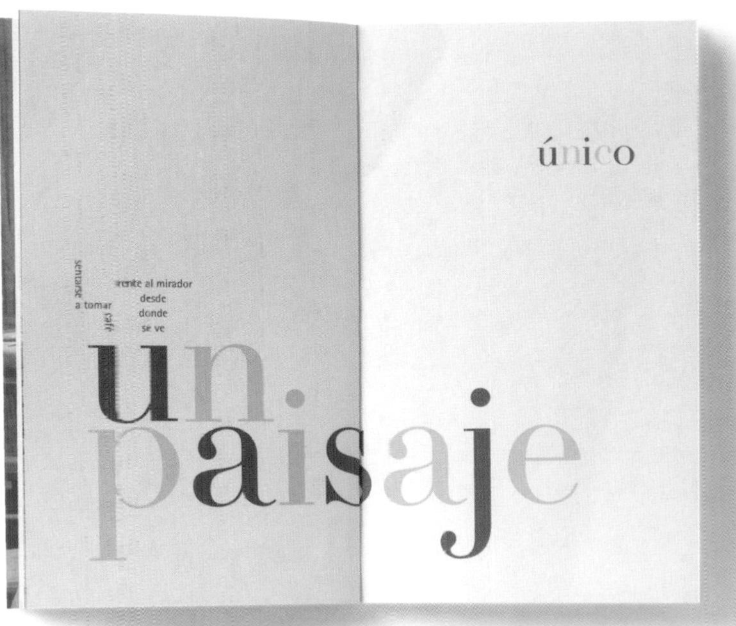

CHANGES IN VALUE and saturation add to the rhythmic typographic color of this page spread.

LSD *Spain*

Color and Hierarchy Applying color to a black-and-white typographic composition will have an immediate effect on hierarchy. For this reason, it's often a good idea to understand how the hierarchy works in black and white first, separating the typographic components through their typographic color—their density and rhythm, linearity and mass. Consider chromatic color as an added bonus, but make sure the hierarchy is clear by virtue of size changes, changes in weight, spacing, and so on. ■ If the different levels of importance in the hierarchy are clearly established, further distinguishing each level with a difference in color can force greater

CHATELET
MUSICAL DE PARIS
Der Ring des Nibelungen
La Tétralogie
de Richard Wagner
Christoph Eschenbach
Robert Wilson
Frida Parmeggiani
Orchestre de Paris
Chœur du Théâtre du Châtelet
Coproduction
Théâtre du Châtelet
Opéra de Zurich
octobre 2005 avril 2006

INTENSE RED CALLOUTS highlight important elements in this posters hierarchy, contrasting with the analogous blue and gray tones that recede in space.

Design Rudi Meyer *France*

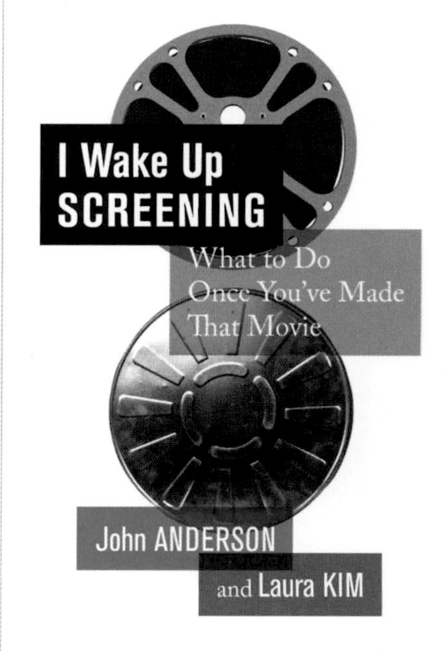

I Wake Up
SCREENING
What to Do
Once You've Made
That Movie
John ANDERSON
and Laura KIM

THE INHERENT optical spatial positions of each colored block reinforce the hierarchy of the typography of this book cover: being warmer, the red block advances over the cooler green and cyan blocks.

Think Studio *United States*

The Program
Welcome | *Christina Lindholm, Dean of VCUQ*
Introduction of Special Guests | *Sandra Wilkins*
Special Showing | *Sarah Takesh* | *Couture Designer*
The Fashion Show
The Golden Needle Awards
Award of Excellence
Presentation of Special Gift to
Her Highness Sheikha Jawaher bint Hamad bin Suhaim Al Thani presentation, May 25th only
Noor Jassim Al Thani
Closing Statement | *Sandra Wilkins*
Reception

BECAUSE THIS PAGE from a fashion show program was produced for a primarily Arabic-speaking audience, the Arabic text is brought into the foreground with bolder weight and a darker, more intense color than is used for the English translation.

VCU Qatar *Qatar*

separation between them. For example, if the information at the top of a hierarchy is set in a deep, vibrant orange-red, while the secondary information is set in a cool gray, the two levels of the hierarchy will be separated visually to a much greater degree. Although the values of the colors are similar, the saturated orange type will advance in space, and the cool gray type will recede. ■ The application of color to the ground within a composition can further enhance the hierarchy. Type of one color, set on a field of another color, will join closely with it or separate aggressively, depending on their color relationship. If the colors of type and background are related, the two elements will occupy a similar spatial depth. If they are complementary in nature, the two will occupy very different spatial depths. It is important to maintain considerable contrast between the type color and the background color so that the type remains visible. ■ Color can also be used to link related informational components within a composition. In a poster for an event, for example, all the information related to the time and place of the event might be assigned a particular color, which may relate to the color assigned to the title of the event. The color relationship of the two components creates a meaningful link for the viewer and serves to clarify the information.

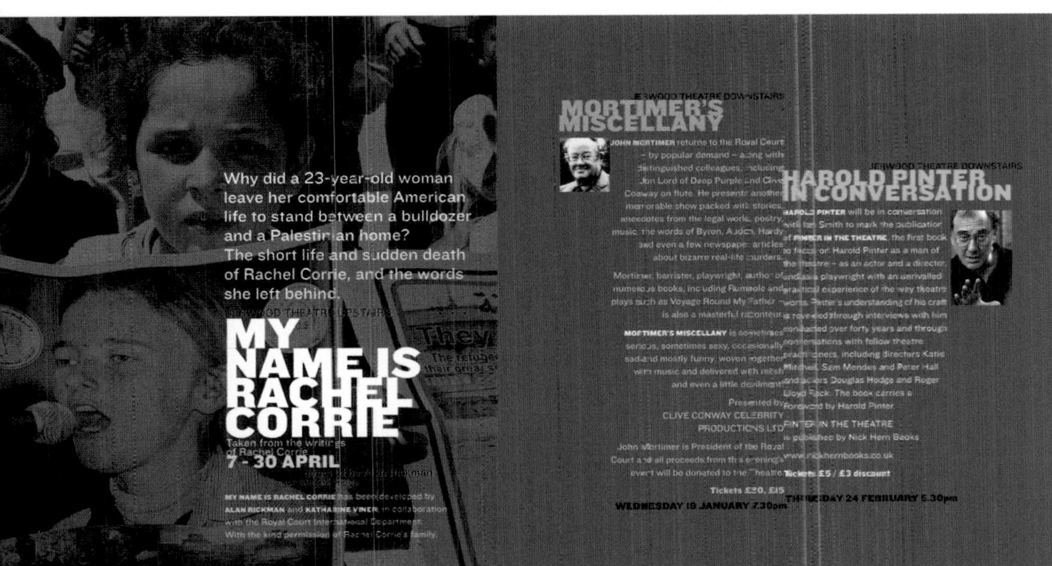

INCREASED VALUE CONTRAST and intensity bring more important elements into the foreground and establish their positions toward the top of the hierarchy.

Research Studios *United Kingdom*

This composition of numbers demonstrates the effect of chromatic color on hierarchy as simply as possible, showing the layout in the same set of colors, but with the colors distributed differently among the numbers each time. The base composition presents the numbers in their natural order, using size, weight, position, and value to define their sequence as a starting point for consideration. The variations that follow swap colors to reorder them despite their initial presentation. While most design projects will likely be more complex, it is easy to see how relationships of hue, value, temperature, and saturation can quickly change not only the apparent spatial depth and presence of elements, but also the sequence in which they are perceived. This knowledge has dramatic implications for how information can be ordered by using chromatic relationships to enhance already-defined hierarchic structure—at the same time potentially delivering color-based messages and creating visual linsk between type and image material.

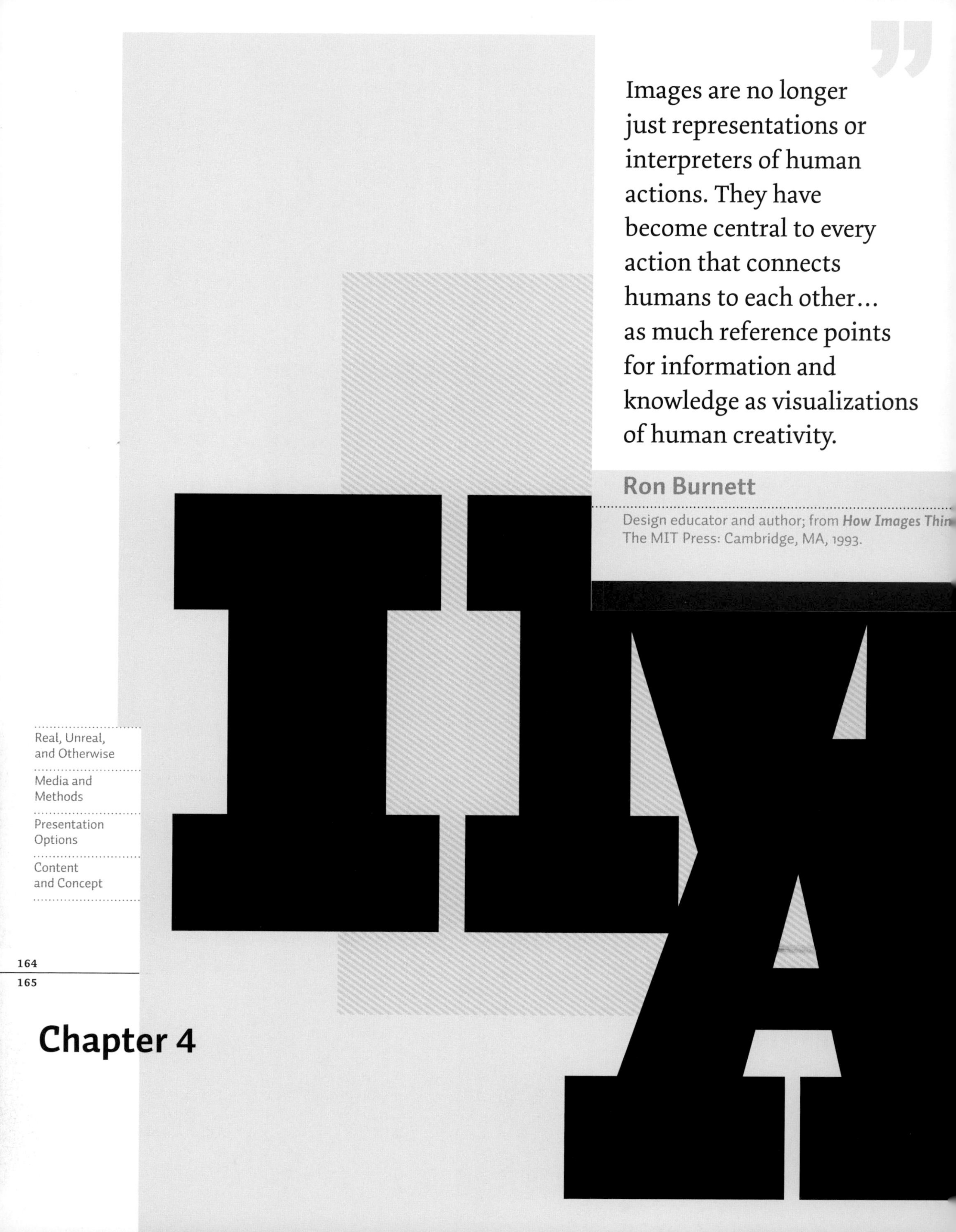

Images are no longer just representations or interpreters of human actions. They have become central to every action that connects humans to each other... as much reference points for information and knowledge as visualizations of human creativity.

Ron Burnett

Design educator and author; from ***How Images Thin***
The MIT Press: Cambridge, MA, 1993.

Chapter 4

THE WORLD OF

What Images Are Image making is perhaps one of the most complex and ecstatically human activities. An image is a powerful experience that is far from being inert—a simple depictor of objects or places or people. It is a symbolic, emotional space that replaces physical experience (or the memory of it) in the viewer's mind during the time it's being seen. This is true of images that are strictly representative of a real place, people, or objects, as well as of images that are artificial—either contrived representations or abstract configurations of shapes. In the hands of a designer who knows how to command composition on a purely visual level, and who can conceptually select and manipulate content, an image is by far the most profound communication tool available. ■ In graphic design, there are myriad image possibilities—symbols and photomontage, drawing and painting, and even type—that perform different functions. Images provide a visual counterpoint to text, helping to engage the audience. Images also offer a visceral connection to experiences described by written language. They can help clarify very complex information—especially conceptual, abstract, or process-oriented information—by displaying it concisely: "at-a-glance." They can add interpretive overlay in juxtaposition with literal text or images. ■ It's foolish to think that simply picking a photograph of a particular object will alone solve a communication problem in its entirety. The relevance of an image to a design solution isn't simply wrapped up in its subject matter. An image becomes relevant when its compo-

CLEVER USE OF LETTERPRESS elements and punctuation to create the gun icon evokes potential conceptual ideas about language and violence.

Sagmeister *United States*

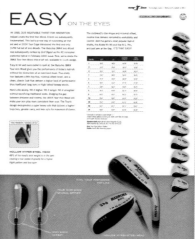

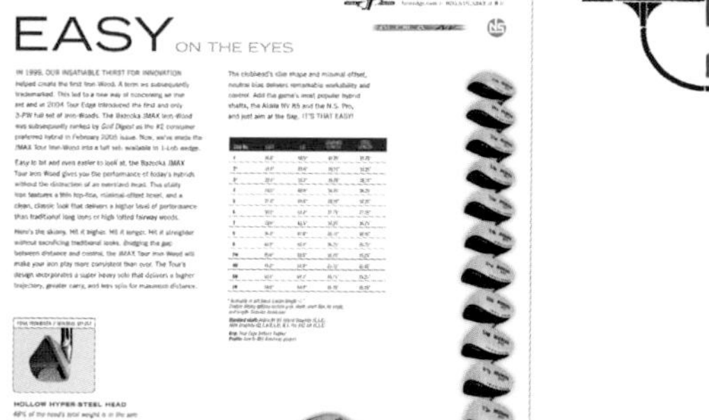

CRYSTAL-CLEAR PHOTOGRAPHY is documentary and credible, considered "real" by the average viewer. These qualities are both appropriate and highly desirable when displaying products.

Rule29 *United States*

THINK PM
OF DESIGN

The presentation of images falls on a spectrum defined at one end by representation and at the other by abstraction. Images that lie closer to the representational end of the continuum are more literal; images that approach abstraction are more interpretive.

LITERAL

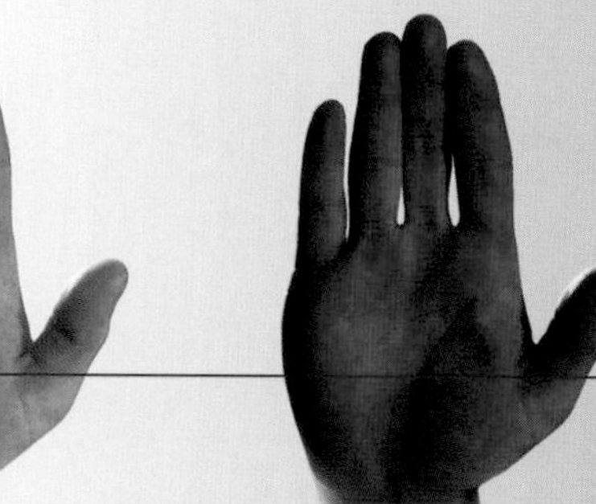

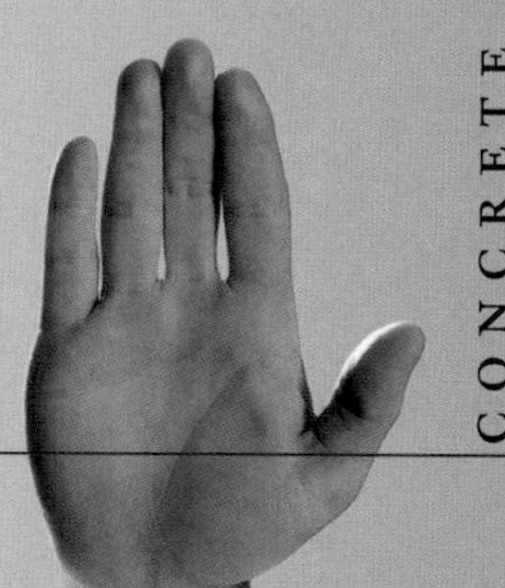

CONCRETE

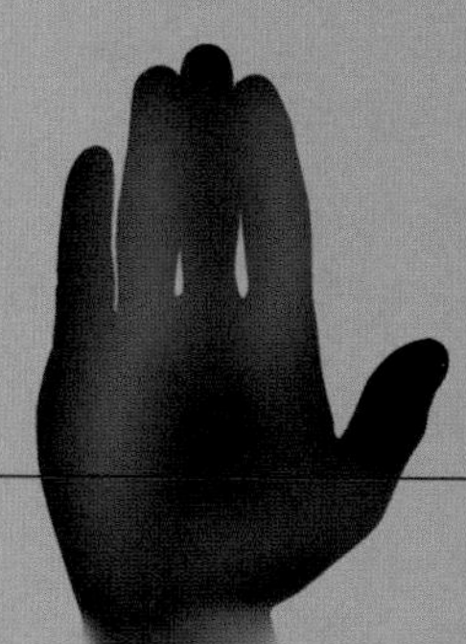

sition and production technique, as well as its subject matter, are working in concert with other material to create an integrated message.

Abstraction and Representation An image might be mostly representational or mostly abstract, but it always will be a mixture of the two. Purely visual, abstract images (as we have seen) communicate ideas that are grounded in the human experience. In the right context, a yellow circle becomes a sun. A composition of lines in dynamic rhythms might communicate a subtler message about movement or energy, not necessarily referring to some literal object or experience. Even a photograph that purports to represent something real is an abstraction on some level—it depicts a state of activity that is no longer happening and flattens it into a two-dimensional form. Portions of it might not even be real, but instead, contrivances set up by the photographer or by the designer directing the creation of the photograph. ■ Using the intrinsic messaging of abstract form described in Chapter 1 to influence a photograph's composition will enhance its messaging potential. Similarly, suggesting concrete, literal experience within an abstract composition will help ground the message in reality for a viewer, making it more accessible without sacrificing the abstraction's simplicity and visceral evocative power.

A LIVELY DIALOGUE between abstract gestural mark and figural representation lends humanity and depth to the illustration.

VCU Qatar *Qatar*

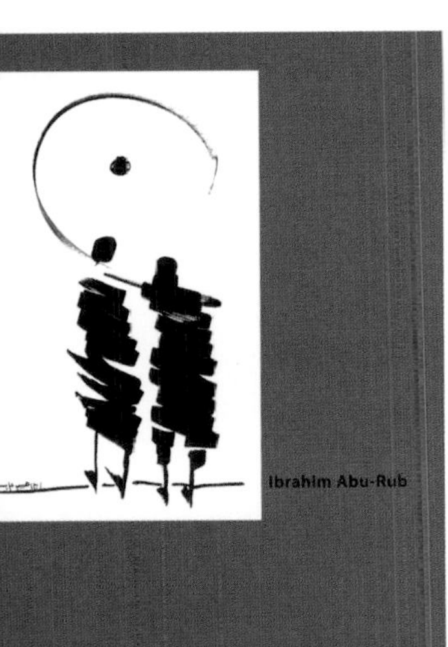

Ibrahim Abu-Rub

SIMPLIFIED representational forms exaggerate the abstract qualities of shape and space; with less naturalistic detail for the viewer to consider, the interplay of diagonals, mass, and contour dominate the image.

Munda Graphics *Australia*

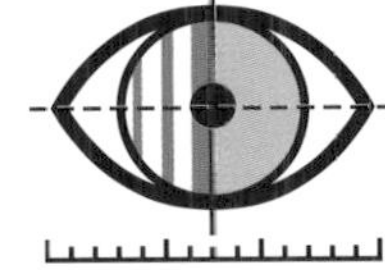

A STYLIZED TRANSLATION of an eye approaches the iconic end of the image spectrum; added graphic elements bring symbolic meaning to the form.

Troy Abel *Iowa State University, United States*

OUR BRAINS ARE hypersensitive to forms that create images of humanity. Note how little information is needed for this image to clearly represent a human face.

TenDoTen *Japan*

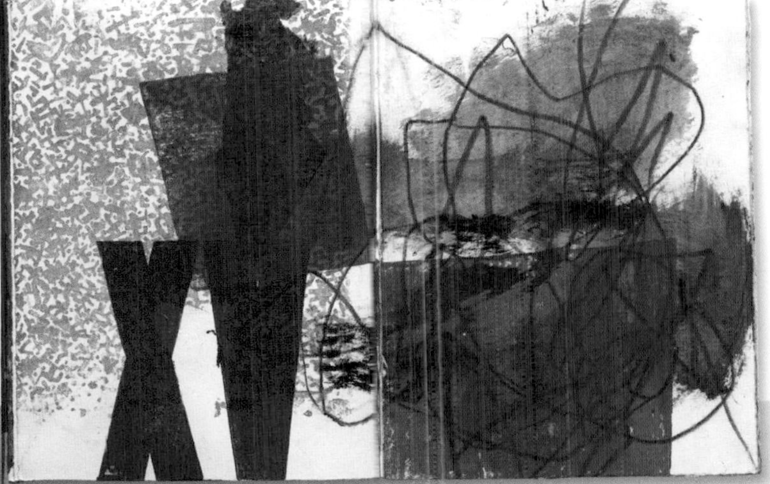

THE ABSTRACT FORMS in this book spread are grounded by the concrete quality of the letterforms, whose style begins to skew the reading of the abstraction toward an environment that might be urban and gritty in character.

Andreas Ortag *Austria*

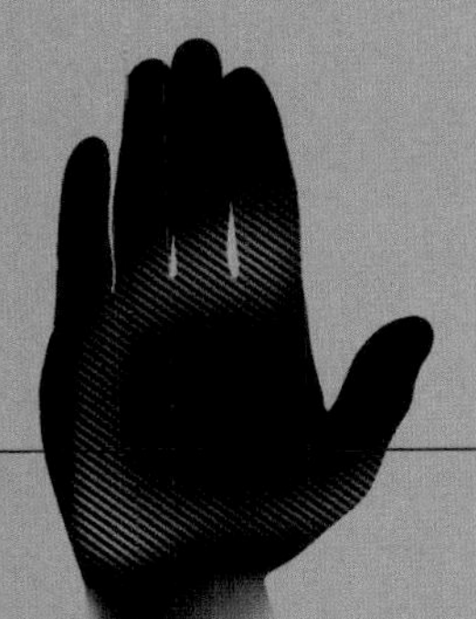

ICONIC

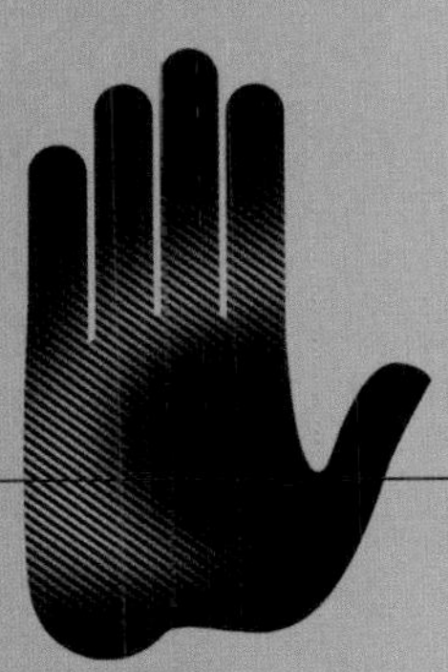

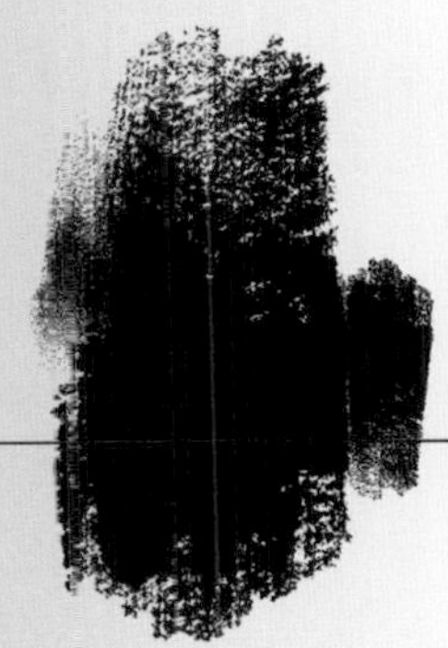

ABSTRACT

Image Modes and Mediation

Regardless of an image's degree of literal representation or abstraction, a designer might choose to represent an idea by using photographs, illustrations (drawings or paintings), or a hybrid: manipulated photographs or drawn images in combination. How a designer decides to involve image results from evaluating the content and its conceptual functions. The images must provide informational clarity, but they must do so in a way that resonates and delivers secondary and tertiary messages—associational or branded messages—as well. ■ The form of an image's representation is called its "mode," and this includes not only its degree of simplicity and abstraction but also its medium. A designer must consider a number of things in choosing the right image mode, or modalities, to use. Among these are the evocative, emotional qualities of the project's content; the number of different modes needed to differentiate specific messages; the expectations of the viewing audience for certain image experiences over others, because of

SYMBOLS ARE highly mediated forms of image, drawing on common understanding and cultural contexts that elevate them beyond mere representation. Consider these two sets of symbols, used as signage to indicate which restroom to use.

Art: Tecaji *Slovenia*

All these images depict the same subject—a figure—but using different modes. The modes range between literal and stylized, and each mode intrinsically mediates the image to varying degrees. The "pure" photograph is the least mediated in this study. The two drawn images are inherently more mediated than the photographic image—the designer has invented his or her own depiction of the subject—but between the two, the naturalistic drawing is less mediated than the other.

their demographic makeup or the social and historical context of the project's content; and production issues, including such technicalities as budget, lead time, and fabrication concerns. How far from its "natural" state the image gets (how much the "pure" depiction of the subject gets altered by the designer) is described as how "mediated" it is. ■ The level of an image's mediation can be evaluated in a couple of ways. First, it can be considered in terms of its physical expression, or how it's made; for example, a realistic drawing shows a greater level of mediation than a photograph of the same subject. Second, an image's level of mediation can be considered in how complex the messaging in the image is—a somewhat literal drawing of an image is less mediated than a highly contrived photograph or collage. ■ The way an image refers to its subject is also an aspect of its form that must be considered by the designer, who might choose to represent, or signify, particular subjects by using images that are realistic or representational but not pictures of the subject itself. This kind of image is called an "index" and refers to its subject through association; an image of an egg, for example, "indexes" a bird.

THE CHOICE OF IMAGE used for one of several wall panels in a French cultural center—Guignol, a puppet character from a child's story—is symbolic of French culture. Its historical stature is altered through mediation: representing the image in a digital pixel pattern that makes it contemporary.

Apeloig Design *France*

A

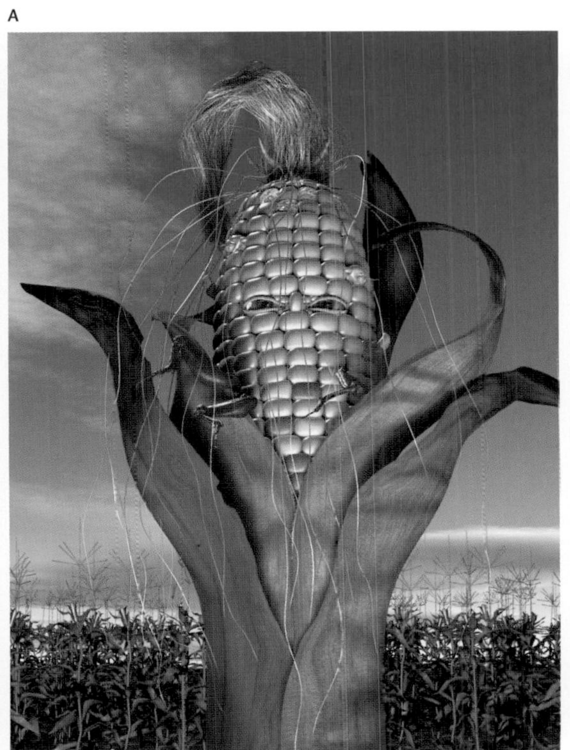

B

THE QUESTION OF MEDIATION and credibility comes to the fore in comparing these two illustrations. Both are fabrications—but which one seems more real? If you decided that the corncob person does, you're probably not alone. Despite the impossibility of this subject matter, it has been rendered in a photographic style that makes it seem more believable as "real" than the abstract, invented space and painterly texture of the drawn image on the right.

A Christopher Short *United States*

B Cyr Studio *United States*

Semiology and Stylization A designer might often need to represent ideas in a stylized way, selecting the most important elements from a subject and arranging them in as concise and simplified a message as possible. The most common occurrence of this kind of image is a logo—an image that is used to identify an organization and differentiate it from competing groups. The purpose of such a distilled, elemental form is quick recognition and easy recall; the more information that can be packed into the shape of the mark, the better. Stylizing an image emphasizes its nature as a "sign"—a visual representation of an idea. ■ The study of relationships between signs and what they represent or "signify" is called "semiology," a branch of anthropology developed in the 1800s. In selecting the details of the idea or subject to be represented, the designer looks for elements that are the most universally recognizable—for example, the fundamental shapes and qualities of a cat (ears, tail, a common posture, whiskers, paws, and so on)—rather than those that are specific—

A RHYTHM OF LINES abstracts a bar code into a graph.

Thomas Csano *Canada*

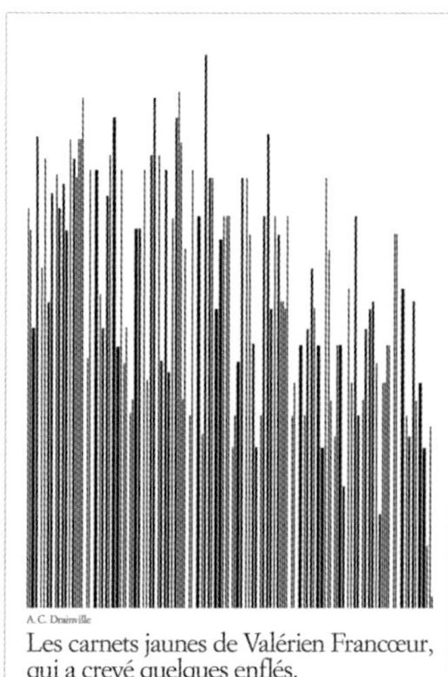

A.C. Desinville
Les carnets jaunes de Valérien Francœur, qui a crevé quelques enflés.

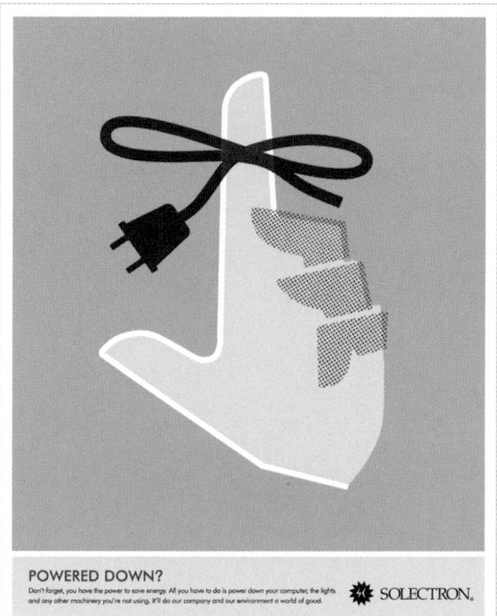

POWERED DOWN?
SOLECTRON.

AN ICON OF A HAND becomes doubly symbolic as the string around the finger—a symbol for remembering something—is transformed into a power cord.

Templin Brink Design *United States*

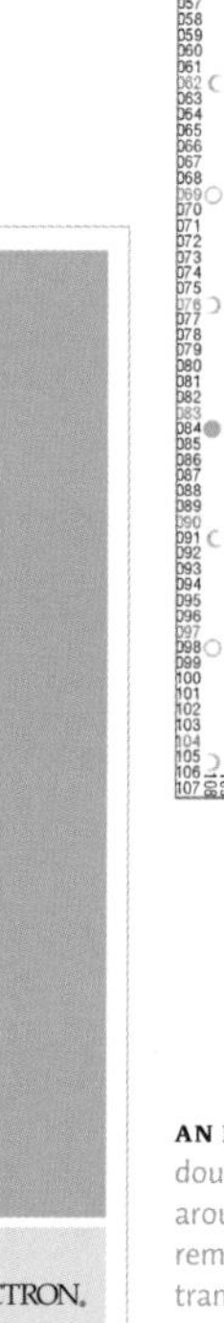

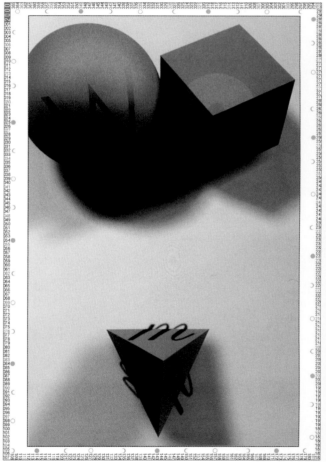

CAREFUL POSITIONING of geometric elements and letterforms creates a concrete anatomical image out of pure form.

Studio International *Croatia*

particular ear shapes, markings, or short or long hair. In arranging the elements, even for that of a recognizable object, the designer's goal is to invent a specific graphic language—an internal logic of positive and negative relationships, an emphasis on curved or angular forms, and an integration of line and mass—that will make the mark live as its own, unified image, rather than simply reproducing the likeness of the object. In one sense, the distilled, stylized mark is neutral because it seeks to communicate on an objective, universal level; simultaneously, however, it must have its own identity as a form.

■ In giving the form its own identity, the designer is selectively interpreting particular aspects of the message and skewing the communication in one direction or another. Following the cat example above, the designer might emphasize a crouching position, possibly communicating readiness for action, or might emphasize the cat's claws, a message that might mean power or aggression. The angularity of the drawing, or how weight is distributed, might add interpretation, such as restful and contemplative, or quick and agile, qualities. The universality of a mark, along with its particular degree of invented stylization, will place the image at different points along the continuum of representation and abstraction. Further, the very selection of the image's subject might involve overlays of meaning that involve conceptual, cultural, or emotional issues.

HIGHLY RESOLVED integration of car and bicycle icons begins to suggest some relationship between them; the addition of the cautionary yellow striping evolves the message further.

Thomas Csano *Canada*

SOME IMAGES ARE complex, visual signs with several layers of meaning; these are called supersigns. The elegant W and M lockup, while still clearly letters, has also formed an iconic representation of wires. In turn, this representation takes on the quality of a symbol when qualified by the client's descriptive title.

Raidy Printing Group *Lebanon*

THIS SUPERSIGN uses a letterform as a base, altered only by the addition of two small dots to create added meaning.

LSD *Spain*

Icon A visual sign that shares a structural similarity with the object it signifies is called an icon. Usually, icons are devoid of detail and are literal representations of their signified object. In these examples, note which elements have been selected and which have been edited out.

Symbol A representational or abstract image whose form is physically unrelated to its signified object or idea is a symbol; it derives its power from the arbitrary agreement of the culture that uses the symbol. A dove, for example, is a symbol of peace in Western culture. The context in which a symbol appears might alter its symbolic meaning: consider the difference in meaning between the same symbol element in these three environments.

Indexical Sign This kind of visual sign points to its signified object indirectly, or "indexes" it—for example, a nest indexes a bird.

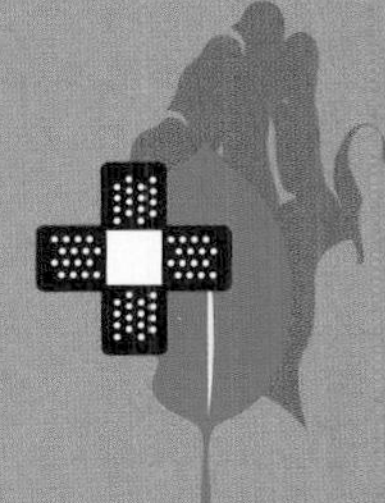

Supersign This is a complex sign that superimposes more than one sign (and often more than one type of sign) in a single, gestalt combination in which all the signs included are visible and accessible immediately; a logo is a good example. A supersign might involve an icon, symbol, index, word, and representation in any combination. The more complicated the supersign, the less effective it is. These three examples show how a particular component might combine with others and thereby take on different functions and meanings.

THE DRAWING OF the house using simple lines becomes symbolic by transforming the lines into circuits.

Drotz Design *United States*

THE VISUAL QUALITY of linear, drawn imagery corresponds closely to the linear quality of typography, especially in this case where the type has been outlined as well.

Finest Magma *Germany*

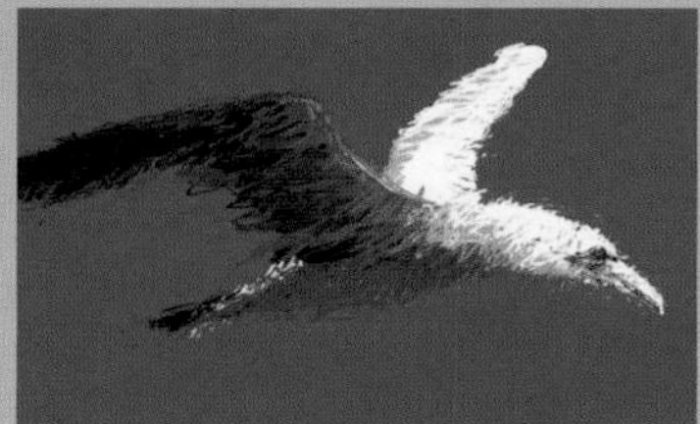

In this study, the same subject is presented in varying degrees of realism and stylization. Toward the realistic end of the spectrum, the subject's literal meaning takes on more importance; as it becomes more stylized, its literal meaning becomes less important, while the gesture, the quality of the marks, and associations or symbolic messaging that these impart become more important.

ILLUSTRATION ALLOWS FOR varying degrees of abstraction and complex, invented spatial arrangements. The flat, hard-edged style of the illustrated elements creates a modern, industrial feel appropriate to the city, while using a map and coat of arms figure adds historical messaging.

Dochdesign *Germany*

AGAIN, ILLUSTRATION doesn't limit the designer in terms of inventing space and combining disparate elements that would otherwise be empirically impossible. In contrast to the Munich poster (left), the style is painterly and representational, but the space is no less abstract.

Cyr Studio *United States*

Illustration The choice of illustration over photography opens up tremendous possibility for transmitting information. The designer is not only unencumbered by the limitations of real-world objects and environment but also given the potential to introduce conceptual overlay, increased selectivity of detail, and the personal, interpretive aspect of the designer's visualization—through choice of medium, composition, and gestural qualities. ■ As with all types of images, an illustration can be concrete, objective, or realistic in how it presents its subject, or it can become abstracted and symbolic; the designer can add details that normally would not exist in a real scene or can exaggerate movement, texture, arrangement, space, and lighting. Choosing illustration for image presentation, however, means potentially sacrificing a kind of credibility or real-world connection for the viewer. Despite the fact that most audiences realize that a photograph might just as easily be manipulated and therefore made misleading, the audiences will still instinctively respond to a photograph as though it were "reality." ■ The power of illustration over photography, however, is to communicate with a visual sensitivity that is emotional, poetic, organic, and innately human. An illustration can also integrate with other visual material, such as type, abstract graphic elements, and even the paper stock or other finishing techniques, on a textural level that is impossible with a conventional photograph. The designer must weigh these aspects carefully and select which mode of representation will best suit the communication.

Drawing and Painting The directness of hand-generated images is universally appealing. Through a drawn or painted image, the designer taps into a viewer's own sense of creativity and connects on an extremely personal level—there is a genuine, honest, and warm quality to an illustration that might be lacking in the slick and seamless realism of a photograph. An illustration's success lies in the appropriateness of its style to the subject matter at hand. The majority of illustration is contracted from specialists, who cultivate a particular style to find a niche in the market, but this doesn't preclude designers themselves from taking on the role of

THE SCRAGGLY OUTLINE and cartoonish forms of this illustration mix humor and pathos.

Ames Bros. *United States*

THE DECISION to illustrate the vegetables on this label, rather than to photograph them, ensures their absolute perfection and freshness.

Wallace Church *United States*

A TEXTURE OF ILLUSTRATED insects reveals a numeral 5 in this panel from a parking garage signage system. Illustrating the insects gives the designer control over their visual presentation, rather than relying on finding or photographing images of real insects.

Studio Works *United States*

illustrator. A designer wanting to illustrate will be intimate with the subject matter of the project and other relevant graphic elements—including type and finishing techniques. As a result, the designer might be able to build images that are even more appropriate and integrated with other elements than would be likely if working through an outside source.

Realism and Beyond An illustration might be a concrete depiction that calls upon the traditions of classical drawing and painting—its goal being to reproduce the empirical world in a way that responds to actual conditions of light, form, and perspective. Alternatively, an illustration might be a graphically stylized image that approaches abstraction, referring to the real world as a grounding point but favoring the expressive qualities of gesture, ambiguous space, and the process of making the image. Between these two extremes lie the possibilities of mixing elements of each state.

SCRATCHY, ALMOST DISTRAUGHT cross-hatching, produced with pen and ink, enhances the mysterious and slightly sinister quality of the image.

Ames Bros. *United States*

THE RICH, ALMOST collagelike mixture of tools used to create this image—airbrush, pen, digital images, flat ink—contributes textural contrast and multiple layers of meaning to consider.

Maciej Hajnrich *Poland*

The Medium Is a Message A line is a line is a line… or not. Every drawing and painting tool makes characteristic marks and affords a designer a specific kind of visual language. The language of the tool has a powerful effect on an illustration's communicative value, not just on its visual qualities relative to other elements in a design solution. Above and beyond the fundamental selection of subject matter components, composition, and degree of stylization, the medium a designer chooses with which to create the illustration carries meaning—in terms of feeling (softness, hardness, fluidity, and stiffness) and, sometimes, conceptually (for example, using a drawing tool native to a certain region or historical period for a project related to that region or period).

Experimenting with the mark-making possibilities intrinsic to different tools shows the endless possibilities of, as well as the opportunities for controlling, the expression of an illustrated image. Here, the same subject is illustrated using different tools to show how powerful the effect of the medium is on communication.

THE SLICK, DIGITAL quality of the linear drawing, gradations in color, and sharply defined silhouetted hands impart a contemporary, technological feel to this poster.

344 Design *United States*

Graphic Translation One particular kind of stylized illustration—known as graphic translation—evolved from the poster tradition of Switzerland and Germany in the early part of the twentieth century. Graphic translation combines some attributes of both icon and symbol. It depicts subjects in a literal way, like an icon, but also in a self-consciously abstract way that takes on symbolic qualities. A translation attempts to convey the concrete, fundamental "truth" of a subject, without details that are specific to that one particular instance of it; for example, a translation of a cat strives to be about the idea "cat," but not about a specific cat; that is, how long its hair is or the markings of its particular breed. ■ Unlike an icon, however, which is strictly about shape, the textural and volumetric qualities of the subject are important considerations in finding an appropriate language with which to

THE GEOMETRIC form language chosen to translate the unicorn's head not only creates the animal's mane but also emphasizes the powerful thrust of the horn.

Sang-Duck Seo *Iowa State University, United States*

Compare the graphic translations (top) of three different objects presented here with examples of the same objects in the form of icons (bottom).

Note the differences in construction, formal complexity, and conceptual overlay between the translation and its respective icon.

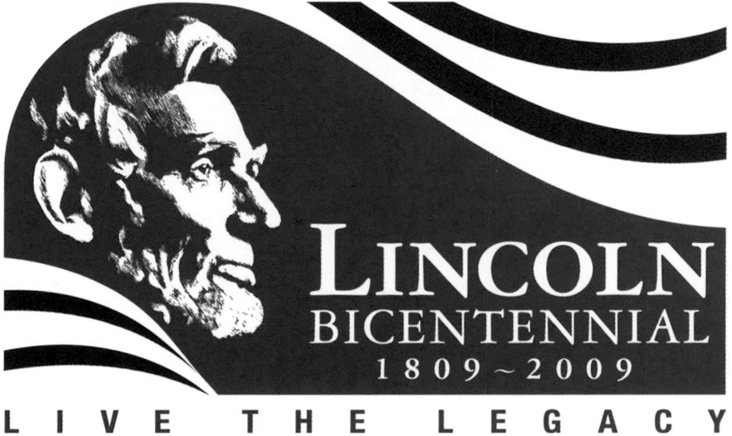

THE TRANSLATION LANGUAGE used to portray U.S. President Abraham Lincoln uses the interaction of light and shadow but renders these shapes with texture that suggests this image is a statue of Lincoln, further enhancing his status as a historical and cultural icon.

Metropolitan Group *United States*

translate it: the cat translation must indicate that cats, in general, are soft or furred, that they are slinky and athletic, and so on. A translation might be simple and stylized, or it might be relatively naturalistic, taking on characteristics such as surface detail or effects of light. ■ Graphic translation differs from conventional illustration in that its visual language, or "form language"—the marks used to make the drawing—is reduced to the point that there's nothing extra, only the shapes and marks needed to describe the subject. ■ The medium used for the drawing is important only if its characteristic marks help describe the subject's form or feeling. A scratchy texture made by charcoal, for example, might be appropriate in describing the fragility or dryness of an autumn leaf, but the texture does not exist for its own sake. ■ Most often, a translation is developed simultaneously with other visual material in a layout—the designer chooses translation as the illustrative option in advance—so that its shape, details, and textural qualities are dynamically integrated with photographs, typeface selection, abstract elements, and their positioning, in combination with the qualities of the translation.

THE REPETITION of concentric black arcs used to describe the butterfly's wings alludes to their movement.

Sohyun Kim *Iowa State University, United States*

These leaf translations all share an overall quality of recognition—the selection of details communicates the idea "leaf" in its simplest, distilled entirety—but the language of the translation is changed in each, affording knowledge of different aspects of the idea "leaf" as well as specifically integrating a given translation with the formal qualities of different typographic options.

THE ICONIC OUTER FORM of the lightbulb is elevated to translation status by virtue of its indistinct, sparkling inner contour—a formal adjustment that suggests the bulb's function. The filament is made symbolic through translation into circuits that also appear to represent leafy branches.

Templin Brink Design *United States*

IN A NOD TO illustration styles of the mid-twentieth century, this translation focuses on a simplified breakdown of light and shadow to clarify the form, while specific details—the bright buttons and the shine of the boot—add information.

Research Studios *United Kingdom*

Collage: Old and New Assembling graphic elements in a free pictorial composition, called "collage," is a relatively recent development in illustration. It derives from the evolution of representation in fine art from depicting a strictly singular viewpoint through the construction of multiple viewpoints, or cubism, into incorporating multiple viewpoints of several, possibly physically unrelated, scenes or references. Collage was initially used to add two-dimensional printed or found material—labels, fabric, bits of newspaper, flat pieces

COLLAGE OFFERS the designer of this book tremendous variety in formal qualities that add contrast and vitality to simple shapes. Typography, found engraving, paint marks, transparent overlays, and crinkled texture all combine to resolve the movement and spatial interaction of the composition.

Andreas Ortag *Austria*

THE CUTOUT LETTERS of the word "democracy" hint at the political dialogue inherent in that social system. The addition of the scissors and the work gloves gives evidence to democracy's constructive nature and creates ambiguous scale and spatial relationships.

Studio International *Croatia*

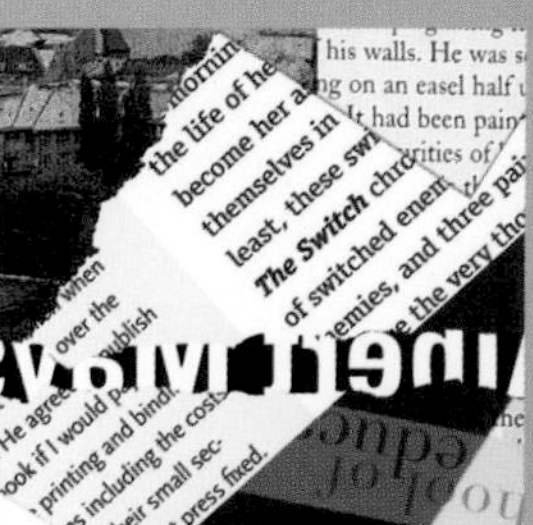

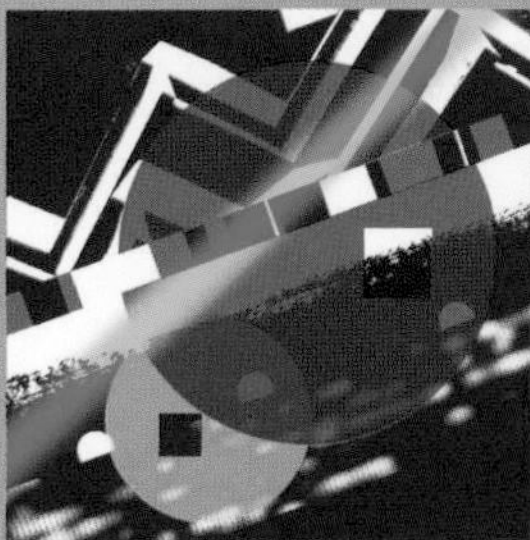

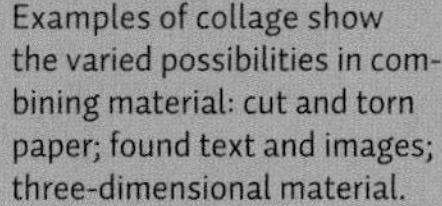

Examples of collage show the varied possibilities in combining material: cut and torn paper; found text and images; three-dimensional material.

Digital collage allows for photographic effects—transparency, blending, blurring, intricate silhouetting, and masking not possible with conventional, cut-and-paste techniques.

of wood, and so on—into paintings, but, with the rise of photography as a medium, it quickly incorporated photographic images. Collaging photographic images, rather than illustrative images, is usually called "photomontage" and has been a popular method of illustration since the 1920s. ■ Collage is a highly intuitive illustrative approach that takes into account not only the possibility of disparate subjects appearing in one space but also the nature of the combined elements—meaning how exactly they were made. Drawn and painted components can coexist with cut or torn pieces of textured paper, cropped images, scraps of fabric, parts of actual objects, and other drawn, painted, or printed material. Given that the pictorial space in a collage is abstract because of its fragmented construction, the designer must resolve compositional issues similar to those in any other image; but he or she must also address each item's internal visual qualities—overall visual activity, flatness of color relative to texture, and recognizability of the source material (such as printed words or croppings of image). ■ In particular, because the source components of a collage might be recognizable, the conceptual relationship between abstract and representational elements is extremely important. Integrating recognizable imagery, with its own subjects and messages, helps direct the message and adds degrees of meaning. ■ Collage is still a common approach to illustration and page layout in the digital environment, where not only scanned images of found or hand-generated material can be combined with photographic material, but also where photographic effects such as transparency, multiple exposure, blurring, and silhouetting—techniques made possible only by the computer—can be investigated.

THIS PROPOSAL FOR a currency design digitally collages complex linear, textural, and typographic material, exploiting the computer's ability to integrate complex color and transparency into the collage process.

Benjamin Myers *Laguna College of Art and Design, United States*

THE MEANING OF the elements brought together in a collage is important—and not just what the images portray but their medium of creation as well. In these two posters for a film festival, the film reel is iconic and modern and both times portrayed as an apple whose symbolic meaning is one of knowledge. The engraved images connote a connection to history, and the photographic transparencies and gradation changes suggest the element of light.

AdamsMorioka *United States*

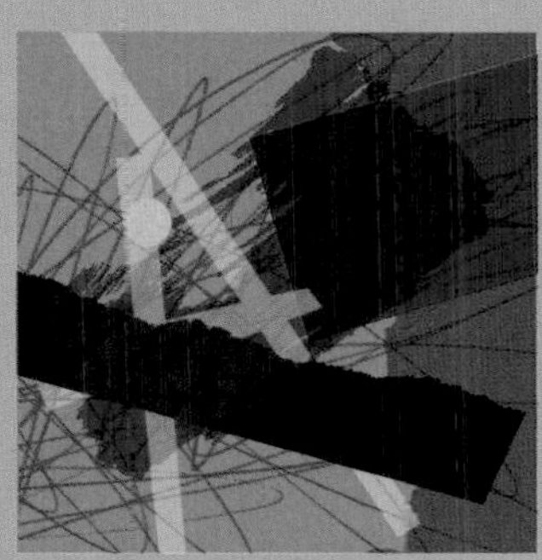

In this study, the message changes as the content of the collage's components are changed. As the content becomes more recognizable, the collage transmits a more literal—and, therefore, more specific—message.

Photography The "pure" photographic image has become the preeminent form of illustration in recent years. One reason for this might be the speed at which photographs transmit information—their realism and directness allow a viewer to enter the image and process it very quickly, rather than get distracted by abstract pictorial issues such as texture, medium, and composition. Access speed in imagery has become important because the flood of visual messages encountered by the average viewer requires images to compete robustly for attention. ■ While composition plays an important role in the quality of the photographic image and its messaging potential, its presence as a mediating phenomenon is much harder to recognize and, therefore, is often overlooked on a conscious level by the viewer. This suggests another reason for the primacy of photographs as communicators: the fact of the image's mediation (or manipulation)—through composition, selective focus, lighting, cropping, and other techniques—is secondary to the acceptance of photographic images as "real." This provides the designer with an upper hand in persuasion, on behalf of a client, because the work of convincing a viewer that he or she can believe or trust the image is already well on its way to being achieved: "I saw it

A

B

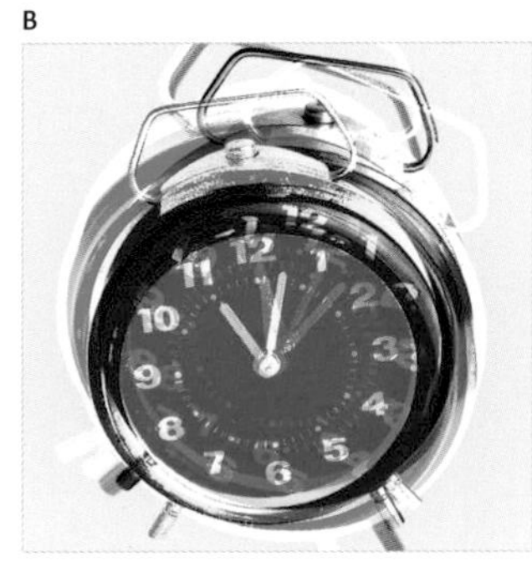

Because photographic images are so readily perceived as depictions of reality, the designer has incredible leeway in manipulating them without sacrificing believability. Despite the surreal situation depicted in the top image (A), for example, viewers will find it easy to accept the scene as credible. Further, this automatic assumption about the veracity of a photograph permits designers to evoke sensory experiences through their manipulation. Presenting a graphically exaggerated photograph of an object, as seen in the lower example (B), trades on its believability and the corrollary common understanding of its function to create an immediately recognizable aural experience.

Josse
De Pauw

Contact
Belgique
jossedepauw@pi.be

18

with my own eyes." ■ Today's average viewer, although much more sophisticated and attuned to the deceptive potential of photography than viewers in previous generations—who were unfamiliar with photography's use to disguise, manipulate, or enhance—is still much more likely to accept the content of a photograph as truth than that of an illustration, simply because the illustration is obviously contrived; the contrivance possible in a photograph is not so readily appreciated.

A

B

C

As with any other imagery, photographic content must be decisively composed. The photographer has two opportunities to control the image's composition, however: first, within the frame of the camera's viewfinder; and second, during the printing process in the darkroom (or in cropping a digital photograph using software). In this study, a minor shift in camera angle produces a variation on an already decisive composition of elements (B). Radically changing the viewpoint (C) creates a very different composition while retaining the identity of the content.

A PHOTOGRAPH IS considered well-shot and compelling when it exhibits a strong and varied tonal range—from deep shadow areas, into rich middle tones, and into bright highlights.

Martin Oostra *Netherlands*

In photography, tonal range—the number and depth of gray values—is of particular concern. Traditionally, a "good-quality" photograph includes a clean, bright white; deep black; detail present within shadow areas; and a fluid range of grays in between. This same range, from darkest shadow to brightest highlight, also is desirable in color photographs. Pushing the tonal range toward generally brighter values decreases the contrast in the image and, to some degree, flattens it out; pushing the tonal range toward the shadow end also tends to flatten the image but increases contrast and causes highlight areas to become brighter and more pronounced. These effects of tonality shift are shown in the accompanying images, in both black-and-white and color. Note the contrast differences between corresponding images.

A Pictorialization
LSD *Spain*

B Pictorialization
Jelena Drobac *Serbia*

C Illustrative pictorialization
Sagmeister *United States*

D Ornamentation
Finest Magma *Germany*

A

B

C

D

Pictorialization When type becomes a representation of a real-world object, or takes on the qualities of something from actual experience, it has been pictorialized. In illustrative pictorialization, forms are drawn to appear to be made out of a recognizable material or to form part of a recognizable object.

Form Alteration Changing the structural characteristics of type elements to communicate a non-literal idea is another strategy. Distorting letter shapes or proportions in an adjective, for example, can change the quality of its description. Such alteration may have a syntactic quality as well; setting the word "exaggerated" with distorted, oversized Gs exploits their sound and the word's meaning.

Pictorial Inclusion Illustrative elements brought into the type forms so that they interact with its strokes or counterforms are said to be *included*. The type retains its essential form, but the pictorial matter is integrated by reversing out of the type or by replacing the counterforms within or between the letters.

Form Substitution Replacing a type form with a recognizable object or another symbol is referred to as a substitution. Many real-world objects share visual structure with letters. Circular objects are often substituted for a letter O, for example. Images aren't the only elements that may be substituted for a type form—replacing a letter with another character is also a common strategy for substitution.

Type as Image When a letter or word takes on pictorial qualities beyond those that define their form, they become images in their own right, and their semantic potential is enormous. Words that are also pictures fuse several kinds of understanding together: they are supersigns. As their meaning is assimilated through each perceptual filter—visual, emotional, intellectual—they assume the evocative stature of a symbol. Understanding on each level is immediate, and a viewer's capacity to recall images makes such word-pictures highly effective in recalling the verbal content associated with them. ■ As is true with so many aspects of strong typographic design, making type into an image means defining a simple relationship between the intrinsic form of the letters and some other visual idea. It is easy to get lost in the endless possibilities of type manipulation and obscure the visual message or dilute it. A viewer is likely to perceive and easily remember one strong message over five weaker ones—complexity is desirable, whereas complication is not. ■ Type can be transformed into an image by using a variety of approaches. Each provides a different avenue of exploration, and several might be appropriate both to the desired communication and to the formal aspects of the type itself.

E

Ornamentation Typography can be transformed with ornaments—borders, dingbats, dots, lines, and geometric shapes—either structural or purely decorative. If the ornaments are symbolic in nature, they might take on the aspect of an inclusion and therefore be more strongly connected to the meaning of the word. An ornament's style might affect the viewer's sense of the historical context of the type; for example, a flourish or antique dingbat from a particular period.

Syntactic Deconstruction Changing the visual relationships between the parts of a word or a phrase is a deconstruction—the inherent structure of the word is called out or changed by being deformed—and the fact that it is related to the nature of meaning makes it a syntactic deconstruction. The cadence of the spoken word, the word's syllables, the prefix, the suffix, and individual letters are all sources for deconstruction.

F

SPARROW
PRODUCTIONS

G

nobody's
perfect

H

I

J

K

L

E Form alteration
Shinnoske, Inc. *Japan*

F Pictorial inclusion
MV Design *United States*

G Form deconstruction
Leonardo Sonnoli *Italy*

H Form substitution
Raidy Printing Group *Lebanon*

I Pictorial inclusions with form substitution
C+G Partners *United States*

J Illustrative pictorialization
Stereotype Design *United States*

K Form alteration
Mixer *Switzerland*

L Form alteration and substitution
Paone Design Associates *United States*

A

B

C

D

The meaning and emotionally evocative aspects of the subject change as a result of the variations' respective compositions. When the figure is presented full-on and positioned with relatively even space around it (A), it is somewhat neutral, or more descriptive; the viewer is looking at the figure. Positioning the figure off center (B), so that the space around it is more dynamic, creates a sense of movement, but also anxiety. Composing the figure as an extremely small element within the format (C) isolates it, increases the viewer's anxiety, and evokes a sense of alienation. Re-cropping the figure (D) so that it extends beyond all sides of the format makes it feel confrontational.

MASSING THE COLLAGED elements along a horizon lends concrete spatial realism to the scene despite its textural and abstract surface qualities. The massing of dark areas also forces a sense of perspective that draws the viewer inward; this triangulated movement is counteracted by the circular title cluster at the top.

2 Fresh *Turkey*

Strategies for Composition Composition in an illustrated image is of great concern. In creating a drawn image—especially one that is naturalistic—designers sometimes forget that they are not bound by the realities of arrangement imposed by the scene they are rendering. Using the formal relationships of figure and ground (see Chapter 1, page 37) on an abstract level—particularly within a realistic representation—contributes to the illustration's power to communicate beyond the literal as well as helps engage the viewer and direct the eye. To simply place the subject in the central area of the illustration, without regard to the subject's outer contour, tension, and contrast of negative space, and so on, prevents the illustration from being resolved and creates a static presentation. ■ Just as cropping, position, relative sizes of elements, and contrast between linearity, mass, angles, and curves are intrinsic to the decisive layout of graphic elements and typography in a page environment, so too is their refinement within an illustrated image of utmost importance—and such considerations apply equally to photographed images.

A representational image is deconstructed here to show the various compositional strategies—beyond the selection of subject and drawing medium—that the designer has considered in creating a well-resolved image. Each aspect of the composition reinforces the others.

Positive and Negative Shapes

Contrast Between Mass and Line

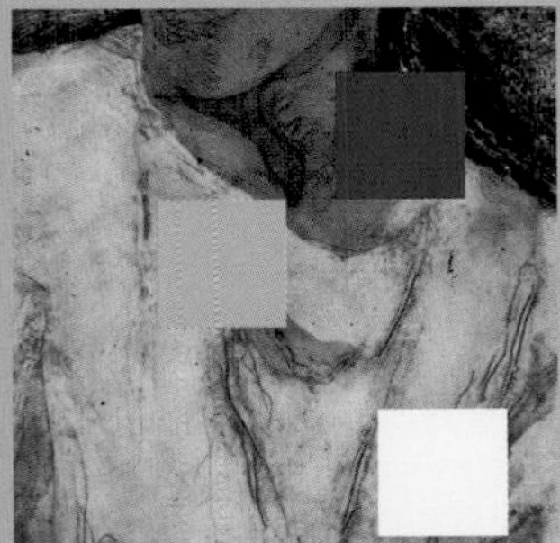
Color Relationships

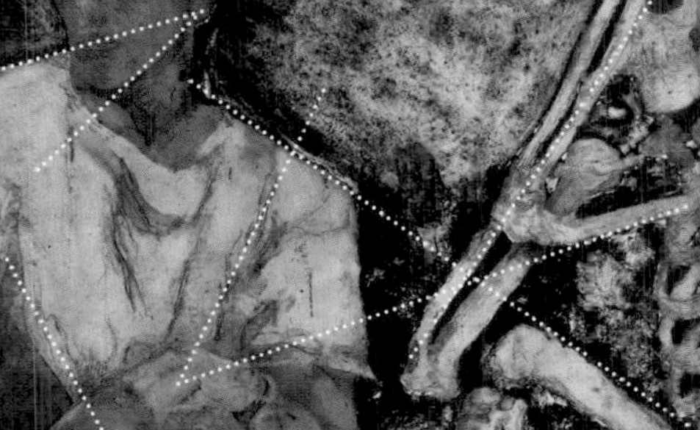
Directional Movement

Optical Weight Distribution

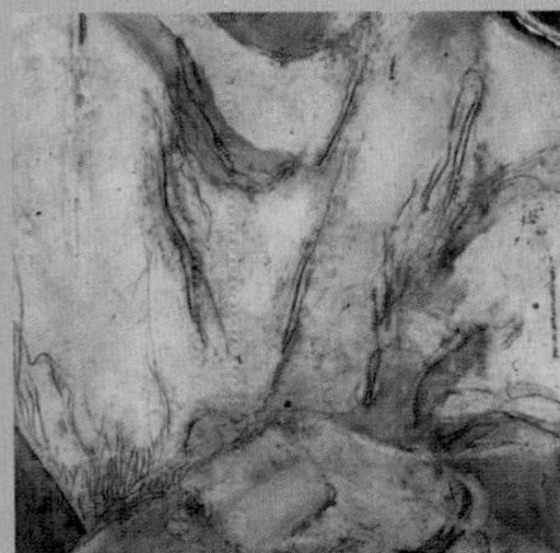
Gesture and Mark Quality

Value Distribution

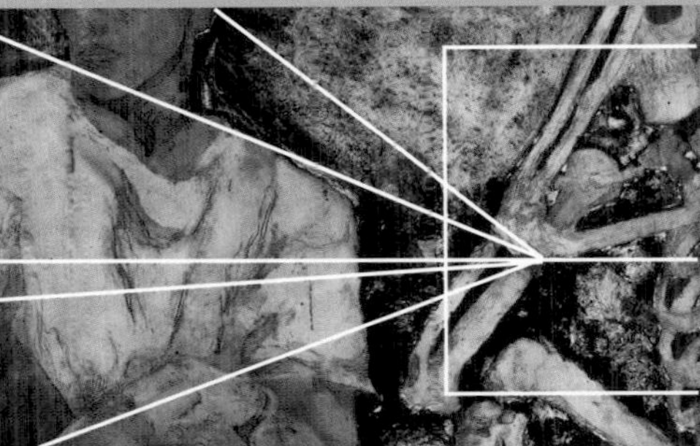
Perspective and Spatial Depth

Mixing Image Styles As with all compositional strategies, creating contrast among visual elements is key to surprising, refreshing, and enlivening layouts—and this is no less true for imagery. Aside from the big-picture contrasts afforded by changing sizes, shapes, color, and spatial arrangement, combining different modes of image offers an important and highly effective method for introducing contrast. Very textural, linear illustration, for instance, will contrast richly with photography—which tends to be continuous in tone—as well as with flat, solid graphic elements. ■ It's important that, while the different styles being combined contrast

This concise (yet by no means comprehensive) table compares the same pair of subjects presented in various combinations of image mode. Evaluate each pairing for similarities, as well as disparities, in visual form; which combinations produce the most unified visual relationships, and which have the most contrast? Then consider which combinations might also be the most useful for comparing related concepts, and which offer the richest interplay of concept.

with each other decisively, they also share some visual qualities. Similar to how these other decisions radically affect communication (as well as compositional quality), the decisions a designer makes regarding image types—icon, symbol, textural drawing, lush photograph—affect communication as well. Each kind of image brings certain associations with it. Photographs are associated with documentation or assumed to represent reality. They are concrete, pure, environmental, and reliable. Illustrations are perceived as "created" and personal, readily showing their method of creation; they evoke fantasy, display impossible or ideal situations, and portray their content in a subjective way—even if they are naturalistic. Icons, symbols, and translations distill and simplify complicated, abstract ideas; they are most often associated with diagrams, navigation, and identification. ■ The designer must combine image styles selectively to support a given purpose, using the qualities of each to appropriately convey intended messages and interact with each other in a unified visual language that assimilates their differences as part of their logic.

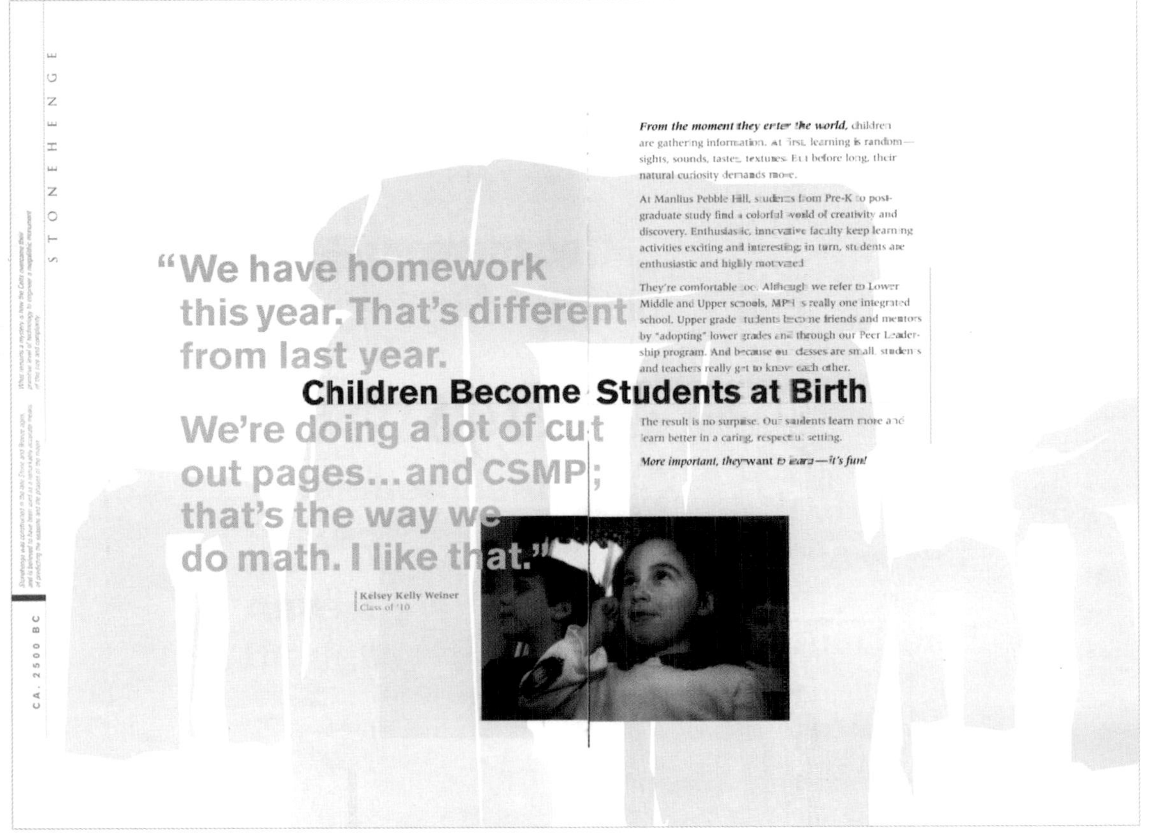

THE DECISION TO present the background image in illustrative form stems from the need to solve two problems. First, the designer wanted to avoid visual conflict between two photographs; the flatness of the illustration style visually separates it from the photograph and causes it to recede into the background. Second, the illustration enhances the temporal metaphor created by the two images—one showing a historical stage in cultural development, the other showing a developmental stage in education.

STIM Visual Communication *United States*

IMAGERY THAT LIES between the abstract and the concrete offers the viewer multiple levels of intrigue. Which is the real image in this poster detail; which is the abstraction? One kind of image, an icon or abstraction of sound waves as seen digitally, is used to create the lights and darks of a larger image: a face.

Mixer *Switzerland*

Selecting and Manipulating Content

A picture, as the saying goes, is worth a thousand words. Which words those are, however, is influenced by the designer and the photographer. The choice of the pictorial elements contained or not within a photograph, regardless of subject matter, has tremendous implications for meaning. Product catalogs—clothing catalogs, for example—often use imagery as a primary means of conveying concepts about lifestyle by showing people wearing the clothes in particular locations or situations. These images serve two purposes: they demonstrate the look of the clothes on real people, and they position the clothes relative to a lifestyle. Similarly, leaving certain facts out of a photograph might be just as influential as choosing what to include.

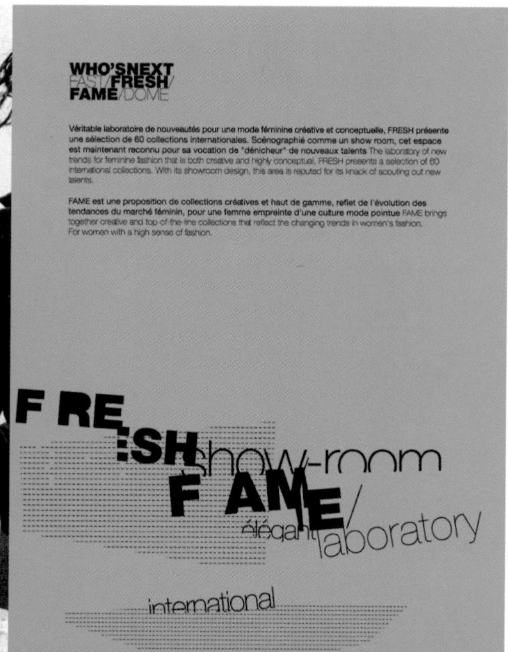

BY FOCUSING ON the indistinct reflection of the figure—and selectively cropping most of the solid figure's back—the designer intensifies the mystery surrounding who will be the next famous designer.

Research Studios *United Kingdom*

A

B

In this study of an image for a mystery novel's cover, the information conveyed by the image is altered—sometimes subtly, and sometimes dramatically—as a result of changes in content and composition. In the first version of the image (A), the content and lighting provide neutral facts: the viewer is in a bathroom, probably at a hotel. In version (B), this content is clarified by the addition of a hotel key—but altered through the addition of the knife and money, signifying foul play. The dramatic change in lighting, from even to more extreme, as well as the unusual direction of the light, enhances the sinister mood and further hints that something is wrong: why is the light on the floor? In the final version (C), a closer viewpoint helps create

The same figure is shown here photographed from the same viewpoint in different environments. Although the figure is the focus of the message, the environment affects the tone of the message, adds secondary meaning, and positions the figure in different relationships to the viewer.

THE ARTIFICE of hanging an award medal around the neck of the bottle dramatizes the quality of the wine and personifies the bottle.

Voice *Australia*

Beresford Wines are hand-crafted to capture the 'essence of McLaren Vale', catering for all levels of consumer preference.
From the entry level to the mid-range, through to the flagship icon brands and reserves, every wine has been crafted with the same attention to detail, representing great value for money and exceptional taste.
BERESFORD
ERESFORD
SHIRAZ

c

a feeling of paranoia—what's happening beyond the frame is unknown—and focuses attention on specific details: the time on the clock, the point of the knife, the money, and the hotel key. The manipulation of the light, as well as selective focus, helps draw attention to elements that may be relevant to the story.

In addition to whatever semantic content an image offers, viewers will project meaning on the image themselves, based on personal, as well as cultural, experience. In the current American cultural context, viewers are likely to project meaning related to "illegal drug use," even though the image doesn't offer any explicit reason for doing so.

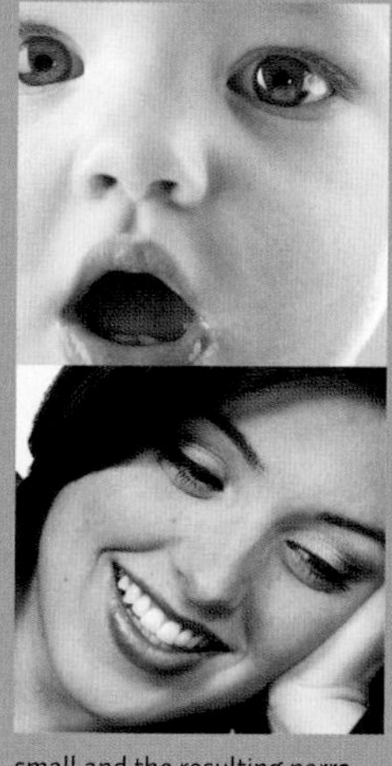

The same image changes semantically—in varying degrees—each time it's paired with an image carrying its own semantic meaning. In the first pair, the semantic gap is quite small and the resulting narrative subtle. In the second pair, the semantic gap creates the same narrative but dramatically alters some assumptions about the meaning of the base image. The third pair offers a semantic gap that forces the narrative in a completely unrelated—and unexpected—direction.

04 Risk

"I DON'T WANT TO TAKE THE RISK OF MOVING TO ITANIUM"

ITANIUM 2 IS A LOW RISK CHOICE FOR ORGANISATIONS – IT'S BUILT ON INDUSTRY STANDARDS AND OFFERS A HIGHLY RELIABLE COMPUTING PLATFORM

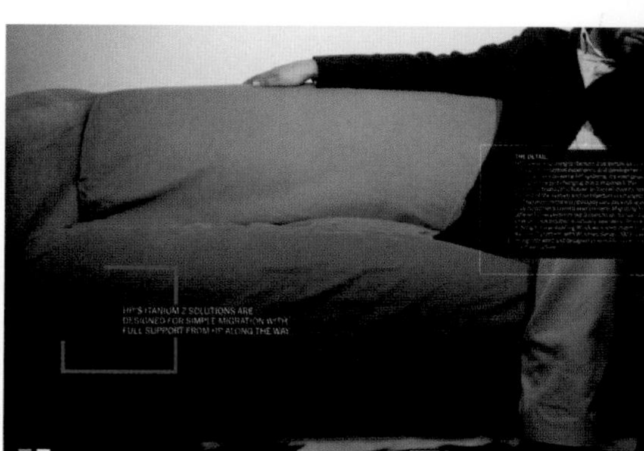

Narrative Interplay A single photograph delivers a powerful punch of "semantic" content—conceptual, verbal, and emotional meaning that likely includes messages that are not literally represented in its subject. Putting photographs together increases their semantic power and creates narrative, or storytelling; the instant two images can be compared, whether juxtaposed or arranged in sequence, a viewer will try to establish meaningful connections between them. ■ Every photograph will influence any others around it, changing their individual meanings and contributing to a progression in narrative as a result. For example, a viewer might see an image of a biker and a second image of a man in a hospital bed and construct a story about a biking accident. Neither image represents this idea; the narrative occurs in the viewer's mind. Even concluding that the man in the hospital bed is the same biker is an assumption the viewer creates. This distance between what is shown in two images and what the viewer makes happen internally is a kind of "semantic gap." Substituting the hospital image for one that shows a biker at the finish line of a race changes the narrative. The semantic gap is smaller and therefore a more literal progression, but the gap exists because the viewer still assumes the two bikers are the same person. ■ As more images are juxtaposed or added in sequence, their narrative reinforces itself based on the increasingly compounded assumptions initially made by viewers. By the time viewers have seen three or four images in a sequence, their capacity to avoid making assumptions decreases and they begin to look for meaning that completes the narrative they have constructed. ■ This "narrative momentum" increases exponentially to the point that viewers will assume the semantic content of any image appearing later in the sequence must be related to that delivered earlier, even if details in the later image empirically contradict those of the first images.

In this comparison of two sequences beginning with the same base image, the narratives are wildly different, but the narrative momentum of each concludes with assumptions that you, the viewer, has made that aren't necessarily true. The rubble in the last image of the lower sequence is not, empirically, that of the building shown earlier in the sequence. What assumptions have been made about the information in the other sequence that cannot be proven true?

SEQUENCING RELATED IMAGES from one spread to the next creates distinct narratives in each set of two page spreads shown at left. In both sequences, the repetition of recognizable, remembered subject components—the cheerleader, the couch—creates narrative momentum: the viewer recognizes a kind of cause and effect because the same object appears in each step of the narrative. In the cheerleader sequence, the semantic or narrative gap is relatively small: the cheerleader is in flight and then is caught and is assumed safe. The gap in the couch sequence is more extreme: we don't see the couch move from one location to the next, but it exists in a very different state in the second spread. We assume that it has been moved and now is being put to use.

Loewy *United Kingdom*

Word and Image: Brainwashing the Narrative Pictures greatly influence each others' meaning... and words, even more so. As soon as words–concrete, accessible, seductive–appear next to an image, the image's meaning is altered forever. Just as there is a semantic gap between images that are juxtaposed, so too is there such a gap between words and pictures. The gap might be relatively small, created by a direct, literal relationship between the two players. Or, the gap may be enormous, allowing the viewer to construct a narrative that is not readily apparent in the image when it appears by itself. The word "death," placed next to an image of a skull, for example, produces a relatively small semantic gap–although not as small a gap as the word "skull" would produce. Consider, however, the same skull image adjacent to the word "love;" the tremendous distance between what is shown and what is told, in this case, presents a world of narrative possibility. ■ Every image is susceptible to change when words appear next to it–so much so that a designer can easily alter the meaning of the same image over and over again by replacing the words that accompany it. In a sequential arrangement in which the same image is repeated in subsequent page spreads but is accompanied each time by a new word or phrase,

ALTHOUGH THE DIFFERENCE between the sharp photograph of the television and the blurred image that follows it creates a sense that the blurred image is a televised image, the juxtaposition of the words creates a different–yet possibly related–meaning for the viewer.

Brett Yasko *United States*

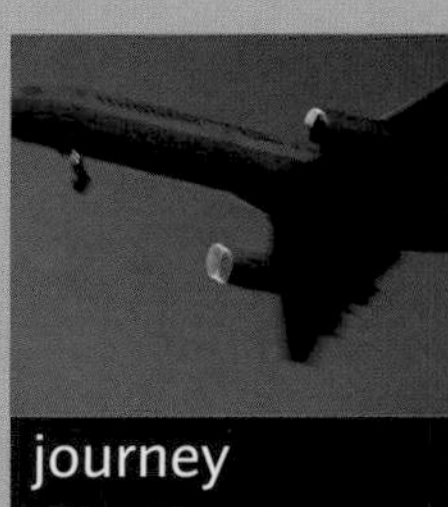

The same image is shown paired with different words. The semantic gap between word and image–the weird, nebulous area wherein the viewer can construct a narrative relationship between the two–is closer in the first pair, wider in the second, and extremely wide in the third.

The brainwashing effect works in reverse. Here, the same word is paired with different images, and the change in semantic gap, as well as in the word's meaning, becomes more pronounced.

new experience and knowledge about the image are introduced to the viewer. Once this knowledge is introduced, the viewer will no longer be able to consider the image in its original context. The meaning of the image, as far as the viewer is concerned, will be the composite meaning that includes all the information acquired through the sequence. ■ Not surprisingly, the ability of images to change the meanings of words is equally profound. This mutual brainwashing effected by words and images depends a great deal on the simultaneity of their presentation—that is, whether the two are shown together, at once, or in succession. If seen simultaneously, word and image will create a single message in which each reciprocally advances the message and neither is truly changed in the viewer's mind—the message is a gestalt. However, if one is seen first and the other second, the viewer has a chance to construct meaning before being influenced. In such cases, the semantic gap is greatly widened and the impact of the change is more dramatic: the viewer, in the short time given to assimilate and become comfortable with the meaning of the first word or image he or she has seen, must give up his or her assumptions and alter his or her mindset.

THE WORD AND the white frame focus attention on the grouping of furniture in the image, transforming it into an altar.

Finest Magma *Germany*

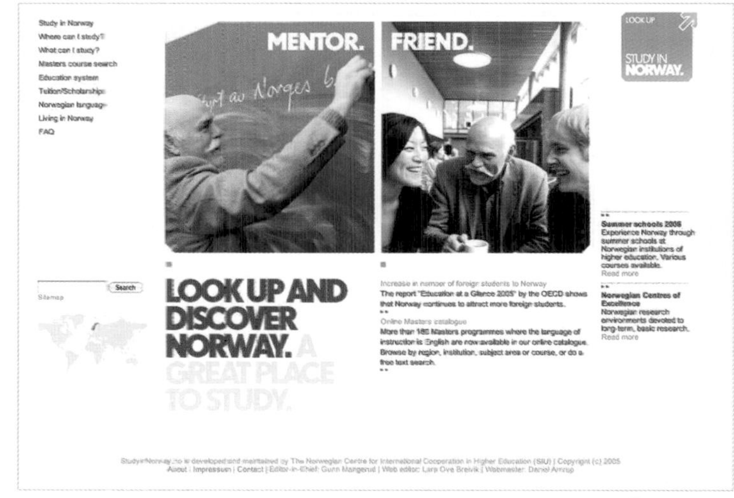

TWO IMAGES OF the same person, juxtaposed with two different headlines, create a double identity for the man as teacher and companion

Cobra *Norway*

THE WORD AND THE IMAGE not only mutually enhance each other's meaning, each depends on the other to communicate appropriately in context.

Paone Design Associates *United States*

Ever Metaphor? In writing and speech, a metaphor is an expression—a word or phrase—that refers to an unrelated idea, creating additional meaning. Images can be used in much the same way: a designer may present an image that means something else entirely, refers to a much broader concept, or combines concepts to evoke a third concept that is not explicit in either of the combinants. ■ A symbol is a simple example (see page 171), but such "visual metaphors" may be very complex in their associations. One option for creat-

211
rfd

Dean, Rebecca F.
Library Science Consultant
beccadean@riseup.net
347 834-6740

THE TYPOGRAPHY of this card is a metaphor for the client's area of practice.

Maris Bellack *United States*

PRESENTING THE NUMERALS as large architectural elements is a kind of photographic pictorialization that metaphorically supports the subject matter of the poster but also transforms the text—verbal ideas—into concrete constructions.

Studio International *Croatia*

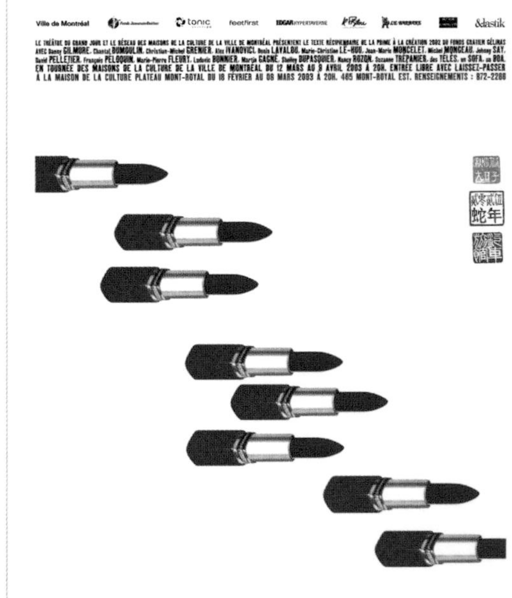

TRANSFORMING lipsticks into bullets creates a metaphorical dialogue about the nature of gender relations and aggression.

Thomas Csano *Canada*

ing a visual metaphor is to use an object to define the form of something else—for example, laying out an invitation to a travel-themed fundraising event to look like an airline ticket, using the type styles, colors, and other visual details of such tickets as a source. Another option is to depict one thing behaving, pictorially, like another—presenting products in an urban cosmetics brochure, for instance, configured as a city skyline. Yet another possibility is to combine two or more seemingly unrelated images to suggest another form with its own meaning, implying some narrative connection between ideas—showing a corn cob with wheels to suggest the idea of plant-based auto fuel. A designer may also consider altering one image by having another act upon it—chopping the first image up, mixing it into a texture, pushing it out of the way, making it vibrate, and so on. ■ There are as many ways to create metaphors as there are ideas and images—in short, an endless array limited only by imagination. While the literal content of images provides a baseline communication, a thoughtful designer can use images to evoke higher-level concepts above and beyond what they merely show. The result is a richer, more inventive, and more memorable and meaningful experience for the audience.

THE GRAPHIC SHAPE of the cigarette creates a focus of attention, letterboxing the action in this sequence of frames from a public service commercial. It also confines and traps the people, and then metaphorically burns them to ash.

2Fresh *Turkey*

IN THIS CONCEPTUAL promotional piece, small cubes of sugar are wrapped in typography that expresses ideas about "sweetness" from a survey and packages them together.

Coma *Netherlands*

THE PLACEMENT of the repeated, green logotype at floor level along the glass wall creates a grassy environment, bringing the outdoors inside and vice versa.

BBK Studio *United States*

PUTTING IT ALL TOGETHER

Chapter 5

> There is no recipe for a good layout. What must be maintained is a feeling of change and contrast.
>
> **Alexey Brodovitch**
>
> Graphic designer and art director

”

Begin with the end in mind.

Lana Rigsby

Principal, Rigsby Design

EVERY ASPECT OF THIS branded literature system consistently reinforces a language of movement and shape while maintaining contrast and flexibility: the angled die-cuts of brochure pages and folder covers; the slanted alignment of text columns; the use of large-scale numerals and titling in varnish; the selection of type styles; and the austere color palette of black, silver, magenta, and orange.

344 Design *United States*

Visual Logic: How Everything Talks to Each Other Design solutions really come together when all the components are clearly interrelated. First off, a format's proportions should begin to evoke appropriate feelings in the viewer—intimate, expansive, or confrontational—right from the moment they come in contact with the work. Content organization should respond to the format, as well as the requirements of the information presented; the selection of images and type styles should support each other stylistically, reciprocally reinforcing mood and concept. The arrangement of type and images should respond to each other visually, and their composition within the format space should again augment the emotions or associations that are more literally apparent in the content of both images and writing. ■ Furthermore, the pacing and sequencing of the content should respond to emphases within the content and create visual highs and lows—alternations of sequences that are dramatic and sedate—to continually refresh the viewer. Thoughtful consideration of typographic and abstract details should be apparent in the way they refer to large-scale compositional elements or spatial interaction. Last, the physical, experiential quality of the work should be considered in the context of its production medium, whether electronic or printed and bound. When a designer sees the project through in all these aspects, the result is a powerful totality of experience: one that is evocative, emotional, useful, enjoyable, and memorable.

A Visual Logic Checklist It's important to consider the big picture of a design solution—the concept and overall layout—in light of its internal components to ensure all of its aspects are interrelated in supporting that concept. At each stage of development, evaluate each aspect in combination.

- ***Does the typographic detail visually relate to image styles, as well as convey messages appropriate to the text?***
- ***Does the form of graphic elements communicate with images?***
- ***Do the images play off each other to enhance intended messages, and does any image or combination thereof deliver unintended messages?***
- ***Does the color system add to the concept?***
- ***What about print techniques, paper, and binding details?***

Image Mode or Style

Image Combination

Compositional Strategies

Physical Aspects

Color

Typeface Selection

Image Content

Organization

Structure

Selection of Forms

Organizational Strategies: Structure and Intuition Figuring out what goes where, in what order, and how it should be arranged from a compositional standpoint demands a lot from a designer. A client might supply some content in a particular order, but the designer really has to understand the content and, potentially, reorder it when necessary to improve its clarity or enhance its conceptual aspects. ■ On a visual level, how much appears at any given time and the actual arrangement are decisions a designer alone must make. As the sequence and pacing of the content is being planned, the designer must also address the specific visual relationships of text and image. How structured, neutral, or documentary does the presentation need to be? What happens if the material is organized in a less structured way? How are the images and the text visually related, and how do they interact within the format? Answering these questions might involve both analytical and intuitive study of the content to see how different methods help or hinder the presentation. ■ A designer must often switch between these two extremes–

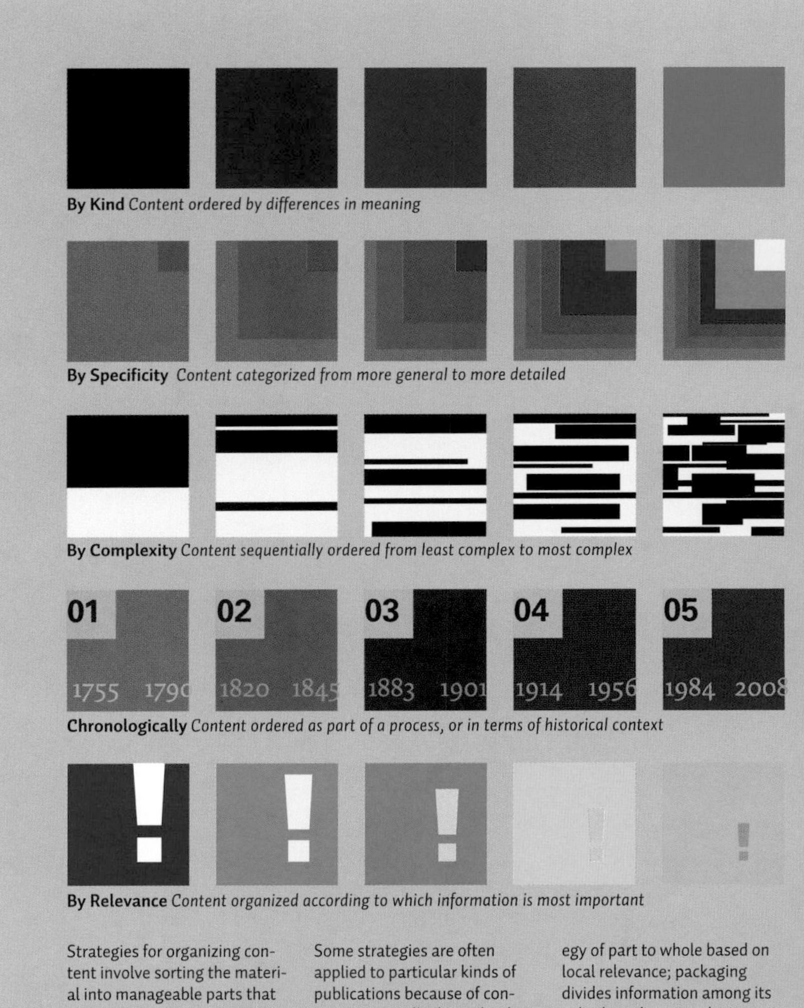

By Kind *Content ordered by differences in meaning*

By Specificity *Content categorized from more general to more detailed*

By Complexity *Content sequentially ordered from least complex to most complex*

Chronologically *Content ordered as part of a process, or in terms of historical context*

By Relevance *Content organized according to which information is most important*

Strategies for organizing content involve sorting the material into manageable parts that are related to each other: by kind; by part to whole; by frequency; by complexity; chronologically; and by relevance. Some strategies are often applied to particular kinds of publications because of convention–usually driven by the expectations of the audience. Newspapers, for example, exhibit an organizational strategy of part to whole based on local relevance; packaging divides information among its sides based on complexity.

messing around with the material to see what's possible, analyzing the visual and conceptual clarity of the results, and then returning to freer exploration to test whether the analysis is accurate or useful. Some basic organizational methods have become common in graphic design practice, especially in regard to typography; some are structurally based, and others respond more intuitively to conceptual and tactile qualities.

STRUCTURED ON A two-column grid, these sample pages from a catalog presenting Dutch playwrights organize the content into sections whose internal structure repeats. The introduction and index of writers follow a similar text-based scheme, with a bold heading used to introduce each section. Within each given writer's section, the bold headline strategy is maintained, and the section is broken down into parts: an image spread of the writer; a biography spread; and then consecutive spreads as needed for a sample of that writer's work.

Martin Oostra *Netherlands*

Introduction

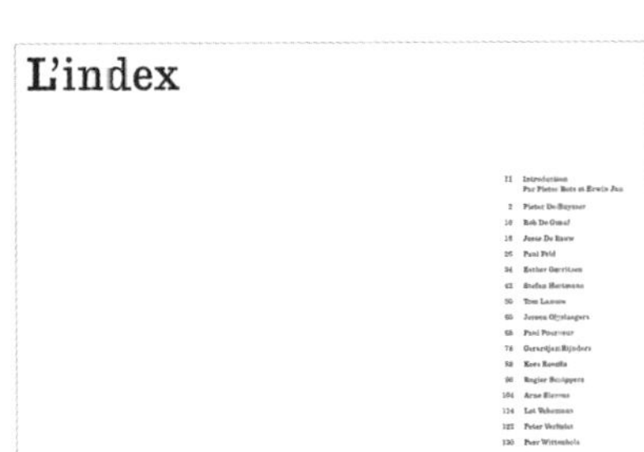

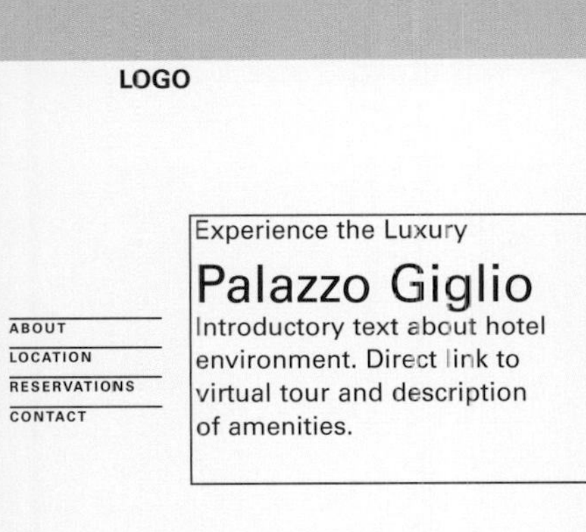

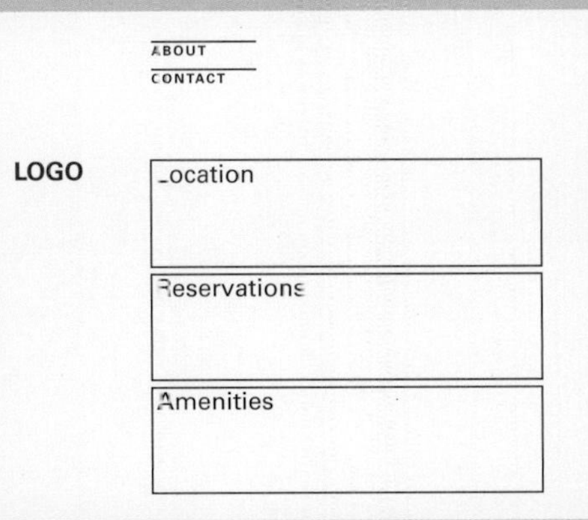

Sorting the same content in different ways might call attention to specific parts over others and thereby affect the emphasis of these specific parts. Whether the content is a website or a printed brochure or book, convention generally dictates that material that comes first should be assumed to have greater significance. Adjusting the order to create a narrative flow that enhances focus on specific content changes the experience, as seen here in these hypothetical examples: alternate options for a hotel's website navigation, shown as wireframe models for the home page.

Structure: The Grid System All design work involves problem solving on both visual and organizational levels. Pictures, fields of text, headlines, and tabular data: all these pieces must come together to communicate. A grid is simply one approach to achieving this goal. Grids can be loose and organic, or they can be rigorous and mechanical. To some designers, the grid represents an inherent part of the craft of designing, the same way joinery in furniture making is a part of that particular craft. The history of the grid has been part of an evolution in how graphic designers think about designing, as well as a response to specific communication and production problems that needed to be solved. Among other things, a grid is suited to helping solve communication problems of great complexity. ■ The benefits of working with a grid are simple: clarity, efficiency, economy, and continuity. Before anything else, a grid introduces systematic order to a layout, helps distinguish between various types of information, and eases a user's navigation through them. Using a grid permits a designer to lay out enor-

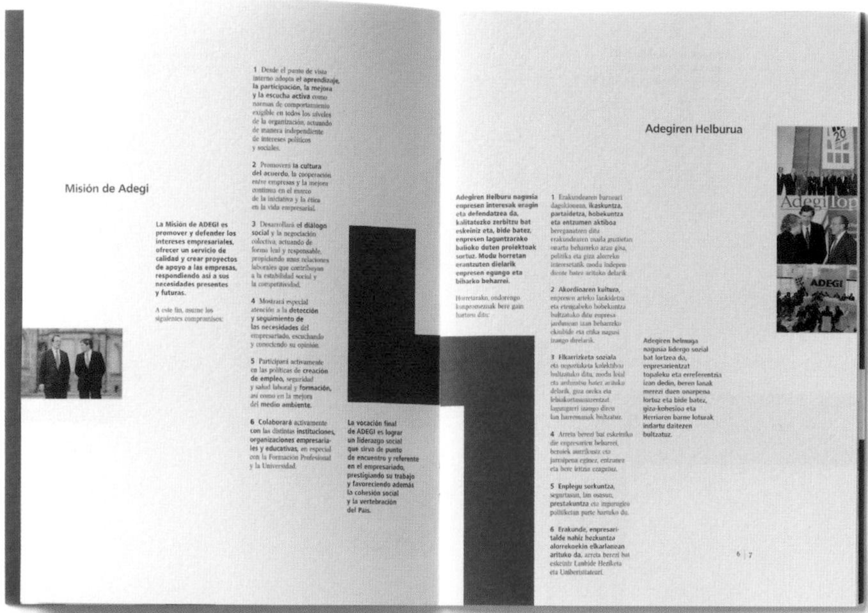

Punto de encuentro de las empresas guipuzcoanas

Gipuzkoako enpresen topaleku

THE TYPOGRAPHY, IMAGES, AND GRAPHIC ELEMENTS are arranged across a structure of four columns. The grid structure creates unity and flexibility among the material, helping to accommodate various amounts or mixtures of content and allowing the designer to lay out the content in variations so that the sequence of pages won't become monotonous. The resulting negative spaces, as well as the type, appear interrelated because they all are based on the same proportions.

LSD *Spain*

mous amounts of information in substantially less time because many design considerations have been addressed in building the grid's structure. The grid also allows many individuals to collaborate on the same project or on a series of related projects over time, without compromising established visual qualities from one instance to the next.

Margins are the negative spaces between the format edge and the content, which surround and define the live area where type and images will be arranged. The proportions of the margins bear a great deal of consideration, as they help establish the overall tension within the composition. Margins can be used to focus attention, serve as a resting place for the eye, or act as an area for subordinate information.

Flowlines are alignments that break the space into horizontal bands. Flowlines help guide the eye across the format and can be used to impose additional stopping and starting points for text or images. There may one flowline, or there may be several. If there are numerous flowlines at regular intervals, breaking the page top to bottom in a repeated proportion, a system of rows is created that intersects the vertical columns.

Spatial zones are groups of modules that form distinct fields. Each field can be assigned a specific role for displaying information; for example, one horizontal field might be reserved for images, and the field below it might be reserved for a series of text columns.

Columns are vertical alignments of type that create horizontal divisions between the margins. There can be any number of columns; sometimes they are all the same width, and sometimes they are different widths, corresponding to specific information. The page diagrammed here shows four columns of even width.

Markers are placement indicators for subordinate or consistently appearing text, such as running heads, section titles, folios, or any other element that occupies only one location in any layout.

Modules are individual units of space separated by regular intervals that, when repeated across the page format, create columns and rows.

Grid Anatomy A grid consists of a distinct set of alignment-based relationships that serve as guides for distributing elements across a format. Every grid contains the same basic parts, no matter how complex the grid becomes. These parts can be combined as needed or omitted from the overall structure at the designer's discretion, and the proportions of the parts is similarly dependent on the designer's needs. This book, for example, is structured on a 17-column grid to address several issues: an optimal column width for running text and captions; a static navigation system at the far left; consistent proportions between diagrams and caption text-widths; and flexibility to size and arrange contributor design projects. While text- and diagram widths necessitate a greater number of columns left-to-right, the need for flexibility in positioning dictates that no flowlines be established top-to-bottom.

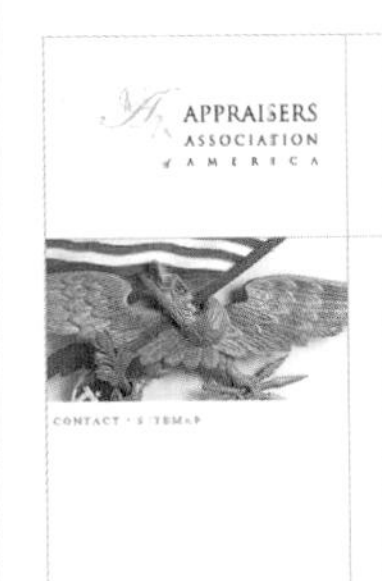

THE THREE-COLUMN GRID in this website portions out content in a clear hierarchy that users can navigate easily. The left column is reserved for branding and imagery; the upper portions of columns two and three define a spatial zone that contains major A-Level navigation and supporting B-Level navigation, respectively. Color changes in the text highlight the user's location in the navigation hierarchy. The bottom portions of columns two and three define a second spatial zone, combined for primary text content.

C. Harvey Graphic Design *United States*

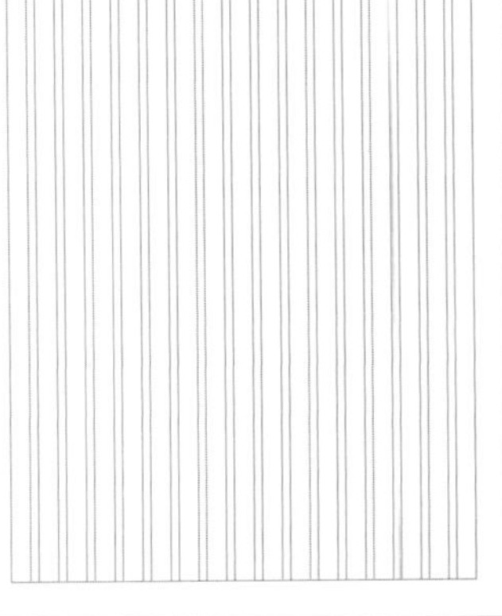

Column Grid Information that is discontinuous benefits from being organized into an arrangement of vertical columns. Because the columns can be dependent on each other for running text, independent for small blocks of text, or crossed over to make wider columns, the column grid is very flexible. For example, some columns might be reserved for running text and large images, while captions might be placed in an adjacent column. This arrangement clearly separates the captions from the primary material but maintains them in a direct relationship. ■ The width of the columns depends, as noted, on the size of the running text type. If the column is too narrow, excessive hyphenation is likely, and a uniform rag will be difficult to achieve. At the other extreme, a column that is too wide will make it difficult for

Any number of columns can be used, depending on the format size and the complexity of the content. Flowlines define horizontal alignments in increments from the top of the page. Within a column grid, a designer has a great deal of flexibility for arranging type and image material. Two- and three-column grids, among the most common used in designing publications, provide great potential for varying typographic width across the columns, integrating images, and differentiating columns with color. Regardless of the number of columns, the body and margins may be related asymmetrically or symmetrically (mirrored), as seen in the fourth column of examples.

the reader to find the beginnings of sequential lines. By studying the effects of changing the type size, leading, and spacing, the designer will be able to find a comfortable column width. Traditionally, the gutter between columns is given a measure, x, and the margins are usually assigned a width of twice the gutter measure, or 2x. Margins wider than the column gutters focus the eye inward, easing tension between the column edge and the edge of the format. This is simply a guide, however, and designers are free to adjust the column-to-margin ratio as they see fit. ■ In a column grid, there is also a subordinate structure. These are the flowlines: vertical intervals that allow the designer to accommodate unusual breaks in text or images on the page and create horizontal bands across the format. The hangline is one kind of flowline: it defines the vertical distance from the top of the format at which column text will always start. A flowline near the top of the page might establish a position for running headers, pagination, or section dividers. Additional flowlines might designate areas for images (specifically) or different kinds of concurrent running text, such as a timeline, a sidebar, or a callout.

[G] IS FOR GREEK

Philanthropic work is a big part of every sorority and fraternity on campus; these groups strive for "social justice and selfless service." During November's Greek Week, they all banded together to raise money and donations for the victims of Hurricane Katrina. Additionally, the groups held a clothing drive for the Store Front — a homeless shelter for San Diego teens — and assembled hygiene kits which were shipped to poverty stricken areas around the world. Also, a campus-wide letter writing campaign to benefit St. Jude's Children's Hospital raised tens of thousands of dollars. Now a new national philanthropic sorority called Alpha Chi Omega has sprung up at USD. The organization has a mission of providing a dedicated career mentor for every member, in order to help deserving USD students further their career pursuits. The sorority's alumnae include U.S. Secretary of State Condoleezza Rice, *Time* magazine's 2002 Person of the Year Sherron Watkins — the Enron whistleblower — and Deidre Downs, 2005 Miss America. To learn more, go to www.alphachiomega.org.

[H] IS FOR HOSPICE

Ann Taylor, who is earning her Ph.D. in nursing at USD, volunteers with the residents who live at Tijuana's Casa Hogar Las Memorias. The home for ex-prisoners and others with HIV/AIDS — where the showers are always cold and sometimes there's no water at all — provides hospice care and helps get the residents off drugs. Taylor has volunteered there since 2000, bringing supplies and doing whatever needs to be done. She also practices healing touch to relax the patients or relieve pain. "I'm the 'white gringo' that comes and does 'the hand thing,'" she says, smiling at their description. She brings them comfort, hope and friendship. She also brings other USD nursing students to help out. They teach the men how to maintain a sterile medical environment and do dressings more effectively. And Taylor teaches symptom management for those who don't have the medication that could prolong their lives. "There are people 30 miles from us who have no shoes, no socks, no winter jackets," Taylor says. "It is quite a place. I love going down there. They've become like my family. They think I come to help them. They help me. They're addicted to drugs. I'm addicted to them." To find out how you can help, call Taylor at (858) 414-6188.

[I] IS FOR IMMIGRANT

Immigrants at both the South Sudan Community Center and the International Rescue Committee's First Things First program benefit from the talents of USD students. FTF offers English literacy help for mothers of preschoolers. At the SSCC, USD volunteers mentor children and offer homework help. Senior Meredith Stocking, USD's site coordinator for both programs, gets inspiration from volunteering. "It gives me a lot of perspective on how blessed I am," she says. Stocking recently helped a woman who is learning English work on health-related vocabulary since she wants to go into health care. "For me, volunteering is about learning and connecting with people."

[J] IS FOR JUVENILES

Downtown San Diego's Toussaint Academy of the Arts and Sciences serves teens in need of a home. USD alum John Weiss '0[illegible] (M.S.E.[illegible]) and fellow alums find teaching self-leadership there extremely fulfilling. "The kids see that we're just average people who are successful." Along with teaching life skills, the group helps out with internships, jobs, grants and letters of recommendation. To learn more, go to www.toussaintacademy.org.

[K] IS FOR KITCHEN

Ever wonder what happens to all the campus food when the students aren't around to eat it? For the past eight years, when Christmas break arrives, Dining Services packs up the perishables from each campus dining outlet and donates them to the Third Avenue Charitable Organization (TACO). The food is then distributed to people in need, including the homeless and local shelters. Go to www.firstlutheransd.org/Outreach/taco.html.

[L] IS FOR LEGAL CLINICS

You're a single mother cleaning houses and you've been hit with a half-million dollar tax bill incurred by your criminal ex-husband who's committed fraud and fled the country. Where to turn for help? USD Legal Clinics exists for situations just like that one, and did, in fact, help the woman rid herself of the bill. Other clinic specialties include helping children get their special needs met by their schools. Call (619) 260-7470.

30 | USD MAGAZINE

SPRING 2006 | 31

THE DESIGNER USES a four-column grid in different ways from page to page. On the left-hand page, longer, more involved text is spread across two-column widths. On the right-hand page, shorter text occupies individual columns, but images might occupy single or multiple column widths.

Barbara Ferguson *United States*

A THREE-COLUMN GRID is used to separate hierarchic components, based on the requirements of the text, relative to each kind of text's importance and optimal reading comfort.

Robert Rytter & Associates *United States*

BRENAU UNIVERSITY

You know you are doing well academically when...

Daniella: I could go back home and have intense conversations about politics, law, government policies, and presidential elections (just to name a few) with my parents' friends who have opposite opinions than I have.

Judith: I got a letter from Dean Halberg congratulating me for making the dean's list.

Annelie: When the good grades started rolling in.

Emily: When my teacher Dr. Webster said that she was proud of me. It was my first "A" on a Spanish test. It was probably the most exciting time of the year. It was a good feeling to know that I was succeeding.

The one teacher you must take while at Brenau is...

Judith: Dr. Barlow. I got so much out of his philosophy of religion class. He's a great teacher. He encouraged me to find out things for myself and he did not push his beliefs on me. To this day I think he is a great person.

Annelie: Dr. Dovile Budryte. Why? She is amazing and very nice. She was my professor but she also took the time to help me to understand this culture.

Daniella: Dr. Casey. She will expose you to a new way of thinking. If you do not share her opinion she will teach you to fight for what you believe in without backing down. I think that is very important nowadays. You have to back up what ever you say with facts. If not you will never survive in the real world.

"I've realized that being a woman is great. I've got so much power. I can do anything I want to do and be anything I want to be — and I don't have to apologize for it."

Judith Pannell '05

With an average student to teacher ratio of just 13-1, you can count on your professors knowing not just your name, but also your personal style, and your aspirations. You'll never be a social security number at Brenau. You'll be a success story.

6

BRENAU UNIVERSITY

Law school, a high paying career or a career in the arts that actually pays—the Brenau education gives you the skills to take on the world. Here, the whole culture is geared toward developing your professionalism, placing you in internships, and helping you land your dream job.

What kind of person does well at Brenau?

Emily: Definitely an active woman. This is a small college with so many leadership opportunities — anyone can go after them. There are so many types of leadership positions you can be at Brenau — art and business and community service. You have to take advantage of that. Also, you have to be a person who wants to succeed. And who wants to feel welcomed. You'll get both here.

Judith: An open-minded, hard-working woman who is serious about her career and her future. A woman with a good heart.

Annelie: A student who enjoys being involved in leadership and organizations. There are all kinds of opportunities.

What's your advice to high school seniors considering Brenau?

Judith: If you are serious about your future and want the best money can offer academically — take a serious look at Brenau.

Emily: Brenau is an easy transition from high school to college. It's going to challenge you, but it's going to be a good feeling when you succeed. And you'll get a ton of support your whole time here.

Kristin: If you want someplace to be called by name, get involved, and experience rich tradition, then Brenau is the place.

Annelie: Come and visit the campus. It is beautiful and the professors are so nice.

Haley: If you haven't visited campus — come and visit. If you don't think you can afford Brenau ask about scholarship options. They will do all they can to see that you can come.

Any regrets about going to Brenau?

Kristin: At Brenau I was able to be in a sorority, play soccer, be in student government, and keep up my scholarship. So it was easier for me on this campus to succeed in those things that I wanted to do in college. I have no regrets choosing Brenau. None at all.

Annelie: Not a one! This has been a wonderful learning experience.

Judith: Looking back, I don't have any regrets whatsoever. I love the faculty, the staff, and my classmates.

Even the squirrels are fearless.

There is a whole population of squirrels on campus that are totally fearless. Normally squirrels run away when you come near. Here, they'll stand there and look you in the eye. They'll scurry up right next to you. The squirrels here are not scared of anything. Normal squirrels are timid and afraid. Here, they don't shy away. Brenau squirrels are completely different from anywhere else. A breed of their own.

— Daniella Riveria

7

Modular Grid Extremely complex projects require even more precise control, and, in this situation, a modular grid might be the most useful choice. A modular grid is essentially a column grid with a large number of horizontal flowlines that subdivide the columns into rows, creating a matrix of cells called modules. Each module defines a small chunk of informational space. ■ Grouped together, these modules define areas called spatial zones to which specific roles can be assigned. The degree of control within the grid depends on the size of the modules.

Smaller modules provide more flexibility and greater precision, but too many subdivisions can become confusing or redundant. A modular grid also lends itself to the design of tabular information. The rigorous repetition of the module helps to standardize tables or forms and integrate them with the text and image material. ■ Aside from its practical uses, the modular grid accords a conceptual aesthetic. Between the 1950s and 1980s, the modular grid became associated with ideal social or political order. These ideals have their roots in the rationalist thinking of both the Bauhaus and Swiss International Style, which celebrates objectivity, order, and

MOST NEWSPAPERS, including this one from Denmark, are constructed on a precise modular grid, which allows for rapid and varied changes in content layout. The text is often situated across multiple column widths, depending on the size and importance of the story; the underlying column width can be found in the negative space at the bottom of the page, between the left-hand paragraph and the square inset image. The depth of the module is defined by the height of the masthead. Note how this proportion repeats in various instances farther down the page.

E-Types *Denmark*

DAGEN

TIRSDAG | 29.10.2002 | No.007 | PRIS: 15 KRONER

Politik A6 | 10 ÅRS INTEGRATION hjalp alt for lidt

Politik A4 | TJETJENIENS LEDERE VIL forhandle med Putin

Politik A2 | "LULA" BRASILIENS SVAR på Tony Blair

EUROPA

EUROPAS FORENEDE STATER

~~DET EUROPÆISKE FÆLLESSKAB~~

DET FORENEDE EUROPA

~~DEN EUROPÆISKE UNION~~

Det Europæiske Konvent sætter for første gang ord på tankerne om en slags EU-forfatning og bryder dermed mange års tabu om emnet. Men faktisk er den forsigtig, denne første skitse til fremtidens europæiske samarbejde

STILSTAND

TRÆNGT MEDICINALBRANCHE SENDER FÆRRE LÆGEMIDLER PÅ GADEN

Ansøgninger om godkendelse af nye lægemidler er halveret i forhold til sidste år

INDEX

Gianni Versace begejstrer briterne

I sit relativt korte liv nåede Versace ikke alene at sætte italiensk mode på den internationale dagsorden men også at skabe et trimm for excentriske udskejelser i moden såvel som blandt branchens topfolk.

B4

Dragen fra Hedehusene – Føljeton

"Nu gider jeg sgu ikke mere pis med jer," siger Claus til klassen og smækker døren efter sig. Næste gang eleverne og lærerne på Flaug Skole ser Claus og Henrik, kører de rundt i skolegården på en stjålet motorcykel.

B6

DAGEN

Here, a variety of modular grid structures shows a range of proportions and precision. The greater the number of modules, the more precise the layout might be; but too many increments become redundant. Variations on the number and stress of the module achieve different kinds of presence for the typographic and image content.

clarity. Designers who embrace these ideals sometimes use modular grids to convey this additional meaning. ■ How does a designer determine the module's proportions? The module could be the width and depth of one average paragraph of the primary text at a given size. Modules can be vertical or horizontal in proportion, and this decision can be related to the kinds of images being organized or to the desired stress the designer feels is appropriate. The margin proportions must be considered simultaneously in relation to the modules and the gutters that separate them. Modular grids are often used to coordinate extensive publication systems. If the designer has the opportunity to consider all the materials that are to be produced within a system, the formats can become an outgrowth of the module or vice versa. By regulating the proportions of the formats and the module in relation to each other, the designer might simultaneously be able to harmonize the formats and ensure they are produced most economically.

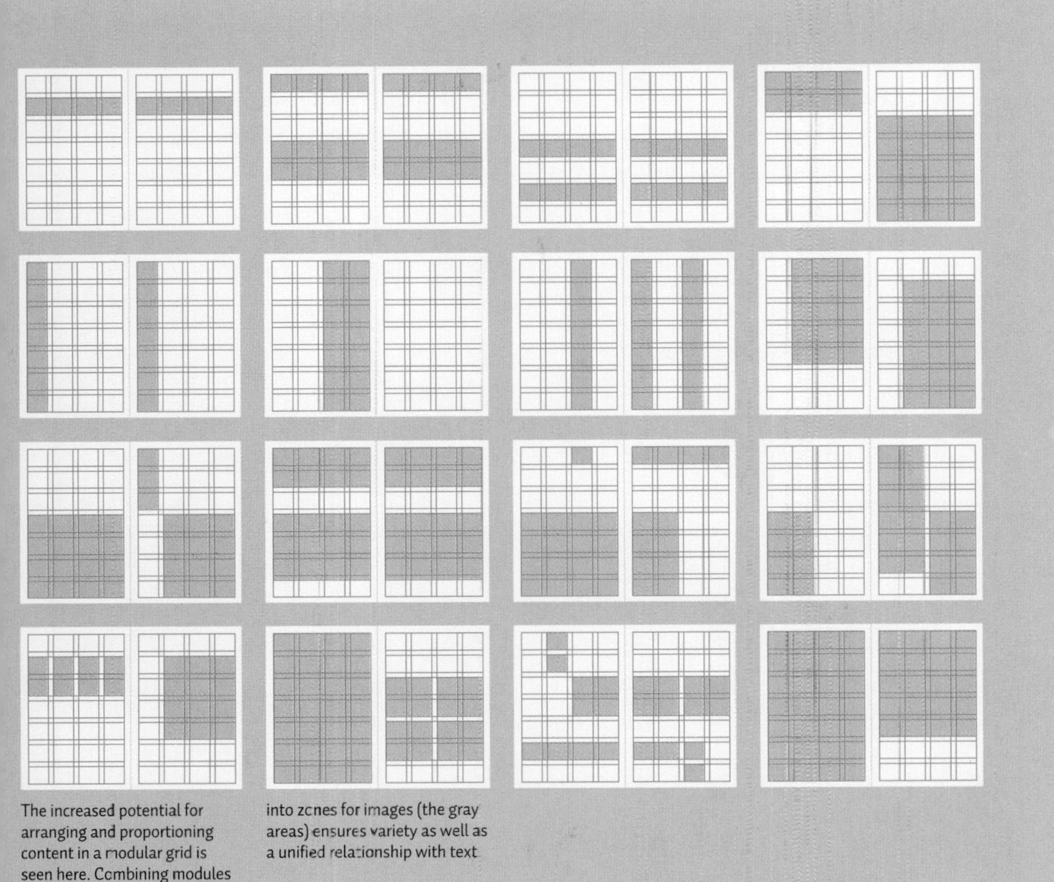

The increased potential for arranging and proportioning content in a modular grid is seen here. Combining modules into zones for images (the gray areas) ensures variety as well as a unified relationship with text.

A SIX-COLUMN MODULAR GRID helps integrate text and images of various sizes to provide contrast and variation but without sacrificing the harmonic proportional unity of the panels.

Clemens Théobert Schedler
Austria

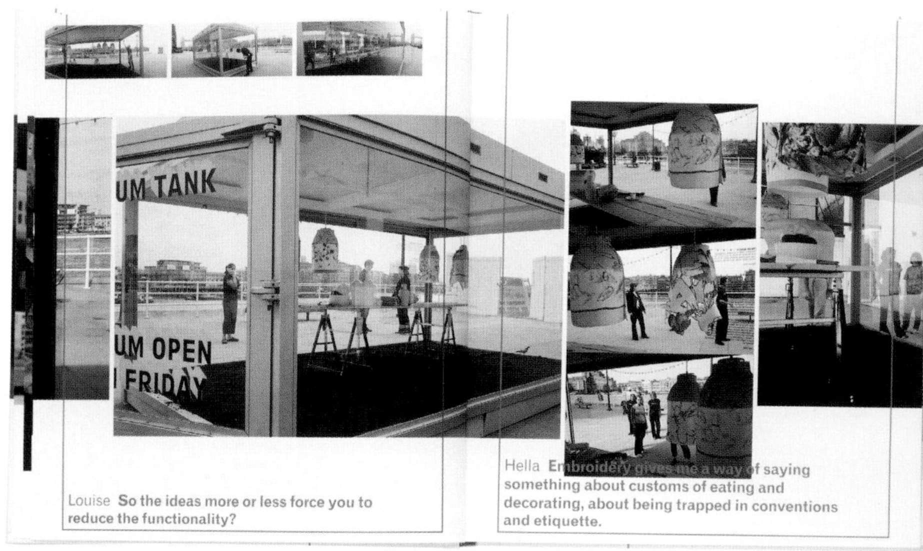

TWO OPPOSING GRIDS are combined in this book to create conflict between text and image areas. The overlap of text and the pushing and pulling of image proportions create a collage-like atmosphere that is edgy and intuitive in feeling.

Coma *Netherlands*

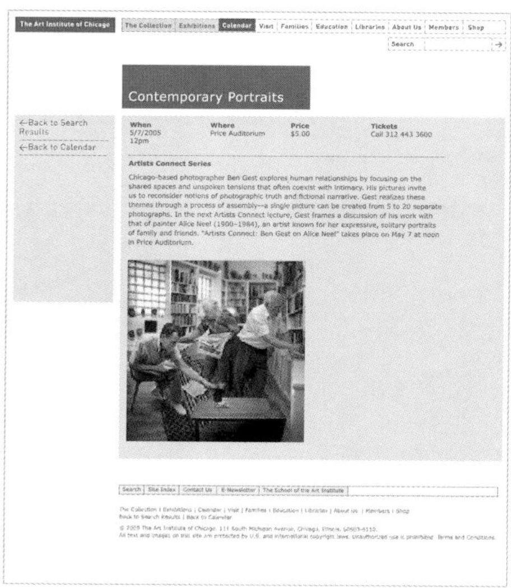

Grid Hybrids and Combinations

Depending on the complexity of the publication, a designer might find that multiple grids are needed to organize the content, within sections or even a single page spread. ■ Working with several grids together can take several directions. First, a grid with a large number of precise intervals might be developed as a basis for a variety of grids used for particular information. For example, a grid with twenty columns to a page might be used to order a five-column, four-column, two-column, and three-column grid with a larger margin for captions in a specific section. In this kind of approach, all the column widths will share a proportional relationship that will also be noticeable in how images relate to text set in these various widths. ■ Another option is simply to use two, three, or more different grids that share outer margins, allowing them to be relatively arbitrary in their relationship to each other. In this approach, the alternation of the grids will be pronounced, since their internal proportions are unrelated; the resulting differences in visual logic between layouts using different grids can make very clear distinctions between sections or types of content. ■ A third option is to combine grids on a single page but to separate them into different areas. For example, primary text or images might occupy a three-column grid in the upper two-thirds of the page, but a five-column grid might hold captions or other secondary content in the lower third of the page.

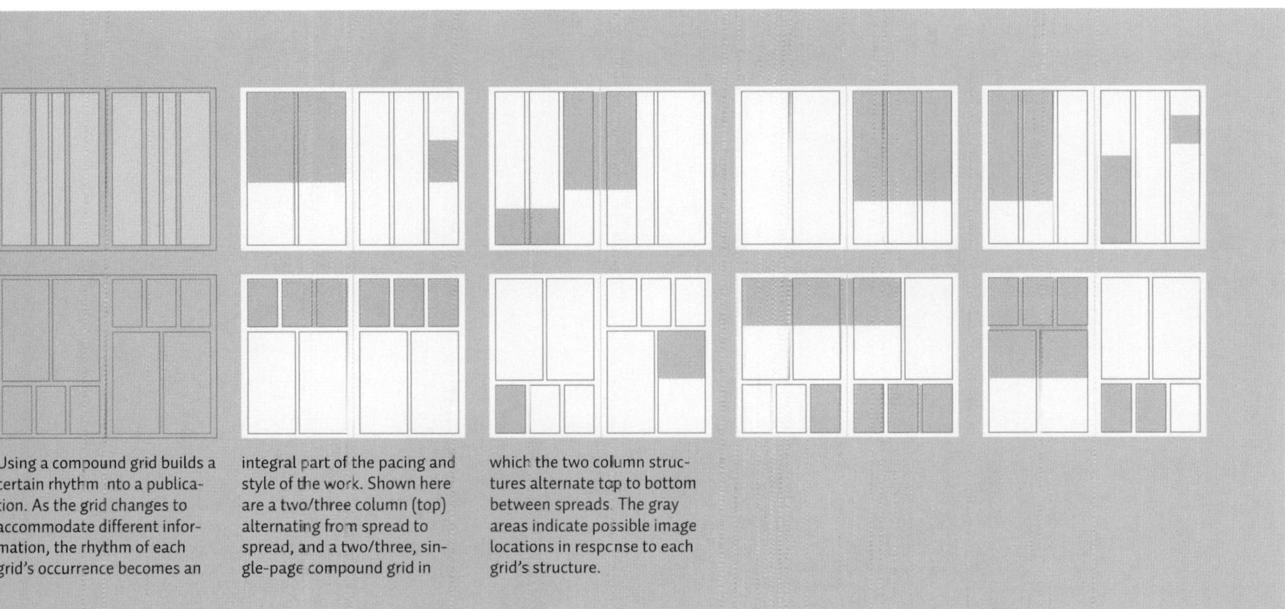

Using a compound grid builds a certain rhythm into a publication. As the grid changes to accommodate different information, the rhythm of each grid's occurrence becomes an integral part of the pacing and style of the work. Shown here are a two/three column (top) alternating from spread to spread, and a two/three, single-page compound grid in which the two column structures alternate top to bottom between spreads. The gray areas indicate possible image locations in response to each grid's structure.

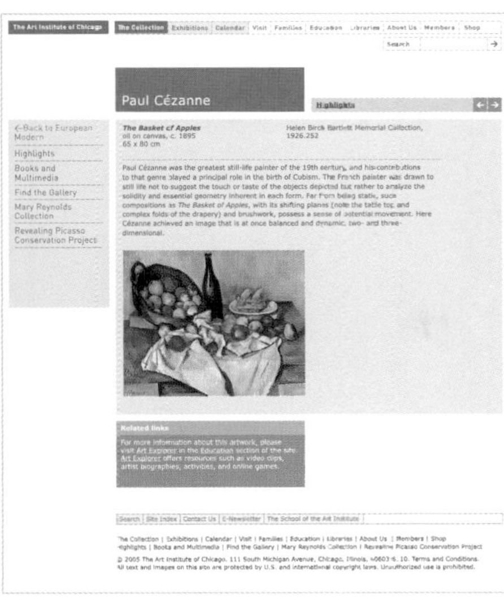

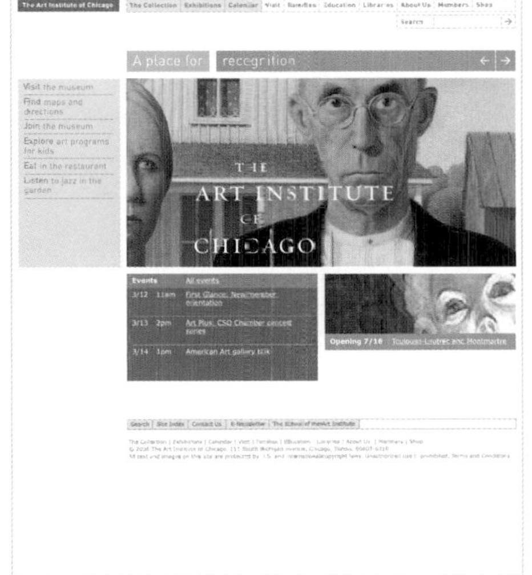

THIS WEBSITE COMBINES multiple column grids, each used in specific areas to organize specific content and navigation, rather than attempting to accommodate all the material on one overly complex grid.

Studio Blue *United States*

Grid Development Building an appropriate grid for a publication involves assessing the shape and volume of the content, rather than trying to assign grid spaces arbitrarily. The shape of the content, whether text or image, is particularly important—its proportions become the source for defining the grid spaces. When considering text as the essential building block, the designer must look at variations in the text setting. ■ Considering image as a source for the grid spaces is another option. If the publication is driven by its image content, this might be a more appropriate direction. The proportions of the images, if they are

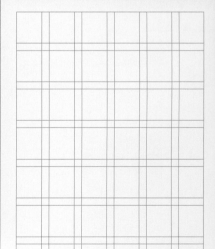

In this hypothetical study, several source images, each with different proportions, are positioned relative to each other to help determine where their depths and widths might correspond.

Shifting the images around each other creates a number of possibilities for distilling a grid that will accommodate them all without having to crop them—a hypothetical "client request."

known, can be used to determine the proportions of columns and modules. The result of both approaches is that the structure of the page develops naturally from the needs of the content, presenting an overall organic, unified sense of space.

Grid by Image A grid might be defined by image content through comparison of its proportions. Beginning with a universal height or depth for the images, and a consistent alignment among them, will allow the designer to assess how varied they are in format–squares, verticals, and horizontals. The designer must then decide how the images are to be displayed in terms of their size relationship to each other: will the images be shown in sizes that are relative to each other, or will they be allowed to appear at any size? If all the images hang from a particular flowline, their depth varying, the designer will need to address the images with both the shortest and deepest depths to determine what is possible for text or other elements below these variations. ■ From these major divisions in space and the logic that the designer uses to govern them, a series of intervals might be structured for the images and for text areas surrounding them. It is also possible to structure the grid based on how images will be sized in succession. Perhaps the designer envisions sequencing the images in a particular way: first bleeding full off one page, then a half-page vertical, then inset, and then a three-quarter bleed. In this case, the proportions of the images as they relate to the format will define a series of intervals.

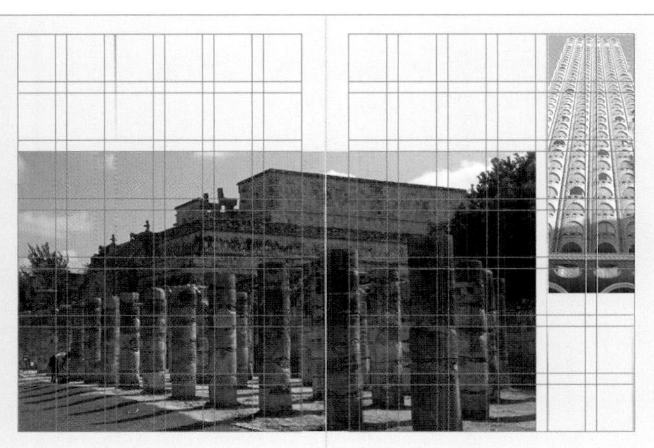

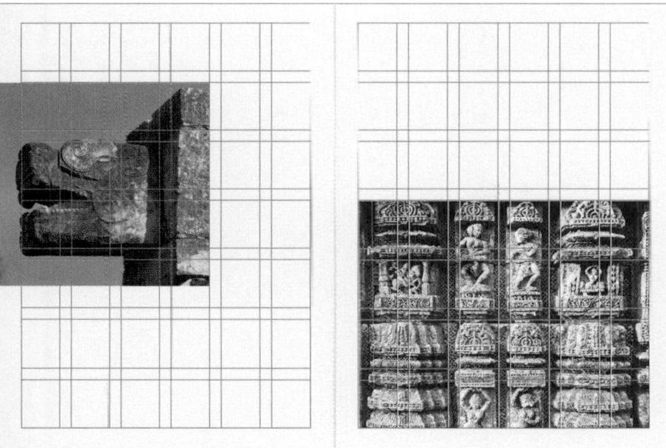

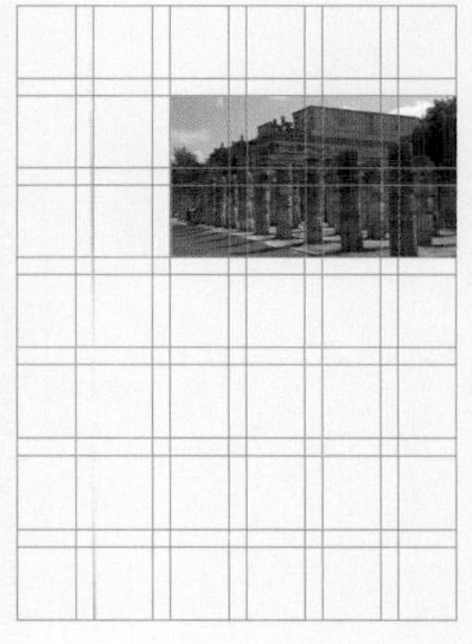

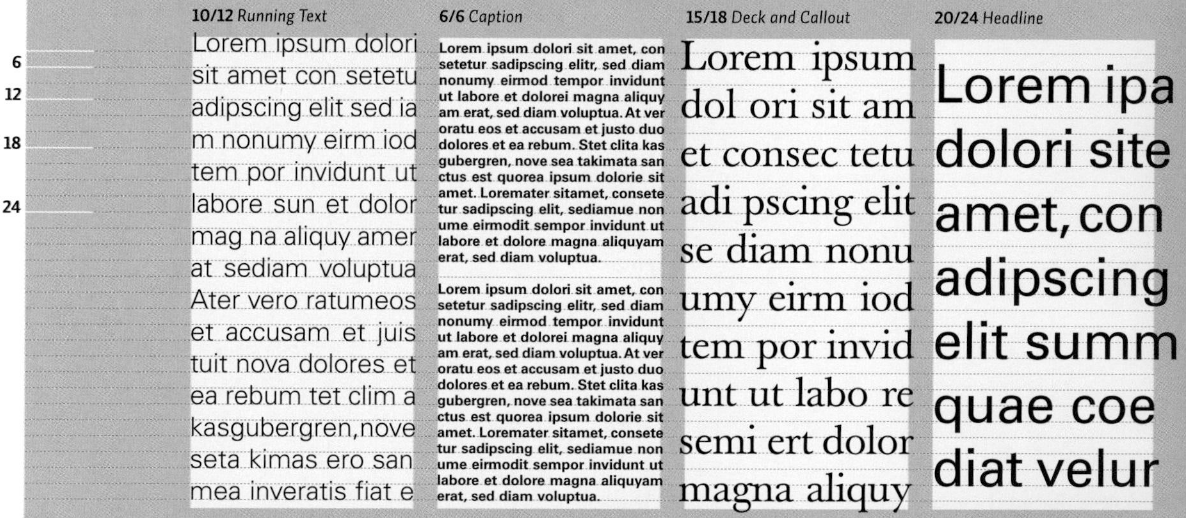

6
12
18
24

10/12 *Running Text*

Lorem ipsum dolori sit amet con setetu adipscing elit sed ia m nonumy eirm iod tem por invidunt ut labore sun et dolor mag na aliquy amer at sediam voluptua Ater vero ratumeos et accusam et juis tuit nova dolores et ea rebum tet clim a kasgubergren, nove seta kimas ero san mea inveratis fiat e

6/6 *Caption*

Lorem ipsum dolori sit amet, con setetur sadipscing elitr, sed diam nonumy eirmod tempor invidunt ut labore et dolorei magna aliquy am erat, sed diam voluptua. At ver oratu eos et accusam et justo duo dolores et ea rebum. Stet clita kas gubergren, nove sea takimata san ctus est quorea ipsum dolorie sit amet. Loremater sitamet, consete tur sadipscing elit, sediamue non ume eirmodit sempor invidunt ut labore et dolore magna aliquyam erat, sed diam voluptua.

Lorem ipsum dolori sit amet, con setetur sadipscing elitr, sed diam nonumy eirmod tempor invidunt ut labore et dolorei magna aliquy am erat, sed diam voluptua. At ver oratu eos et accusam et justo duo dolores et ea rebum. Stet clita kas gubergren, nove sea takimata san ctus est quorea ipsum dolorie sit amet. Loremater sitamet, consete tur sadipscing elit, sediamue non ume eirmodit sempor invidunt ut labore et dolore magna aliquyam erat, sed diam voluptua.

15/18 *Deck and Callout*

Lorem ipsum dol ori sit am et consec tetu adi pscing elit se diam nonu umy eirm iod tem por invid unt ut labo re semi ert dolor magna aliquy

20/24 *Headline*

Lorem ipa dolori site amet, con adipscing elit summ quae coe diat velur

The leading of the body text, decks, callouts, and captions might have some proportional relationship based on their sizes. For example, the body text might be 10 points, set on a leading of 12; captions might be 6 points, set solid on a leading of 6; decks might be 15 points, set on a leading of 18. The numeric relationship between these leading measurements is 6 points; a certain number of lines of each text component will, at some depth interval, share the same top and lower baseline, and this depth interval might very well indicate the depth of a module. This is the method used here: 10 lines, or a leading of 60 points, defines the depth of the module; the gutter measure between rows reflects a hard return between caption paragraphs. The column is defined by the caption's optimal width.

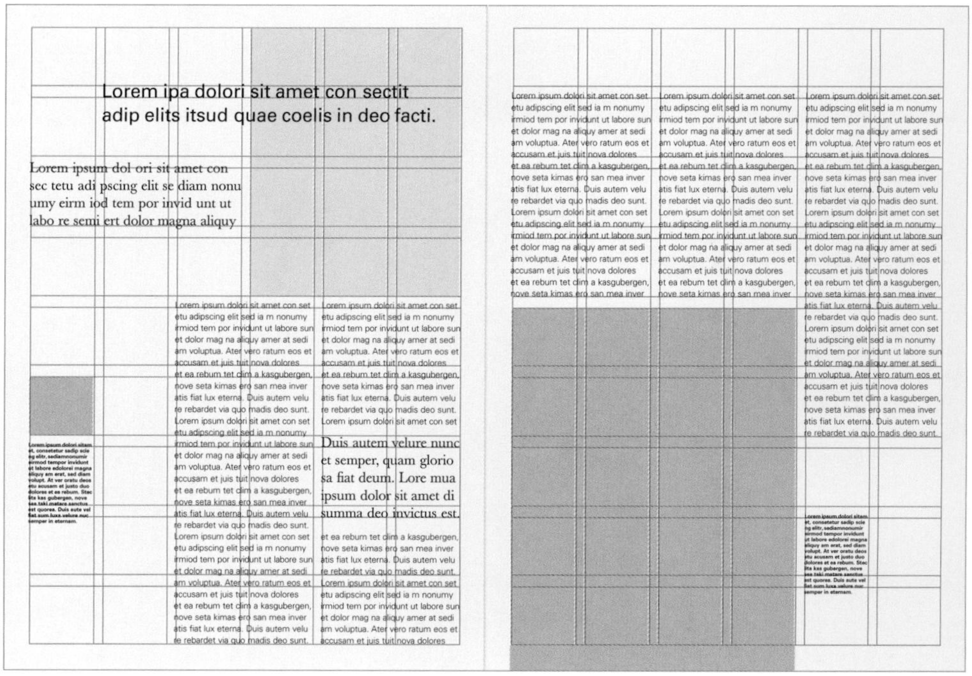

Lorem ipa dolori sit amet con sectit adip elits itsud quae coelis in deo facti.

Lorem ipsum dol ori sit amet con sec tetu adi pscing elit se diam nonu umy eirm iod tem por invid unt ut labo re semi ert dolor magna aliquy

Duis autem velure nunc et semper, quam glorio sa fiat deum. Lore mua ipsum dolor sit amet di summa deo invictus est.

Grid by Text Alternatively, the designer might approach the grid from the perspective of the text shape and volume. The sheer amount of text that the publication must accommodate is an important consideration; if each page spread must carry a particular word count to fit a prescribed number of pages the designer will have some sense of how many lines of type must appear on each page. This variable might eventually affect the column width or depth, but the optimal setting is a good starting point. Achieving an optimal setting for text at a given size and in a given face will indicate a width for columns, and, from there, the designer can explore how many columns will fit side by side on a single page. Adjusting the size of the text, its internal spacing, and the gutters between columns will allow the designer to create a preliminary structure that ensures optimal text setting throughout. From this point, the designer must evaluate the resulting margins—head, sides, and foot—and determine whether there is enough space surrounding the body to keep it away from the edges of the format. Since optimal width can vary a little with the same text setting, the designer has some leeway in forcing the columns to be wider or more narrow, closer or further away from each other, until the structure sits comfortably on the page.

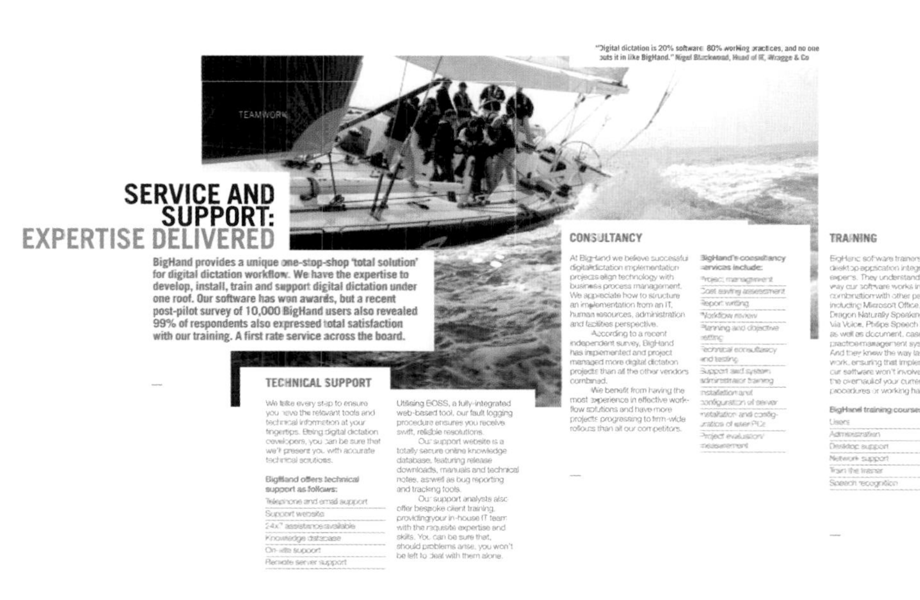

THE GRID IN THIS BROCHURE was developed based on the proportions of the type sizes given to each level of information in the hierarchy and the resulting mathematical relationship between the baselines of their leading. Comparing the baselines of larger text elements with those of smaller text elements reveals that they correspond on a regular basis, hinting that the grid is modular as well as columnar.

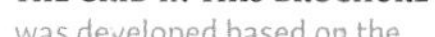

Loewy *United Kingdom*

Column Logic and Rhythm on a Grid

The way in which columns of text interact with negative space is an important aspect of how a grid is articulated. The spaces above and below columns play an active part in giving the columns a rhythm as they relate to each other across pages and spreads. The options available to a designer are endless but can be described as fitting into three basic categories: columns that justify top and bottom; columns that align vertically at top or bottom and rag at the other end; and columns that rag top and bottom. Each kind of logic has a dramatic impact on the overall rhythm of the pages within a publication, ranging from austere and geometric to wildly organic in feeling—all the while ordered by the underlying grid. ■ Changing the column logic from section to section provides yet another method of differentiating informational areas. The designer, however, must carefully consider the rhythm of that change.

A

B

Columns justified to the head and foot margins, or to a specific module depth, create a rigidly geometric band of text. Hanging columns provide a measure of consistency, balanced by their changing depth.

Columns that change hangline and depth offer the most organic (and flexible) option for arranging text, especially in terms of integrating images.

The differences in interval between column beginnings and endings must be decisive and considered for their rhythm. The heads and feet of the columns might be decided spontaneously or determined by the existence of flowlines or modules in the columns.

Some regularity or system must clearly exist in the alternation of column logic to be meaningful; otherwise, the audience simply recognizes the change but not its significance. ■ When columns begin to separate vertically, shifting up and down past one another—or dropping to different depths while adhering to a single hangline above—consider the relationship between lines of text across the gutter separating the columns.

In a grouping of columns set justified, with no line breaks (or a hard return of the same leading) between paragraphs, the baselines between columns will align. Any other situation, and the baselines between columns will not align. ■ In hanging columns, text will align between columns until a paragraph change. Because the depth of the hanging columns changes, this might feel appropriate. A problem will occur in a page spread set with columns justifying top and bottom, however, if the paragraph space introduces an uneven line: the lines of text at the foot margin will be noticeably off.

C

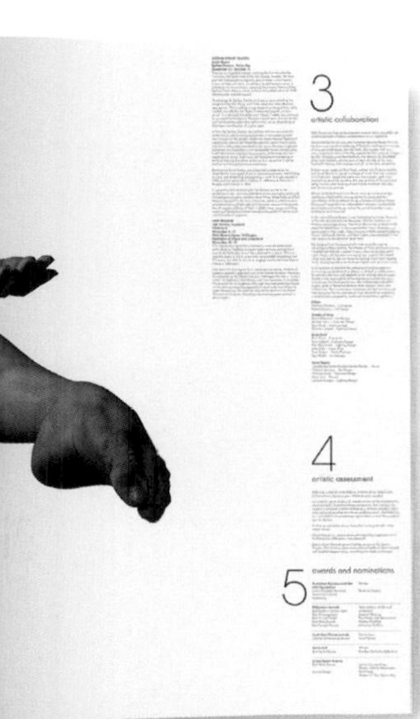

TEXT COLUMNS IN THIS sequence of brochure spreads are allowed to move up and down and be different depths as needed to create rhythmic interplay with the photographs. Note the similarity in hangline drop between the columns in the first spread (A), the hangline of the rightmost column, as well as the space between paragraphs in spread (B). The columns appear to hang from the tops of modules. This assumption is further supported in the last spread (C) by the alignment of the numeral 6 with the numeral 2 in (A) and the location of the numeral 8 relative to the end of the first column in spread (B).

Frost Design *Australia*

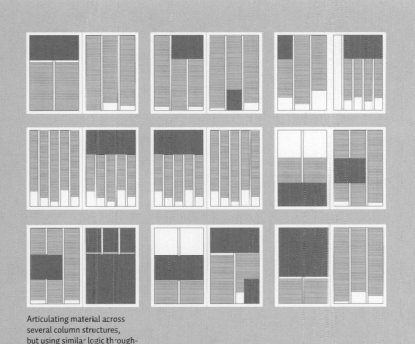

Articulating material across several column structures, but using similar logic throughout, creates tremendous difference in the overall rhythm of the layouts while retaining a certain unity.

Variation and Violation A grid is truly successful only if, after all the problems have been solved, the designer rises above the uniformity implied by its structure and uses it to create a dynamic visual narrative of parts that will sustain interest page after page. ■ The greatest danger in using a grid is to succumb to its regularity. Remember that the grid is an invisible guide existing on the bottommost level of the layout; the content happens on the surface, either constrained or sometimes free. Grids do not make dull layouts—designers do. Once a grid is in place, it is a good idea to sort all the project's material spread by spread to see how much will be appearing in each. A storyboard of thumbnails for each spread in the publication can be very helpful. Here, the designer can test layout variations on the grid and see the result in terms of pacing—the rhythm of the layouts. Can there be a visual logic to how elements interact with the grid from page to page? Do pictorial elements alternate in position from one spread to another? Perhaps the sizes of the images change from spread to spread, or the ratio of text to image changes sequentially. Even simply placing images toward the top of the pages in one spread and then toward the

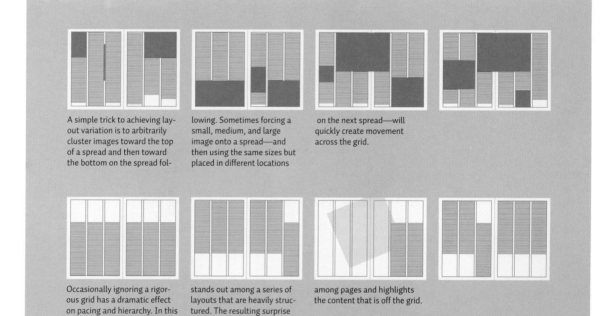

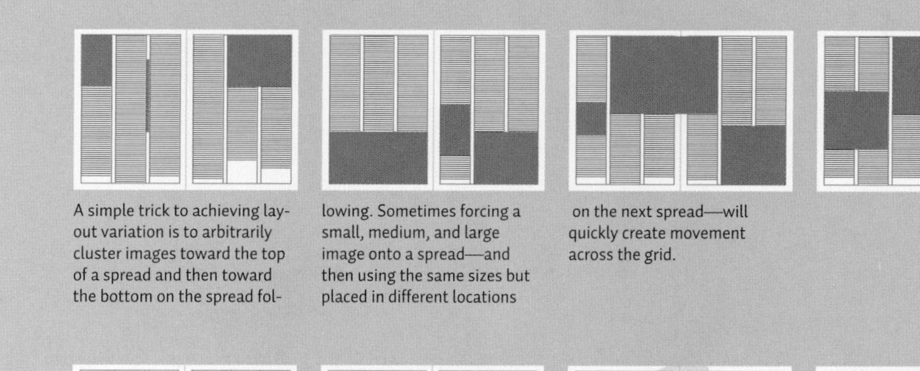

A simple trick to achieving layout variation is to arbitrarily cluster images toward the top of a spread and then toward the bottom on the spread following. Sometimes forcing a small, medium, and large image onto a spread—and then using the same sizes but placed in different locations on the next spread—will quickly create movement across the grid.

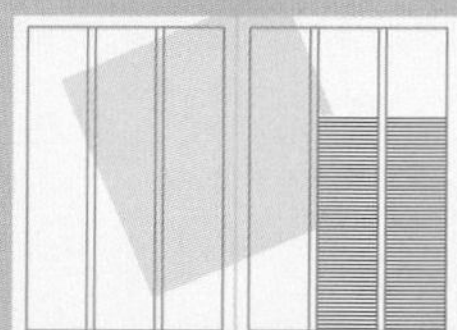

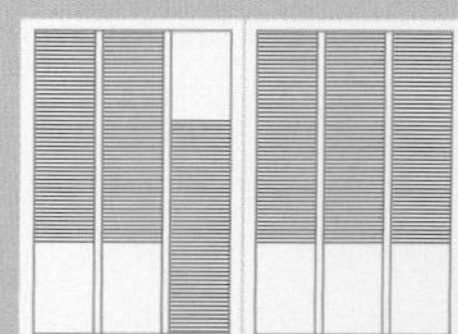

Occasionally ignoring a rigorous grid has a dramatic effect on pacing and hierarchy. In this study, just such an instance stands out among a series of layouts that are heavily structured. The resulting surprise breathes life into the pacing among pages and highlights the content that is off the grid.

God prosjektstyring er en sentral faktor for å forbedre lønnsomheten i bygg- og anleggsbransjen. Veidekke har til enhver tid rundt tusen ulike prosjekter løpende – alle med sine unike kjennetegn og problemstillinger. Prosjektgjennomføringen er en kompleks prosess som involverer et stort antall aktører. Oversikt og kontroll i alle ledd av prosessen er derfor avgjørende for å sikre effektiv gjennomføring og god kvalitet.

For å kunne levere denne tryggheten til våre kunder er vi helt avhengig av godt lederskap på byggeplassen. Vi trenger prosjektledere som er til stede på byggeplassen, og som er engasjerte i byggeplassdrift, kvalitet, kunder og leverandører. Ledere som bruker av sin erfaring i både utviklings-, prosjekterings- og produksjonsfasen. Ledere som er i dialog med kunden og ser løsninger i stedet for begrensninger. Derfor er lederutvikling en prioritert oppgave i Veidekke, og vi er i dag en ledende opplæringsbedrift på vårt område.

I tillegg til godt lederskap er vi avhengig av riktig verktøy for prosjektstyring. Ved hjelp av vårt styringssystem lager vi unike planer for alle delene av prosjektet. Slik holder vi kontroll med faktorer som kostnader, produktivitet og kvalitet.

faktor 4: prosjektstyring

Langt på vei er entreprenør- og eiendomsutviklingsvirksomhetens hovedprodukt prosjektstyring og logistikk

Erfaring har likevel lært oss at vi må forvente det uventede. Vi skal derfor alltid ha noe gjennomføringskapasitet i reserve. Slik er det mulig å takle de uventede utfordringene som alltid dukker opp ved gjennomføringen av et komplekst prosjekt, uten at det får store konsekvenser for prosessen.

Oversikt og kontroll gjennom godt lederskap og riktige verktøy minker totalrisikoen i prosjektene, bedrer marginene og bidrar til økt kundetilfredshet og økt grad av gjenkjøp. Prosjektstyring er derfor en av våre viktigste kjernekompetanser, og bidrar til å styrke vår posisjon som en ledende skandinavisk entreprenør.

bottom of the pages in the next achieves a powerful sense of difference while still ensuring overall visual unity. ■ Violating the grid is a necessity of designing, sometimes because circumstance dictates it—content that must occupy a specific spread won't quite fit—or because it is visually necessary to call attention to some feature of the content, or to create some surprise for the reader. Within a rigorous grid structure, violations must be relatively infrequent or relatively small, or they begin to undermine the reader's sense of the grid's consistency. Any specific item or general layout that violates the grid will be very dramatic. Disturbing the regularity of a column of text by allowing an element to jut out past the alignment not only will be instantly noticeable but also will cause the wayward element to shift to the top of the hierarchy; it becomes the most important item in the layout because it is clearly the only thing out of order. Designing a two-page spread that ignores the grid established for the remaining pages of a publication ensures that spread will be memorable. The problem facing the designer in making such a dramatic decision is that of integrating the layout into the publication's overall visual logic: what defines this spread as belonging to the same publication? Usually, using the same typefaces as are used elsewhere will do so, as will application of similar colors as on other pages; but these alone will not unify the altered spread with the others that clearly follow an established structure. The designer must create some reference to the established structure even as he or she violates it—perhaps a typographic element from the previous spread continues onto the unique spread. In addition, the designer must consider the transition back into the grid-structured pages following the violation; if the pages following this particular spread are a continuation of its content, the designer might add smaller violating elements that recall the major violation while restating the regular structure.

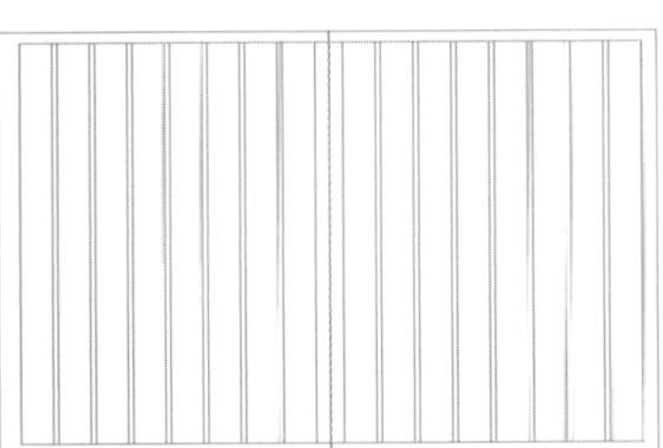

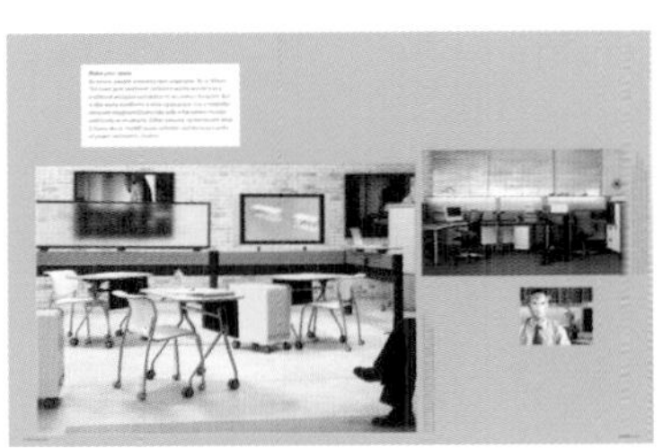

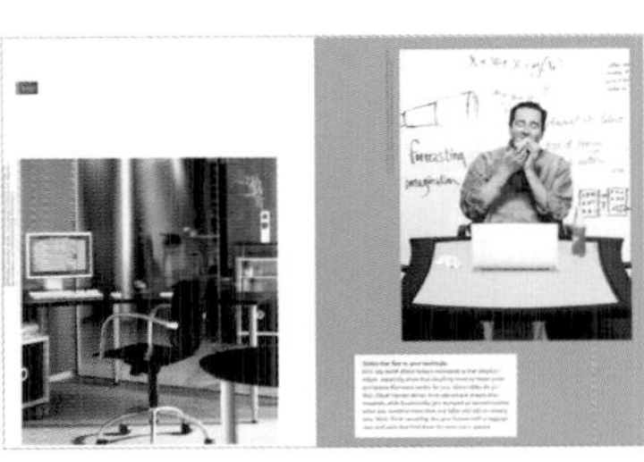

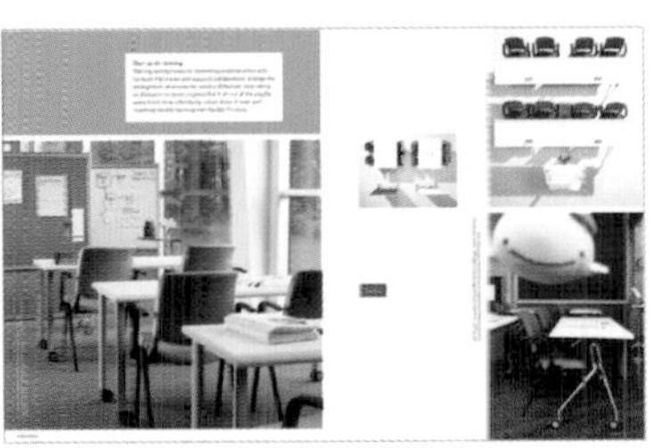

THESE PAGES, selected from several related brochures, use a relatively tight column structure as a means of radically altering margin, image, and text proportions from page to page. The greater number of columns means that simple blocks of content can shift around dramatically, but the proportions of the negative spaces and content objects remain unified in feeling.

BBK Studio *United States*

COMPARE THE LOCATION of spatial breaks from left to right across this page spread with the grid diagram; although the majority of typographic and image content responds to the column structure, several items noticeably shift off the structure to introduce visual surprise and focus attention.

Cobra *Norway*

Exploring Other Options: Nonstructural Design Approaches Grid structure in typography and design has become part of the status quo of designing, but, as recent history has shown, there are numerous ways to organize information and images. The decision whether to use a grid always comes down to the nature of the content in a given project. Sometimes that content has its own internal structure that a grid won't necessarily clarify; sometimes the content needs to ignore structure altogether to create specific kinds of emotional

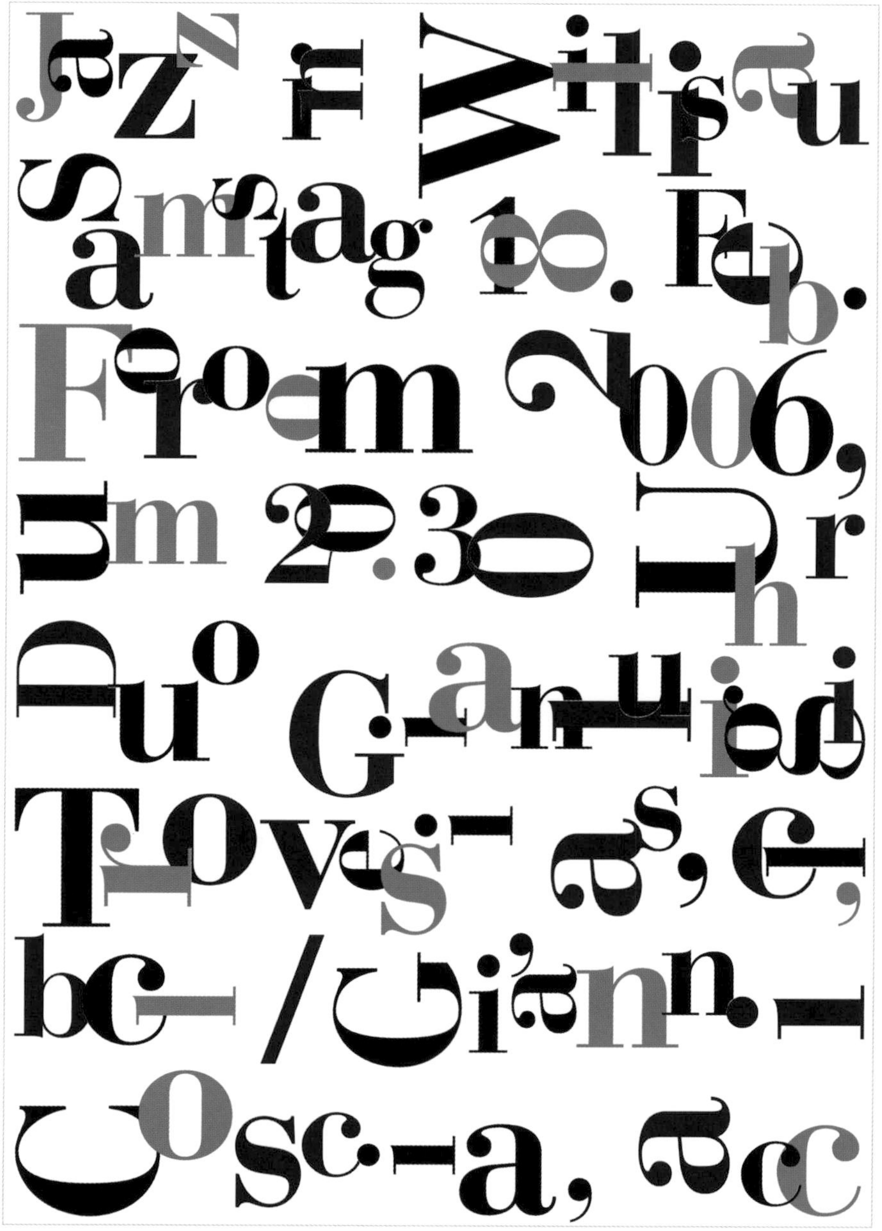

THE MATERIAL IN THIS POSTER is organized intuitively and spontaneously in an almost collage-like or painterly fashion, considering the visual qualities of the components in a more organic way.

Niklaus Troxler *Switzerland*

reactions in the intended audience; and sometimes a designer simply envisions a more complex intellectual involvement on the part of the audience as part of their experience of the piece. ■ Our ability to apprehend and digest information has become more sophisticated over time as well; constant bombardment of information from sources such as television, film, and interactive digital media has created a certain kind of expectation for information to behave in particular ways. One has only to look at television news broadcasting or reality-based programming, where several kinds of presentation—oral delivery, video, still images and icons, and moving typography—overlap or succeed each other in rapid succession to understand that people have become accustomed to more complex, designed experiences. In an effort to create a meaningful impression that competes with—and distinguishes itself within—this visual environment, designers have pursued various new ways of organizing visual experience.

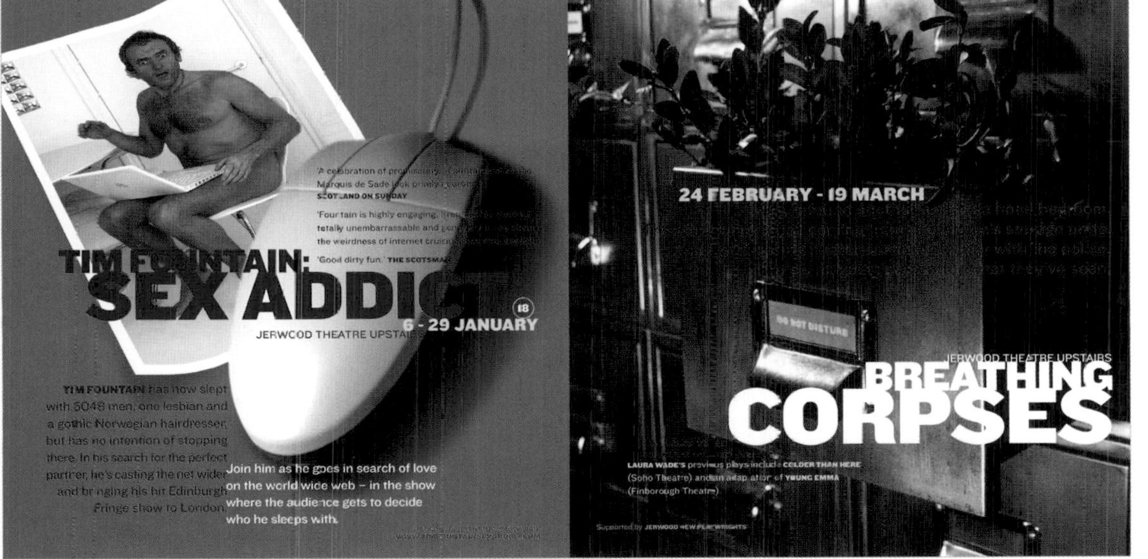

THESE TWO SPREADS from a theatrical season brochure respond to a 3 x 3 module structure as a base—seen in the opening contents spread—but the module alignments appear to shift, forcing the type into new alignments. This approach is called a deconstruction; it takes a structure and then deforms it.

Research Studios *United Kingdom*

Grid Deconstruction The first option is splitting apart a conventional grid, even a very simple one. A structure can be altered in any number of ways. A designer might "cut apart" major zones and shift them horizontally or vertically. It's important to watch what happens when information that would normally appear in an expected place—marking a structural juncture in the grid—is moved to another place, perhaps aligned with some other kind of information in a way that creates a new verbal connection that didn't exist before. The shifted information might end up behind or on top of some other information if a change in size or density accompanies the shift in placement. ■ The optical confusion this causes might be perceived as a surreal kind of space where foreground and background swap places. A conventional grid structure

SHIFTING columns and exaggerated textural qualities harmonize the type with the images.

Hyosook Kang *School of Visual Arts, United States*

Hendrik Nicolaas Werkman born in 1882 in Leens in the north of Holland

Tribute to HN W

In the 1920s, Werkman directed a large printing company in Groningen, a city where, between 1923 and 1926, he published nine editions of the magazine **The Next Call**, which was in economic format, print and paper type, but completely original in character and content.

For this magazine, Werkman himself wrote visual poetry, designed manifestos with provocative titles and effected innovative compositio with typographical materials with wood type, lines in brass and le blocks, managing to obtain – despite severe economic constraints – wide variety of printed stuff which even today strikes the viewer with sense of vitality. At first, **The Next Call** was distributed only to a restrict circle of artist friends in Groningen, but from '24, it reached Paris, B grade, Prague, becoming fully recognized as one of the most innovative ternational vanguard magazines.

In the 1930s, Werkman developed new technologies for the application on paper of his poetic visions, which he was able to exhibit in De Ploeg **- a group of artists which aspired to** Die Brücke **and to the freedom of cultural expressionism.**
He commenced to manually intervene in the printing itself, with stamps and shaped moulds, using the roll directly to provide ink in the form of the brush, while also using its external part.

VERK

MAN.

With the advent of the war and the encounter with F.R.A. Henkels, a protestant pastor, confined him to design and print for the clandestine editions of **De Blauwe Schuit**, which documented the cultural resistance against the oppressors.

In 1941, he printed the "**Sendbrief an die Christen im Niederland**" which was written by Martin Luther in 1523, with strong parallelism between the burning at the stake of the first Christian martyrs and the events of that epoch.

In the same year he published the 1942 **Turkenkalendar** which was an anthology in the form of poems and short prose, creating a reference between the Turkish expansion in 1453 and the oppression which the people of Holland were being subjected to.

In 1942, he worked for other clandestine editorials, such as **In agris Occupatis**, which were published in sufficiently small volumes that they would fit into a wallet.

When, at the end of 1944, it was no longer possible to find or procure norm paper, editors and printers continued their activity by using brown wrapping per, pages which had been taken from ledgers found in households, and wh ever else they could find. Werkman almost ceased completely to print as types were confiscated, the electricity cut-off and the lack of heat resulted the ink being frozen. He terminated his work with a few paintings and design his last calendar.

Sixty years have passed since 1945 in which Werkman was arrested by the secret police on 13 March, and executed on the 10 April, thus paying with his life for the freedom of the Press.
Only many years later was the extent of his influence on entire generations of graphic project designers understood, the poetic rebellion of a humble Dutch printer.

SLIGHT OVERLAPS IN columns, changing column widths, and column rotation create movement and geometric spaces reminiscent of the design work and historical context of the poster's subject without copying his style or showing any of his own projects.

Leonardo Sonnoli *Italy*

repeated in different orientations could be used to explore a more dynamic architectural space by creating different axes of alignment. ■ Similarly, overlapping grids with modules of different proportions, or which run at different angles in relation to each other, can introduce a kind of order to the spatial and directional ambiguity that layering creates, especially if some elements are oriented on both layers simultaneously.

Shifting or breaking apart grid modules or columns so that they begin to overlap, even while they carry sequential information (like running text), can create a perception of layers within the compositional space. The textures of different columns interacting as they run over each other can create a sense of transparency in which the viewer perceives the columns of text, or other elements, to be floating in front of each other.

"Brother, can you spare a dime?"

THE CHANGING WIDTHS and spatial intervals, as well as changing interline space within the text and proportions of the image, deconstruct a conventional column grid to create tension, discomfort, and spatial conflict that evoke the feeling of uncertainty in a particular historical period.

Travis Simon *School of Visual Arts, United States*

IN A REMARKABLY funny twist, typographic elements are deconstructed off the "grid" of the walls in hotel rooms to create an amusing spatial environment for guests

E-Types *Denmark*

82% of all European hotel rooms feature a romantic landscape painting

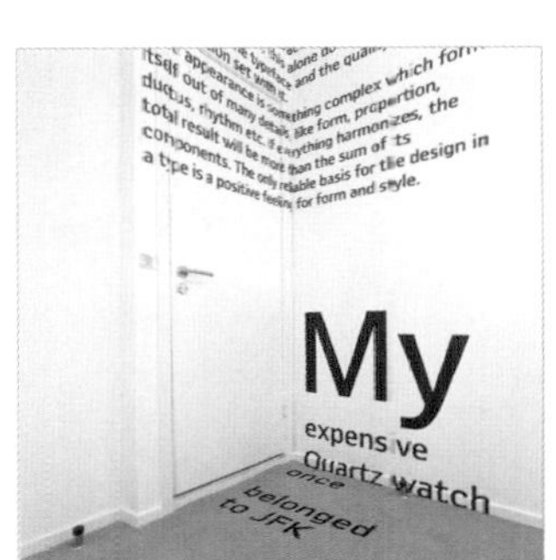

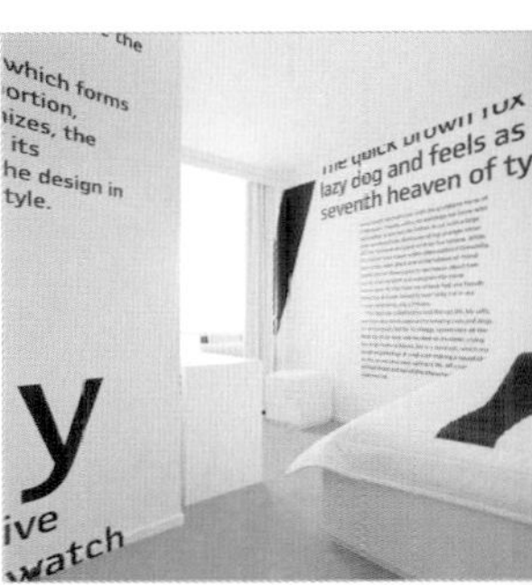

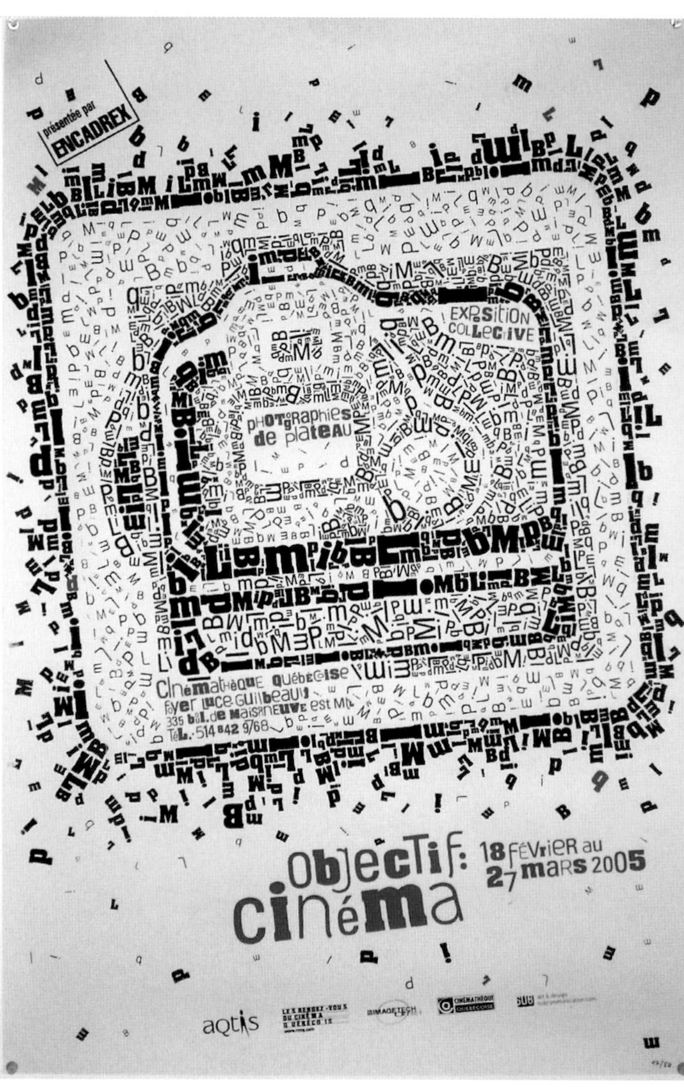

CUT-AND-PASTE typographic texture is distributed in both spontaneous and ordered ways in this poster.

SubCommunication *Canada*

THIS POSTER ORGANIZES typographic material loosely and organically, showing evidence of the designer's attention to tension and contrast relationships in proximity, clustering, overlap, edge-to-format spacing, and angular versus curvilinear logic.

Cally Keo *The Art Institute, Orange County, United States*

Spontaneous Optical Composition

Far from being random, this compositional method can be described as purposeful intuitive placement of material based on its formal aspects: seeing the inherent visual relationships and contrasts within the material and making connections for the viewer based on those relationships. Sometimes designers will use this method as a step in the process of building a grid, but its use as an organizational idea on its own is just as valid. ■ This approach starts fast and loose: the designer works with the material much like a painter does, making quick decisions as the material is put together and the relationships are first seen. As the different optical qualities of the elements begin to interact, the designer can determine which qualities are affected by those initial decisions and make adjustments to enhance or negate the qualities in whatever way is most appropriate for the communication. The method's inherent liveliness has an affinity with collage; its sense of immediacy and directness can be inviting to viewers, providing them with a simple and gratifying experience that is very accessible. The result is a structure that is dependent on the optical tensions of the composition and their connection to the information hierarchy within the space.

THE DESIGNER HAS CREATED a shifting maze of positive and negative shapes to contain, as well as work around, the text elements. The shapes take on the attributes of road signs and architecture but appear to move about, as heavy masses, open spaces, and texture collide and separate.

I Just Might *United States*

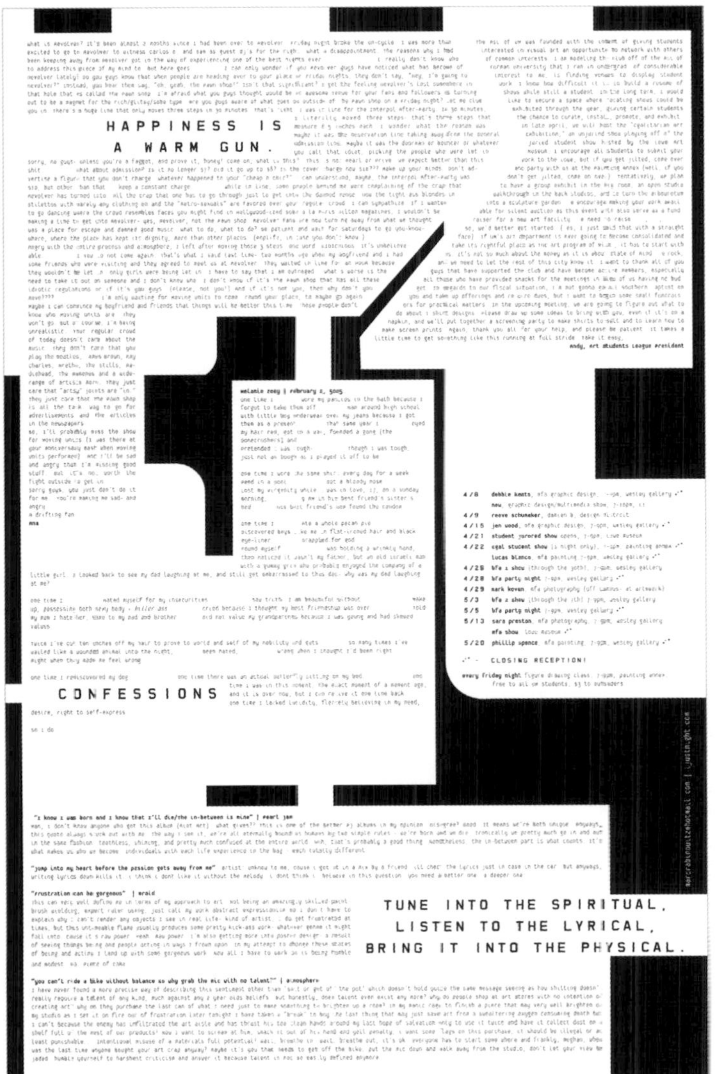

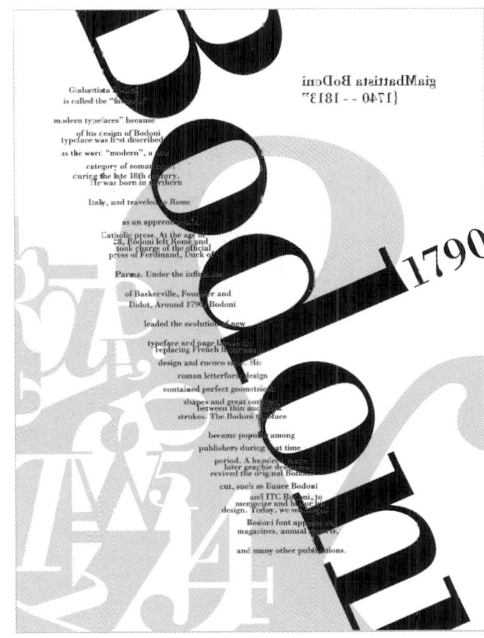

EXTREME SCALE CHANGES, contrast in weight among the strokes of the large title, and the textural qualities of the diagonally aligned paragraph and background elements create dynamic foreground and background relationships and a very colorful set of contrasts.

Ko-Hsing Wang *The Art Institute, Orange County, United States*

Conceptual or Pictorial Allusion Another interesting way of creating compositions is to derive a visual idea from the content and impose it on the page format as a kind of arbitrary structure. The structure can be an illusory representation of a subject, like waves or the surface of water, or can be based on a concept, like a childhood memory, a historical event, or a diagram. ■ Whatever the source of the idea, the designer can organize material to refer to it. For example, text and images might sink underwater or float around like objects caught in a flood. Even though no grid is present, sequential compositions are given a kind of unity because of the governing idea. Margins, intervals between images and text, and relative depth on the page might constantly change, but this change has recognizable features that relate to the overall idea; these might even be called allusive structures. ■ In projects of a sequential nature, like books or walls in an exhibit, visual elements relate to each other in time, as though in frames of a film. Images might move across a format or otherwise be changed from page to page, affecting other images or text that appear later. A simple example of this visual kinesis might be a sequence of pages where text appears to advance forward in space because its scale changes incrementally every time the page is turned. Using sensory experiences of space and time as organizing principles can be a powerful tool for evoking a visceral, emotional response from viewers.

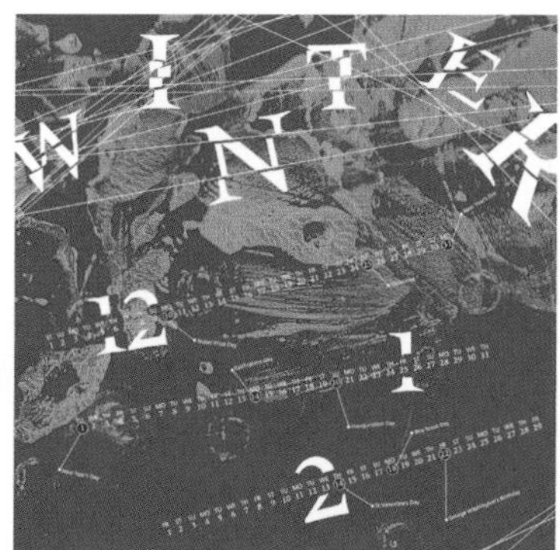

THE DESIGNER OF these seasonal calendar panels expresses the feeling and energy of each season through abstract images. The typography responds not just formally but conceptually, alluding in different instances to falling rain, leaves, and snow.

Hae Jin Lee *School of Visual Arts, United States*

LITTLE EXPLANATION is needed to clarify the image that is being created by the configuration of justified text blocks in this foldout brochure.

LSD *Spain*

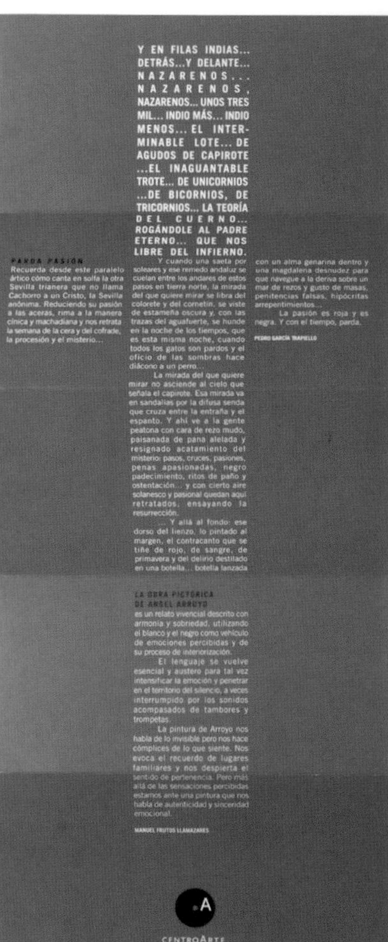

Y EN FILAS INDIAS... DETRÁS...Y DELANTE... NAZARENOS... NAZARENOS, NAZARENOS... UNOS TRES MIL... INDIO MÁS... INDIO MENOS... EL INTERMINABLE LOTE... DE AGUDOS DE CAPIROTE ...EL INAGUANTABLE TROTE... DE UNICORNIOS ...DE BICORNIOS, DE TRICORNIOS... LA TEORÍA DEL CUERNO... ROGÁNDOLE AL PADRE ETERNO... QUE NOS LIBRE DEL INFIERNO.

PARDA PASIÓN

Recuerda desde este paralelo ártico cómo canta en solfa la otra Sevilla trianera que no llama Cachorro a un Cristo, la Sevilla anónima. Reduciendo su pasión a las aceras, rima a la manera cínica y machadiana y nos retrata la semana de la cera y del cofrade, la procesión y el misterio...

Y cuando una saeta por soleares y ese remedo andaluz se cuelan entre los andares de estos pasos en tierra norte, la mirada del que quiere mirar se libra del colorete y del cornetín, se viste de estameña oscura y, con las trazas del aguafuerte, se hunde en la noche de los tiempos, que es esta misma noche, cuando todos los gatos son pardos y el oficio de las sombras hace diácono a un perro...

La mirada del que quiere mirar no asciende al cielo que señala el capirote. Esa mirada va en sandalias por la difusa senda que cruza entre la entraña y el espanto. Y ahí ve a la gente peatona con cara de rezo mudo, paisanada de pana alelada y resignado acatamiento del misterio: pasos, cruces, pasiones, penas apasionadas, negro padecimiento, ritos de paño y ostentación... y con cierto aire solanesco y pasional quedan aquí retratados, ensayando la resurrección.

Y allá al fondo: ese dorso del lienzo, lo pintado al margen, el contracanto que se tiñe de rojo, de sangre, de primavera y del delirio destilado en una botella... botella lanzada con un alma genarina dentro y una magdalena desnudez para que navegue a la deriva sobre un mar de rezos y gusto de masas, penitencias falsas, hipócritas arrepentimientos...

La pasión es roja y es negra. Y con el tiempo, parda.

PEDRO GARCÍA TRAPIELLO

LA OBRA PICTÓRICA DE ANGEL ARROYO

es un relato vivencial descrito con armonía y sobriedad, utilizando el blanco y el negro como vehículo de emociones percibidas y de su proceso de interiorización.

El lenguaje se vuelve esencial y austero para tal vez intensificar la emoción y penetrar en el territorio del silencio, a veces interrumpido por los sonidos acompasados de tambores y trompetas.

La pintura de Arroyo nos habla de lo invisible pero nos hace cómplices de lo que siente. Nos evoca el recuerdo de lugares familiares y nos despierta el sentido de pertenencia. Pero más allá de las sensaciones percibidas estamos ante una pintura que nos habla de autenticidad y sinceridad emocional.

MANUEL FRUTOS LLAMAZARES

CENTROARTE

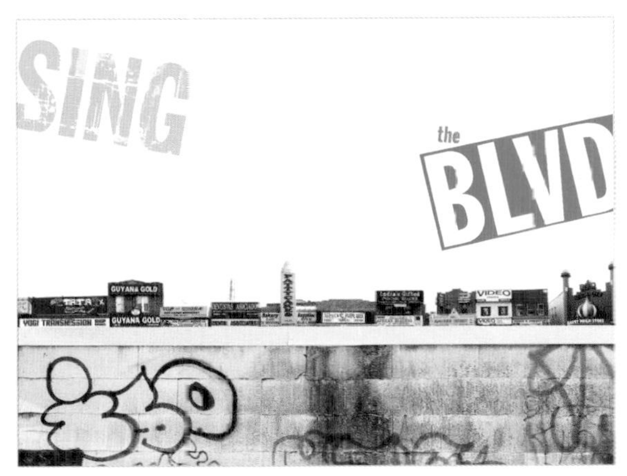

BOTH TYPEFACE STYLE AND POSITIONING allude to a specific urban environment, creating a narrative of travel and experience.

EarSay/W.W. Norton
United States

VEILS OF COLORED TEXTURE and transparent type—running in two directions—evoke the veil of Arabic culture and reference that language's reading direction in contrast to that of Western reading.

Leonardo Sonnoli *Italy*

Visual Relationships Between Words and Pictures

Visual Relationships Between Words and Pictures Getting type to interact with imagery poses a serious problem for many designers. The results of poorly integrated type and image fall into two categories. The first category includes type that has nothing in common with the images around it or is completely separated from the image areas. The second category includes typography that has been so aggressively integrated with image that it becomes an illegible mass of shape and texture. ■ Images are composed of lights and darks, linear motion and volume, contours, and open or closed spaces, arranged in a particular order. Type shares these same attributes. It is composed of lights and darks, linear and volumetric forms, and contours and rhythms of open and closed spaces, also arranged in a particular order. The task is finding where the specific attributes of both come together.

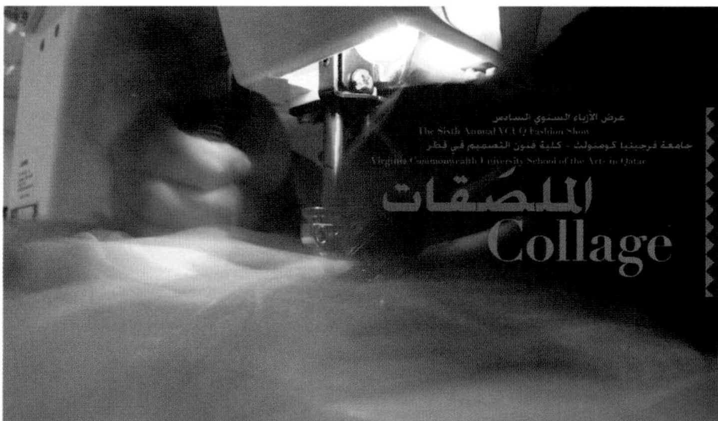

THE STAGGERED MOVEMENT and size change of the type correspond to the vertical movement of the sewing machine needle—contrasting it with horizontal motion—and the flow of fabric through the sewing machine.

VCU Qatar *Qatar*

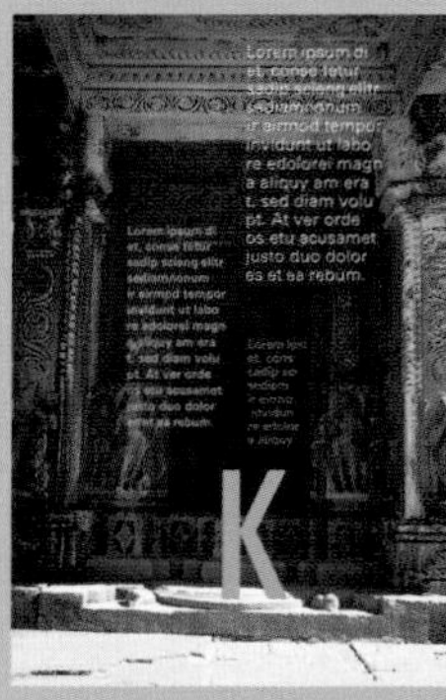

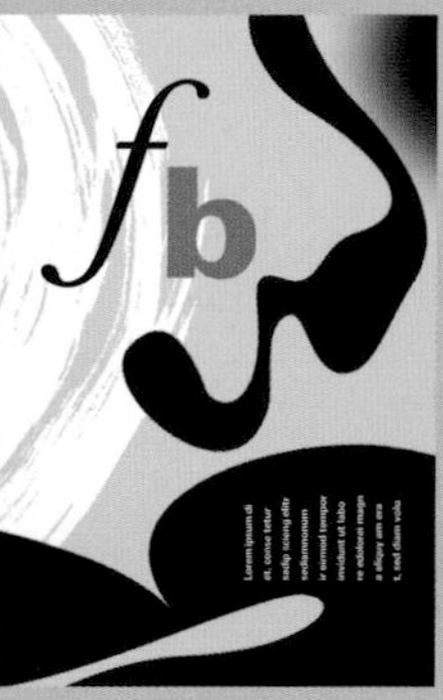

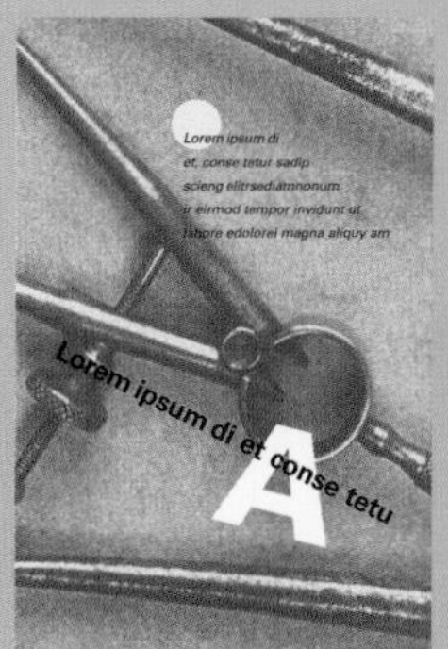

Placing the type directly onto the image permits a quick comparison of the shapes within both elements. In these examples, the type responds to the scale changes, directional movement, and the tonal variations found in the images.

THE IMAGE OF the spiral staircase, symbolizing career evolution, is visually similar to the spiraling geometric shapes in the logo.

C. Harvey Graphic Design *United States*

■ Laying type into or across an image is a quick way of finding visual relationships. Their immediate juxtaposition will reveal similarities in the shape or size of elements in each. The rag of a short paragraph might have a similar shape as a background element in a photograph. An image of a landscape with trees has a horizon line that might correspond to a horizontal line of type, and the rhythm and location of trees on the horizon might share some qualities with the type's ascenders. ■ At the opposite end of the spectrum, the image and the typographic forms might be completely unrelated—in opposition to each other. Opposition is a form of contrast that can be an equally viable strategy for integrating the two materials. A textural and moody image with great variation in tone, but no linear qualities, might work well with typography that is exceptionally linear, light, and rhythmically spaced. The contrast in presentation helps enhance the distinct qualities of each.

THE DIRECTIONAL MOVEMENT of the delicate, curving feather form is supported by the back-and-forth shifting of the poster's title while its vertical structure is restated by the rotated type elements. Careful attention has been paid to the locations of visual stress and openness within the image in considering the placement of the type elements to interact with it.

Paone Design Associates *United States*

ALTERNATING DARK AND LIGHT typographic elements in the upper portion of this brochure cover repeat the dark and light value breaks in the landscape image.

Andreas Ortag *Austria*

THE TEXTURAL COLLAGE of changing typefaces and sizes echoes the graffiti on the wall in the photograph.

Barbara Ferguson *United States*

Formal Congruence Similarities between type elements and pictorial elements make a strong connection between the two. Every image portrays clear relationships between figure and ground, light and dark, and has movement within it. Objects depicted in photographs have a scale relationship with each other and proportional relationships with the edge of the image. When typographic configurations display similar attributes to an adjacent image, or expand on those attributes, the type and the image are said to be formally congruent.

A

B

C

D

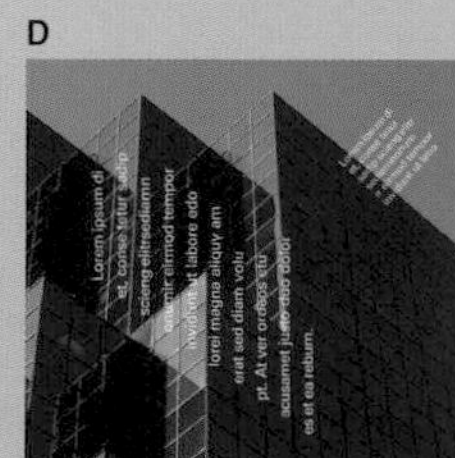

The type in this series of studies is related to the image alternately through: position (A); repetition of linear movement and alternation of weights (B); mimicry of depth and perspective (C); and the angle of its alignment (D).

The numerals and the figure have similar shapes and movement. Note how the position of the numeral 3 highlights the mass of the shoulder and the curve of the torso.

The light and dark areas of the image show similarity to the locations, shapes, sizes, and tonality of the type forms.

www.augustinum.de

THE DESIGNER USES typographic texture in the background—and its color—to correspond formally with the chain in the silhouetted image but uses the violet type to formally oppose the image. This violet type, however, shares a formal quality—contrast in stroke weights—with the light, textural script.

Finest Magma *Germany*

There are an unlimited number of ways for type to become congruent with an image. The selection of a particular face for the type might relate to tonal or textural qualities in the image. Instances in which type extrapolates the formal qualities in an image create powerful emotional and intellectual responses in the viewer. Type that is adjacent to an image also can be formally congruent in terms of its position relative to the image. In this kind of formal congruence, the image exerts an influence on the composition of the page as a whole. Even if the type retains its natural architecture, it may still react to the compositional architecture within the image. All three elements—image, format, and type—appear to share the same physical space.

Formal Opposition Relating typographic elements to images by contrasting their visual characteristics is also a viable way of integrating them. Although seemingly counterintuitive, creating formal opposition between the two kinds of material actually can help clarify their individual characteristics. Contrast is one of the most powerful qualities that a designer can use to integrate material—by their very difference, two opposing visual elements become more clearly identified and understood. Within a letterform combination of an M and an O, for example, the fact of the M's angularity is reinforced by the curved strokes of the O. The movement within each form is made more pronounced, and the two elements essentially fight for dominance. The caveat is that some congruence between the elements must also exist so that the opposing characteristics are brought clearly into focus. In the same way that a hierarchy is destroyed if all the elements are completely different, the strength of the contrast in opposing forms is weakened if all their characteristics are completely different.

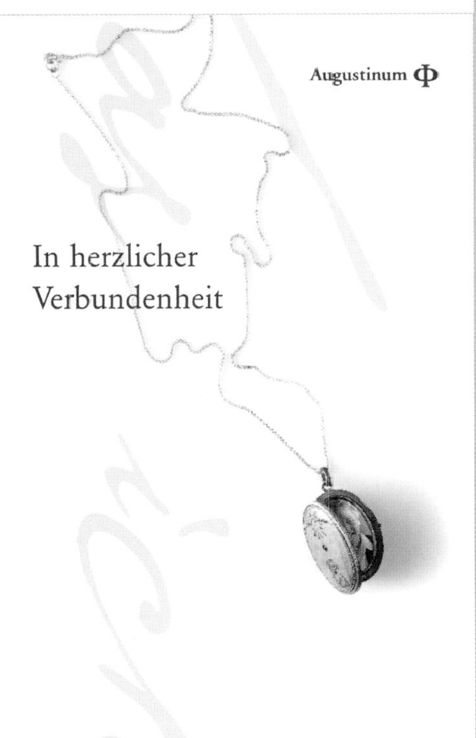

In these three examples, the visual relationship between type and image is one of opposition, but the choice of type style and treatment in each example shares some formal relationship with the image.

1: A soft-focus photograph with muted detail and light tonal values overall is contrasted by a bold-weight sans serif typeface, but the subdued color of the type shares a tonal and color relationship with the image.

2: A regular-weight modern serif face with a great deal of contrast in the strokes—the opposite of the photograph's lack of contrast. The geometric quality of the typeface responds to shapes apparent in the image.

3: A lightweight text with very active details; the type's stylized quality counteracts the passive, neutral character of the image, but its arrangement within the image responds to areas of light and dark.

A study of letterform combinations reveals both congruence and opposition. The inherent differences between the O and M are made more pronounced by changing the posture, weights, styles, and positions of the letters, yet the combinations in which they share one—or two—aspects seem richer. The inherent similarities of the A and K allow for more dramatic opposition because their structural similarity is so powerfully congruent.

Positioning Strategies Consider the location of the type relative to the image and the attributes of the image's outer shape in relation to the format. An image cropped into a rectangle presents three options: the type might be enclosed within the image; the type might be outside, or adjacent to the image; or the type might cross the image and connect the space around it to its interior. Type that is placed within the field of a rectangular image becomes part of it. Type adjacent to a rectangular image remains a separate entity. Its relationship to the image depends on its positioning and any correspondence between its compositional elements and those in the image. The type might align with the top edge of the image rectangle, or it might rest elsewhere, perhaps in line with a division between light and dark inside the rectangle. Type that crosses over an image and into the format space becomes both part of the image in the rectangle and part of the elements on the page. Its location in space becomes ambiguous.

THE VERTICAL, OVERLAPPED TITLE—as well as the geometric blocks of white and yellow—appears to float in front of and over the image on an invisible foreground plane, thanks to their enormous scale and tremendous value contrast with the image. Oddly, the subtitle occupies a space inside the white bar at the top.

Thomas Csano *Canada*

BECAUSE OF ITS LINEARITY, transparency, and low value contrast, the typography on this page layout seems to become part of the sky space within the image.

Finest Magma *Germany*

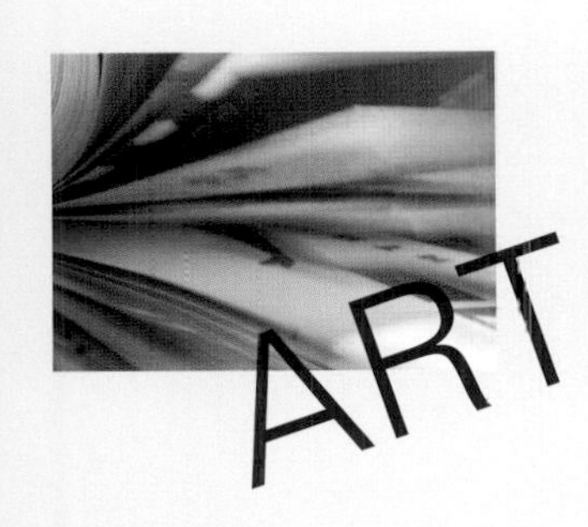

Type will appear to change spatial relationships when placed on, in, or next to a cropped image. This spatial ambiguity might also involve the space around the cropped image, creating a connection between the field, image, and type that brings them together in space. The type at top left is part of the image. In the layout at upper right, the type leaves the image; it enters the format space and moves into the foreground. The type crossing the image, lower left, joins image and space by crossing the image. At lower right, the type responds to the rectangular shape of the image, relating it to the format shape.

COMBINING VERTICAL and horizontal positioning of type elements helps integrate the linear movement of both type and image, as well as permits the currency's denomination to be read when the bill is held at either angle.

Marcia Lisanto *Laguna College of Art and Design, United States*

FOR ALL APPEARANCES, the chapter title on this book spread is situated on the gallery wall at the back of the image.

Finest Magma *Germany*

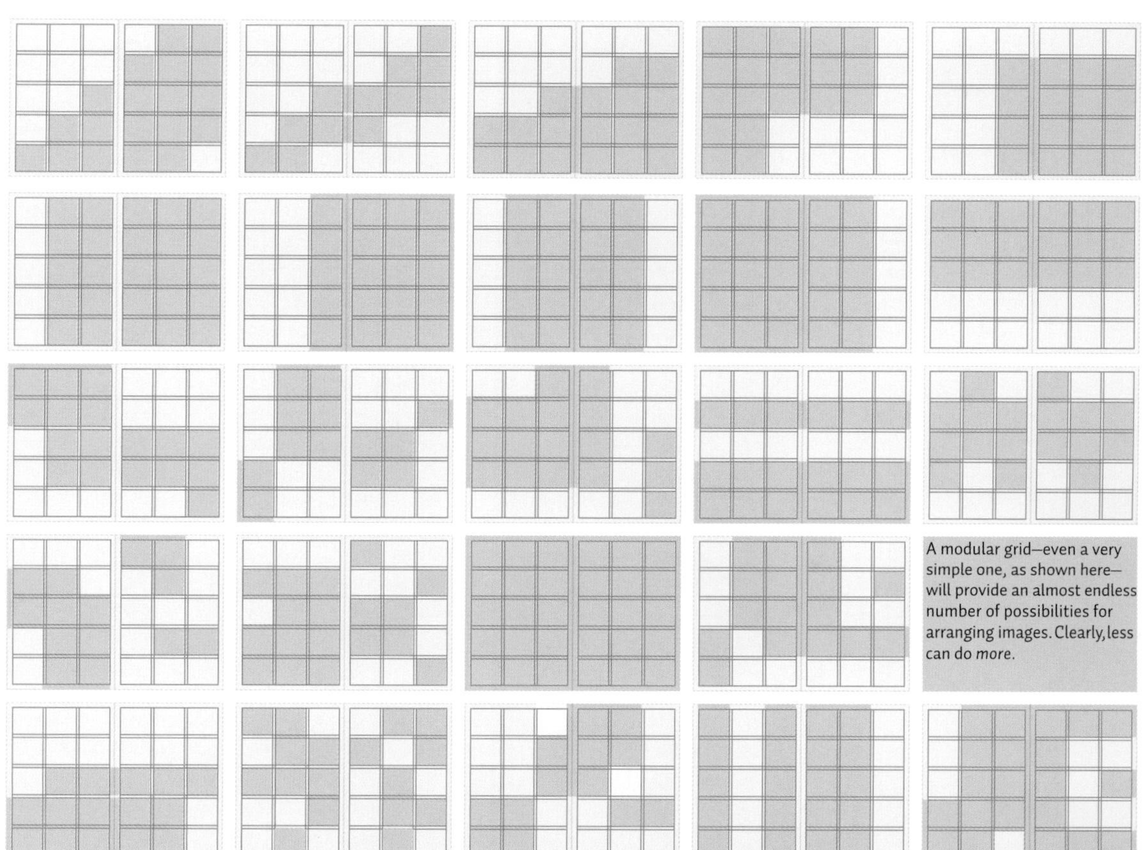

A modular grid—even a very simple one, as shown here—will provide an almost endless number of possibilities for arranging images. Clearly, less can do *more*.

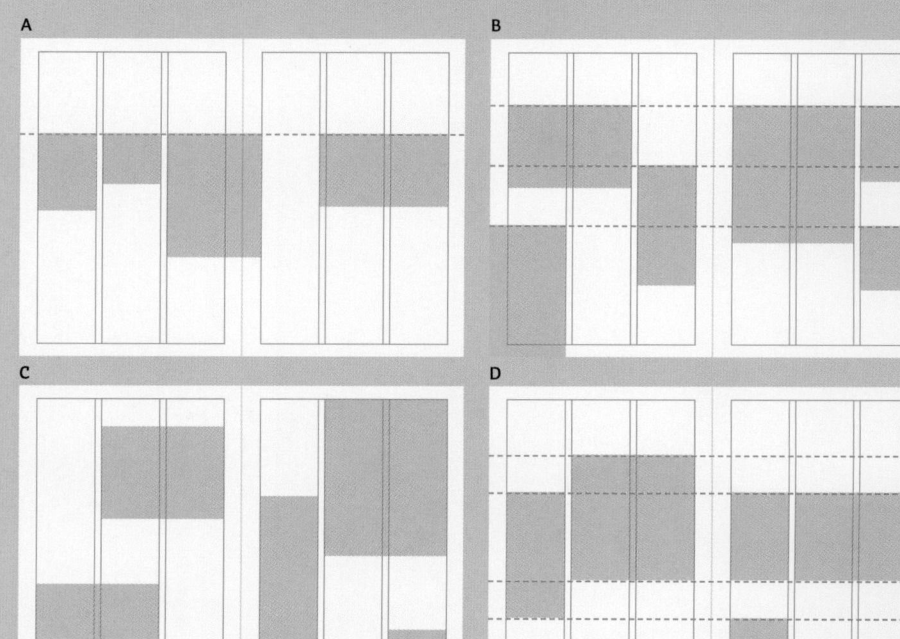

Strategies for integrating images on a simple column grid revolve around the relationship of the images to flowlines—whether the images hang from one (A); hang from several (B); appear anywhere vertically, conforming only to the column widths (C); or stretch between flowlines in a more rigid approach (D).

Integrating Images with a Grid Using a grid structure to organize pictures and text means bringing them in line with the natural horizontal and vertical axes created by columns and blocks of text. By organizing images into a grid that repeats these attributes, a designer chooses to deemphasize their internal visual qualities in favor of the structural proportions of the page. ■ A designer may use either a column grid without modules, or a modular column grid, to provide locations and proportions for images. As images increase in size, based on the widths of columns or modules, their internal visual qualities become more pronounced, and the structural quality of the type begins to contrast the image. As images shrink relative to the grid, their internal visual qualities become less pronounced, and their shapes as geometric objects within the text structure become more important. This fluctuation is another compositional attribute imparted by the grid. ■ Even though using a grid to organize images might seem to stifle their visual potential, remember that a grid has a kind of built-in, organic flexibility to it. A simple column grid has consistent width intervals that pictures can traverse—the more columns, the more possible widths for images—but it also allows a variety of depths for the images. Images might be allowed to meet a system of flowlines if they are established as part of the column grid. Modular grids, which at first appear to limit possibilities for images, actually provide enormous flexibility for how images might interact on a page. Each module can contain an image, and groupings of modules in any combination may also contain images—2 x 3, 1 x 6, 3 x 5, and so on, all the way up to full-bleed images and large divisions of the overall spread.

THE GRID USED TO structure this layout defines the scale and orientation of the images and affects their presence related to type. A smaller image relates visually to the module, and hence to the overall page structure; the larger the image becomes, the more its internal visual qualities dominate, creating contrast with the structure and surrounding type.

Studio Works *United States*

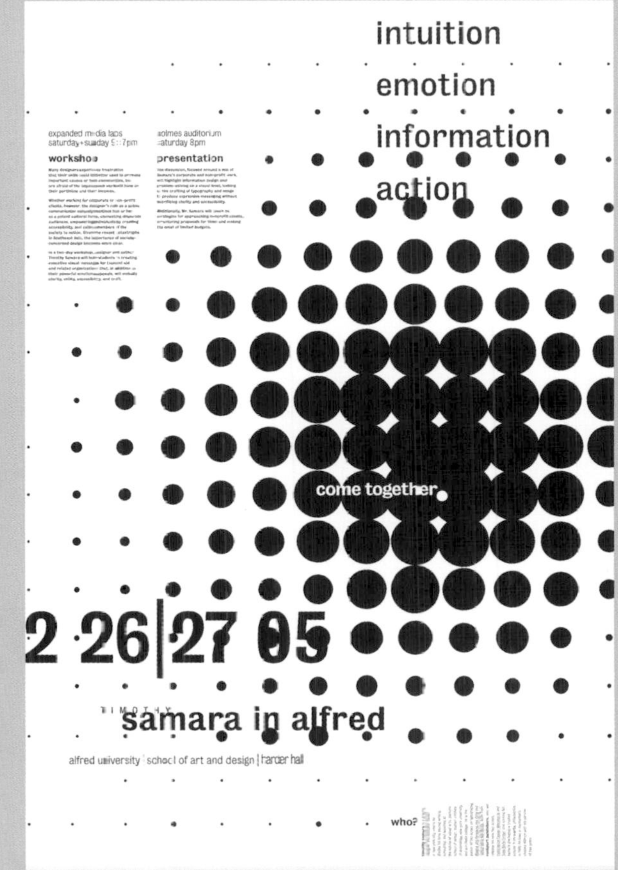

Even within a single-format piece, such as a poster, a grid is a useful strategy for organizing material, whether pictorial or typographic. In this poster, for example, the various elements are arranged on a hierarchic grid based on a proportion derived from the inset images. All the spatial intervals between text components, as well as between text and major formal elements—such as the dot grid—adhere to this internal proportional system. The grid-based intervals are hierarchic in that their sizes relative to each other are determined by the relative importance of the material they govern.

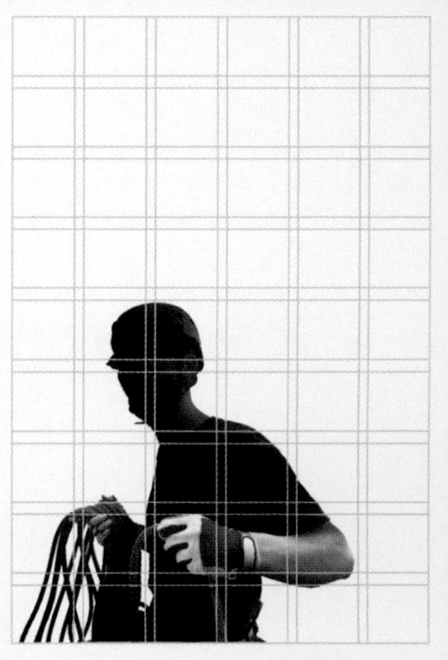

Silhouetted images contrast sharply with rigid grid structures by virtue of their irregular outer contours. Still, the designer must position silhouetted images with respect to the grid so that they don't seem out of place but, rather, flow smoothly into the geometry surrounding them. Although such images are irregular in shape, the designer must ensure that they "feel" as though they're proportioned and situated like grid-structured images, yet retain their inherent organic quality without feeling stiff or awkward.

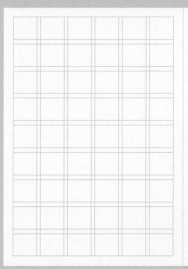

THE SILHOUETTED IMAGE is a welcome break from the geometric regularity of the text columns and tinted blocks.

Martin Oostra *Netherlands*

fiscaal

Ontslagen Wat nu?

slaguitkering benutten om een nieuwe onderneming op te zetten, of u in te kopen in een andere BV. benutten om een nieuwe onderneming op te zetten, of u in te kopen in een andere BV. benutten om een nieuwe onderneming op te zetten, of u in te kopen in een andere BV. benutten om een nieuwe onderneming op te zetten, of u in te kopen in een andere BV.

EIGENZORG

om een nieuwe onderneming op te zetten, of u in te kopen in een andere BV. benutten om een nieuwe onderneming op te zetten, of u in te kopen in een andere BV. benutten om een nieuwe onderneming op te zetten, of u in te kopen in een andere BV. benutten om een nieuwe onderneming op te zetten, of u in te kopen in een andere BV – wat in de tekst gerommeld.

Ontslaguitkering, WW en de fiscus
Even leek het erop dat de ontslaguitkeringen zouden worden gekort op de werkeloosheidsuitkering van de werknemer. Het kabinet heeft inmiddels met de sociale partners (vakbonden en werkgeversorganisaties) afgesproken dat de regeling vooralsnog in haar geheel komt te vervallen. Ook is het plan om de werknemer te verplichten zijn ontslaguitkering in één keer met de fiscus af te rekenen in de ijskast gezet. Wij houden u uiteraard op de hoogte van de ontwikkelingen in deze.

IB-tarieven 2004

over uw inkomen boven het onderstaande bedrag	*betaalt u dit percentage als u jonger bent dan 65 jaar*	*betaalt u dit percentage als u ouder bent dan 65 jaar*
50.652	52%	52%
29.543	42%	42%
16.25	40,35%	22,45%
0	33,40%	15,50%

IB-tarieven 2005

50.652	52%	52%
50.652	52%	52%
50.652	52%	52%
29.543	42%	42%
16.25	40.35%	22,45%
0	33,40%	15,50%

24 FiscAlert maand 2000

fiscaal

tip
Alleen bij massief gouden handdrukken loont het om een stamrecht-BV op te richten. De administratieve rompslomp en de kosten zijn de beperkende kostenfactor. Als vuistregel geldt dat een ontslaguitkering van minder dan een ton euro de kosten van oprichting en instandhouding van de vennootschap niet opwegen tegen de baten. U moet niet alleen zelf het vermogensbeheer voeren, u moet ook jaarlijks een jaarrekening opstellen en aangifte vennootschapsbelasting doen. Als u voor deze zaken iemand zou inhuren worden de kosten nog groter.

conclussie
Het antwoord op de vraag of u uw ontslaguitkering moet afrekenen, storten in een lijfrente of moet gebruiken voor een stamrecht-BV, hangt af van verschillende zaken: of u het geld direct nodig heeft, de hoogte van het geldbedrag, en of uitstel van uitkering in de vorm van een lijfrente of stamrecht tariefsvoordeel oplevert. Heeft u een stevige handdruk van een paar jaarsalarissen, maar krijgt u binnenkort een vorstelijk pensioen? Dan lijkt afrekenen de beste oplossing. Zit u daarentegen op dit moment ruim in de hoogste belastingschaal, maar valt uw inkomen straks terug naar, zeg, 20.000 euro bruto? Wacht dan nog even met het betalen van belasting.
Let verder op of de belastingvoordelen van het kopen van een lijfrentepolis of het creëren van een stamrecht-BV opwegen tegen de kosten en de beperking van uw keuzevrijheid. Eventueel kunt u, als compromis, deels direct afrekenen en de rest van het kapitaal wegzetten.
Let verder op of de belastingvoordelen van het kopen van een lijfrentepolis of het creëren van een stamrecht-BV opwegen tegen de kosten en de beperking van uw keuzevrijh. Hier okok wat in gerommeld.

Dreigend ontslag?
Wilt u juridische bijstand of weten hoe hoog de ontslaguitkering kan zijn? Dan kunt u onder meer hier terecht:

www.goudenhanddruk.nl als u te maken krijgen met een ontslaguitkering, van welke aard ook

www.intermediair.nl voor het berekenen van de hoogte van uw ontslaguitkering, plus een juridische vragenservice bij vragen over uw ontslag

www.ontslag.nl is de site van een gespecialiseerd advocatenkantoor (ook telefonisch te bereiken op 0900-404 01 23, 50 cpm)

En wat krijgt u mee naar huis?
Uw werkgever kan proberen u af te schepen met een ontslaguitkering van één maandsalaris bruto. In uw plaats zouden wij dat weigeren, want voor de hoogte van de ontslaguitkering wordt in de regel aansluiting gezocht bij de zogenaamde 'kantonrechtersformule' die werd ontwikkeld om tot een uniforme en redelijke ontslagvergoeding te komen. Werkt u langer dan een jaar voor het bedrijf dat uw ontslag aanvraagt wegens reorganisatie, dan moet het gek lopen wil de rechter niet op een hoger bedrag komen. De kantonrechtersformule luidt A maal B maal C, waarbij A = aantal dienstjaren, B = bruto maandsalaris en C = correctiefactor.

A wordt onderverdeeld in jaren waarin u jonger was dan 40 (A1), de leeftijd van 40 jaar had bereikt maar jonger was dan 50 (A2) en 50 of ouder (A3). Deze jaren worden respectievelijk met een factor 1, 1,5 en 2 vermenigvuldigd, bij elkaar opgeteld en gedeeld door D, het totaal aantal dienstjaren. In formuleform:
A = { A1 + (1,5 x A2) + (2 x A3) } / D

B is ééntwaalfde deel van het huidige bruto jaarsalaris, inclusief dertiende maanden, tantièmes, vakantiegeld en andere vaste loonbestanddelen.

C is de correctiefactor, die afhankelijk is van de omstandigheden waaronder het ontslag heeft plaatsgevonden. In C worden zaken uitgedrukt als de verwijtbaarheid van het ontslag (van zowel de werkgever als de werknemer), de herplaatsbaarheid van de werknemer, het functioneren, het toekomstperspectief van de werknemer en de wijze waarop het ontslag is totstandgekomen. Als er niets bijzonders aan de hand is, wordt deze factor op 1 gesteld. Bij ernstige verwijtbaarheid van de werkgever kan de factor op bijvoorbeeld 2 gesteld worden en bij verwijtbaarheid van de

maand 2000 FiscAlert 25

Integrating Silhouettes Silhouetted images—whose contours are free from enclosure in a rectangle—share a visual relationship with the rags of paragraphs or columns but also share an opposing relationship with their alignments. Type adjacent to a silhouetted image offers more or less contrast, depending on its location relative to the image. If the rag leads into the image contours, the two elements flow together, and the type might seem to share the spatial context of the image. Bringing the vertical alignment of a column into proximity with an image's irregular contour produces the opposite effect: the type advances in space and disconnects itself from the spatial context of the image. The strong contrast between the aligned edge of the type and the contour of the image might then be countered by the irregular contour of the column's rag.

In the first version of the spread (left), the size of the silhouetted image, along with its strict adherence to the margins and column guides, causes it to seem small, weak, and somewhat stiff. Resizing the image—and adjusting its orientation so that it optically relates with other grid-structured images—not only makes it seem more at home in the structure with the surrounding elements, but also enhances its irregularity with regard to creating contrast to the structure's clear geometry.

The relationship between the image shape and the rag becomes dominant if the rag enters into the image's contour; the geometric alignment in the same block of text will naturally counter the irregular forms within the silhouetted image.

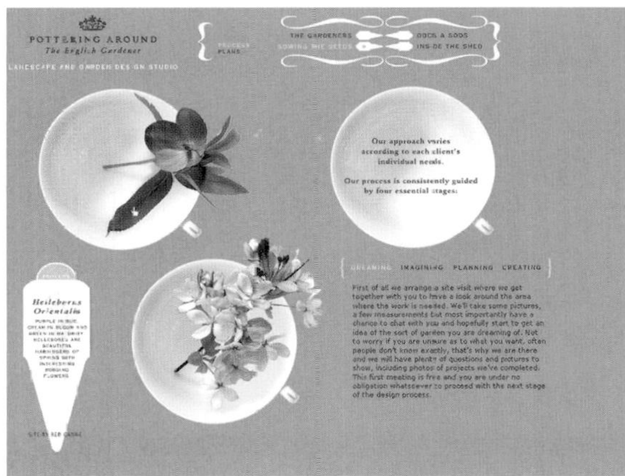

GEOMETRIC SILHOUETTES— the circular teacups and the triangular potting marker—are contrasted by the irrgular silhouettes of the flowers and leaves. Both types of silhouettes contrast the angular and linear aspects of the type structure.

Red Canoe *United States*

Design as a System The vast majority of designed works—printed, interactive, and environmental—are systematic in nature; the existence of a single-format, one-off design piece is exceedingly rare. A website, for example, consists of multiple pages that interact; consider, too, the pages of a book in sequence, all of which must relate to each other, as well as to the exterior of the book as an object itself. Most publications are produced serially—meaning that new issues are produced periodically, as with magazines or newsletters—or sequentially—meaning that they are either a family of separate, but related, items that are produced all together, or that they are individual publications whose information is augmented or supported at different times, such as families or series of brochures. Advertising campaigns, too, are systematic: a single format might be used serially, placed in sequential issues of a magazine, or the ads within a campaign might appear simultaneously in multiple

TYPOGRAPHIC STYLE, use of white space, and consistent application of colors and grid structure mark these branded collateral materials as coming from the same source. The neutrality of the structure is flexible and will be useful in streamlining production for complex publications, as well as allow designers to accommodate new kinds of materials without having to reinvent the wheel.

Grapefruit *Romania*

USING PORTIONS OF the client's logotype at tremendous scale in a retail environment creates a simple system that can easily adapt to changing store layouts.

A10 Design *Brazil*

publications, but in different formats–single page, double-page spread, half-page vertical or horizontal, and so on. Even environmental design work is systematic in that it addresses the integration of information and visual experience among multiple spaces, for example, the exterior and entry lobby of a building, a set of exhibit spaces, or public areas such as restaurants, shopping centers, or mass transit stations. ■ Because of this aspect, a designer's understanding of the visual language he or she is creating for such work is terribly important. It not only ensures the user's or viewer's unity of experience from one space to another but also helps direct them through changing levels of information and provides flexibility in visual presentation appropriate to whatever such changes may be. Being able to control variations within the system also prevents the experience from becoming monotonous for the audience.

Consistency and Flexibility Establishing tension between repeated, recognizable visual qualities and the lively, unexpected, or clever manipulation–even violation–of those qualities in a system-oriented work is a difficult task. At one extreme, designers risk disintegrating the visual coherence that makes for a unified and memorable experience by constantly altering the project's visual language in his or her effort to continually refresh the viewer. At the other extreme, treating material too consistently will kill the project's energy. In some instances, it might also do the material a disservice by constraining all elements into a strangled mold that decreases the clarity of either the concept or informational relationships by not allowing these to flex as they must. The renowned designer, Massimo Vignelli–known chiefly for his rigorous use of grid structures–put it this way: "A [structure] is like a cage with a lion in it, and the designer is the lion-tamer; playing with the lion is entertaining and safe for the viewer because of the cage, but there's always a danger that something will go wrong:.. and the lion-tamer has to know when to get out so he doesn't get eaten."

SYSTEMATIC THINKING most often is associated with branching and corporate identity-focused communications, the hallmark of which is consistency. In the case of this logo, the form remains consistent, but a variable color scheme allows for flexibility in relating the logo to accompanying imagery, reinforcing itself yet refreshing itself every time it is seen.

Research Studios *United Kingdom*

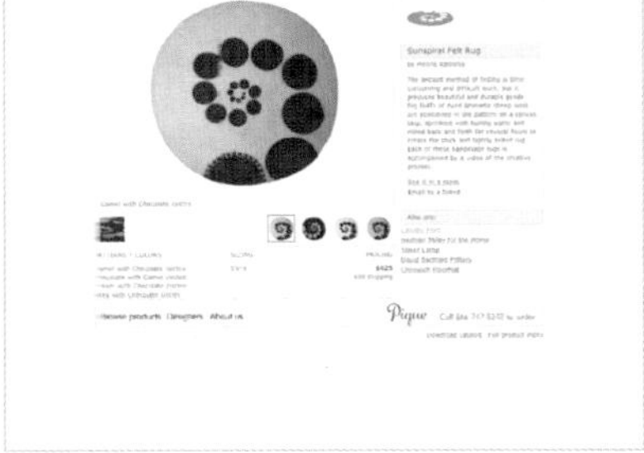

SYSTEMATIC USE of a grid structure in this website allows different combinations of content–and content of varying widths and complexity–to be updated quickly and without sacrificing the overall unity of the pages.

BBK Studio *United States*

SIMILAR PHOTOGRAPHS and a specific color palette create unity among a series of print collateral applications, but each image is varied with a different illustrative detail.

Loewy *United Kingdom*

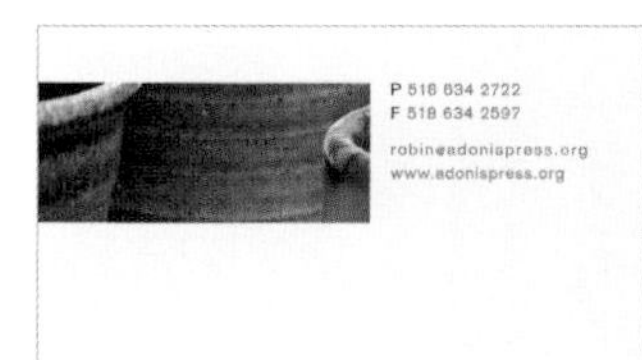

THE DESIGNER CREATES flexibility in this simple stationery system by altering the orientation and proportion of image components as well as the application of color to the typography—whose style and treatment remain consistent throughout.

Maris Bellack *United States*

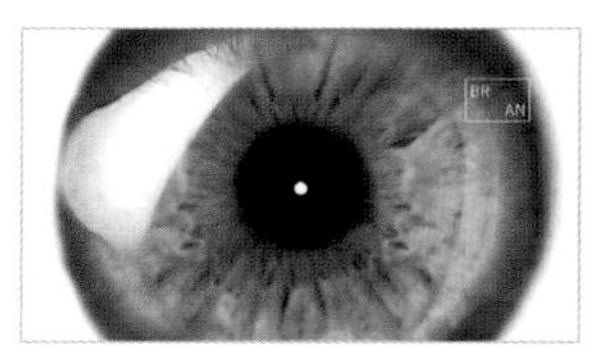

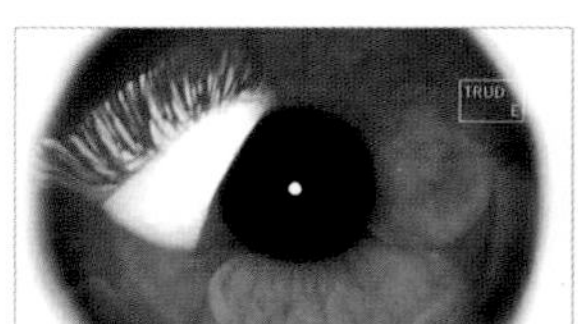

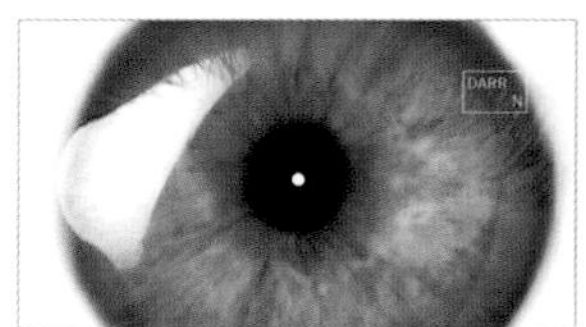

A SIMILAR STRATEGY is employed in this series of business cards. The size and position of elements, both on the front and the back of each card, remain the same, but the color palette changes.

Fishten *Canada*

In-depth study of the potential formal variation possible for even one aspect of a project's visual logic can be time-consuming, but the results of even an hour or two of experimentation can open up a wild range of possible solutions (as well as solutions for other projects with which the designer is struggling). "Serious study" means looking for a range between extremes within a particular variable—very light versus very dark, for example—and taking into account off-shoots of logic that potentially could lead to a truly original solution. Even if the study isn't rigorously organized or the actual composition of the studies isn't totally resolved, just seeing the possible permutations can be invaluable. A rough composition study for a poster series yields a multitude of possibilities for a consistent, yet flexible, visual language. In each set of examples, one aspect of the visual language has been called out for variation without disturbing any of the other aspects. In the first, scale change

Finding Flexibility There are two fundamental variables in any project that a designer can investigate while looking for strategies to keep the work visually consistent as well as flexible. The first variable has to do with the way material is presented, what its actual form and colors are. Within a given project, there may already be a range of possibilities that the designer has established—the options within a selected color palette presents one possibility of changing the presentation of material; the kinds of images the designer chooses to use might also offer a range of options. The second variable is pacing—altering the frequency of different page components in some kind of pattern so that the kinds of images or shapes, the number of images, and the amount of specific colors from within the palette are constantly changing.

is the variation that is exploited for flexibility; in the second study, the shape of the organic forms changes, but their essential identities remain recognizable; in the third, position of elements is the only variation.

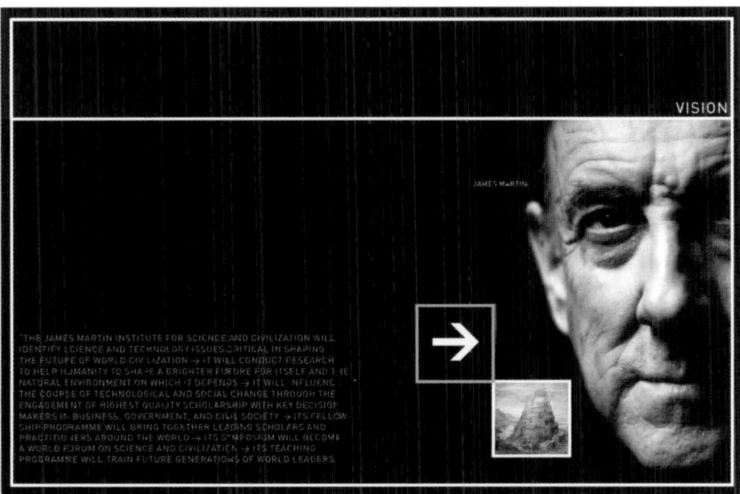

A GRID STRUCTURE provides harmonic and consistent relationships in text and image proportions, and the individual treatment of text components—typeface selection, size, and weight—is also rigorously applied. However, the locations of the elements as well as their organizational complexity change dramatically.

Loewy *United Kingdom*

Formal Variation As noted earlier, a designer's understanding of the internal logic of the visual language he or she is creating is paramount; one variable a designer can look at to create flexibility is variation in the visual language's internal logic. The first step is to consider what the components of that visual logic are, and, if necessary, make a written list of them. Asking simple questions of oneself is a great way to begin the evaluation process—and answering such questions as simply as possible is equally important. "What are the visual components of this project?" "What kind of images am I using?" "Is geometry important in the shapes or relationship?" "Is there spatial depth, and, if so, what creates it—transparency, scale change, overlap?" "Do I sense movement, and, if so, is it lateral, vertical, frenzied, calm and repeated?" Once the designer has answers to these questions, focusing on one or two of the variables—scale change and color family, for example, or texture, organic shapes, and overlapping—might lead to establishing rules for how these variables might be altered without changing their fundamental character.

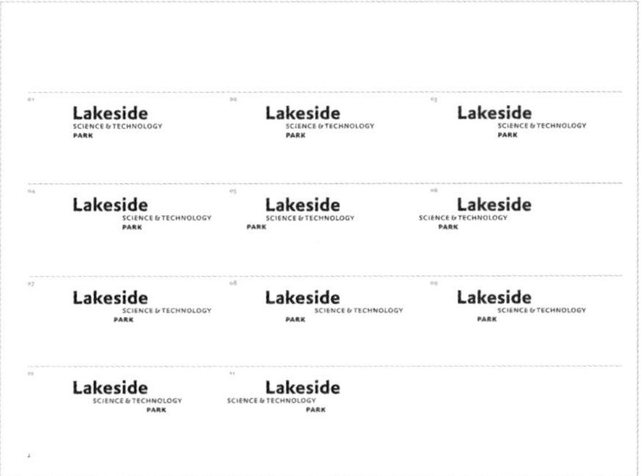

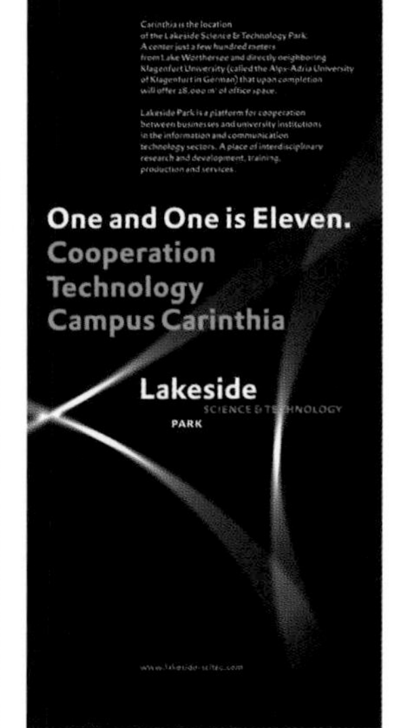

ALTHOUGH THE TYPOGRAPHY throughout this identity program is rigidly styled on a consistent grid, the designer has introduced flexibility in form at every level: variations in the visual shape of the logotype lockup; a series of abstract linear illustrations that can be used in a number of ways; and a strong color palette of analogous hues with varying levels of intensity.

Clemens Théobert Schedler
Austria

TO CREATE FLEXIBILITY in this packaging system, the design team varies the form language of the linear illustrations and the color coding of each item.

Templin Brink Design
United States

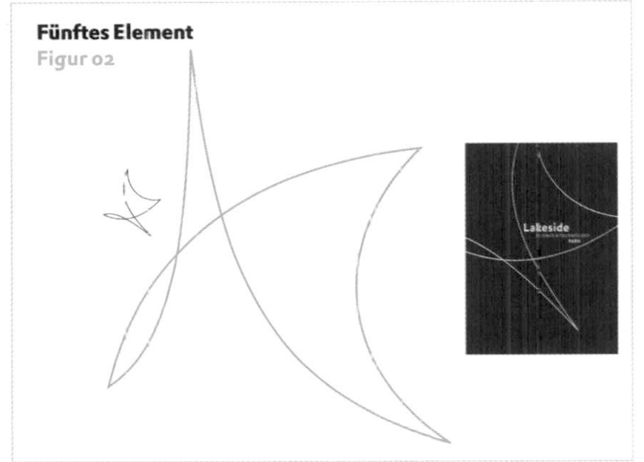

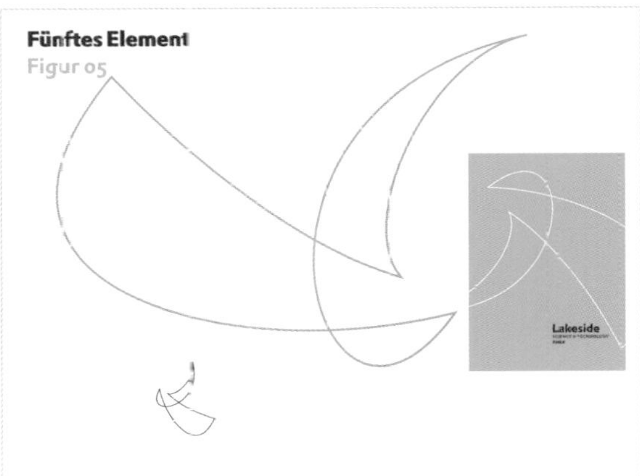

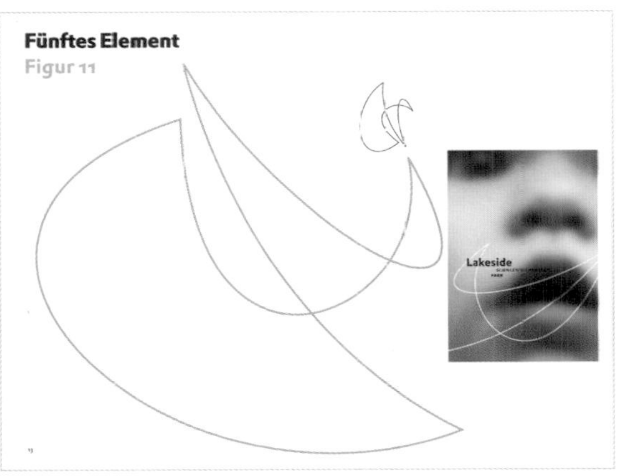

Riesenrad & Hightech
Einladung zur Eröffnung
Lakeside Science & Technology Park
22. April 2005
13.00 bis 17.00 Uhr
Zeit & Ort
Freitag, 22. April 2005 | 13.00 bis 17.00 Uhr
Der Eintritt ist frei
Lakeside
SCIENCE & TECHNOLOGY
PARK

Structural Variation Changing How Content Is Arranged

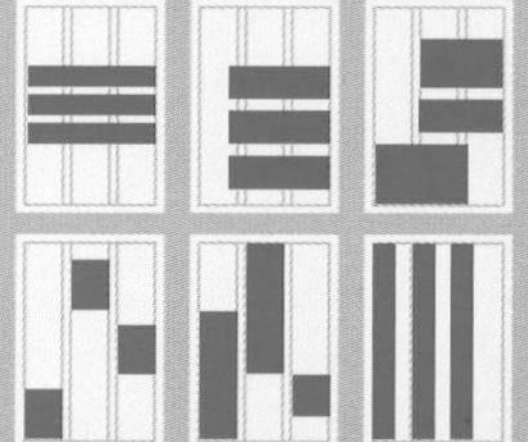

Overall Progressive Sequencing This strategy articulates image and text on a grid beginning with one type of logic and progressively changing the logic spread by spread. The result is a continuous transition in the pacing over the course of the entire project.

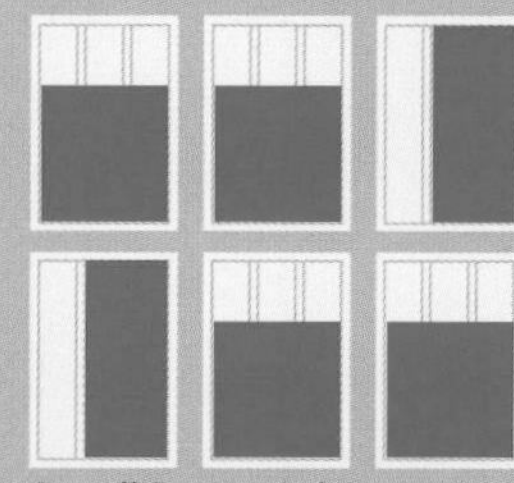

Overall Syncopated Sequences In this approach, content is articulated on a grid using one type of logic for a particular sequence of page spreads; altering the logic for a second sequence of spreads; and then returning to the previous logic. This strategy can become more complicated—instead of the A·B·A rhythm described, a rhythm of A·B·A·C·A might be used, or A·B·C·B·C·D·C·D·E, for example.

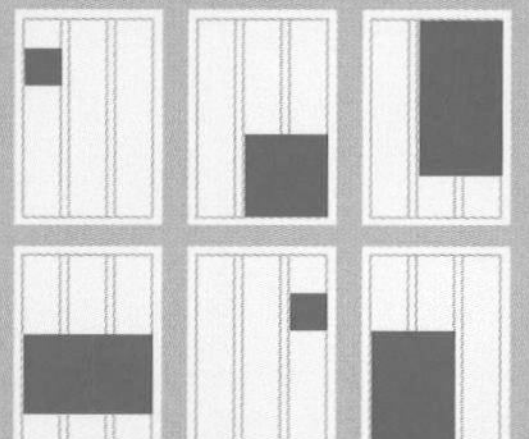

Continuous Variation This is an approach in which the articulation of content continuously changes from spread to spread. The change might focus on the relative position of elements or on the proportions of spatial zones given to specific informational components.

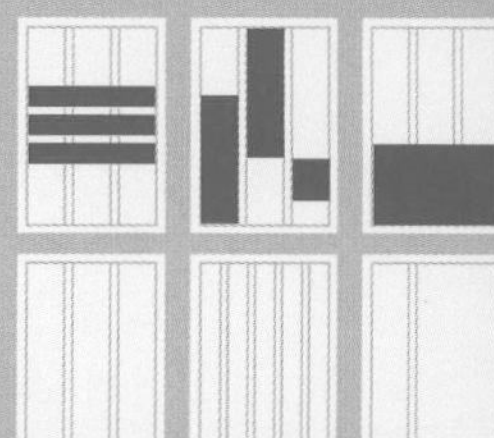

Section Variation The same grid is articulated using a specific logic in one sequence of page spreads, another logic in the following sequence, and another logic in the sequence after, without repetition. Or, completely different grids might be used in each section.

Content Presentation Changing the Content's Visual Attributes

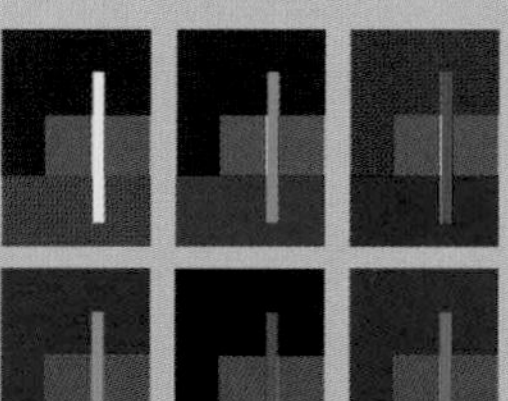

Color Progression or Syncopation In this visual strategy, page sequences exhibit a distinct color scheme, either varying completely between sequences or tied together by a color or two that are universal. The color schemes might progress—from cool to warm, or neutral to vibrant—or they may alternate in a particular rhythm—cool, warm, cool, warm.

Scale Progression or Syncopation Similar to color progressions, this variation focuses on scale change from spread to spread or from sequence to sequence. Images might grow in scale over a sequence of pages; or their scales might alternate between page spreads or sequential sections. Scale-based pacing might or might not be influenced by grid variation.

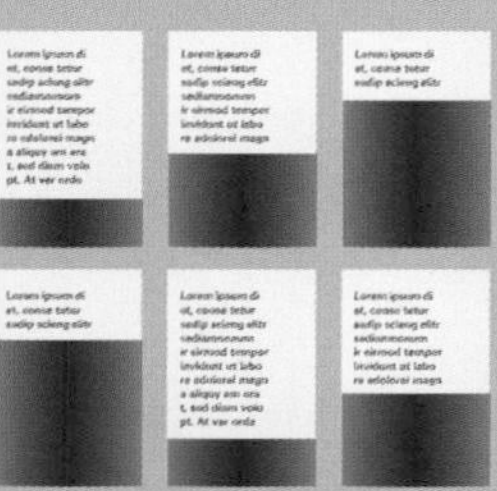

Text Versus Image The relationship between the amount of text and the amount of image material changes, either progressively or in a distinct rhythm.

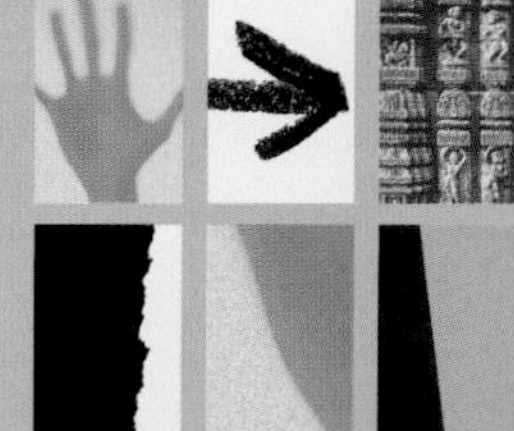

Image Treatment Progressions or Syncopation This approach presents changes in image treatment or mode between spreads or sequences; for example, progressing from representational to abstract, or alternating between photographs and graphic icons. The complexity of the material may be reflected as a progression—for example, simple to complex—or as a syncopation—simple/complex/simple/complex.

Since every project is different, the ways in which a designer might address pacing in a specific project are unlimited. However, most pacing strategies can be distilled into two basic overall approaches.

Structural Variation Regardless of the content's treatment in terms of color, imagery, or typography, the structure of a publication can be articulated in a variety of ways.

Content Presentation Aside from varying structure, the designer might exploit formal variation and opposition within the content to create pacing changes: its color, scale, photographic or illustrative treatment, and its complexity. Sometimes such pacing changes coincide with structural variation; for example, changing the scale of images over a page sequence might reflect a change in grid logic. At other times, changes to content treatment for pacing might be independent of any structural variations.

Pacing and Sequencing Building off the idea of variation, the order in which a designer delivers content—or, the order in which the formal variation occurs—can be a powerful method for creating variation without disturbing the essential logic of the visual language. The sequence of a multipart project creates a particular rhythm, or pacing. ■ Pacing can be understood as a kind of cadence or "timing" the reader will apprehend from part to part—whether from homepage to subpage within a website, or between page spreads in a magazine, or between brochures in a literature system—almost like a film. By varying this rhythm from slow to fast, or from quiet to dynamic, for example, the designer can accomplish several goals. One result achieved is strictly visual: each turn of a page engages the reader in a new way by varying the presentation. Another result might be that the reader is cued to a significant content change; the informational function is clarified by the pacing. ■ Periodic publications, such as magazines, present specific concerns regarding pacing. Much of a publication's flow will be determined by its overall structure. Magazines, for example, are often divided into sections: a series of "department" pages that recur in the same order every issue and a sequence of feature stories that changes every issue. Within each section, too, the designer must establish visual variation so that the reader, while recognizing a consistent structure, doesn't become bored. ■ On a conceptual level, the pacing and sequencing contribute a tremendously to the message delivered by content. Indeed, such organization may be an intrinsic part of the concept that governs the visual presentation of the content. Sometimes, content organization derives directly from the designer's common-sense understanding of the content's

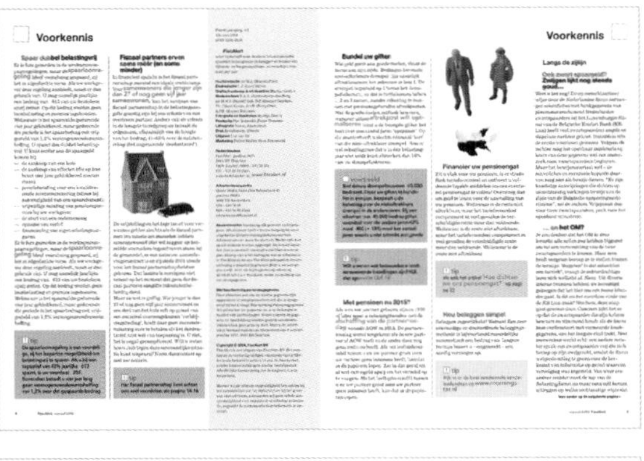
Voorkennis

Voorkennis

fiscaal

Betaal minder belasting door slim te schuiven

huis & hypotheek

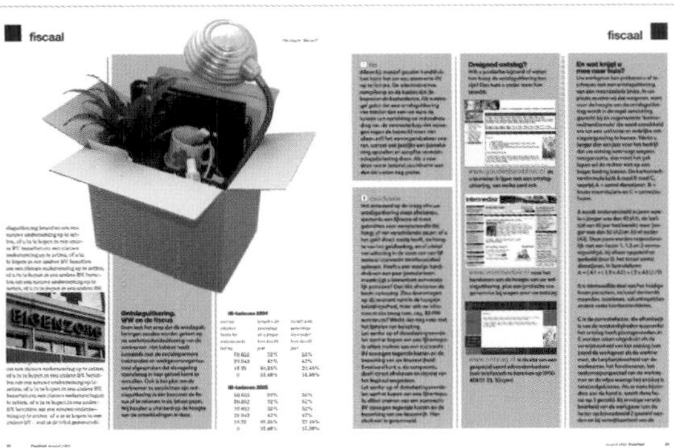
fiscaal

huis & hypotheek

Hypotheek 7 keer goedkoper

schenken & erven

Geef lijfrentetermijnen aan uw kinderen

THIS NEWSLETTER employs a clear, simple strategy to create rhythmic pacing from spread to spread: changes in the sizes, proportions, and placement of photographs. Using tinted blocks to call out specific portions of text also introduces constant change in the presence of the type.

Martin Oostra *Netherlands*

structure, or from generally accepted (even legally required) conventions as to how particular content ought to be delivered. In the first instance, for example, the general public assumes that the upper levels of a Web site's content will be more general, each directing them toward more specific content as they delve further into the site. Conventions abound for publications such as books or periodicals, where the average reader assumes a certain kind

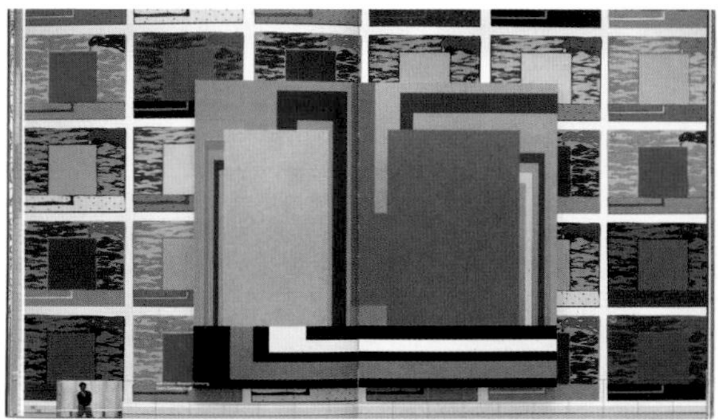

FULL-BLEED PHOTOGRAPHS of a gallery environment lead viewers experientially thorugh an exhibit, moving them from room to room and then close-up to artworks on individual walls. Content travelling horizontally through a spatial zone at the bottoms of the pages provides commentary on the exhibit and organizational strategies used by the artist in his work.

Coma *Netherlands*

of introductory sequence, followed by sections or chapters that group related or sequential content. In the second instance, an annual report is legally required to present brand-related content separately from financial date, and the date must appear in a specific order. ■ Most projects, however, benefit from evaluating the expected method of delivery and finding whether it will best serve the content as defined, or if a better sequence is more appropriate. Designers must always investigate this aspect of a project—the fundamental relationship of all the content's parts—on a case by case basis, and in association with their conceptual goals and their client's communication goals.

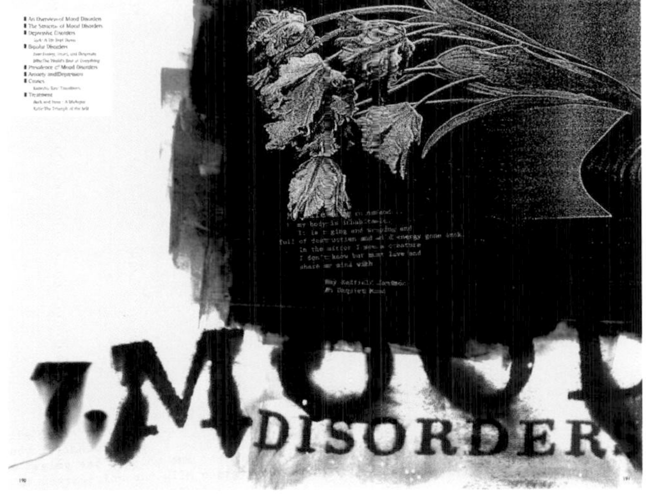

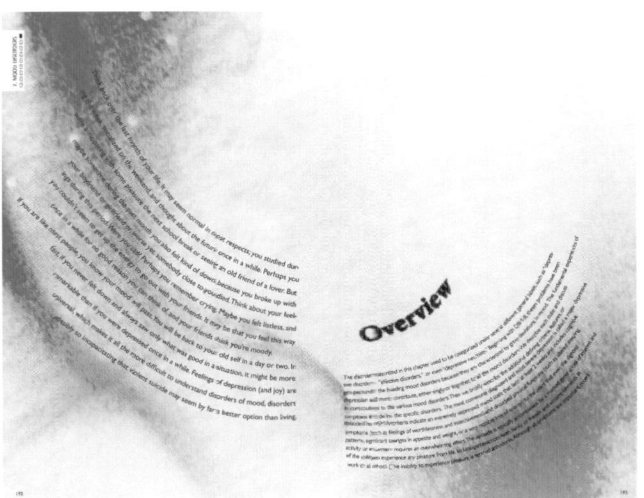

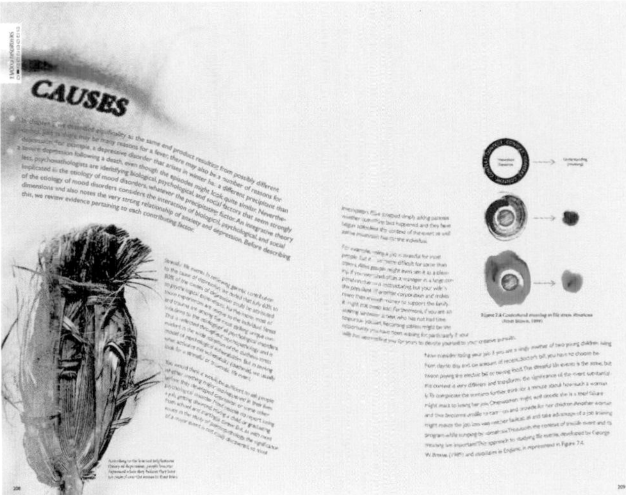

THE SPREADS IN each chapter of this book on abnormal psychology progress from arrangements of image and type that communicate the quality of a given disorder to a state of grid-based resolution that describes various treatment options and successful case studies.

Hae Jin Lee *School of Visual Arts, United States*

Appendix A

The Right Design Choices

Twenty Reminders for Working Designers

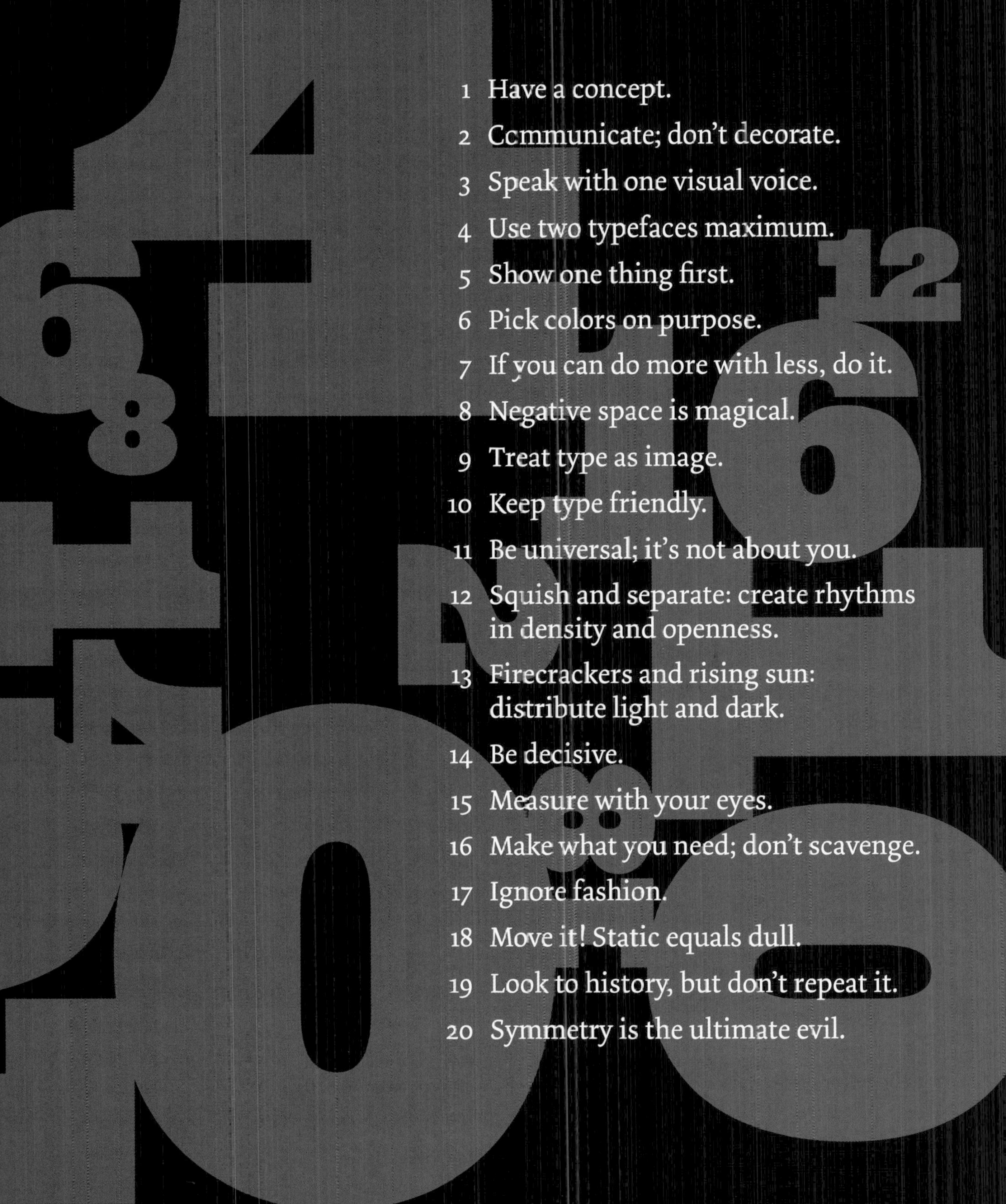

1. Have a concept.
2. Communicate; don't decorate.
3. Speak with one visual voice.
4. Use two typefaces maximum.
5. Show one thing first.
6. Pick colors on purpose.
7. If you can do more with less, do it.
8. Negative space is magical.
9. Treat type as image.
10. Keep type friendly.
11. Be universal; it's not about you.
12. Squish and separate: create rhythms in density and openness.
13. Firecrackers and rising sun: distribute light and dark.
14. Be decisive.
15. Measure with your eyes.
16. Make what you need; don't scavenge.
17. Ignore fashion.
18. Move it! Static equals dull.
19. Look to history, but don't repeat it.
20. Symmetry is the ultimate evil.

If a design doesn't feel good in your heart, what the mind thinks doesn't matter.

April Greiman

Graphic designer, author, and educator

Appendix B

Causin' Some Troub

When and Why to Challenge Anything in This Book

Rules in graphic design exist as guidelines to help establish a way to evaluate what's good and what's not; but, more importantly, they serve to help designers avoid problems that interfere with communication. It is often said, however, that rules are made to be broken, and this is never truer than in design. No two projects are alike: every project comes with different requirements, different messages and ideas that must be expressed, and different—sometimes very specific—audiences. No design approach is ever out of bounds or "illegal"—thou shalt not, on pain of death. In breaking rules, it is important for designers to understand what a rule means and, most importantly, what will happen when the rule is broken. Some rules are less flexible than others; for example, a really dark gray word printed on an even darker background will likely be illegible or close to it. This is not to say that making some type difficult to read can't be an appropriate part of the design; it's just a matter of context: Is making type difficult to read appropriate to that project, and why? Which type elements will be difficult to read? When breaking a rule, there is likely to be a trade-off—something will be gained, and something lost. The designer must decide whether the sacrifice is acceptable and ultimately be prepared to accept the consequence of the decision. Once a designer feels confident that he or she understands how the rules work and what the effects of breaking them will be, a designer must decide why, when, and how. Some of the greatest innovations in graphic design will happen when the designer knowingly—and intelligently—throws the rule book away.

"Don't expect theory to determine how things look."

Michael Rock

Principal of 2x4, New York; graphic designer and educator

Sometimes a designer needs to get out of the way to let the content speak with as little interference as possible. This is true in the case of pure information design–in forms, for example, where the content's only requirement is to get seen and understood very easily–but might also be true for other project types as well. Being neutral and having no concept, that is, selecting a pleasing color scheme, neutral typefaces, and a pleasant paper stock–almost to the point of being purely decorative–can result in a quickly accessible, informative, and functional object, which is not without its appeal.

Have a concept.

Breaking It

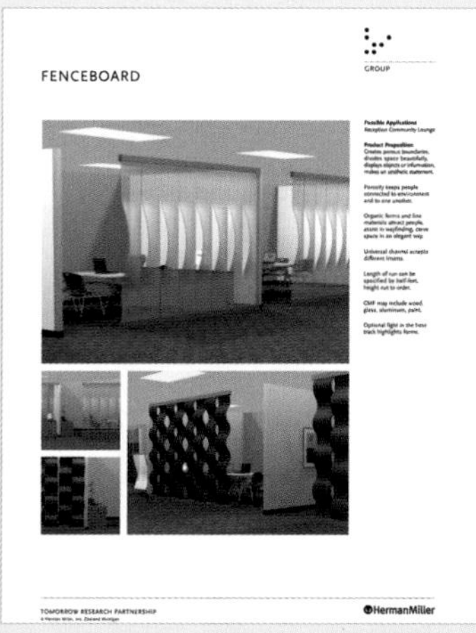

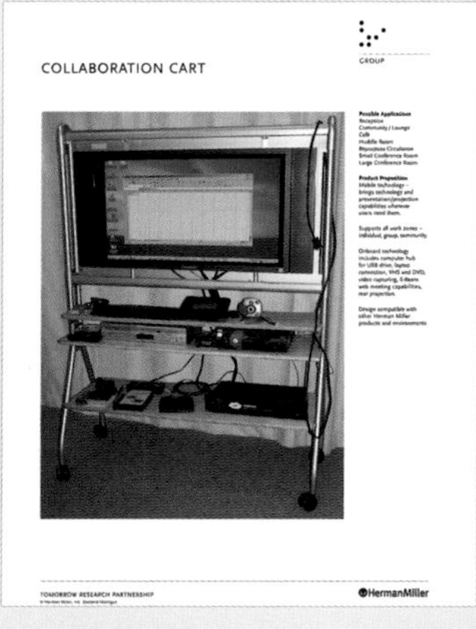

Much of designing is simply problem solving: how to set up a system for information that is easy to use, easy to recreate, and gets the job done. Such is the case for these office-furnishing sell-sheets. No concept, just clear hierarchy, thoughtful treatment of type with weight and size to distinguish informational components, pleasantly decisive margin proportions, and a grid to accommodate one image or multiples.

BBK Studio *United States*

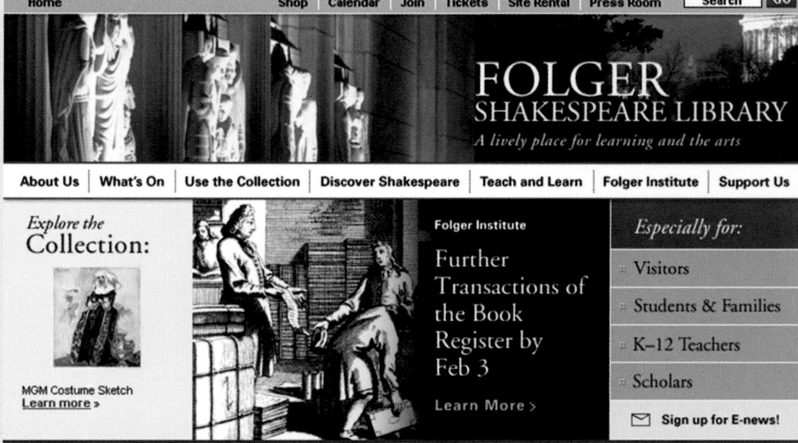

The artifacts collected in the client museum are their own content and concept, and there's no need to embellish that fact in the website. Instead, the design team has focused on developing a strong and easily navigable structure that separates different content areas, is flexible for presenting different combinations of content, and is scalable for future updates. An analogous scheme of greens and pale beige unify the feeling of the site, further help distinguish navigational elements, and generally leave the fanfare to the striking images from the museum's collection.

Swim Design *United States*

This poster promotes a video production studio, but one might not know that from the selection of collaged elements, which are unrelated to the subject matter—except for a hint of film reels in the central area. Instead, the selection of collage elements plays off the abstract notion of the tag line, "Music for the Eyes," and creates references to cultural and stylistic attitudes that might be appropriate to the audience.

Thomas Csano *Canada*

Breaking It

Communicate—don't decorate.

When the message warrants it, use form willy-nilly, without regard for its meaning. This, in itself, might be interpreted as a message and—on rare occasions—that message is appropriate as part of a design solution. A project concerning Baroque architecture or Victorian aesthetics, for example, might very well benefit from extremely decorative treatments that would otherwise constitute a crime against nature.

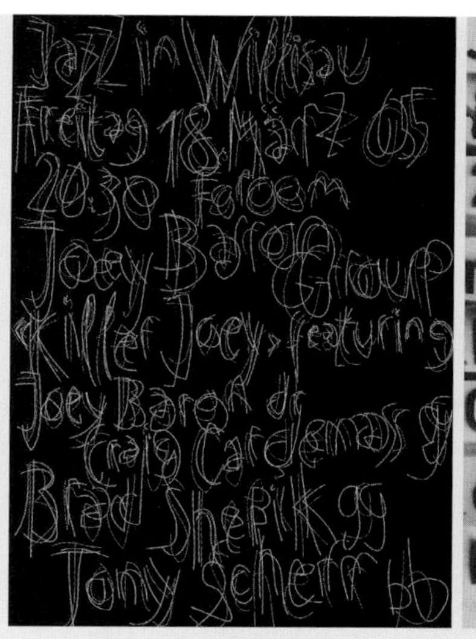

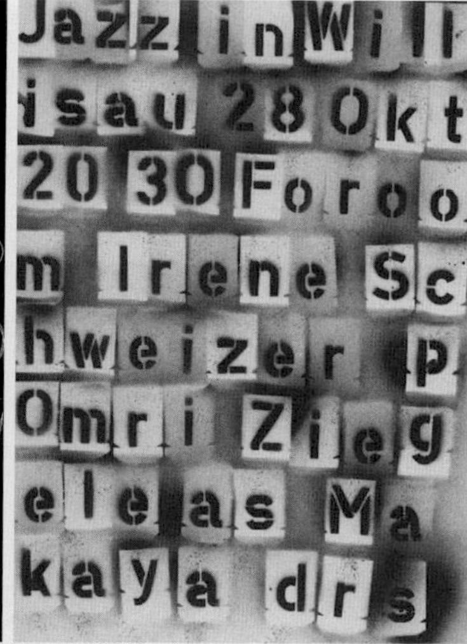

These posters are part of a series promoting events during one season of a jazz festival. Unlike most event branding schemes, however, they don't offer any similarities in color, type style, spatial arrangement, or form language. In this case, violating the cardinal rule of consistency expresses the improvisational nature and individuality of each performance. Another benefit is that potential patrons won't be likely to mistake one performance announcement for another and accidentally miss something they would like to see.

Niklaus Troxler *Switzerland*

Breaking It

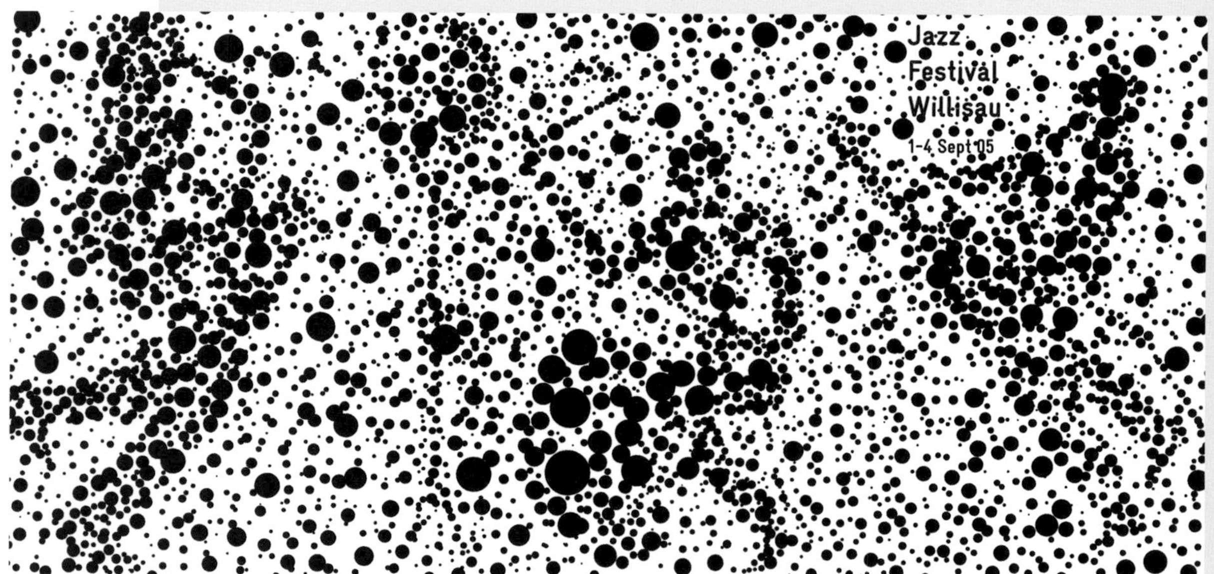

The quickest way to draw attention to a particular element is to make it different from everything else around it, and this can be highly effective as a communication strategy. Disharmony among visual elements—whether stylistic, or in terms of spatial arrangement or color relationship—is also a message unto itself.

Use two typeface families maximum. OK, maybe three.

Breaking It

An extremely complex text, with a great many parts, will be clarified by strong, varied changes in type style. Sometimes you'll need many different typefaces working together to create a certain kind of texture, a busy-ness, that conveys something really important about the client, the subject of the project, or the project's relationship to some other context. Thinking outside the type-box can be difficult, especially if you're comfortable with a select set of typefaces: so take a deep breath, close your eyes, and click the font list at random to see what happens. You might be surprised.

A tremendous variety of typefaces shares space in this music publication. The constant change in typographic style relates to the various musical genres and will appeal to younger audiences that culturally expect a constant shifting of stylistic language in their visual diet.

Ames Bros. *United States*

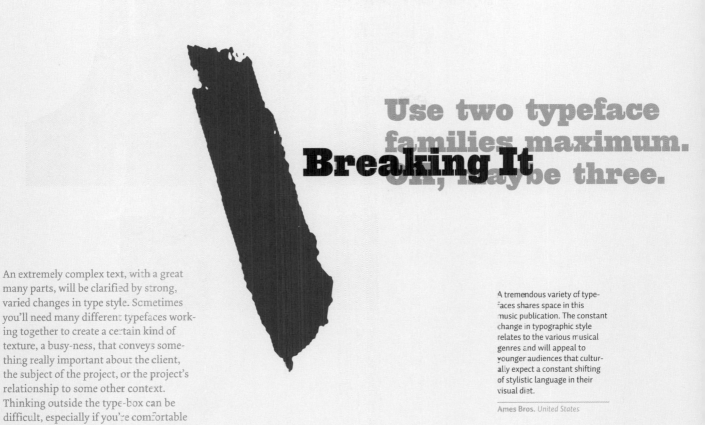

The composition of this page spread is dynamic and decisive, with the size and placement of images corresponding to a strict six-column grid. The energetic change in scale, clustering, overlapping, and horizontal or vertical proportions creates enough activity that focusing on any one element is difficult—and this is the designer's intention. The interval of years in this timeline is statically and consistently called out by regularly spaced year markers, but the designer wants to portray the energy and continuity of historical developments and events by allowing them to interact. From an informational standpoint, the designer has also indicated spans of years for particular developments or processes by allowing images to overlap from year to year. The result is a complex diagram of interrelationships that allows the reader to get a quick overview, enjoy the dynamic composition on the page, and pick out the events that interest him or her the most in whatever order is desired.

Spin *United Kingdom*

Breaking It

Use the one-two punch!

Presenting a multitude of items for simultaneous consideration is usually a no-no, but, in some instances, it helps get the information out front quickly, leaving the viewers to pick which thing interests them most or which is most important at a particular moment. Letting the viewers decide, instead of pointing the direction out for them, can be a good way of engaging them—making them participate in getting the information, rather than handing it to them on a plate. If they have to work for it, they might enjoy it and remember it more easily later.

6

Pick colors on purpose.

Breaking It

Being completely random with color selection—or choosing colors whose usual association purposely conflicts with expectation—for a project is a viable method that can achieve some surprising results. After a time, choosing color using familiar methods yields combinations that are, at the least, somewhat expected and, at the worst, completely uninteresting. Purposely selecting colors that feel awkward in combination or disharmonious might present unexpected options that, despite their seeming randomness, retain some chromatic relationship. Additionally, a random color choice might sometimes aid in communication, depending on the nature of the project. Seeming randomness, like other messages, can be valid given the concept the designer intends to convey.

B

A

They say you're scared.
They say
you don't care.
They say you
won't stop AIDS.
You know different.
Get real.
Get tested.
Get your results.
www.youknowdifferent.org
nyac
NATIONAL YOUTH ADVOCACY COALITION

Each of these two projects explores color in a relatively random or contradictory way. The public service advertisement (A) uses a jarring combination of intense colors that are unrelated in value and temperature to create contrast and enhance the stark directness of the message. The currency design, however, avoids the color cliche usually associated with China in favor of a cool, vivid scheme of analogous hues that calls to mind, fruit, water, sky, and leaves.

A Metropolitan Group *United States*

B Maggie Vasquez *Laguna College of Art, United States*

So much for Modernism! This set of collateral for a fund-raising event, guided by a surreal theme, uses as much illustration, ornament, and typographic change as possible (layered into deep, textural space) to make references to childhood literature in an overly complicated, rich, Victorian way.

Lexicon Graphix and STIM Visual Communication
United States

By all means, add extra stuff if it helps the message. Intricate, complicated, layered, maze-like arrangements of form, even though somewhat daunting at first, can be very engaging–and will appeal to specific audiences. Including apparently unrelated forms or images can be frustrating to a viewer, or they may add an important subtext that, in the end, helps support the primary messages in the project. Since the connection with the audience is really of utmost importance, this rule is breakable when that resonance will be enhanced by an overload of form or texture.

If you can do it with less, then do it.

Breaking It

OK, there's really no good way to break this rule. An absence of negative space is a disaster and always will be. That said, allowing visual material in particular segments of a project to overwhelm the compositional space—on occasion, in response to other segments in which negative space is used liberally—can be an excellent strategy for introducing dramatic rhythm and helping separate out simpler material for special attention.

8
Negative space is magical—create it, don't just fill it up!
Breaking It

Speaking of overdoing it: This book appropriately and excitingly delivers its content, an exploration and showcase of a design trend called Maximalism, in which the more ornament, texture, complexity, and surface treatment, the better. The pages revel in overblown patterns, layers of texture, abstract graphic elements, and color; yet somehow the images and text are presented in a masterfully clear way.

Loewy *United Kingdom*

The focus of this brochure is the client's architecture, both in elevation and image. The designer respectfully shuts up and lets the architect's work do the talking. At the same time, however, the designer provides a clear and consistent hierarchy of sizes, weights, and locations for informational components.

Not From Here *United States*

Treat the type as image, as though it's just as important.

There are always times when typography needs to shut up and get out of the way of the pictures—especially when the type accompanies catalogued artwork or is acting in support of images that are carrying the brunt of the communication burden. In such instances, treating the type as quietly and as neutrally as possible can be most appropriate. Even so, the relationship of the typography to the format will bear some consideration, as will consideration of its size, spacing, and stylistic presentation.

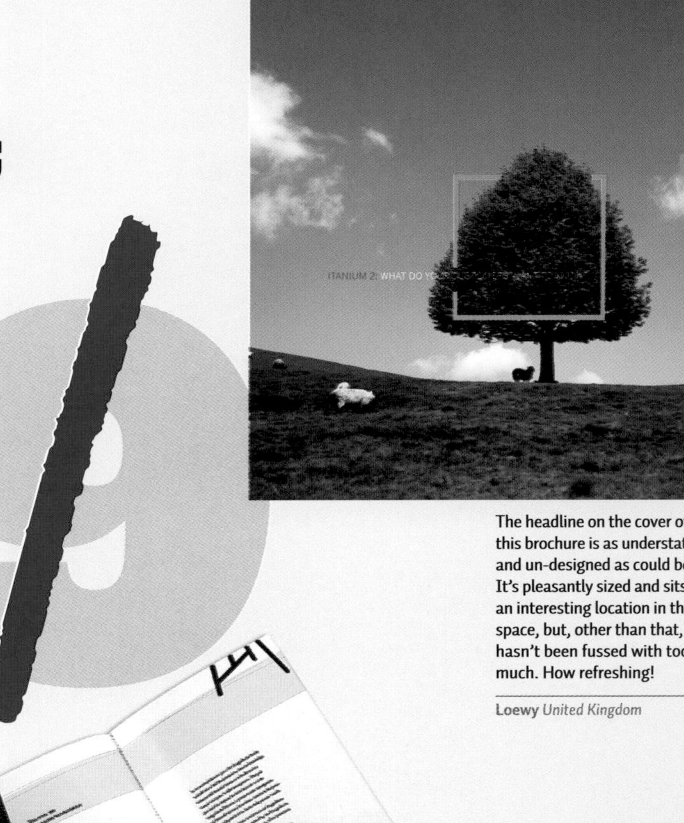

The headline on the cover of this brochure is as understated and un-designed as could be. It's pleasantly sized and sits at an interesting location in the space, but, other than that, it hasn't been fussed with too much. How refreshing!

Loewy *United Kingdom*

The relationship between the typography and the images in this brochure is absolutely neutral; they completely contrast with each other in quality and are independent of the other's compositional strategy. This, in itself, is a very clear kind of logic and perfectly acceptable when it's done with understanding.

Carregal Pease *United States*

In a perfect world, everyone would be friendly and every message we read would be about how friendly we are. Sadly, this is not the case—and many messages are not particularly friendly. As you might guess, the relative accessibility of type greatly depends on the message being conveyed. Making portions of type illegible, overbearing, aggressive, sharp and dangerous, nerve-wracking, or fragile is perfectly acceptable—indeed, preferable—when the job calls for it. There is no excuse for typography that doesn't viscerally communicate in an appropriate way, even if this means frightening, frustrating, or confusing viewers in service of the right concept.

Breaking It

Type is only type when it's friendly.

It's bold, it's strong, it's intriguing, and it's not immediately legible... but the typography in this poster is clearly interested in expressing a design firm's personal vision, idiosyncratic language, and search for originality. Typography of this kind plays well with specific audiences that enjoy being challenged by aggressive visual messaging and participating in the attitude it conjures.

Dochdesign *Germany*

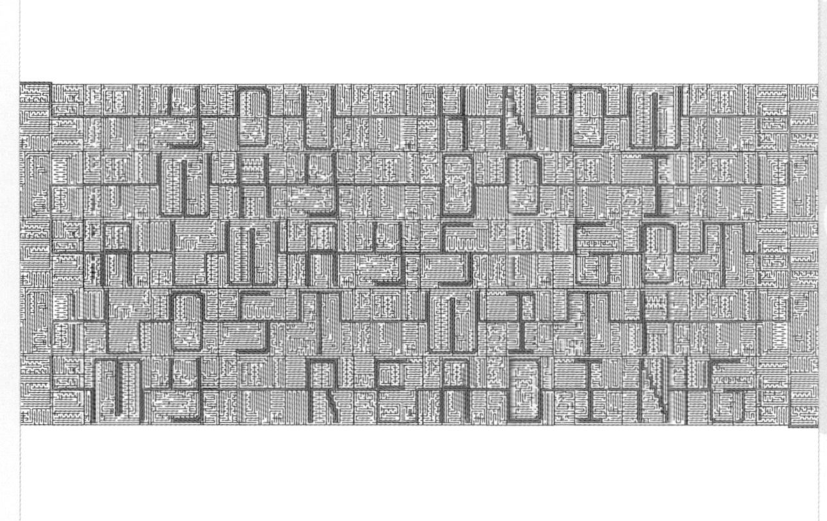

A tricky, textural exploration of legibility and access occurs in this experimental typographic layout. The concept, appropriately supported by the difficulty in reading the type, is about getting lost in information.

Munda Graphics *Australia*

This CD-ROM packaging trades on the designer's unique visual sensibility and interpretation of a specific performer's style or genre of music. The illustration of the artist is rendered in a flat linear style that conflicts with the dimensionality of the type on the back cover, and the designer's own idiosyncratic visual language of swirling dot forms accompanies the other graphic materials. Since music is such a personal experience, both for the artist, the designer and their mutual audience, such personal styling is not only appropriate for a project such as this, but also much appreciated by all concerned.

344 Design *United States*

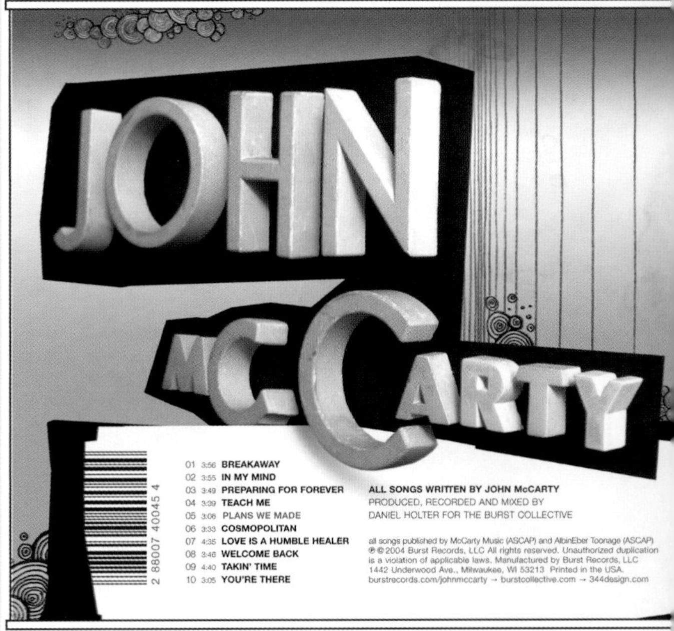

JOHN
MC.CARTY
01 3:56 BREAKAWAY
02 3:55 IN MY MIND
03 3:49 PREPARING FOR FOREVER
04 3:39 TEACH ME
05 3:06 PLANS WE MADE
06 3:33 COSMOPOLITAN
07 4:35 LOVE IS A HUMBLE HEALER
08 3:46 WELCOME BACK
09 4:40 TAKIN' TIME
10 3:05 YOU'RE THERE
2 88007 40045 4
ALL SONGS WRITTEN BY JOHN McCARTY
PRODUCED, RECORDED AND MIXED BY
DANIEL HOLTER FOR THE BURST COLLECTIVE
all songs published by McCarty Music (ASCAP) and AlbinEber Toonage (ASCAP)
℗ © 2004 Burst Records, LLC All rights reserved. Unauthorized duplication is a violation of applicable laws. Manufactured by Burst Records, LLC
1442 Underwood Ave., Milwaukee, WI 53213 Printed in the USA.
burstrecords.com/johnmccarty → burstcollective.com → 344design.com

Always tailor the message to the audience; this includes ignoring the usual imperative to communicate with the widest possible constituency to speak directly to a very small audience in culturally specific ways. For a small audience whose cultural expectations of visual messaging are closely related—a CD cover or music poster, as opposed to a large-scale, general-public branding campaign—using visual metaphor, idiosyncratic stylistic treatments of type or image, and color that references their shared context will resonate more personally and evocatively than images and color that are designed to speak to as broad a group as one is able.

Dynamic, ever-changing, rhythmic movement is highly engaging and most often desirable as a way of attracting and holding attention. Still, a pronounced lack of movement or tension creates an altogether different feeling in a project and, when it makes sense for the message, is quite appropriate. Sometimes, constant visual activity and bouncing movement will adversely distract viewers from focusing on the content. Consistency in rhythm and arrangement is a message that can also communicate.

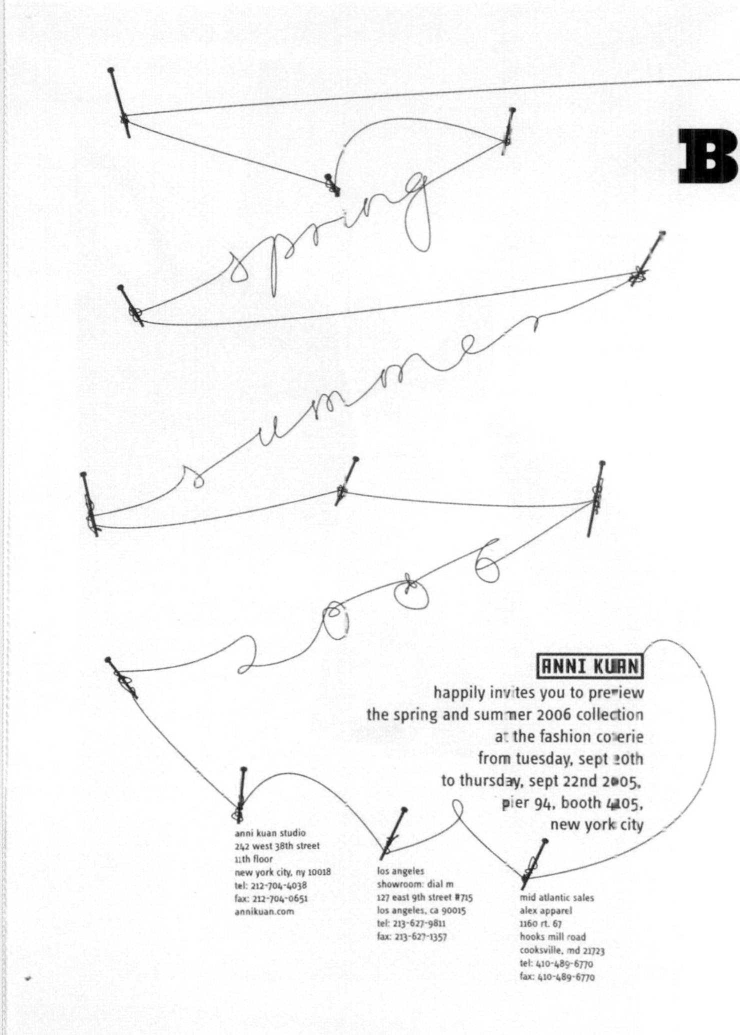

Although there are some areas of tension and density in this poster invitation (try finding a good piece of design where there's absolutely no contrast whatsoever!), the tension is minimal. Overall, almost all the negative spaces created by the back-and-forth motion of the thread line are similar in size, shape, and presence. Almost all the elements are equidistant from the format edges. And all the elements are linear, with only mild changes in weight and size. The result is a very quiet, casual, lackadaisical expression that is unpretentious, comfortable, and charming.

Sagmeister *United States*

A

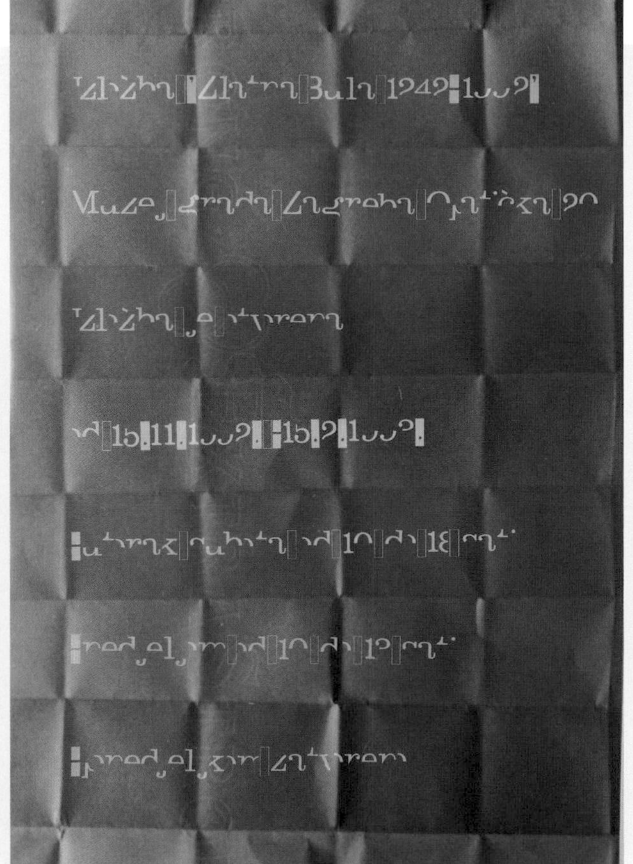

B

C

All three projects here—two posters and a website—purposely play down tonal contrast to achieve restful and contemplative results. The blue poster presents a political message for careful consideration rather than as a call to action; the construction company's website is uncharacteristically soft, detailed, and precise; and the black poster creates a very quietly glamorous, almost sinister, tactile sensuality in service of a fashion collection with textural black illustrations and a metallic surface.

A Studio International *Croatia*

B E-Types *Denmark*

C 2Fresh *Turkey*

Subtle tonal shifts, like consistent spatial rhythm, are a strong vehicle for messaging. Among competing visual material with strong contrast, a tonally quiet, soft presentation in which contrast between light and dark, or between chromatic relationships such as value and intensity, might be just as effective in garnering attention and creating space that helps separate viewers from surrounding visual activity. Low-contrast images and typography tend to be perceived as more contemplative and elegant, rather than urgent or aggressive.

Breaking It

13 Distribute light and dark like firecrackers and the rising sun.

Ambiguity, after all, can be a good thing. While clear visual and conceptual relationships are usually favored for the sake of quick, accessible communication, introducing mixed states of being among elements—elements that appear to be in the foreground, as well as in the background, as a simple example—can create an impulse on the part of the viewer to question and investigate more thoroughly. The gap between the concrete idea and the ambiguously presented image that refers to it can provide more complex avenues of interpretation and a rich, engaging experience that yields deeper, more complex understanding.

Breaking It

Be decisive. Do it on purpose, or don't do it at all.

A jarring grid of checkered spaces gives way to a set of ellipses that change the pattern's density to create type forms. The change also creates a strange, somewhat translucent quality and an ambiguous optical separation between the title and the background.

Leonardo Sonnoli *Italy*

Hello No, I'm not talking about art. Useful objects have a rich history. They are saturated with references to specific contexts and specific moments in history. If you refer to that history explicitly and include all the associations in a new story, then you are communicating something, and it's something about useful objects.
Louise Then you're talking about art.

Two conflicting grids—one for text, one for images—encourage bizarre overlaps of type and pictures, as well as linear elements, in this book spread. Take a look at the not-quite-aligned relationship between the images themselves. The indecisive quality of these structural details elicits questions from the viewer, rather than attempting to answer questions in advance or persuade them of some truth.

Coma *Netherlands*

Any time the form elements are tightly locked together and arranged systematically, as in an intricate pattern or grid structure, mathematical measurements and alignment become unavoidable—and likely, more appropriate conceptually. Optically aligning, spacing, or sizing material that is very tightly arranged will call attention to misalignments, uneven spaces, or elements that are not quite the same size, even though they are intended to be perceived that way.

15

Breaking It

Measure with your eyes: design is visual.

The intended message of media integration—the client's core service—as well as the visual allusions to video screens, file tabs, and pixels, all depend on precise mathematical alignments. Rather than "eyeballing" to assess scale and positioning relationships, the designer relies on measured guidelines within the layout software to ensure the elements create the pattern as envisioned.

STIM Visual Communication
United States

Time is money, it is often said; and the time it takes to research truly effective stock images can burn a hole in a designer's budget faster than you can say "Ow!" True, finding an image to stick into a layout tends to be quicker; but this is still not a good reason to use images that already exist because the existing image will never be as closely tied to the project's message as it really needs to be. Sometimes, however, purposely using banal, almost meaningless or kitsch images from stock sources can be great fun, especially if the project calls for a tongue-in-cheek approach or if the designer is conceptually referring to the ubiquity of image content and the influence of day-to-day pop culture. But the real benefit of scavenging is acquiring pieces and parts that can be used to create custom images quickly. Still, proceed with caution. Even presenting a group of found images, but customizing them to integrate formally and conceptually with other material, is preferable to using them as is.

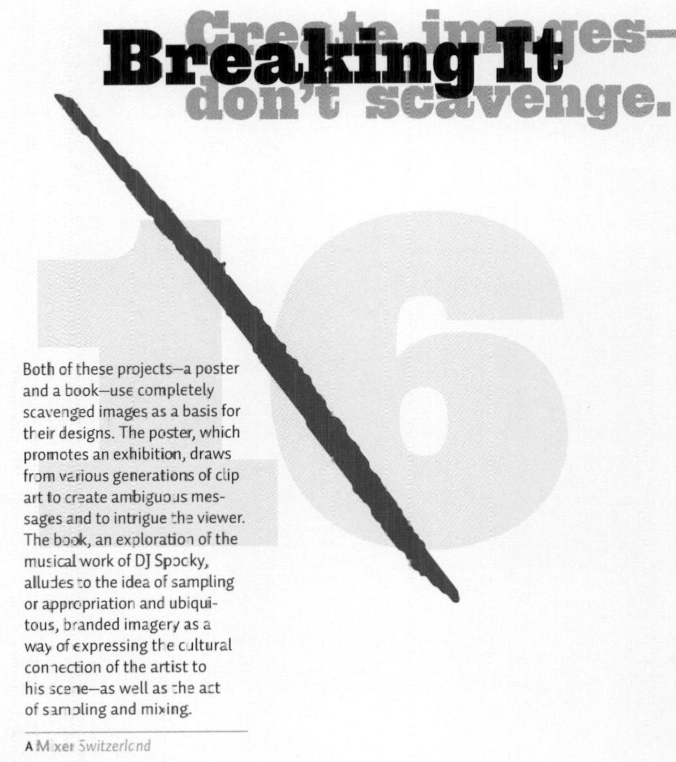

Breaking It

16 Create images—don't scavenge.

Both of these projects—a poster and a book—use completely scavenged images as a basis for their designs. The poster, which promotes an exhibition, draws from various generations of clip art to create ambiguous messages and to intrigue the viewer. The book, an exploration of the musical work of DJ Spooky, alludes to the idea of sampling or appropriation and ubiquitous, branded imagery as a way of expressing the cultural connection of the artist to his scene—as well as the act of sampling and mixing.

A Mixer *Switzerland*

B Coma *Netherlands*

A

Wunderliches im Schtei
Bonjour Madame
Nanie
Samstag
8. Oktober 2005
20.30 Uhr

B

Riding the current stylistic trend has occasional benefits. In choosing to do so, a designer is opting to speak more personally and directly to an audience whose expectations of visual messaging coincide with a particular thematic metaphor and which, as a result, is likely to bypass visual material that doesn't appear to speak to them. This is especially true when communicating to adolescents, who identify with very specific visual styles at any given moment, and will ignore anything else.

17 Ignore fashion. Seriously.

Breaking It

A

B

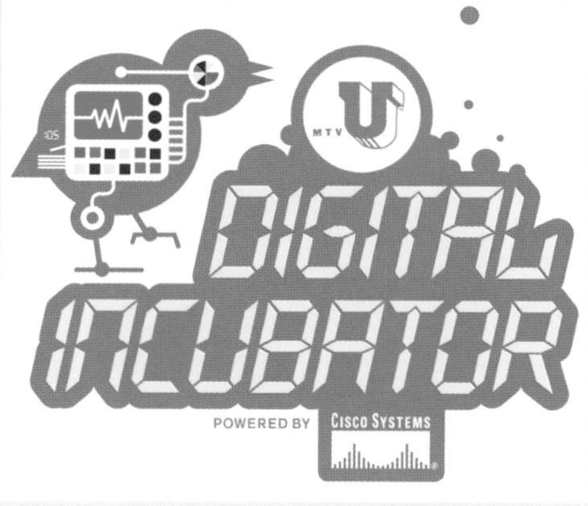

As ephemeral as fashion may be, it is a powerful communicator in today's youth market, especially in the entertainment industry. These three items trade on current trends in the illustrative realm of design: super-stylized, retro-techno graphics and type; highly idiosyncratic and personal drawing; and the iconography of electronics and video gaming.

A SubCommunication *Canada*

B Ames Bros. *United States*

C Sergio Gutierrez *Spain*

C

MIENTRAS LA TERMINAMOS PUEDES ESCUCHARNOS
LOS MARTES DE 22,30 A 23,30 EN EL
107.5 FM_
MADRID (ZONA SURESTE)
ONDAS DEL ESPACIO EXTERIOR .COM
contacto
lista correo

This page spread from a monograph on the work of British design concern WhyNot Associates offers a contemplative introduction to the book and a historical overview of their output in recent years. Low-contrast imagery, printed in muted metallic silver on an absorbent textured paper, combines with undifferentiated margins and a single type treatment to create a quiet moment of review before launching into the firm's dynamically colored, textural design work.

WhyNot Associates
United Kingdom

Breaking It

As with all the rules, proceed with caution when breaking this one. The primary danger here is causing viewers to disengage, because it is dynamic visual activity–stimulating the eyes and brain to move about–that generally holds their attention. Static arrangements of material, however, can be very focused and restful, an alternative to dramatic movement and deep spatial illusion, and in that sense can be useful at times. As part of a pacing scheme that alternates with clearly dynamic movement, static arrangements can provide areas of rest, visual punctuation to aggressive presentation, and contrasting moments of focus and introspection.

Breaking It

Look to history, but don't repeat it.

There will be an endless number of communication projects that present history as a theme or overall context in which a given message will participate. Books or exhibitions that focus on historical subjects, or invitations to period-themed events, for example, are perfect vehicles for exhuming visual style from the vaults of antiquity—even if that antiquity is only twenty years old. The fun for designers in such situations is to assimilate a period's characteristic visual details, colors, typefaces, and image styles into their own visual sensibility, not so much copying the style outright as sampling portions thereof, adjusting them, and reorganizing them so they become new again—while still capturing the essence of the period and, in appropriate contexts, celebrating it.

A

B

A CD-ROM cover and a series of stickers for an auto manufacturer's promotion revel in their appropriation of period design styles without succumbing to being wholly derivative—a difficult line to walk. The CD-ROM cover invokes the design sensibility of Blue Note jazz albums from the 1950s and 1960s in its use of slab serif typefaces and blue-and-black color scheme. The confrontational close-up image is a decidedly contemporary treatment that makes the layout fresh and inventive and likely resonates deeply with its audience. The stickers use color schemes, typography, and illustrative styles associated with clip art and stock-car graphic detailing of the 1970s, a Me Generation salute to the contemporary consumer's environmental activism embodied in the positioning of the car's hybrid energy system.

A **Stereotype Design** *United States*

B **Ames Bros.** *United States*

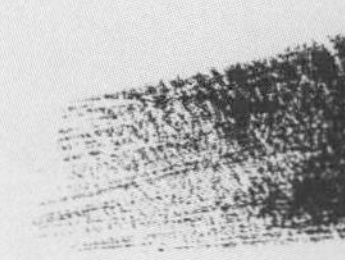

The symmetrical arrangement of type and imagery in this poster is counteracted by irregular graphic elements and stark changes in contrast and rhythm, avoiding any possibility of a static layout that will fail to engage the viewer.

MV Design *United States*

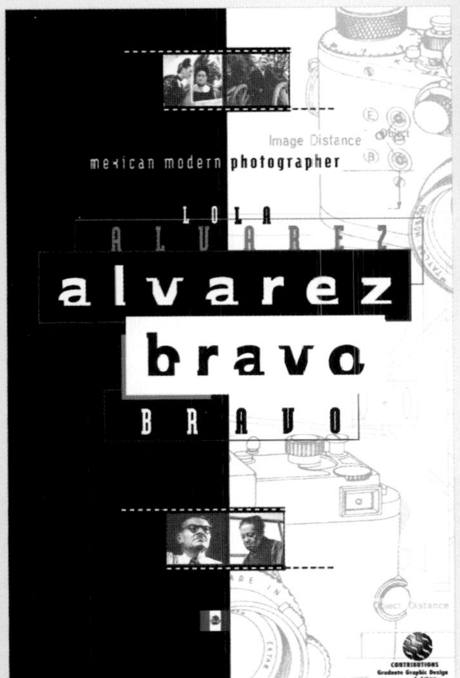

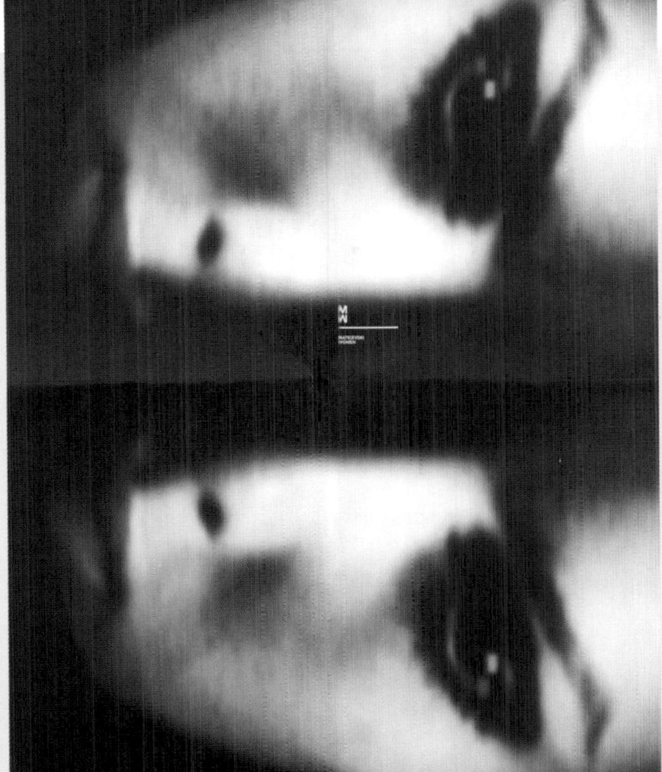

The layout of this large-format tabloid poster responds to the symmetrical midpoint of both the vertical and horizontal page dimensions but accomplishes an unexpectedly dynamic twist in rotating the main image—also symmetrical—horizontally. The tremendous scale and aggressive cropping of the face offer a deep perceptual space that contrasts with the sharp, detailed typographic element that defines the poster's vertical axis.

There *Australia*

Although situated in an asymmetrical location relative to the package's format, the label area for this food product is nonetheless a masterful study in typographic tension and contrast around a centered axis. Each element changes presence through scale, weight, density, style, and color; but the designer has implemented these changes while keeping some formal congruence between the elements.

Wallace Church *United States*

In all its manifestations, symmetry is a compositional strategy to be approached with caution. Along with its inherent quietness, inflexibility, and disconnect from most other kinds of form, symmetry brings with it a set of classical, stuffy, old-world, elitist messages that, in the context of the past fifty years or so of design work, can immediately skew communication away from a feeling of relevance. It is precisely because of this effect, however, that symmetry can be a powerful approach to designing very formal, historical, and serious material—as well as material that requires a very simple, clear separation of image and typography, strong contrast between dynamic, textural content, or rigid presentation of a great deal of similar content. When working with symmetrical relationships—whether those of text configuration or image placement—the tension between spatial intervals, density and openness, and light and dark becomes critical in maintaining visual activity so that the symmetry becomes elegant, lively, and austere, rather than heavy-handed, stiff, and dull.

2 Fresh
Maslak, Beybi Giz Plaza, K:26
34396, Istanbul/Turkey
contact@2fresh.com
184, 195, 262

344 Design, LLC
101 N. Grand Ave. #7
Pasadena, CA 91103 USA
www.344design.com
049, 054, 175, 198, 260

A10 Design
170 Helena St., 4th Floor
São Paolo, 04552-050 SP
Brazil
www.a10.com.br
015, 106, 236

Troy D. Abel
c/o The Art Institute,
Orange County
3601 West Sunflower Avenue
Santa Ana, CA 92704 USA
da301@stu.aii.edu
167

Adams Morioka
8484 Wilshire Blvd. Suite 600
Beverly Hills, CA 90211 USA
www.adamsmorioka.com
006, 020, 063, 072, 101, 105, 131, 135, 179

Ames Bros.
2118 8th Ave.
Seattle, WA 98199 USA
www.amesbros.com
026, 085, 173, 174, 253, 266, 268

And Partners
159 West 27th St. 7th Floor
New York, NY 10001 USA
www.andpartnersny.com
011, 076, 121

Apeloig Design
41 Rue La Fayette
75009 Paris, France
www.apeloig.com
026, 036, 066, 110, 127, 169

Art:Tecaji
Miklosiceva 38
1000 Ljubljana, Slovenia
www.art-tecaji.com
168

BBK Studio
648 Monroe Ave. NW Suite 212
Grand Rapids, MI 49503 USA
www.bbkstudio.com
007, 071, 072, 084, 087, 111, 195, 217, 237

Maris Bellack
172 South 4th St. #3
Brooklyn, NY 11211 USA
www.marismaris.com
194, 238

C+G Partners, LLC
116 East 16th St., Floor 10
New York, NY 10003 USA
www.cgpartnersllc.com
018, 047, 061, 140, 183

C. Harvey Graphic Design
415 West 23rd St.
New York, NY 10011 USA
www.charvey.com
013, 051, 069, 129, 203, 226

Carolyn Calles
c/o The Art Institute,
Orange County
3601 West Sunflower Avenue
Santa Ana, CA 92704 USA
cnc303@stu.aii.edu
cncalles@yahoo.com
082

Carregal Pease Design
1390 S. Dixie Hwy. Suite 2217
Coral Gables, FL 33146 USA
www.carregalpease.com
258

Myung Ha Chang
c/o School of Visual Arts
209 East 23rd Street
New York, NY 10010 USA
mchang4@sva.edu
104

Tammy Chang
2225 Ridgefield Green Way
Richmond, VA 23233 USA
www.design.cmu.edu
151

Cheng Design
2433 East Aloha St.
Seattle, WA 98112 USA
www.cheng-design.com
070, 136

CHK Design
8 Flitcroft Street
London WC2H 8DL
United Kingdom
71, 122, 134

Christine Chuo
c/o Carnegie Mellon
University
5000 Forbes Ave.
Pittsburgh, PA 15213 USA
www.cmu.edu
151

Cobra
Karenslyst Allé gB
NO-0278 Oslo, Norway
www.cobra.no
019, 034, 100, 146, 155, 193, 217

Coma
Saxenburgerstraat 21-1
1054 KN Amsterdam
The Netherlands
www.comalive.com
027, 195, 208, 244, 263, 265

Thomas Csano
3655 St. Laurent
Montreal, Quebec H2X 2V6
Canada
www.thomascsano.com
010, 035, 061, 076, 102, 112, 119, 170, 171, 194, 230, 251

Cyr Studio
P.O. Box 795
Stroudsburg, PA 18360 USA
www.cyrstudio.com
025, 169, 172

Design Rudi Meyer
27 rue des Rossignols
F-91330 Yerres, France
design.rudi-meyer@
easyconnect.fr
014, 075, 162

Dochdesign
Kidlerstrasse 4
81371 Munich, Germany
www.dochdesign.de
029, 172, 259

Jelena Drobac
9 Siva stena St.
11000 Belgrade, Serbia
www.d-ideashop.com
010, 101, 127, 182

Drotz Design
1613 12th Ave. SW
Puyallup, WA 98371 USA
www.drotzdesign.com
079, 099, 172

E-Types
Vesterbrogade 80B, 1
1620 Copenhagen V
Denmark
050, 117, 206, 221, 262

Earsay
P.O. Box 4338
Sunnyside, NY 11104 USA
www.earsay.org
139, 148, 153, 225

Barbara Ferguson
10211 Swanton Dr.
Santee, CA 92071 USA
zoographics@earthlink.net
205, 227

Finest Magma
Suedenstrasse 52
76135 Karlsruhe, Germany
www.finestmagma.com
043, 143, 172, 182, 193, 228, 230, 231

Fishten
2203 32nd Ave. SW
Calgary, Alberta T2T1X2
Canada
www.fishten.com
238

Form
47 Tabernacle St.
London EC2A 4AA UK
www.form.uk.com
007, 052, 061, 079

Frost Design, Sydney
Level 1, 15 Foster St.
Surry Hills, NSW 2010
Australia
www.frostdesign.com.au
021, 038, 113, 153, 215

Grapefruit
Str. Ipsilanti 45
Intrare Splai, Ia_i 700029,
Romania
www.grapefruit.ro
127, 129, 236

Sergio Gutierrez
Povedilla, 10, Esc. 2, Apt. 6-I
Madrid, Spain E28943
beezual@hotmail.com
266

Maciej Hajnrich
Browarna 23/30
Bielsko-Biala 43-400 Poland
www.nietylko.net
174

Helmut Schmid Design
Tarumi-cho 3-24-14-707
Suita-Shi, Osaka-FV 564-0062
Japan
www4.famille.ne.jp/~hsdesign
127, 156

Diana Hurd
18 Northwood Dr.
Timonium, MD 21093 USA
dianaceleste14@gmail.com
093

I Just Might...Design
4747 Collins Ave. #707
Miami Beach, FL 33140 USA
www.ijustmight.com
129, 223

Igawa Design
3726 Clark Ave.
Long Beach, CA 90808 USA
www.igawadesign.com
129

John Jensen
2925 Grand Ave. Apt. 10
Des Moines, IA 50312 USA
john@onpurpos.com
039

JRoss Design
90 South Main St.
Alfred, NY 14802 USA
www.jrossdesign.com
033, 048, 102, 106, 158

Hyosook Kang
School of Visual Arts
23 Lexington Ave. #1533
New York, NY 10010-3748 USA
Yellowapple79@hotmail.com
220

Cally Keo
c/o The Art Institute,
Orange County
3601 West Sunflower Avenue
Santa Ana, CA 92704 USA
222

Sohyun Kim
2516 Aspen Rd. #4
Ames, IA 50010 USA
lovemoi@iastate.edu
111, 177

Kropp and Associates
105 Sycamore Studio 609A
Decatur, GA 30030 USA
www.kroppassociates.com
096

Hae Jin Lee
32-32 36th St., 3rd Floor
Astoria, NY 11106 USA
chocoicecream@hotmail.com
224, 245

Lexicon Graphix
304 South Franklin St.
Suite 304
Syracuse, NY 13202 USA
www.lexicongraphix.com
011, 256

Vicki Li
c/o Lisa Fontaine
Iowa State University
College of Design
Ames, Iowa 50011-3092
fontaine@iastate.edu
036

Marcia Lisanto
c/o Laguna College of
Art +Design
2222 Laguna Canyon Road
Laguna Beach, CA 92651 USA
www.lagunacollege.edu
231

Loewy
147a Grosvenor Rd.
London, SWIV 3JY UK
www.loewygroup.com
United Kingdom
017, 059, 160, 191, 213, 237, 239, 257, 258

LSD
San Andrés 36, 2° p 6
28004 Madrid, Spain
www.lsdspace.com
007,016, 037, 057, 059, 075, 076, 087, 098, 148, 161, 171, 182, 202, 224

Made In Space, Inc.
818 South Broadway
Suite 1000
Los Angeles, CA 90014 USA
www.madeinspace.ca
053, 060, 078, 082, 127

Metropolitan Group
519 SW Third Ave., Suite 700
Portland, OR 97204 USA
www.metgroup.com
079, 176, 255

Mixer
Löwenplatz 5
CH-6004 Lucerne Switzerland
www.mixer.ch
183, 187, 264

Monigle Associates
150 Adams St.
Denver, CO 80206 USA
www.monigle.com
042, 068, 075

contribut

Muller
Unit 307, Studio 28
28 Lawrence Rd.
London, N154EG UK
www.hellomuller.com
007

Munda Graphics
11/113 Alison Rd.
Randwick, NSW 2031 Australia
www.geocities.com/
munda_gallery
042, 167, 259

Mutabor Design GmbH
Grosse Elbstrasse 145B
D-22767 Hamburg, Germany
www.mutabor.com
007, 025, 061, 069

MV Design
10 Thunder Run 6-D
Irvine, CA 92614 USA
atiragram3@hotmail.com
183, 269

Benjamin Myers
c/o Laguna College of
Art +Design
2222 Laguna Canyon Road
Laguna Beach, CA 92651 USA
www.lagunacollege.edu
179

Niklaus Troxler Design
Bahnhofstrasse 22
Willisau, CH-6130 Switzerland
www.troxlerart.ch
043, 218, 252

Not From Here Inc.
101 Summit St. #3 Third Floor
Brooklyn, NY 11241 USA
www.norfromhere.com
048, 091, 258

Marek Okon
3836 Ponderosa Ln.
Mississauga, Ontario L5N
6W3 Canada
www.marekokon.com
028, 151

Martin Oostra
Donker Curtivsstraat 25D
Amsterdam 7057JM,
Netherlands
studio@oostra.org
086, 133, 181, 201, 234, 243

Andreas Ortag
Parkstrasse 5
A-3822 Karlstein/Thaya
Austria
www.ortag.at
024, 040, 137, 167, 178, 227

Paone Design Associates
242 South Twentieth St.
Philadelphia, PA 19103 USA
www.paonedesign.com
**022, 083, 092, 118, 132,
160, 183, 193, 227**

Sunyoung Park
2505 Jensen Ave., #413
Ames, IA 50010 USA
sunyoung@iastate.edu
038

Michelle Pinkston
2627 Kent #6
Ames, IA 50010 USA
pink12@iastate.edu
129

Raidy Printing Group S.A.L.
St. Antoine St.
Beirut PC 20713203 Lebanon
www.mariejoeraidy.com
082, 088, 129, 130, 171, 183

Gunter Rambow
Domplatz 16
D-18273 Güstrow, Germany
gunterrambow@web.de
095, 111

Red Canoe
347 Clear Creek Trail
Deer Lodge, TN 37726 USA
www.redcanoe.com
028, 055, 098, 112, 235

Research Studios
94 Islington High St.
London, N18EG UK
www.researchstudios.com
**036, 078, 089, 096, 147, 152,
159, 163, 177, 188, 219, 237**

Robert Rytter & Associates
14919 Falls Rd.
Butler, MD 21023 USA
www.rytter.com
131, 205

Pamela Rouzer
c/o Laguna College of
Art + Design
2222 Laguna Canyon Road
Laguna Beach, CA 92651 USA
pamelarouzer@
lagunacollege.edu
056

Roycroft Design
7 Faneuil Hall Marketplace
Boston, MA 02109 USA
www.roycroftdesign.com
060

Rule29 Creative
303 W. State St.
Geneva, IL 60134 USA
www.rule29.com
166

Sagmeister Inc.
222 West 14th St.
New York, NY 10011 USA
www.sagmeister.com
056, 105, 166, 182, 261

Clemens Théobert Schedler
Hirschberggasse 6
A-3411 Scheiblingstein, Austria
c.schedler@sil.at
025, 037, 141, 156, 207, 240

Sang-Duck Seo
4815 Todd Dr., Apt #74
Ames, IA 50014 USA
sdseo@iastate.edu
176

Shinnoske, Inc.
2-1-8060-2 Tsuriganecho,
Chuoku
Osaka City, Osaka 540-0035
Japan
www.shinn.co.jp
090, 183

Christopher Short
P.O. Box [illegible]
Stroudsburg, PA 18360 USA
www.chrisshort.com
169

Travis Simon
120 South 2nd St.
Brooklyn, NY 11211 USA
nvudesign@gmail.com
221

Matt Smith
c/o Laguna College of
Art +Design
2222 Laguna Canyon Road
Laguna Beach, CA 92651 USA
www.lagunacollege.edu
255

Leonardo Sonnoli
Via G. Rossini 16
Trieste 34132 Italy
leonardosonnoli@libero.it
**047, 062, 105, 119, 161,
133, 220, 225, 263**

Spin
12 Canterbury Court,
Kennington Park
1-3 Brixton Rd.
London SW9 6DE UK
www.spin.co.uk
254

Stereotype Design
39 Jane St. 4A
New York, NY 10014 USA
www.stereotype-design.com
027, 067, 091, 154, 183, 268

Stressdesign
1003 West Fayette Street
Floor One
Syracuse, NY 13204 USA
www.stressdesign.com
023, 056, 154

**STIM
Visual Communication**
436 West 22nd Street, No. 4C
New York, NY 10011 USA
stim@visual-stim.com
**011, 065, 109, 157, 187,
256, 264**

Studio Blue
800 W. Huron St., Suite 3N
Chicago, IL 60622 USA
www.studioblue.us
103, 110, 209

Studio International
Buconjiceva 43
10 000 Zagreb Croatia
www.studio-international.com
**029, 051, 055, 078, 106,
170, 178, 194, 262**

Studio Works
838 Broadway
New York, NY 10003 USA
www.studio-works.com
033, 058, 173, 233

SubCommunication
24 Av. Mont-Royal West #1003
Montreal, Quebec H2T2S2
Canada
www.subcommunication.com
094, 222, 266

Michael Sui
3808 John Carroll Drive
Olney, MD 20832 USA
msuimsui@gmail.com
151

Swim Design
8040 Georgia Ave., Suite 100
Silverspring, MD 20910 USA
www.swimdesign.com
097, 123, 250

Templin Brink Design
720 Tehama St.
San Francisco, CA 94130 USA
www.tbd-sf.com
012, 095, 170, 177, 241

TenDoTen
Vira Biance #504 2-33-12
Jingumae
Shibuya-ku Tokyo 150-0001
Japan
www.tententen.net
167

There
Level 1, 16 Foster St.
Surry Hills
Sydney NSW 2010 Australia
www.there.com.au
060, 269

Think Studio, NYC
234 West 16th St.
New York, NY 10011 USA
www.thinkstudionyc.com
066, 162

**UNA (Amsterdam)
Designers**
Kurte Papavarweg 7A
Amsterdam, the Netherlands
una@unadesigners.nl
042, 108, 144

**Virginia Commonwealth
University (VCU) Qatar**
P.O. Box 8095
Doha, Qatar
www.qatar.vcu.edu
033,111, 162, 167, 226

Voice
217 Gilbert St.
Adelaide, South Australia
5000 Australia
www.voicedesign.net
**013, 044, 061, 072, 099,
125, 141, 147, 157, 189**

Wallace Church, Inc.
330 East 48th St.
New York, NY 10017 USA
www.wallacechurch.com
173, 269

Ko-Sing Wang
c/o The Art Institute,
Orange County
3601 West Sunflower Avenue
Santa Ana, CA 92704 USA
223

Why Not Associates
22C Shepherdess Walk
London N1 7LB UK
www.whynotassociates.com
267

Brett Yasko
2901 Smallman St., #5D
Pittsburgh, PA 15201 USA
www.brettyasko.com
035, 039, 109, 134, 192

Acknowledgments

Books of this kind depend on the time and effort of a lot of very busy people. My thanks to all the designers who took time from their often hectic schedules to help illustrate the ideas within and provide a sampling of the ongoing evolution of the graphic design field. Once again, I'd like to thank the team at Rockport, who–as always–work tirelessly to make sure things turn out the way they're supposed to. This book is dedicated to Sean, my parents and friends, and all my students.

about the author

Timothy Samara is a graphic designer based in New York City, where he divides his time between teaching, writing, lecturing, and consulting through STIM Visual Communication. His fifteen-year career in branding and information design has exposed him to projects as diverse as print, packaging, environments, user interface design, and animation. Mr. Samara is currently a faculty member at the School of Visual Arts, NYU, Purchase College, and Parsons School of Design. He is the author of *Making and Breaking the Grid, Typography Workbook, Publication Design Workbook,* and *Type Style Finder.*